Cross-Platform Development Using Visual C++

By Chane Cullens & Ken Blackwell

M&T Books
A Division of MIS:Press, Inc.
A Subsidiary of Henry Holt and Company, Inc.
115 West 18th Street
New York, New York 10011

Library of Congress Cataloging-in-Publication Data

Cullens, Chane.
    Cross-platform development using Visual C++, Ken Blackwell.
        p. cm.
    ISBN 1-55851-428-7
    1. Cross-platform software development. 2. C++ (computer program language) 3. Microsoft Visual C++. I. Blackwell, Ken. II. Title.
QA76.76.D47C84   1995
005.13'3--dc20   95-8850
                                                                   CIP

98 97 96 95   4 3 2 1

Editor-in-Chief: Paul Farrell
Managing Editor: Cary Sullivan
Development Editor: Michael Sprague
Copy Editors: Winifred Davus
Technical Editor: Don Johnson
Production Editor: Anthony Washington

Table of Contents

Preface

Why is Cross-Platform Development Important?

In today's software marketplace, more and more customer environments consist of a variety of hardware platforms and operating systems. Some of the reasons for these heterogeneous environments include the following:

- Customers want to use the best tool for each type of job. For example, product designers might require high-end UNIX workstations, whereas personal computers might be better suited for accounting departments.

- Many customers are moving from a mainframe environment toward a client-server environment in which end users have Windows-based personal computers but use powerful UNIX servers to run their applications.

- Customers want to take advantage of new technologies such as Windows NT or PowerMac without replacing all of their existing hardware or software.

But no matter how many different platforms customers use, there are many applications they want to run on all of their platforms, allowing users on different operating systems to use the same applications and share the same information. Therefore, it is becoming increasingly important for software developers to provide products that work the same way on a variety of platforms.

Cross-platform development (developing software for more than one target platform) can be crucial to the success of a software product. However, it can also be quite expensive in terms of the resources and time it takes to develop a product initially and to maintain it into the future. Therefore, it is important to choose the best cross-platform development strategy.

Why Use Visual C++ for Cross-Platform Development?

There are a wide variety of cross-platform development environments available today. This book discusses only one: Microsoft Visual C++. There are several reasons why Visual C++ is the best choice for cross-platform development.

The most important reason to use Visual C++ for cross-platform development is that Visual C++ is the standard development environment for both Windows and Windows NT platforms. Visual C++ and the Microsoft Foundation Class (MFC) Library provide an architecture that reduces the complexity of your application and the time required to maintain it. Using Visual C++ for cross-platform development allows you to leverage existing code instead of rewriting your code to a proprietary cross-platform interface. Developers are already widely familiar with the Visual C++ framework, so they don't need to learn a different interface for cross-platform development. Using Visual C++ provides significant cost savings, since you can do all your development on low-cost personal computers, using UNIX workstations only for compiling and debugging the UNIX versions of your application. Another important consideration is that proven tools for porting Visual C++ applications based on the MFC Library are already available, and Visual C++ 2.0 is based on the Windows NT portable operating system.

What are the Potential Problems for Cross-Platform Development?

Even with the tools available, however, using Visual C++ for cross-platform development is not simply a matter of writing an application with Visual C++ and recompiling it on all the target platforms. Customers expect their applications to take advantage of all the features available on each supported platform. For example, the Windows version must have the Windows look and feel and must provide Windows features such as OLE. An application can no longer be competitive if it is limited to functionality that is common to all platforms.

This requirement is not limited to the graphical user interface (GUI); you must also consider data portability and data interchange. For example, the UNIX version of an application must be able to read data created by the Windows or Macintosh version. The application must also be able to exchange data with other applications via the clipboard, DDE, and OLE.

Good cross-platform development requires you to understand how the many differences between target operating systems, hardware architectures, and even C++ compilers can impact your application and to plan for those differences when you initially develop your application.

There are essentially three categories of cross-platform development:

- Developing for the same operating system but different hardware (for example, developing for Windows NT on Intel, Alpha, and MIPS systems)
- Developing for different operating systems on the same hardware (for example, developing for Windows 3.1 and Windows NT on Intel systems)
- Developing for different operating systems and different hardware (for example, Windows NT on Intel systems, UNIX on RISC systems, and Macintosh on PowerPC systems)

This book addresses the issues that you should be aware of when using Visual C++ for the third type of cross-platform development. It points out the areas in which you should pay particular attention when designing your application, and it provides examples of how to resolve potential problems. By understanding potential portability problems, you can design for cross-platform development and then minimize cross-platform issues during porting. (All code examples discussed in the book are included on the accompanying CD-ROM.)

The first chapters of this book introduce you to some of the general problems you can expect to encounter when you are developing cross-platform applications. Chapter 1 describes some of the different strategies for cross-platform development, including the development team, the build environment, and quality assurance testing. Chapters 2 and 3 address cross-platform development issues for the Macintosh and UNIX environments, respectively. Chapter 4 addresses the features of the MFC library that make it well-suited as a cross-platform development technology.

The rest of the book describes a variety of portability issues in detail. The portability issues discussed in this book include the following:

- Data persistence issues, encountered when creating a database that can be read by all versions of an application (Chapter 5)

- Potential problems with using a single dialog on all target platforms (Chapter 6)

- Potential issues with system services such as resi=ource management and system information API's (Chapter 7)

- Graphics device interface (GDI) issues, such as how the underlying software impacts performance and how to identify graphics bottlenecks (Chapter 8)

- Potential User API issues, such as threads, messages, and window creation and management (Chapter 9)

- On-line help issues, such as how to create a single help source file base that can be used on all target platforms (Chapter 10)

- Solutions for adding networking capabilities to cross-platform applications (Chapter 11)

In addition, the book discusses other important cross-platform development issues, such as managing your build environment and implementing rigorous and consistent testing methods to ensure high-quality products on all target platforms (Chapter 12).

CHAPTER 1

Developing a Cross-Platform Strategy

As with most software development projects, a solid strategy for your cross-platform project is essential for success. In most respects, the planning and management of a porting project are similar to a new development project. There are, however, some important differences that you should consider early in the planning process. This chapter describes the issues to be considered when you are planning a cross-platform development project:

- Personnel
- Code management
- Code design
- Build environment
- Quality assurance

Personnel

By far the most frequent mistake that companies make when beginning a cross-platform development effort is assigning the wrong people to the job. It's easy to see how this can happen because there are many technical skills needed, including knowledge of the source platform, the destination platform, the tools used for porting, and the product being ported. Considering that finding an employee with all these skills is extremely difficult (and costly), which of these skills are most important?

There are really two cases to consider: porting an existing Windows application and doing cross-platform development in parallel.

Porting an Existing Project

Porting an existing Windows application to another platform, such as the Macintosh, is the most common porting scenario (especially when dealing with Visual C++/MFC). There are tens of thousands of Windows applications already developed, and only a fraction of that number for any other GUI platform. These numbers indicate that cross-platform development usually means porting existing Windows applications to other platforms. Answering the following questions should help you identify the right people for the porting project.

Should existing employees do the job or should you hire outside consultants? One mistake frequently made in cross-platform development is hiring consultants on a temporary basis and releasing them at the end of the project without first gaining sufficient in-house knowledge of the ported project to handle support and ongoing development. Before hiring a consultant, managers must identify the ongoing needs for maintenance, future development, and support. If you expect any significant ongoing development, maintenance, or support requirements, you should consider dedicating existing employees to the port. If you use consultants, be sure to plan for a sufficient transition period at the end of the project.

Who should lead the project? Ideally, either the project leader or a senior developer from the Windows development team should lead the porting project. In general, hiring an outside consultant to lead the project does not work. Although there are many things to learn about the Win32 cross-platform toolkits and many platform-specific issues to deal with, the most challenging work in the development is testing and debugging the application being ported. The internals of the application are usually much more complex than the GUI front-end subsystem, so detailed knowledge about the product is usually more valuable than extensive knowledge of the tools being used to port it.

What is the right number of engineers to assign to a porting effort? What should the mix of skills be? To answer these questions, you must consider several factors:

- How large is the product? Many mature Windows applications are now 1 million lines of code or more. Just compiling an application this large can sometimes take several man-weeks.

- Is the product divided into subsystems that can easily be tested individually? If so, multiple engineers can work in parallel. We discuss parallel development later in this chapter.

- If you are hiring new people, the porting effort will probably take significantly more time. Engineers who are familiar with the Windows version will be able to port and test faster because they know how the product is supposed to work. Having a Windows PC sitting next to the target platform and going through the product serially to make sure that all of the screens look the same is not effective. Good testing and debugging requires someone who knows intuitively whether the product is working correctly.

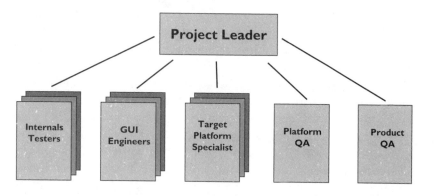

Figure 1.1 Suggested project team organization.

- The project leader should be someone from the Windows development team. Because it is essential that the project leader be very familiar with the application, the project leader should be someone who has been through the complete development cycle of the Windows application. It is also an advantage if the project leader has some experience with the target platform.

- The internals tester should know the details of internal, non-GUI-related subsystems of the application. Depending on the size of the application and whether all versions are being developed in parallel or whether the Windows version is being ported, your development team should have one or more internals testers. These team members must be able to test the internal non-GUI subsystems independently of the GUI component. Some typical tasks that an internals tester performs include verifying binary file compatibility, testing internal database I/O, and verifying interfaces to external subsystems (including networking/communications, mail, and security).

- The GUI engineer should know the GUI-compliance requirements of the target platform. Because the GUI engineer needs to ensure that the application GUI works as it should, knowledge of the Microsoft Windows GUI is a plus, as is knowledge of a Win32 cross-platform tools (especially MFC). As with the internals testers, your development team may need one or more GUI engineers, depending on the size of the application and whether all versions are being developed in parallel.

- The target platform specialist should know the target platform well and understand deployment issues like security, performance, and usability requirements. This person's job is to make sure that, for example, the Motif version of the ported application is, to users, indistinguishable from a native Motif application, the Macintosh version is indistinguishable from a native Macintosh application, and so on. This person must also understand what features are available on the target platform that the application might be able to exploit. For example, rather than porting the entire security subsystem of a Windows application, it might be easier to use the security features of the target platform. Such a solution might save time in the port and make the application integrate with the target platform more cleanly. This person and the project leader should work together on architectural issues; this person might be one of the GUI engineers. You may want a target platform specialist for each target platform.

Parallel Cross-Platform Development

Although there are many existing Windows applications being ported to other GUI platforms, the introduction of Visual C++ 2 and MFC 3 will certainly accelerate the development of new applications. Also, Visual C++ 2 and MFC 3 finally bring power Windows programming to the masses. No longer will sophisticated Windows applications be provided by only the major software companies. With Visual C++ 2 and MFC 3, a small in-house MIS development team can easily provide a sophisticated cross-platform 32-bit GUI application with features such as OLE 2, ODBC, and MAPI.

Certainly for the next couple of years, the main thrust of cross-platform development will be migrating Windows applications to other platforms. However, the best strategy is still to do all cross-platform development in parallel so that the big issues can be identified early and can be solved in a cross-platform-friendly manner. In theory, it is best to progress development in parallel on all target platforms.

The reality, however, is that Microsoft Windows outsells the other Win32-hosted platforms by huge margins. From an engineering perspective it might seem that the best solution is to keep development in parallel, but the marketing reality is usually that the Windows version must ship as soon as possible because it generates much more revenue. When this is the case, pragmatism usually dictates that the secondary platforms suffer while the Windows version is completed.

The good news is that using Visual C++ and MFC, rather than a third-party proprietary application builder and class library, solves both of these requirements. The focus is on the primary platform; codevelopment of the other target platforms is relatively painless and can be executed in parallel or may lag the Windows development by a few weeks. Visual C++ and MFC assure maximum compatibility on the other platforms, so you can be assured that the code will port relatively easily.

Why is parallel cross-platform development better than porting an existing application? Because you can use a methodical design exercise for cross-platform development, rather than a brute force approach. You can use preemptive/proactive design techniques rather than reactive techniques. The principal developers of the code (the ones who really understand it) can solve cross-platform issues, instead of developers who are attempting to port an existing product and who too often really don't understand a product's design at the start of the job.

What should a parallel development team look like? Not much different than a purely Windows application team. Where it differs the most is that all developers compile and test their code on all platforms, rather than writing it for Windows, and they rely on other team members to port the code to other platforms. Your parallel development team may have the following:

- The project leader must know the problem being solved by the application. The project leader should also know Visual C++/MFC and have a basic understanding of all target platforms.

- The platform architects must know the target platform well and understand the Win32 cross-platform tool. These team members must know the capabilities and limitations of the tool. They are also responsible for platform look and feel and other compliance issues.

- The development engineers must understand the problem being solved by the application. They should also know Visual C++/MFC very well, in order to use it as effectively as possible. Development engineers should not do anything outside of MFC without first consulting with platform architects.

- The product QA engineer should know how to test the product's capabilities. If you are porting an existing Windows application, the product QA engineer should ideally be a member of the Windows development team who understands the features of the application and how to test them.

- The platform QA engineer should be familiar with the target platform and should be able to test the application's compliance with the target platform.

Code Management

How do you keep the Windows version of your application up-to-date with changes made when porting to other platforms? This issue is not as important when developing in parallel because all code is tested on all platforms when it is written. When you're porting an existing application, however, a different team of programmers is usually working on the next Windows version while the porting team migrates the code to other platforms. This time lag can make code management challenging because it is difficult to incorporate portability changes into the Windows code.

The best solution that we have found is to proliferate only the really important and complex changes, not simple syntax changes, and so onthat result from compiler differences. This means that some work will have to be redone when the next version of the Windows code is ported (this is the added cost of porting an existing application instead of developing in parallel), but the risks to the schedule of the next Windows version are significantly reduced. Tools, either homegrown or provided by the porting tool, can be a big help in filtering the source code for simple compiler issues. As you will see in later chapters, these are differences in compilers among the various Win32-hosted platforms although identifying these differences is relatively straightforward in filter programs.

Although the syntax issues might not be worth the risk of proliferating into the future Windows version as it is developed, any architectural and functional changes that are necessary in the port should certainly be addressed in the future Windows version. These are the changes that require redesign of code and take up the most time in the port.

Some examples of these types of changes include the following:

- Work-arounds for features unsupported by the target operating system, graphics subsystem, or porting tool
- Changes necessary for taking advantage of advanced features that are unavailable under Windows
- Modifications made for better compliance with target operating system conventions

When these types of big changes are made, the porting and development teams should get together, go over the changes, and decide how to integrate them into the Windows source base. Because of the significance of the changes, they certainly introduce risk into the Windows application schedule, so care should be taken to minimize this risk. The Windows developers, not the porting team, should migrate the changes into the source base. Having the Windows developers do this gives them familiarity with the changes and allows them to anticipate side effects in other parts of the code.

Another technique that makes code management easier is to organize your application components into portable and platform-specific source files. You will find that most of the classes in MFC applications will easily port to other platforms, but a few will be very platform-specific. Isolate these platform-specific modules into separate files so that the portable files are not affected when moved to other platforms.

Code Design Issues

When porting an existing application, most programmers typically go about porting code by jumping right in and compiling, debugging, and testing. As already described, this method is not very efficient because it causes some parts of the application to be rewritten if they do not adequately take into consideration cross-platform issues. Although this brute force approach generally works for porting existing applications, there are much more efficient methods when the development team is organized for parallel cross-platform development.

The key to maximizing productivity, meeting development schedules, and producing a good cross-platform product is *designing for portability*. Most issues encountered when developing for cross-platform use an be identified early in the design phase when you can develop an effective design to work around these issues. Although there will still be a temporary need for porting existing applications, never do it twice! Get your projects on the parallel development method as soon as possible.

Portable Language Issues

Although syntax/compiler issues are relatively simple to solve, the sheer number of them in a major project can take quite a bit of time to correct. Tools, such as **porttool** or the Wind/U **prepare_source** utility, are certainly helpful in this area. Still, a good understanding of the relevant language standards is important for everyone on the development team. Invest some time in teaching developers the ANSI C and C++ draft standards. Knowing these standards is especially important because PC compilers, although generally supporting the standards, also provide many extensions that are not portable to other platforms. The risk of using nonportable features is not as great when porting to the Macintosh, because the Visual C++ Mac solution uses the same compiler front-end for Windows, Windows NT, and Macintosh. When porting to UNIX, however, the compilers adhere to the standards much more strictly.

Adhering to established standards not only makes your code more portable, it improves overall quality. Even if you never intend to support a different platform, your code will be of much higher quality if you invest the time to compile it under one or more different platforms. You'll be surprised what different compilers will identify as problems that the compiler that you are using does not identify.

Isolating Subsystems

The beginning of most porting projects is like drinking from a fire hose. The developers spend anywhere from a day to a couple of weeks getting all of the code to compile and link, depending on the size of the applications. They then run the application to see what happens. The problem with this approach is that applications often have too many interdependencies to allow testing of individual subsystems. For example, most Windows applications are a GUI front-end to a database. At their core, word processors, spreadsheets, GUI builders, design tools, and so forth, are all a GUI front-end to a database.

Many of these applications are designed so that operation of the GUI is completely dependent on the correct operation of the underlying database engine. Likewise, there is rarely a front-end to the underlying database other than the GUI provided by the application, creating a Catch 22 situation. All subsystems have to be debugged in parallel, making it impossible to isolate bugs to a particular subsystem. Debugging all subsystems at once doubles (at least) the amount of work required for the port.

Instead, try providing a simple stub database that allows the GUI to be at least partially exercised, independent of the real underlying database. Likewise, create a simple character front-end to the database that allows its basic operation to be exercised without involving the complexity of the actual application GUI front-end.

The GUI and database subsystems are just two examples. Try to separate out communications subsystems such as network database connections, file I/O subsystems, and GDI intensive components. Also, if the GUI is very complex, try splitting it into separate testable components. For example, if your GUI contains custom controls, try writing independent test cases that exercise just the individual controls. These small test cases are easier to debug than the entire application, and the entire application is easier to test after its individual subsystems are independently tested.

Having independent test environments also allows for better parallelism in development because different developers can work on difference pieces. This approach even makes the skills mix for the development team easier to satisfy because with the monolithic approach, you need someone who is both a GUI and database expert, which can be very expensive.

This approach will save you a significant amount of time. Porting the application all at once, instead of breaking it into individually testable modules, is the single biggest mistake that people make when designing for cross-platform use. You should even consider having QA engineers test the GUI and underlying database independently of each other; this is a very good way to isolate problems.

Build Environment Issues

After you have initially compiled and linked your application, build it frequently on all target platforms. Building frequently ensures not only that any changes you make do indeed fix the problems they were intended to fix on all target platforms, but also that you identify any possible side effects caused by your changes. The easiest way to build frequently on all target platforms is to find tools that make batch building of all platforms possible. Figure 1.2 shows a typical scenario in which the application is built nightly for all platforms on a Windows NT server.

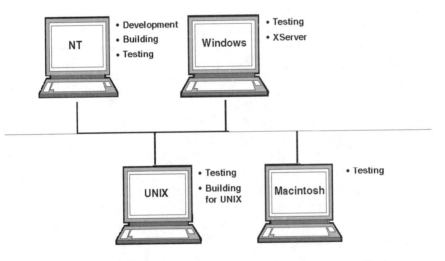

Figure 1.2 Typical build environment.

In a cross-platform development environment, source control becomes extremely important. Choose only one system in your build environment as the source control system. Windows NT and UNIX systems are the best choices for source code control because they can act as servers for multiple developers and platforms. In addition, a wide selection of source code control tools are available for these multiuser development environments.

All development team members must have access to the source code control system over the network. Before developers commit any changes, they must build and test the application on all platforms. Again, organizing your application into individually testable modules makes this process much easier and faster. Testing the application on all platforms means more than simply building and running the module. Use a code debugger to walk through the code on all platforms to verify that the execution path is consistent and that no conditional compilation errors cause problems.

In some applications, compiling on every target platform might not be feasible. In these environments, another approach is to require developers to test on at least two platforms before committing changes. Although not as fool-proof as testing on every platform, this approach still identifies many portability problems.

Building your application frequently for all platforms, using a single source code base shared by all developers, reduces the risk of introducing unwanted side effects into your application. It also reduces the risk that changes made by one developer will cause problems for other developers. It is also a good idea to run some type of automated test after each build to verify some minimal level of functionality before the new build is unleashed on the entire development staff.

The Cross-Platform QA Plan

Just as you need a good design for effective cross-platform coding, you need a good plan for cross-platform testing. Separate the plan into common testing components and platform-specific components. Common components include normal operation of the application from the user's perspective. Exceptions to this are look-and-feel issues that are defined by the target platform rather than by the application.

Identifying Platform-Specific Testable Items

One type of a platform-specific subsystem is any subsystem dependent on data files or network components that are a different word size or byte ordering on different platforms.

One subsystem that is particularly platform-specific is file I/O. Because of differences in the way different platforms store data, you must thoroughly test file I/O to ensure that data written by your application on one platform can be read by your application on a different platform. Your code cannot make any assumptions about byte ordering.

Network components are also very platform-specific because the network data is susceptible to byte ordering, word sizes, and structure packing differences. Chapter 11 will describe networking issues in detail.

Just as we have overcome 16-bit versus 32-bit issues with Windows NT and Windows 95, along comes DEC Alpha/OSF1, which is a 64-bit operating system. (Windows NT on Alpha runs in 32-bit mode.) You cannot make any assumptions in your code about data type sizes. This issue is very important when testing an application's capability to read and write data correctly.

Another platform-specific component that must be thoroughly tested is shared libraries. Shared libraries are implemented differently on virtually all platforms. Because much of your application is likely to be implemented in shared libraries, it is especially important that you test them carefully on all target platforms.

Security is another important platform-specific component that you must test carefully. Although Windows and Macintosh environments are single-user, Windows NT and UNIX are both multiuser operating systems. An important issue to consider in a multiuser environment is application licensing. It is much easier for end users to circumvent licensing terms in distributed GUI systems. Therefore, you may want to implement network licensing schemes in high-end markets, such as Windows NT and UNIX.

Another important platform-specific testing concern is the fact that, in distributed computing environments such as NT and UNIX, your application will be run remotely from servers. Data may not be stored on the same system as the application. Unlike PC or Macintosh environments, where all the hardware is virtually identical, in these environments, your application must be able to run remotely over a network and access data correctly across a variety of platforms. It is important that you test all possible combinations.

Testing Tools

There are cross-platform testing tools that are useful. Some products are not on all platforms, but there are roughly equivalent tools for each. For example, Purify is a UNIX equivalent to Nu-Mega BoundsChecker on the PC. When you can afford to, buy different tools for different platforms to get the greatest benefit from them. Sometimes one will identify problems that another overlooks. For automated test tools, however, a tool that is available across platforms is a better choice because you can use the same test scripts on all platforms. Examples of this type of tool are XRunner and QA Partner.

As indicated above, automated test tools are useful not only in the QA phase of development, but also in the code phase to test periodic builds of the application. For example, QA test tools can be integrated with the application build tools to provide a nightly build and "sniff test" to verify a minimal level of functionality. If the nightly tests fail, then the developers can know early in the day and begin looking for the problem (and the developer that introduced the bug!).

When testing on all platforms, you will likely find that one platform is very stable, but there are problems identified on another. Should you hold up further development or release of the stable platform until the unstable one is fixed? This can be a tough decision to make, particularly when revenue depends on product delivery. Unfortunately, there is no magical formula for solving this problem. Most managers end up trusting in the developers' intuition as to whether a problem is specific to a particular platform.

Chapter 12 discusses cross-platform testing in greater detail.

Summary

As with all software engineering, it is always better to be preemptive and proactive rather than reactive. Effective cross-platform development is an issue for product architects and principal developers, not an afterthought for a removed porting group. To be completely successful, you must plan and allocate resources for cross-platform development just as you would any other development project.

CHAPTER 2

Porting to the Macintosh

This chapter describes how to use the Windows Portability Library for cross-platform development of Visual C++ applications. In particular, it addresses the following topics:

- The requirements for Visual C++ for the Macintosh
- How to build Win32 applications for the Macintosh
- How to debug your Macintosh applications
- Special issues caused by differences between Windows and the Macintosh
- Macintosh extension APIs

As the largest developer of applications for the Apple Macintosh, no company has more of an interest for easy cross-platform development between Windows and Macintosh than Microsoft. To help address the problem of portability between Macintosh and Windows, Microsoft recently released Microsoft Visual C++ version 2.0 Cross-Development Edition for Macintosh.

The Visual C++ Cross-Development Edition for Macintosh is a set of add-on tools for Visual C++ version 2.0 running on Microsoft Windows NT version 3.5. Visual C++ for Macintosh allows you to do all of your development work for Windows, Windows95, Windows NT, and Macintosh in Visual C++ version 2.0.

Running and debugging applications created with Visual C++ for Macintosh requires an Ethernet AppleTalk connection between your Windows NT version 3.5 computer and your Macintosh. Visual C++ for Macintosh includes utilities for transferring compiled objects from your Windows NT system to the Macintosh, as well as facilities to remotely debug the application using the familiar Visual C++ integrated debugger, class browser, and other tools.

Requirements for Visual C++ for the Macintosh

Using Visual C++ for Macintosh requires two computers. First, you will need a Windows NT version 3.5 PC with Visual C++ version 2.0 and Visual C++ Cross-Development Edition for Macintosh installed. Note that Visual C++ for Macintosh is only available for *x*86-class PCs; not DEC Alpha, MIPS, or other Windows NT version 3.5 systems.

The PC requirements for running Visual C++ for Macintosh is essentially the same as for doing native Win32 development for Windows, Windows95, and Windows NT. You will need at least a VGA monitor, an 80386 or higher processor (80486 recommended), 16 MB of system RAM (20 MB recommended), a Windows NT compatible CD-ROM, and between 10 and 24 MB of free hard disk space (depending on setup options chosen).

The one exception to the standard Windows NT version 3.5 setup is that you will need to configure the AppleTalk protocol on the PC when you install Windows NT version 3.5. You will also need a network card in the PC to access the AppleTalk network.

It is also possible to connect the PC to your Macintosh via a serial cable between the serial ports of the two computers. Using the serial port requires a null-modem cable, and either 9 or 25 pin connectors depending on the connectors on the two computers. While handy for a quick proof-of-concept, using a serial port between the PC and Macintosh is not recommended for normal use on large projects due to the slow connection provided by the serial cable solution. You will find that a relatively small investment in an Ethernet card will pay off very quickly.

For your Macintosh system, you will need a Macintosh from the II family or Quadra series with at least a 68020 processor and System 7 or later operating system installed. Also, the Macintosh components of Visual C++ for Macintosh are installed from a 3.5-inch, 1.44-megabyte floppy disk. The Macintosh should have at least 5 MB of memory, and enough free disk space to hold the compiled object files that you will be creating using Visual C++ for Macintosh.

As with the PC, you will need an AppleTalk compatible Ethernet adapter or a properly configured serial cable connection to the PC.

Components of Visual C++ for the Macintosh

Visual C++ for Macintosh comes with two installation disks. The PC components are installed from a CD-ROM, while the Macintosh components are installed from a single 3.5-inch high density floppy disk. Each disk includes a setup program that makes installation very straightforward.

Macintosh Components

The Macintosh floppy disk installs the following components into a folder named Visual C++ 2.0:

- A Visual C++ File Utility which works with MFILE on the PC to transfer files from the PC to the Macintosh.

- A WLM Debug Output application that displays debug messages from the Windows Portability Library. (The acronym WLM is a reference "Windows Library for Macintosh", a pre-release name for what is now called "Windows Portability Library.")

- A Tracer program that works like the Visual C++ MFC Trace Options utility in the PC environment. Tracer allows you to set the tracing options for Microsoft Foundation Class Library for Macintosh.

- The Visual C++ Debug Monitor allows you to configure the Macintosh side of the remote debugging connection (either AppleTalk or serial cable) between the PC and Macintosh.

- Microsoft Help for Macintosh is a utility for viewing Windows help files on Macintosh.

PC Components

The Visual C++ for Macintosh installation manuals assume that you have already installed the PC with Windows NT version 3.5 and Visual C++ version 2.0. The PC components of Visual C++ for Macintosh come on a single CD-ROM and are installed into the same subdirectory as Visual C++ version 2.0.

The following directories are copied to your Visual C++ version 2.0 directory on your PC (assuming that you choose a full installation):

- /BIN—contains dynamic link libraries that are used by the Visual C++ integrated debugging environment for debugging Macintosh applications remotely.
- /M68K/BIN, /M68K/INCLUDE, /M68K/LIB—contains the 68K compiler, including files and libraries (including Windows Portability Library for Macintosh) necessary for compiling 68K binaries from within Visual C++. These components are generally referred to as the *68K back-end* to the Microsoft C/C++ version 8 compiler.
- /MFC/LIB—contains Microsoft Foundation Class Library for Macintosh.
- /SAMPLES—contains sample programs for Win32 applications, MFC applications, and Macintosh specific samples for Visual C++ for Macintosh.
- /HELP—contains the Visual C++ for Macintosh reference manuals in Windows Help format.

Visual C++ for Macintosh Tools and Libraries

Microsoft designed Visual C++ version 2.0 to allow for multiple targets when compiling Win32 applications. Visual C++ 2.0 includes the Project dialog box which allows you to choose the target platform to compile for. Standard Visual C++ 2.0 includes Win32 on Intel platforms (Windows 3.1, Windows 95, and Windows NT) and MIPS platforms running Windows NT. Microsoft has also released Visual C++ for DEC Alpha, which allows Visual C++ 2.0 to generate applications for DEC-Alpha–based systems running Windows NT.

With the Visual C++ for Macintosh extension, Visual C++ 2.0 can now also generate applications for Apple Macintosh from true Win32-based source code. When Visual C++ for Macintosh is installed on your Windows NT version 3.5 system with Visual C++ 2.0, about the only thing different that you notice in the Visual C++ environment is that the targets *Macintosh Release*, and *Macintosh Debug* show up in the target dialog along with MIPS and Intel platforms.

While the user interface of Visual C++ 2.0 does not change much when Visual C++ for Macintosh is installed, the architecture of Visual C++ for Macintosh is significantly different from the other target platforms. These differences exist because Visual C++ for Macintosh allows for remote debugging of Macintosh applications from the Macintosh test computer to the Windows NT development system. All other currently supported Visual C++ targets are tested on the same system on which they are compiled.

68K C/C++ Compiler

Visual C++ for Macintosh includes a 68K back-end to the Visual C++ C/C++ compiler. The MS C/C++ compiler is comprised of two components. The "front-end" is responsible for compiling C and C++ source code into a intermediate, architecturally neutral format. The front-end is the same regardless of the ultimate binary being produced. The *front-end* implements the MS compiler's ANSI compliance, as well as most of the MS compiler language extensions.

The *back-end* translates the intermediate code into platform-specific objects. Currently, MS supports Intel *x*86, Macintosh 68K, DEC Alpha, and MIPS objects. Support has been announced for the PowerPC. Visual C++ for Macintosh includes the 68K *back-end* for generating 68K objects that will run on the Macintosh.

The architecture of the MS C/C++ compiler is important to you as a programmer because, since the *front-end* is architecturally neutral, your source code is guaranteed to compile for all platforms that the C/C++ compiler supports. The compiler front-end is tied to the language; the back-end is tied to a processor and operating system.

Most of the options that are available in the *x*86 mode of the C/C++ compiler are also available in the 68K mode through the C/C++ tab in the Project Settings dialog box.

68K LINK

Visual C++ for Macintosh includes a linker that works identically to the standard Visual C++ linker, except that it generates native 68K Macintosh program objects. As with the C/C++ compiler, most of the options that are available in the *x*86 mode of the linker are also available in the 68K mode through the Link tab in the Project Settings dialog box.

Macintosh Resource Compiler

The resource compiler that comes with Visual C++ for Macintosh is based on the Win32 resource compiler, but has been modified for the Macintosh. Visual C++ for Macintosh also includes a PC-based implementation of the Macintosh Rez resource compiler, called MRC. This utility provides a method of compiling native Macintosh resource files into your application within the PC development environment. See the documentation for Visual C++ for Macintosh for further information on this utility.

Help Compiler and MacHelp

HC35.EXE is an implementation of the Windows Help compiler with extensions for the Macintosh. MacHelp is a Macintosh implementation of Windows WinHelp. It opens and displays Windows help files on the Macintosh. See Chapter 10 for details on creating on-line help for the Macintosh version of your application.

Windows Portability Library for the Macintosh

The Windows Portability Library for the Macintosh provides an implementation of a subset of the Win32 API for the Macintosh. With the Windows Portability Library, most Win32-compliant code can compile and execute on the Macintosh with few, if any, changes.

The Windows Portability Library implements the Macintosh user-interface conventions. As we shall see later, adhering to the Macintosh user interface might require that you change some Windows source code for the Macintosh environment. There are a few instances as well where native Macintosh features are not supported through the Win32 API, and you may need to call out to the native Macintosh Toolbox. The Windows Portability Library allows you the flexibility of writing Win32 code and also of bypassing the Win32 API when necessary and calling directly into the Macintosh Toolbox.

MFC 3.0

While the Windows Portability Library provides good portability for Win32 based code, the more elegant solution to cross-platform development is MFC 3.0. With MFC 3.0, you get the portability of C++, a powerful and versatile C++ class library, a robust and feature rich GUI builder in Visual C++, and cross-platform portability to Macintosh with Visual C++ for Macintosh.

Most of the reasons for modifying your Win32 C code go away with MFC 3.0, because MFC 3.0 abstracts most platform dependencies from your application. For instance, most Win32 API applications must at some point deal with drive letters, directory separators, and file system naming schemes. With MFC 3.0, all of this platform specific logic is abstracted from your application through the CFile and CArchive classes. MFC 3.0 also includes support for advanced Microsoft technology such as ODBC and OLE 2.0, which is very difficult to implement with low-level Win32 API code.

Building Win32 Applications for the Macintosh

Before you use the Windows Portability Library to port an application to the Macintosh, it is important that the application compile and run correctly under Windows. If your application already runs under Windows NT or Win32, you will have a much easier time porting to the Macintosh since you will have already solved most of the problems related to 16-bit versus 32-bit portability.

If the Windows version of your application is still 16-bit, then be sure to use the 16-bit tools, libraries, and header files from version 3.1 or later of the Windows SDK and compile your source code for Windows using the /DSTRICT option. Make any changes required to compile correctly using that option. By converting to STRICT compilation under Windows, you can identify and fix many of the problems that you might encounter when moving to a new platform.

Port to Macintosh

With the Windows Portability Library, you can port Windows code to the Macintosh platform with minimal changes. Your resulting Macintosh application will adhere to the Macintosh user interface conventions and style, and will therefore have the same look and feel as other Macintosh applications. There are a few places where Windows and Macintosh conventions conflict; in these cases, the Macintosh conventions will apply.

As you port your application, keep in mind that the Windows Portability Library is not a complete implementation of Microsoft Windows for the Macintosh. Parts of Windows are not implemented at all under the Windows Portability Library, and other parts differ from standard Windows. However, the Windows Portability Library provides a substantial and useful subset of the

Windows Win32 API. Most well-written Windows code should run under the Windows Portability Library without requiring any modification whatsoever.

You can use the VCPort utility to identify which Windows APIs and C run-time functions in your existing Windows code are supported on the Macintosh, which are not, and which are supported but may require code changes. The Windows Portability Library implements core Windows APIs residing in the KERNEL, GDI, and USER subsystems, along with APIs from the COMMDLG subsystem. The first release of the Windows Portability Library does not support other subsystems and extensions, such as multimedia subsystems, DDEML, and OLE. In general, the Windows Portability Library does *not* support any of the following:

- API functions not included in the Win32 API
- Task API functions
- Communications API functions
- Sound API functions
- Profiling API functions
- Most module-management API functions
- Messages between applications
- Obtaining information about windows or processes of other applications

Add Macintosh Specific Code

Because of the strict GUI compliance expectations of most Macintosh users, most applications ported with the Windows Portability Library will need to include some Macintosh-specific code in order to deal with Macintosh-specific problems. To take a simple example, the Macintosh can change screen-color depth while an application is running, whereas Windows applications generally check color depth settings only at boot time.

The Windows Portability Library provides the programmer with direct access to the Macintosh Toolbox. In instances where the Windows API does not provide the capability to be completely Macintosh GUI-compliant, it should always be possible to bypass the Windows Portability Library and call the Macintosh Toolbox directly. The Windows Portability Library includes a number of special APIs to facilitate this kind of mixed programming.

Avoiding Function Name Conflicts

If you do use Macintosh Toolbox or Operating System functions, you will probably need to include one or more of the standard Macintosh operating system header files, in addition to the Windows Portability Library version of the **WINDOWS.H** file. When you do so, name conflicts may arise between the Windows and the Macintosh interfaces. For example, both systems define a function called GetMenu (defined in **WINUSER.H** under Windows, and in **Menus.h** on the Macintosh).

The Windows Portability Library provides two ways of avoiding function name conflicts when you include Macintosh operating system include files. The first way is to use the name mappings provided by the **MACNAME1.H** and **MACNAME2.H** header files. When you include a Macintosh header file, bracket it with include statements to **MACNAME1.H** and **MACNAME2.H**. These name mappings require that you add a Mac prefix to every Macintosh function having a conflicting name. For example, in the following code fragment, the Macintosh GetMenu function is called as MacGetMenu:

```
#include <windows.h>
#ifdef _MAC
#include <macname1.h>
#include <Menus.h>
#include <macname2.h>
#endif
    ...
// shared menu code
    DrawMenuBar(hwnd);
    hmenu = GetMenu(hwnd);          // Windows GetMenu
    ...
// mac-specific menu code
#ifdef _MAC
    MenuHandle hmm;
    hmm = MacGetMenu(ridMac);       // Macintosh GetMenu
    SetItem(hmm, 0, "\pMacintosh");
    ...
#endif
```

This method is best suited for porting existing Windows code to the Macintosh, where you will use relatively few native Macintosh operating system and ToolBox calls.

The second method of avoiding name conflicts, which works best when porting existing Macintosh code to the Windows Portability Library, is to define a symbol called _MACNAMES before including the Windows Portability Library header file, WINDOWS.H. When _MACNAMES is defined, every name in WINDOWS.H that conflicts with a Macintosh name is given an Afx prefix.

Using this method, you must add an Afx prefix in your source code to every Windows Portability Library API with a conflicting name. The following example shows how you could call the Windows version of GetMenu as AfxGetMenu, while also including Menus.h:

```
#ifdef _MAC
#define _MACNAMES
#include <windows.h>
#include <Menus.h>
#else
#include <windows.h>
#endif
...
// shared menu code/

#ifdef _MAC
    AfxDrawMenuBar(hwnd);       // Windows DrawMenuBar on the
                                //   Macintosh

    hmenu = AfxGetMenu(hwnd);   // Windows GetMenu on the Macintosh
#else
    DrawMenuBar(hwnd);          // Windows DrawMenuBar under Windows

    hmenu = GetMenu(hwnd);      // Windows GetMenu under Windows
#endif


    ...
// mac-specific menu code
```

```
#ifdef _MAC
   MenuHandle hmm;
   hmm = GetMenu(ridMac);        // Macintosh GetMenu

   SetItem(hmm, 0, "\pMacintosh");
   ...
#endif
```

This approach works well for porting existing Macintosh code that contains many calls to operating system and ToolBox functions with conflicting names.

Setting Up the Build Environment

As with all the Visual C++ for Macintosh tools, the Windows Portability Library requires that the PATH and INCLUDE environment variables point to the \BIN and \INCLUDE subdirectories, respectively, so that the correct toolset is used when you build. Most of the tools and header files used by Microsoft Visual C++ for Macintosh have the same name as the corresponding files used by Visual C++ for Windows NT. If the environment variables are not correctly set, the wrong tools or header files may be invoked by mistake.

If you install Microsoft Visual C++ for Macintosh using the normal Visual C++ setup utility, these dependencies will be handled transparently to you. You need only set the PATH and INCLUDE environment variables yourself if you are compiling for the Macintosh outside of the Visual C++ environment (that is, from the DOS command line or external makefile).

When building Windows Portability Library applications that include the Macintosh system header files, it is important to set the INCLUDE environment variable correctly to avoid a conflict between the main Windows Portability Library header file, **WINDOWS.H** and the Macintosh OS header file, **Windows.h**. If you place the INCLUDE\MACOS directory in your INCLUDE variable, be sure that it follows the base INCLUDE directory for Visual C++ for Macintosh. In source files that need to include the Macintosh OS header file, **Windows.h**, it is best to use a statement such as the following:

```
#include <macos\Windows.h>
```

Macintosh Compiler Flags

Most of the compiler flags for the Visual C++ for Macintosh compiler are the same as for the Intel version of the Visual C++ compiler. The following sections describe which Visual C++ for Macintosh compiler options to use when compiling code that calls the Windows Portability Library:

Compiler Options for Debug Builds

For a debug build, a command line using options such as the following is recommended for use with the Windows Portability Library:

```
CL /AL /Gt1 /Zi /Q68m /Q68s /Od /D_MAC /DSTRICT /c EXAMPLE.C
```

The following table briefly describes these options:

Table 2.1 Compiler Options for Debug Builds

/AL	Turns on the far Apple calling convention, which allows individual code segments and total global data to exceed 32 Kbytes.
/Gt1	Causes all global variables to be addressed with "far" references. This switch may not be necessary for small applications.
/Zi	Causes debugging information to be included in the object files.
/Q68m	Turns on MacsBug symbols.
/Q68s	Generates swapper prologs and epilogs.
/Od	Turns off optimizations.
/D_MAC	Controls conditional inclusion of Macintosh-specific code in your application.
/DSTRICT	Turns on strict type-checking in the Windows header files.
/c	Compiles to an object file without automatically invoking the linker.

Compiler Options for Ship Builds

For a ship or retail build, a command line using options such as the following is recommended:

```
CL /AL /Gt1 /Oxw /Q68s /D_MAC /DSTRICT /DNDEBUG /c EXAMPLE.C
```

Two of the ship-build options above would not be used for a debug build:

```
/Oxw       Turns on aggressive optimizations.
/DNDEBUG   Turns off asserts.
```

Linking Macintosh Applications

Use the Visual C++ for Macintosh **LINK.EXE** to link your Windows Portability Library application. The Windows Portability Library requires the Visual C++ for Macintosh Swapper library, and automatically links to **SWAP.LIB**. In addition, because the Windows Portability Library uses floating point calculations internally, you must also link it with **SANES.LIB**. Any runtime or toolbox libraries that your application uses should be the swappable versions (such as **LIBCS.LIB**).

The following example shows a typical link command line for a Windows Portability Library application:

```
LINK /OUT:PROG.EXE PROG1.OBJ PROG2.OBJ ... WLM.LIB
    PROG.RSC PROGMAC.RSC WLM.RSC [COMMDLG.RSC]
```

Note that the Windows Portability Library includes header files that are nearly identical to the standard Win32 header files. Win32 APIs not supported by the Windows Portability Library are still included in the header files. This means that if your application uses APIs that are not supported by the Windows Portability Library, your application will compile, but it will not be able to link. Accordingly, you will see link errors until you have removed all references to APIs not supported by the Windows Portability Library.

If your project contains both Win32 and Macintosh targets, the Use MFC in a Shared DLL (**MFC30.DLL**) option causes the project to link dynamically with MFC on Win32; however, when building the Macintosh project, Visual C++ 2.0 silently links MFC in a static library. You can view the specific library used in the General tab of the Project Settings tab dialog box.

Using Windows Resources on the Macintosh

A Windows Portability Library application typically uses two different types of resources. The first consists of standard Windows resources (such as menus, dialog boxes, bitmaps, and so forth) that have been compiled into Macintosh resources using the Windows Portability Library version of RC.EXE, the Windows resource compiler. The second type consists of resources needed for the Macintosh version of the application, but not used under Windows (such as BNDL or SIZE resources). These are defined in an Apple Rez language text file with an **.R** extension, and are compiled using **MRC.EXE**, the Visual C++ Cross Development version of the Macintosh resource compiler.

Windows resource scripts are typically kept in files with an **.RC** extension, and are compiled using the Windows Portability Library version of the Windows Resource Compiler, **RC.EXE**, into binary resource files having an **.RSC** extension.

The Windows Portability Library provides a version of **RC.EXE** that can compile a Windows resource script into a Macintosh format. (This version of **RC.EXE** can only be used to create Macintosh resources.) The output file will have a normal **.RSC** extension. For example, the following command line generates a Macintosh-targeted **RSCFILE.RSC** from **RSCFILE.RC**, provided that the Windows Portability Library version of **RC.EXE** is used:

```
RC /R /D_MAC RSCFILE.RC
```

The **/D_MAC** component is not necessary to produce a Macintosh resource, but may be useful for controlling conditional statements in your resource script. Once compiled to a Macintosh-specific **.RSC** file, you can pass such Windows resources to the Visual C++ for Macintosh Linker, or you can attach them to the Macintosh application by including them in a Macintosh-specific resource (.R) file that is processed by the **MRC.EXE** tool.

NOTE   Be sure that your PATH environment variable is set correctly to point to the version of the **RC.EXE** tool that you need to use. Using the Windows Portability Library version when you intend to compile for Windows, or the Windows version when you are targeting the Macintosh, will not generate usable resources.

Debugging Your Macintosh Application

Just as Visual C++ for the Macintosh allows you to use your knowledge of the Windows API to develop applications for the Macintosh, it allows you to use your knowledge and familiarity with the Visual C++ graphic environment when monitoring and debugging your Macintosh applications. Visual C++ for Macintosh contains a distributed debugger; part of it runs on the target Macintosh system, and the other part runs as a components of Visual C++ on the Windows NT 3.5 build machine. These two components transfer status and commands between the two systems either on an attached LAN via the AppleTalk protocol or through a serial port connection between the two machines. Figure 2.1 depicts the architecture of the Visual C++ distributed debugger.

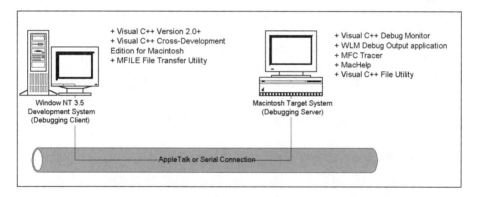

+ Visual C++ Version 2.0+
+ Visual C++ Cross-Development Edition for Macintosh
+ MFILE File Transfer Utility

+ Visual C++ Debug Monitor
+ WLM Debug Output application
+ MFC Tracer
+ MacHelp
+ Visual C++ File Utility

Window NT 3.5
Development System
(Debugging Client)

Macintosh Target System
(Debugging Server)

AppleTalk or Serial Connection

Figure 2.1 Visual C++ For Macintosh Distributed Debugger

The debug version of the Windows Portability Library validates the correctness of parameters to most APIs and sends a warning to the debugger if a parameter is invalid. This validation does take time, and if you find that the debug version of your application runs too slowly, you can turn validation off in specific areas with the WlmDebug API. The Windows Portability Library also provides many debugging messages that warn you about potentially nonportable, unsupported, or incompatible usage of the Windows API. Most of these messages will halt you in MacsBug or the Visual C++ for Macintosh debugger. However, some messages are only warnings and will not stop you in the debugger. If you are not using the Visual C++ for Macintosh debugger, you will notice these warnings because your Macintosh will briefly display the MacsBug screen and then flip back to the normal display. You can use the interrupt switch on your Macintosh to break into MacsBug and see what the warning was. You can also rerun your application and hold down the **Control** key as you execute the operation that caused the warning, which will cause the Windows Portability Library to halt in the debugger instead of continuing execution.

Output from Debugging API Functions

On the Macintosh, the Windows debugging API functions send their output to MacsBug—an assembly language debugger provided by Apple. Before sending output to MacsBug, however, the debugging APIs first check for the presence of the Gestalt selector WLMD, and if present, interpret the value returned by the selector as a function pointer to be called and passed to the output string. A simple debugging output monitor called WLM Debug Output is provided with the Windows Portability Library. WLM Debug Output registers a WLMD Gestalt selector and writes debugging output to a text window.

Debug Preference File

The debug version of the Windows Portability Library checks a preference file named WLM Preferences to set certain debug options. The Windows Portability Library Preferences file is located in the Preferences folder inside of the System Folder. The Options:Debug string can contain a number from 0 to 3, with the following meanings:

Value	Meaning
0	Disables all asserts and slow handle validation
I	Enables slow handle validation only
2	Enables asserts only
3	Enables asserts and handle validation

Dealing with Differences between Windows and the Macintosh

The Windows Portability Library does a very good job of masking most Macintosh environmental differences from your application. However, there are some differences that are too difficult to hide inside the library due to functional limitations on the Macintosh or because of performance issues.

System Differences

There are a few low-level operating system differences that might become issues when porting your Windows application to Macintosh. System differences include things like file system differences, application resources differences, and system information API functions.

File System Differences

Differences between the Windows and Macintosh file systems create porting issues for almost all applications. Not only are file names, directory names, drives, and volume names handled differently on the two systems, there are also many features of the Macintosh file system that do not exist under Windows. For example, creator types, file types, directory IDs, and Macintosh file system specifications do not exist in Windows. Therefore, it is particularly important for Windows developers to familiarize themselves with the Macintosh file system before attempting to port an application.

Code that parses and manipulates pathnames under Windows will not work on the Macintosh, and must be rewritten. In dealing with this problem, you may find the Windows Portability Library WrapFile and UnwrapFile API functions useful for gaining direct access to the Macintosh file I/O APIs in the Macintosh version of your application. Another useful approach is to design a file-handling layer that sits between your application and the native Win32 file APIs, and then write a Macintosh version of this layer.

In the Windows Portability Library, the file I/O functions normally do not manipulate full pathnames. Instead, they work with a formatted data buffer that contains a filename, directory ID, and a volume identifier. This data buffer is not a valid file system path and is not useful for display purposes. Although the file I/O functions also support Macintosh pathnames, this usage is discouraged, since it is not as robust as the default formatted data buffer.

The *volume identifier* in a formatted data buffer contains the volume name and creation date, and both of these data are used to generate a volume reference number when needed. Therefore, you can safely save a formatted data buffer to a permanent storage location and reuse it to locate a file on subsequent boots of the Macintosh. Also, because the data buffer is both null-terminated and guaranteed not to contain any null characters, you can use the normal C Run-Time library string functions to copy it or determine its length. You may also pass a full or partial filename to the file I/O functions, which will look for the file starting in the current directory.

Similarly, the search path used by OpenFile is specific to the Macintosh. Another minor difference affects such Windows Kernel APIs as OpenFile and ReadFile. Under the Macintosh file manager, files open for writing only are actually opened for reading and writing. As a result, if you use OpenFile to open a file for writing only, and then depend on the "write-only" mode to prevent subsequent reads from succeeding, your code will not work properly on the Macintosh.

In spite of these differences, most Windows applications that use the Common Dialog library will port to the Macintosh without significant difficulty.

Resource Differences

Resources on the Macintosh are fairly similar to Windows resources, but there are a few differences. The Windows Portability Library currently provides no access to modules outside of the executing application. As a result, the resource APIs ignore the hModule parameter, and address only resources within the application.

If you use a C string to identify a custom resource type, the Windows Portability Library uses the first four characters of the string to create a corresponding Macintosh resource type. The **RC.EXE** utility provided with the Windows Portability Library also uses this technique to name the Macintosh resources which it creates.

Because the Windows Portability Library uses the first four characters of a resource name to create the corresponding Macintosh resource type, the first four custom resource names in your application must be unique. Otherwise, two or more custom resource types can be assigned the same name. You should review your application carefully to make sure that your custom resource names are only four characters long, or that they are all unique in their first four characters. This restriction does not apply to std resources.

System Information

Although the Windows Portability Library supports most selectors to GetSystemMetrics, some supported selectors are inherently nonportable due to differences between the Macintosh and Windows user interfaces. Some of the colors returned by GetSysColor are approximations at best. Very few of the selectors to SystemParametersInfo are supported.

Multiple Monitor Support

Windows APIs do not generally address multiple-monitor issues. You should familiarize yourself with multiple monitor support on the Macintosh and review your code carefully for related issues. Windows Portability Library API functions refer to the primary monitor by default.

When Graphics Device Interface (GDI) functions draw across multiple monitors, they draw at the greatest color depth currently set on any one of those monitors. This can cause problems, particularly when drawing is occurring across a color and a monochrome monitor, for example.

GDI Differences

The following sections describe differences in the Windows Portability Library Graphical Device Interface (GDI) API functions. For more details on these differences, see Chapter 8.

Bitmaps and Device-Independent Bitmaps (DIBs)

Bitmaps and DIBs are well-supported by the Windows Portability Library, but there are a few things to be aware of when porting your bitmap or DIB code:

- The Macintosh allows the screen depth to change while your application is running. If screen-compatible bitmaps are displayed when the screen depth changes, they will no longer be compatible afterwards.

- Be aware that you may need to re-create your bitmaps in response to a WM_SYSCOLORCHANGE message.

- Be careful about deleting bitmaps that are selected in HDCs. This was illegal under Windows, but did not always cause a General Protection Fault. It will definitely cause such a condition under the Windows Portability Library.

- Unlike Windows, the Windows Portability Library must allocate a good deal of extra memory to provide for drawing on a bitmap. Applications can save this memory by marking a bitmap read-only, using the Windows Portability Library SetBitmapReadOnly API. This is particularly important for applications that use many bitmaps.

Pen Shape

When drawing lines, Windows uses a round pen whereas the Macintosh uses a rectangular pen. End-points and line joints on Windows look round, while on the Macintosh, end-points and line joints look square. Similarly, when drawing the outline around a RoundRect, Windows does not maintain a line of constant thickness when tracing the round corners, whereas the Macintosh does. This difference should be noticeable only with very wide pens.

Polygons

The Windows Portability Library does not support the WINDING fill mode polygons since the Macintosh only supports ALTERNATE mode. The Windows Portability Library does not support PolyPolygons.

Color Resolution

When resolving RGB colors to monochrome devices, Windows uses a method called "luminance matching" to decide whether to use black or white to represent a specific color. For example, yellow maps to the color white on monochrome devices.

The Macintosh also uses luminance mapping to resolve colors, but the luminance threshold is in a different place than it is under Windows. Of the fully saturated colors (blue, green, cyan, yellow, red, magenta), only yellow maps to the color white on the Macintosh. Under Windows, a fairly wide range of fully saturated colors around yellow will also map to white. Note also that the Macintosh palette is different than most Windows display drivers. For example, dark red (RGB(0x80,0x00,0x00)) does not exist in the standard Macintosh 16-color palette.

Palettes

There are a number of areas in which Macintosh and Windows palette handling is quite different. See Chapter 8 for complete details on the Windows Portability Library palette implementation.

Transparent BitBlt Extensions

On color QuickDraw systems, the Windows Portability Library supports the transparent BitBlt extensions from **MMSYSTEM.H**. GetDeviceCaps(hdc, CAPS1) returns **C1_TRANSPARENT** if transparent BitBlts work. SetBkMode(hdc, NEWTRANSPARENT) enables the transparent BitBlt. BitBlt uses the current background color as the transparent part of the bitmap. Note that this only works for the SRCCOPY raster operation. The following example shows how transparent BitBlt extensions might be implemented:

```
#include <windows.h>
#include <mmsystem.h>

// transfer non-gray pixels to the screen
if (GetDeviceCaps(hdc, CAPS1) & C1_TRANSPARENT)
{
    SetBkMode(hdc, NEWTRANSPARENT);
    SetBkColor(hdc, RGB(0xc0,0xc0,0xc0));
    BitBlt(hdc, x, y, cx, cy, hdcButton, 0, 0, SRCCOPY);
}
else
{
    ...   // old mask and blt code
}
```

Binary Raster Operations: ROP2 and "Background Mode"

On the Macintosh, QuickDraw does not support the full range of binary raster operations available under Windows. Windows also supports the concept of background mode, which determines how the white bits in two-color patterns mix with the existing display surface background. The binary raster operation is set with SetROP2, and the background mode is set with SetBkMode. See

Chapter 8 for a complete list of the Binary Raster Operations supported by the Windows Portability Library.

BitBlt Ternary Raster Operations

Windows supports a large number (256) of ternary raster operations in the BitBlt (and related) operations. These operations allow for arbitrary logical operations combining the source, destination, and current brush pattern. Although this set of raster operations is comprehensive, many of the operations are never used in practice. Because Apple did not implement so general an interface on the Macintosh, the Windows Portability Library supports only a small subset of the Windows raster operations. See Chapter 8 for a complete list of the Ternary Raster Operations supported by BitBlt and related API functions.

Color inversion (that is, XOR operations) on the Macintosh results in different color combinations than you would expect on Windows. If the inverted colors are black or white, however, then you will get the same mapping.

StretchBlt Modes

Both Windows and the Macintosh allow bitmaps to be stretched (either shrunk or expanded) if a destination rectangle is a different size than its source rectangle. However, although the stretching algorithm used on the Macintosh is similar to that used by the COLORONCOLOR mode under Windows, the results of stretching are not identical on the two systems. On the Macintosh, StretchBlt does not support image reflection (that is, the source rectangle is oriented differently than the destination rectangle).

Font Handling

Fonts in Windows are complex entities, defined by a dozen or so different parameters. Everything from the facename and height to the clipping precision and output quality can be used to pick a font. Fonts are also device-specific; one device may not support the same set of fonts as another. The process of mapping a logical, device-independent font to a physical, device-dependent font is called "font resolution." The "font mapper" finds the physical font that most closely matches a requested logical font.

The native Macintosh font model is simpler. An output font is specified by its facename, height, and attributes. The Macintosh font manager can simulate all the font attributes and can scale font heights on all output devices, so there is no need for a complex font mapper. With the development of TrueType outline fonts, many of the scaling and font mapping problems in Windows have been simplified as well.

Character Sets

While the Visual C++ for Macintosh compiler does not perform character mapping for strings within your source code, the Windows Portability Library **RC.EXE** resource compiler does map the Windows ANSI character set to the Macintosh character set wherever appropriate. So, if you have strings that have characters in the 0x00–0x1f or 0x7f–0xff range, move them into the resource file string tables so that the resource compiler will translate them properly.

Text Metrics

The Windows TEXTMETRIC structure supplies some font information that is not available from the Macintosh font manager. To the extent possible, the Windows Portability Library uses "best guess" values to fill in unavailable metrics. The following table shows fields that are not necessarily identical to the Windows values:

Table 2.2 Text Metric Differences Between Windows and the Macintosh

TEXTMETRIC field	How it is set under the Windows Portability Library
tmInternalLeading	A guess value that may or may not be accurate, computed so that the font "size" can be derived by subtracting tmInternalLeading from tmHeight.
tmWeight	FW_BOLD or FW_NORMAL; no other values are returned.
tmDefaultChar	Always a space.
tmBreakChar	Always a space.
tmPitchAndFamily	Font family is only filled in if the application supplies a 'FFAM' resource. If no 'FFAM' resource is present for a given facename, then the font family is FF_DONTCARE. The pitch and outline bits should be accurate. The vector and device bits are always 0.
tmCharSet	For most fonts, OEM_CHARSET. For Japanese, Korean, or Chinese fonts, one of the Far East _CHARSET constants, as appropriate.
tmOverhang	For italic text in bitmap fonts, the overhang is equal to ascent/2; otherwise it is 0.

Both EnumFonts and GetTextMetrics will return the TEXTMETRIC structure as noted above. EnumFonts, in addition, returns a LOGFONT structure with similar differences:

Table 2.3 LOGFONT Differences

LOGFONT field	How it is set under the Windows Portability Library
lfEscapement	Always 0.
lfOrientation	Always 0.
lfWeight	FW_BOLD or FW_NORMAL.
lfCharSet	Always OEM_CHARSET or one of the Far East character sets.
lfOutPrecision	Always 0.
lfClipPrecision	Always 0.
lfQuality	Always 0.
lfPitchAndFamily	Unless the application supplies an 'FFAM' resource, the font family is always FF_DONTCARE, but the VARIABLE_PITCH and FIXED_PITCH parts are set correctly in either case.

It works best to use negative lfHeight fields in the LOGFONT structure to specify font sizes to the Windows Portability Library GDI, and specify 0 for the lfWidth field. All fonts are assumed to be in the OEM character set, not the ANSI character set. The Macintosh does not have vector fonts.

Font Mapping

The Windows Portability Library GDI tries to map Windows font names into equivalent Macintosh font names. The font mapping table used to do this mapping is contained the FTAB 17000 resource in the application's resource fork. The font mapping table is used only if the requested facename cannot be found in the list of installed fonts. The format of the 'FTAB' resource and the recommended font mappings can be found in **FTAB.R**, located in the \M68K\INCLUDE\MRC subdirectory. If you do not want facename mappings to occur, simply remove this resource from your application.

Font Resources

The Windows Portability Library supports modified versions of the AddFontResource and RemoveFontResource functions. They both accept formatted FSSpec (Macintosh file system specification) filenames, which should refer to a resource file that contains the FONT and optionally, the sfnt resources. The AddFontResource and RemoveFontResource functions only add and remove fonts for your application, they do not affect the list of system fonts.

Metafiles

Most metafile APIs have been implemented on the Macintosh, but with some significant restrictions. Extended metafile APIs are not supported. Metafiles are implemented using Macintosh Pictures, which works well for rendering graphics to the clipboard, since a Picture is the standard format for data interchange on the Macintosh. Although Macintosh Pictures and Windows metafiles are similar in concept, they differ significantly in so many details that it is prohibitively expensive to implement many of the Windows metafile APIs completely.

For a complete description of metafile support on the Macintosh, please refer to Chapter 8.

Windows

The following sections describe differences in the Windows Portability Library Window Manager Interface API functions. For more details on these differences, see Chapter 9.

Resizable Top-Level Windows

In some cases, the behavior of top-level window is different under the Windows Portability Library than under Windows, because of interactions with the Macintosh window manager. For example, you cannot change the state (size, position, or z-order) of a top-level window without redrawing the window. As a result, if you use the **SWP_NOREDRAW** flag when calling SetWindowPos on a top-level window, the flag is ignored.

Instead of a thick frame, the Macintosh uses a "size box" in the bottom right corner of a window to indicate the window is resizable. This difference causes many problems with applications that have placed user interface elements in this corner of their windows. By default, the Windows Portability Library only draws a size box in a top-level window if the window is resizable (that is, has the **WS_THICKFRAME** style bit set), and the top-level window or one of its children has at least one frame scroll bar turned on (that is, has the **WS_HSCROLL** or **WS_VSCROLL** style bit set), and that scrollbar is aligned to the bottom or right side of the top-level window. The purpose of these restrictions is to ensure that the Windows Portability Library only draws a size box if it is guaranteed that it will not be drawing the size box over a portion of the top-level window that could be drawn on by the application.

Even if the size box is not drawn, however, the bottom right corner of a resizable window still hit-tests as a resizing area. This means that even if your application places a user interface element such as a control in this area, when the user clicks there, the Windows Portability Library will enter a resizing mode for the top-level window instead of passing the click on to your application. For this reason, it is best to redesign your user interface if your existing application uses this corner of a resizable top-level window. If the Windows Portability Library does not automatically draw a size box for you, you may wish to create a scroll bar control with the **SBS_SIZEBOX** style bit and place it in this area. A scroll bar created with this style bit draws itself as a size box instead of a scroll bar, and gives the user a visible indication that the window is resizable. Another alternative is to use the **WS_EX_FORCESIZEBOX** extended window style with CreateWindowEx. This window style forces the Windows Portability Library to draw a Macintosh grow icon in the bottom right corner of the window. You should only use this window style on top-level windows.

Top-Level Child Windows

A child window created with a caption (**WS_CAPTION**) is represented as a separate Macintosh window instead of being drawn inside its parent window. The child window will be freely movable by the user and may be moved outside the bounds of its parent window. When the parent window moves or scrolls, the child window does not move. Clicking on the client area of such a top-level child window does not change the z-order of the child; you must call SetWindowPos (possibly by way of BringToFront) to change the child's z-order, just as in Windows. If your ported application creates top-level child windows that you want to be contained by their parent windows, create the child windows without a caption and provide your own nonclient-area painting to make the child look like a moveable window with a caption.

Some Windows-based applications override the **WM_NCCALCSIZE,** **WM_NCPAINT, WM_NCACTIVATE** and other **WM_NC...** messages to create their own non-client area (frame) styles. For example, many applications implement windows with tiny title bars for their tool palettes. Under the Windows Portability Library, if your application changes the frame of a top-level window, the window must be created with an initial style specifying only **WS_BORDER.** This prevents the Macintosh from drawing a window frame, and gives your application complete control over nonclient painting.

Minimized Windows

The Macintosh does not support minimized windows, and neither does the Windows Portability Library. Passing one of the **SW_SHOWMIN...** commands to ShowWindow results in the appropriate display and activation of the window, but the window remains in its current size and position and does not minimize.

Window Style Restrictions

Not all combinations of window styles are supported when creating a window (see Chapter 8). Some uses of SetWindowLong to change the style or extended style of a window are not supported, because they would require changing the Macintosh implementation of the window. For example, the Windows Portability Library does not allow adding the **WS_CAPTION** style to a child window that does not have a caption or system menu, because this would change the child from being drawn inside its parent window to having its own Macintosh window. If you attempt such a change, the Windows Portability Library warns you that changing the host implementation is not allowed and refuses to make the change. Similarly, you can not use SetParent on the Macintosh to make the desktop the parent of a child window.

Multiple Document Interface (MDI) Windows

Multiple Document Interface (MDI) is an area where the Windows Portability Library makes many assumptions about your application in order to achieve reasonable Macintosh behavior. As a result, you may encounter compatibility problems where these assumptions are not correct for your application.

The Windows Portability Library requires that an MDI frame window be maximized at all times, to achieve good results when maximizing child windows and positioning child windows of the frame window, such as toolbars and status bars. To enforce this requirement, the Windows Portability Library always maximizes the frame window whenever ShowWindow is called with a show command other than SW_HIDE. Also, the DefFrameProc API overrides the **WM_WINDOWPOSCHANGING** message and changes the window location and size to match the maximized position.

When DefFrameProc receives a **WM_ACTIVATEAPP** message indicating that the application is being deactivated, it hides all children of the MDI frame window other than the MDICLIENT control. This is done in accordance with the Macintosh user interface convention that windows such as toolbars, status bars, and floating palettes be hidden while the application is in the background. Windows that were hidden by DefFrameProc are shown when DefFrameProc receives an activating **WM_ACTIVATEAPP** message. If you have a child window of the frame window that you do not want to be hidden, add the **WS_EX_NOAUTOHIDE** style bit to the child's extended style flags when you call CreateWindowEx.

To work properly, your application must pass the following messages through to DefFrameProc:

- WM_GETMINMAXINFO
- WM_WINDOWPOSCHANGING
- WM_WINDOWPOSCHANGED
- WM_ACTIVATEAPP

The MDI standard for Windows requires that only one child window can be maximized at any time. The Windows MDI APIs enforce this standard by restoring the unmaximized state of the current maximized child whenever a different child is activated, and by maximizing the newly active child. The Windows Portability Library does not support this standard. On the Macintosh, MDI APIs only change the maximized state of MDI children in response to the **WM_MDIMAXIMIZE** and **WM_MDIRESTORE** messages. The **WM_MDIMAXIMIZE** message handler does not restore any previously maximized child.

The Macintosh window corresponding to an MDI frame window is never made visible, even if the frame window is visible. This means that the MDICLIENT control is not visible either. If your application depends on having a "desktop" area on which to draw, design an alternate user interface, or preferably create a child window on which to draw.

Menus

Since there is only one menu bar on the Macintosh system, there is only one menu bar visible on the screen at any given time. In general, the Windows Portability Library inserts a window's menu into the Macintosh menu bar when the top-level window becomes active.

It is possible to prevent the normal menu-bar replacement and force another non-active window's menu into the Macintosh menu bar by intercepting the **WM_MACINTOSH(WLM_SETMENUBAR)** message. This should be used with caution, however, since many Windows application do not expect to receive **WM_COMMAND** messages when the application window is in an in-active state.

Top-Level Menus

The Windows Portability Library does not support the **MF_OWNERDRAW** or **MF_BITMAP** styles in top-level menus and all menu items in the top-level menu must be **MF_POPUP** (that is, you cannot have active buttons in the top-level menubar). Also, the Macintosh does not automatically make a menu taller and wrap around when it gets too wide. If a menu bar gets wider or taller than the Macintosh screen, it will be truncated and may cause other problems.

Menu Keyboard Accelerators

In a standard Macintosh user interface, the "Command" key (the clover symbol) is used for all menu accelerators. To specify the clover character, use "\021" in your menu item string:

```
MENUITEM "Copy\t\021C"
```

Also, change any accelerator tables you have in your resource file to match the accelerators you give in your menus. For example, a Windows .RC file might contain the following:

```
POPUP "&File"
BEGIN
```

```
            MENUITEM "E&xit", ID_APP_EXIT
    END
```

The corresponding Macintosh .RC file would contain the following:

```
POPUP "&File"
BEGIN
            MENUITEM "&Quit\t\21Q", ID_APP_EXIT
    END
    IDR_MAINFRAME ACCELERATORS
    BEGIN
            "Q", ID_APP_EXIT, VIRTKEY, ALT
    END
```

Macintosh-specific resources can be created and maintained as a part of Visual C++ 2.0 projects. For more information on the steps used to create separate accelerators for the Macintosh, see Chapter 1 of the *68K Programmers Guide* that accompanies Visual C++ for the Macintosh.

Help Menu

Top-level menus created with the MF_HELP bit set are automatically appended to the end of the Macintosh System 7.0 Help menu. Help menu items must not use **MF_BITMAP, MF_OWNERDRAW**, or custom checks, and must not have noncommand key keyboard accelerators. The system software, not the Windows Portability Library, draws the menu items in the System 7.0 Help menu. The system software does not support drawing bitmap or ownerdrawn menu items, menu items with custom checks, or menu items with anything other than standard command-key keyboard accelerators.

If your application inserts items in the balloon Help menu (using **MF_HELP** menus, or with the "HELP" keyword in the .RC file), set up balloon Help strings using a special 'hmnu' resource in your .R resource script file. Macintosh 'hmnu' resources may be used to assign balloon Help for items in the enabled, disabled, checked, or marked state. Because the Windows Portability Library does not support the marked state, leave that entry blank. The Help menu uses kHMHelpMenuID as the resource number.

Menu Tracking

When tracking the mouse in menus, an application receives **WM_MENU SELECT** messages over enabled and disabled menu items. Windows applications can force Windows to stop menu tracking at any time by send the **WM_CANCELMODE** message to the menu's owner. This message does not work on the Macintosh. Once the user has started tracking the menus with the mouse, there is no way to stop menu tracking until the user releases the mouse button.

System Menu

Macintosh windows do not include system menus. However, your application can modify the Apple menu using the GetSystemMenu API. The standard list of items in the Apple Menu folder is always appended to the end of the menu owners system menu. If the menu bar owner does not have a system menu, the Windows Portability Library provides a default system menu consisting of a simple About string that an application usually replaces with its own About MyApp command. The default About menu item has a command ID of **SC_DESKACCESSORY**.

When the user chooses a menu item in the Apple menu, the Windows Portability Library sends a **WM_SYSCOMMAND** message with **SC_DESKACCESSORY** in the LOWORD of the wParam. The lParam contains the menu offset of the DA item chosen. When DefWindowProc sees the **SC_DESKACCESSORY** system command, it launches the appropriate desk accessory for the application. If lParam is 0, then the message is for the default "About" command mentioned above.

Disabled Menu Bars

The standard Macintosh user interface allows for menus to be in the "disabled" state when a dialog box is displayed. When a dialog box is active, the menus are typically completely dimmed, unless there is an edit control in the dialog box, in which case the Cut, Copy, and Paste commands are left enabled.

To implement this kind of interface in your application, you can override the **WM_MACINTOSH (WLM_MENUSTATE)** message in the window that owns the menu. If your application returns **MD_ENABLE** from this message, you get the normal, ungrayed user interface. If your application returns **MD_DISABLE** the menu is disabled and beeps when you click on it. If you return **MD_GRAY**, the entire menu bar is disabled and drawn gray. If you return **MD_GRAYCCP**, the entire menu bar is drawn gray except for Cut, Copy, and Paste.

Note that in the **MD_GRAYCCP** state, **WM_COMMAND** messages are not sent to the window that owns the menu bar. Instead, **WM_COPY**, **WM_CUT**, and **WM_PASTE** messages are sent to the active window.

The Windows Portability Library dialog box manager uses the **WLM_HASCCP** message to implement the standard Macintosh menu user interface when Windows Portability Library dialog boxes are active. When a dialog box is activated, the **WM_MACINTOSH** (**WLM_HASCCP**) message (has cut, copy, and paste) is sent to it. The default handling of this message is to send it to all child windows. If any of them return **TRUE**, then the dialog box returns **TRUE** as well. Since you can cut, copy and paste into edit controls, the edit control returns **TRUE** in response to this message. If you want to disable this feature, intercept the **WLM_HASCCP** message and return **FALSE**.

Dialog Boxes

Differences in the standard dialog box interfaces used by the Macintosh and Windows can introduce significant incompatibilities. By default, dialog boxes managed by the Windows Portability Library follow Macintosh conventions, which differ from Windows dialog boxes in several significant ways. See Chapter 5 for a complete description of Macintosh dialog differences.

Message Differences

There are several general porting issues relating to the handling of Windows Portability Library messages:

- Mouse-moved events are generated synchronously; they are not generated at input time and posted into the input queue, but are created when the application calls WaitMessage, PeekMessage, or GetMessage.
- There is a new field in the MSG structure, lPrivate, which should not be modified by the user.
- **WM_QUIT** messages are returned only when the message queue is empty, as under Windows. However, the Macintosh event queue need not be empty for a **WM_QUIT** to be returned.

- PeekMessage can return a **WM_MACINTOSH (WLM_MACEVENT)** message in several circumstances that may require changes to message latching or message filtering code.

Keyboard Messages

Keyboard messages under the Windows Portability Library differ in several respects from their Windows counterparts. To begin with, the MSG structure has a new field in it, lPrivate, which is maintained by the Windows Portability Library and used by TranslateMessage to generate the correct **WM_CHAR** message. As a result, an application can not explicitly fill in the fields of a MSG structure with a **WM_KEYDOWN** or **WM_KEYUP** message and pass the MSG to TranslateMessage. However, an application can use PostMessage to post a **WM_KEYDOWN** message to a window, in which case the Windows Portability Library can determine the appropriate contents for the private field and fill in the MSG structure.

Message Latching and Filtering

One of the most significant differences in all of the Windows Portability Library is its implementation of PeekMessage(). On the Macintosh, several event types such as update, disk, activate, suspend/resume, and high-level are generated which do not have equivalent Windows messages. Under the Windows Portability Library, PeekMessage(..., **PM_NOREMOVE**) returns a **WM_MACINTOSH (WLM_MACEVENT)** message so that your application can stop passing **PM_NOREMOVE** to PeekMessage and can instead call GetMessage or PeekMessage(..., **PM_REMOVE**). PeekMessage also returns the **WM_MACINTOSH (WLM_MACEVENT)** message if an event is converted into a corresponding Windows message that does not match the HWND or message filters passed to PeekMessage. As a result, it is possible under the Windows Portability Library that a call to PeekMessage(..., **PM_REMOVE**) will not find a message just returned by PeekMessage(..., **PM_NOREMOVE**). See **WLM_MACEVENT** for more information.

Cursor and Icon Differences

The Windows Portability Library does not support color cursors on the Macintosh. When reading a cursor from a resource file, the Windows Portability Library gives first preference to 16 x 16 monochrome cursors, followed by 32 x

32 monochrome cursors (which are then scaled down to 16 x 16). You may want to design a custom 16 x 16 monochrome cursor for use in the Macintosh version of your application. The **IDC_ICON** and **IDC_UPARROW** system cursors are not supported.

The Clipboard

Macintosh clipboard format names are only four characters long. You should convert all your Clipboard format names to the equivalent four-character strings used on the Macintosh. For example:

```
#ifdef _MAC
    cf = RegisterClipBoardFormat("RTF ");
#else
    cf = RegisterClipBoardFormat("RichTextFormat");
#endif
```

Clipboard viewers only update when the viewer application is the front-most application on the Macintosh's desktop. While your application is in the background, clipboard changes caused by other applications do not show up in your viewer. If the clipboard changes while your application is inactive, change notifications occur when your application is reactivated.

The Macintosh has a much smaller set of standard clipboard formats than Windows. The CF_TEXT format is mapped to the Macintosh's TEXT format, and CF_METAFILEPICT is mapped to PICT. Note that there is no unique format for CF_BITMAP, CF_DIB, and CF_PALETTE formats. The Windows Portability Library supports these formats, but maps them all to the PICT format. Unless your application does not support CF_METAFILEPICT, you should disable your application's code that renders or accepts CF_BITMAP, CF_DIB and CF_PALETTE formats.

Macintosh Extensions

Of course, there are some aspects of the Macintosh that are not available in Windows. The Windows Portability Library provides a variety of extensions to the Win32 API designed to bridge the gap between Windows and the Macintosh operating system. The APIs listed in the following table provide access to native Macintosh ToolBox and operating system functions.

Table 2.4 Macintosh Extension APIs

CheckinHandle	Checks back in a Macintosh handle corresponding to a local or global allocation.
CheckinMenu	Checks in a Macintosh menu corresponding to a given popup menu.
CheckinPict CheckoutPict.	Checks in the Pict (Macintosh picture) previously checked out by
CheckinPort	Checks back in a Macintosh graphics port (GrafPort).
CheckinPrint	Checks back in a Macintosh print record.
CheckinRgn	Checks back in a Macintosh RgnHandle.
CheckoutHandle	Retrieves the Macintosh handle corresponding to a local or global allocation handle.
CheckoutMenu	Retrieves a Macintosh menu handle corresponding to a specified menu item.
CheckoutPict	Checks out a Pict (Macintosh picture) from a specified metafile.
CheckoutPort	Checks out the Macintosh GrafPort that corresponds to a given DC.
CheckoutPrint	Checks out the Macintosh print record corresponding to a given printer DC.
CheckoutRgn	Checks out a Macintosh RgnHandle associated with a given Windows region.
CreateMacPattern	Creates a Windows HBITMAP corresponding to a Macintosh Pattern.
GetHandleWrapper	Retrieves the local or global allocation, if any, corresponding to a Macintosh handle.
GetWindowWrapper	Returns the Windows-style window handle, if any, corresponding to a specified Macintosh window.
GetWrapper ContainerWindow	Returns the Macintosh window that contains a specified Windows-style window.
GetWrapperHandle	Retrieves the Macintosh handle corresponding to a local or global allocation.
GetWrapper Window	Returns the Macintosh window corresponding to a specified Windows-style window handle.

Table 2.4 Macintosh Extension APIs (continued)

UnwrapFile	Converts a special formatted string into a Macintosh file system specification (FSSpec).
UnwrapFileHandle	Converts a Win32 file handle into a Macintosh FSSpec.
UnwrapHandle	Converts a local or global allocation back into a Macintosh handle.
UnwrapPict	Removes a Macintosh picture handle from a Windows metafile and deletes the metafile.
UnwrapPort	Frees a device context handle created using WrapPort.
UnwrapPrint	Destroys a printer device context created by WrapPrint.
UnwrapRgn	Removes from around a Macintosh region the wrapping that was performed by WrapRgn.
UnwrapWindow	Destroys a Windows-style window handle without affecting the underlying Macintosh window.
WrapEvent	Converts a Macintosh event into the corresponding Windows message.
WrapFile	Converts a Macintosh FSSpec into a special formatted buffer.
WrapFileHandle	Converts a Macintosh File Manager reference number into a Windows file handle.
WrapHandle	Converts a Macintosh handle into a handle that can be manipulated by local or global allocators.
WrapMenu Command	Converts a Macintosh menu ID and item index pair into a WM_COMMAND message.
WrapPict	Creates a metafile corresponding to a Macintosh picture.
WrapPort	Creates a device context handle to draw on a Macintosh GrafPort.
WrapPrint	Creates a device context equivalent to a Macintosh print record.
WrapRgn	Creates a Windows region out of an existing Macintosh region.
WrapWindow	Creates a Windows-style window handle from an existing Macintosh window.

Memory Handle Transformations

The Windows Portability Library provides the CheckoutHandle, CheckinHandle, WrapHandle, UnwrapHandle, GetHandleWrapper, and GetWrapperHandle APIs for converting between global and local memory allocations and Macintosh handles.

Files

The Windows Portability Library provides several APIs for translating between Macintosh file management structures and Windows Portability Library structures. Use the WrapFile and UnwrapFile APIs to move between an FSSpec and a data buffer. Both UnwrapFileHandle and GetMacFileInformation convert a file handle into an FSSpec and a Macintosh file system refNum. The TranslateFileError API converts a Macintosh file system error into a Windows NT error.

Strings

The standard Char..., IsChar..., and lstr... Windows APIs assume that their input text is in the system script. The Windows Portability Library provides extended versions of these APIs that take an extra parameter specifying the script of the text. For example, CharNextScript(sz, smJapanese) assumes that sz is in the Shift-JIS Japanese double-byte character set instead of the character set of the system script.

On the Macintosh, you should not use the lstrcmp, lstrcmpScript, lstrcmpi, or lstrcmpiScript functions to compare filenames. The Macintosh file system uses a hard-coded comparison routine to compare filenames, and this routine cannot be localized for different sorting rules. The functions listed above use a comparison that adapts to the sorting rules of the current localization. If you need to compare filenames, you must write Macintosh-specific code that calls one of the EqualString or RelString APIs.

For non-US markets, you must be careful about the string comparison function you use. Under the Macintosh, comparisons for string equality may be different than comparisons for string sort order (in fact, in some European systems, it is possible for unequal strings to be sorted as "equal" in the sort order). The Windows Portability Library maps lstrcmp, lstrcmpScript, lstrcmpi, and lstrcmpiScript to the equivalent Macintosh sort order comparison, and therefore should not be used for testing string equality. Instead, use the Macintosh international routines IdenticalString and IdenticalText.

Fonts

The Macintosh allows the user to have fonts from multiple script systems (English, Japanese, Arabic, and so on) installed at the same time. When presenting a list of available fonts, the Macintosh convention is that the fonts are grouped by script system, sorted by name within each script, and drawn using the system script of each script system. The Windows Portability Library assists in the first two of these tasks by enumerating fonts with the correct grouping and sorting. Therefore you probably want to remove the LBS_SORT or CBS_SORT style bit from any list box or combo box that displays fonts, so that the default ordering of fonts returned by the Windows Portability Library is used for display.

The WM_MACINTOSH Message

The Windows Portability Library uses a new message, the WM_MACINTOSH message. The low word of the wParam of the message is a selector indicating the particular kind of message. The high word of the wParam and the lParam vary depending on the value of the selector. Usually, these messages are sent and used internally by the Windows Portability Library, and are handled by DefWindowProc.

Table 2.5 Message Descriptions

WLM_BALLOONHELP	Sent when it is time to display balloon help.
WLM_CHILDOFFSET	Sent to all child windows of a window being moved.
WLM_DEVICECHANGED	Sent to every window having a Macintosh window on a GDevice that changed.
WLM_HASCCP	Menu management code sends this to ask a window if the Edit menu Cut, Copy, and Paste items should be enabled.
WLM_MACEVENT	Sent to the application when a Macintosh event that does not correspond to any Windows message is removed from the event queue.
WLM_MENUSTATE	Menu management code sends this before drawing the menubar to query for the menubar disable state.
WLM_PARENTACTIVATE	Sent when the highlighted state of the window frame of a top-level or top-level child window changes.
WLM_PARENTCHANGED	Sent to a window and all of its children when the parent of the window is changed using the SetParent.
WLM_SETMENUBAR	Sent when it is time to change the contents of the menubar (with a call to SetMacMenuBar).

Macintosh Windows

The Windows Portability Library provides a number of window-related extensions for the Macintosh that do not exist in the Win32 API.

Window Handles

The Windows Portability Library GetWindowWrapper API finds the HWND corresponding to a Macintosh window. The GetWrapperWindow and GetWrapperContainerWindow APIs translate the opposite direction, from an HWND to a Macintosh window. You can use the WrapWindow and UnwrapWindow APIs to turn a WindowPtr into an HWND and vice versa.

Coordinate Mappings

The ClientToGrafPort and GrafPortToClient APIs perform coordinate mappings from client coordinates of an HWND to local coordinates of the Macintosh GrafPort containing the HWND, and vice versa. These APIs may be particularly useful if you are drawing the contents of an HWND using Macintosh QuickDraw graphics instead of GDI.

Rectangles

The WindowToGlobalPortRect API converts between the window RECT of an HWND and the portRect, in global coordinates, of a similarly positioned Macintosh window. The GlobalPortToWindowRect performs the opposite conversion. These APIs are not generally useful, but you may need them in some rare circumstances. For example, if you receive a SetData AppleEvent instructing you to change the bounding rect of a window, you can use GlobalPortToWindowRect to convert the new bounding rect into a window rect, and then pass the window rect to SetWindowPos.

Foreign Windows

The Windows Portability Library provides two APIs, IsForeignWindow and SubclassForeignWindow, that are used to manipulate the special foreign window. The Windows Portability Library creates this window at startup. Whenever the Windows Portability Library encounters a Macintosh window that does not have a corresponding Windows HWND, it temporarily records the Macintosh WindowPtr as being associated with the foreign window, and uses the foreign window as a placeholder. For example, if a non-Windows Portability Library window becomes active and is sent an activate event, the Windows Portability Library intercepts the event and sends **WM_NCACTIVATE** and **WM_ACTIVATE** messages to the foreign window.

If you receive an HWND from the Windows Portability Library, you can use IsForeignWindow to determine if the HWND is the foreign window. In some cases, you may want to have control over what happens when the foreign window receives a message; for example, you may want to install your own special menu bar when a desk accessory becomes active. In this case you can use SubclassForeignWindow to install your own wndproc in the foreign window. When you receive a **WM_ACTIVATE** event, use SetMacMenuBar to install your own menus.

MFC Resource (.RC) Files

There are various changes that you can make to the resources of a Windows MFC application so that its user interface conforms more closely to Macintosh user-interface standards. The Macintosh MFC sample applications contain changes of this kind. For example, most of the samples do not use a gray dialog background on the Macintosh. Also, the menus have been edited to add Macintosh-specific accelerators, and to substitute Macintosh terms, such as *Quit*, for Windows terms, such as *Exit*.

Do not make changes of this sort by entering conditional statements directly into the .RC text file. Although the **RC.EXE** resource compiler supports such conditional statements, Visual C++ 2.0 strips them out whenever you edit the resource. Instead, use Visual C++ 2.0 to create Macintosh-specific resources.

In the .MAK project window, double-click the .RC file containing the resources that you need to change for the Macintosh. Visual C++ 2.0 preprocesses and compiles the resource file, loads the resources, and opens an .RC resource file edit/browser window. In this .RC file window, take the following steps for each resource requiring changes:

To create a Macintosh version of a resource:

1. In the .RC window, copy the resource to be changed and paste the copy into the same resource folder as the original.

2. Rename the copy with the form "name$(_MAC)," where name is the name or ID# of the original resource.

3. Open the new resource, make the required changes, and save them.

Look-and-Feel Extensions

The extensions in the following table make a Macintosh application look and act more as it would under Windows.

Table 2.6 Look-and-Feel Extension APIs

DS_WINDOWSUI	Style for creating a dialog box and all its child controls with the WS_EX_WINDOWSUI style.
GetMenuUnderline	Retrieves the current underline state of the current menu.
MU_OFF	Specifies the menu state in which menu items are not drawn with underlines beneath accelerator characters.
MU_ON	Specifies the menu state in which menu items are drawn with underlines beneath accelerator characters.
SetMenuUnderline	Sets the underline state of the current menu.
WS_EX_FORCESIZEBOX	Forces a Macintosh grow icon to be drawn in the bottom right corner of the window.
WS_EX_MDICLIENT	Prevents an MDICLIENT-equivalent window from being created on the Macintosh.
WS_EX_MDIFRAME	Prevents an MDI frame window from being shown on the Macintosh.
WS_EX_NOAUTOHIDE	Prevents a window from being hidden.
WS_EX_SMCAPTION	Causes a Macintosh floating window to be created.
WS_EX_WINDOWSUI	Causes the third state of a tri-state checkbox to be drawn using the Windows rather than the Macintosh user interface convention.

Other WPL Extensions

The APIs listed in the following table provide various services specific to the Macintosh.

Table 2.7 Miscellaneous Extension APIs

InitDC	Resets a specified Macintosh device context to its original default state.
WlmDebug	Sets the WPL debug validation state.
WlmVersion	Returns the WPL version number.

OLE

The Windows Portability Library does not currently provide wrapper functions for the Macintosh implementation of Microsoft Object Linking and Embedding (OLE). However, you can include Macintosh-specific code in an application to use OLE on the Macintosh. For more information about Microsoft's native Macintosh OLE implementation, see documentation included with the Microsoft OLE 2.01 Software Development Kit for the Macintosh. For an overview of the OLE dispatch interface, see the OLE Quick Reference.

## CHAPTER 3

Porting to UNIX

This chapter describes how to use the Wind/U portability toolkit for cross-platform development of Visual C++ applications. In particular, it addresses the following topics:

- The benefits of using a technology such as Wind/U for cross-platform development
- An overview of how Wind/U works
- Procedures for using Wind/U for cross-platform development
- Portability issues you may encounter when porting with Wind/U and how to resolve them

Porting Technologies Available

There are a wide variety of cross-platform tools on the market today. Many of them, however, require you to write your application to a proprietary API. If you have already written your application, you must rewrite it to the cross-platform API. Other porting technologies support only those features available on all target platforms—the "lowest common denominator" approach. Some tools, such as Wind/U from Bristol Technology, implement the Microsoft Windows API, including the Microsoft Foundation Class (MFC) library, on UNIX platforms. With this type of technology, you do not have to rewrite your existing

Visual C++ applications to a proprietary interface. You also do not have to give up features on one platform in order to port your application to another platform that does not support those features.

Wind/U is a full and robust implementation of the Microsoft Windows API, the Microsoft Foundation Class (MFC) library, and their concepts on UNIX. In addition to offering those features available within both Windows and Motif, Wind/U extends Motif's functionality by offering Dynamic Data Exchange (DDE), Multiple Document Interface (MDI), on-line help (HyperHelp), PostScript and PCL printing (Xprinter), and Windows equivalent Common Dialogs.

Wind/U not only helps you create a Motif version of your Visual C++ application, it allows you to produce a better Motif application than you could create using standard Motif and X Window System APIs.

Another advantage of using Wind/U is that, since its development is based in part on Microsoft Windows source code, you can be confident that it implements Windows functionality as closely as possible to the way it is implemented in Windows. Therefore, the UNIX version of an application, ported with Wind/U, is quite consistent with the Windows version.

Wind/U Benefits

There are considerably more Windows applications than there are graphical applications for Motif. There are many reasons for this gap, including the following:

- The market for Windows software is larger than the market for Motif; therefore, Windows attracts more developers.
- ISVs must spend their resources keeping up with the intense competition in the crowded Windows applications market; they cannot afford to divert resources to develop applications for Motif.
- The Motif environment has less functionality than the Windows environment.

Wind/U offers developers the benefit of maintaining only one source code base for both Windows and Motif, as well as the added benefit of using Windows as the primary development platform. Figure 3.1 shows the development model for creating applications in Windows and using Wind/U to compile them for UNIX systems.

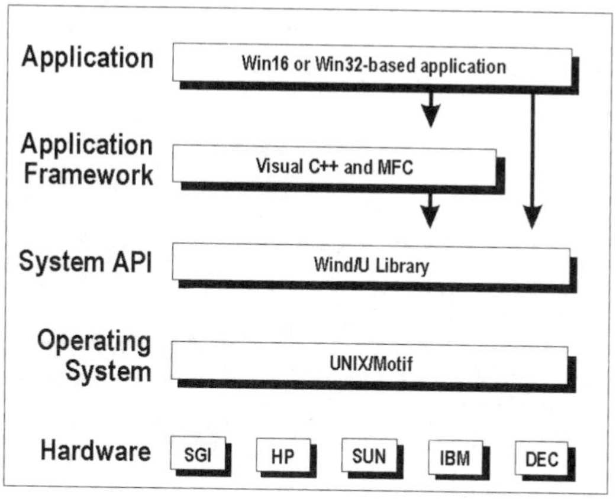

Figure 3.1 Wind/U development model.

Added Functionality to Motif

Wind/U brings added Microsoft Windows functionality to the X Window System and Motif. Some features available in Windows—but not in Motif—include the following:

- Interface widgets, such as the Multiple Document Interface (MDI)
- Common Dialogs for File Open/Save As, Printing, Choose Color, Choose Font, Find, and Replace
- Dynamic Data Exchange (DDE)
- Dynamic Link Libraries (DLLs)
- Unified imaging model between the display and the printer
- Complete C++ Application Framework (MFC)

Wind/U provides all of these features under Motif in a UNIX environment. Wind/U also performs extensive mapping of low-level X Window System events to equivalent Windows messages. By relying on Motif widget set translation and on callbacks to implement higher-level window messages unsupported in the Xlib layer, Wind/U can provide features such as the following:

- Menu item selections
- Button selections
- Edit controls
- Clipboard operations

Since Wind/U is built on top of Motif, Wind/U provides all of the above functionality in a manner compliant with Motif and the X Window System.

Cross-Platform Development Process Overview

Porting a Windows application with Wind/U requires the following steps:

1. Copying Visual C++ source files to a UNIX workstation
2. Copying Windows resource files to the UNIX workstation. You can generate your resource files with App Studio.
3. Using Wind/U utilities to convert your source to UNIX conventions and create a makefile for compiling and linking your application in UNIX
4. Compiling the source files with an ANSI C++ compiler
5. Compiling resource files with the Wind/U resource compiler
6. Linking compiled source files, compiled resource files, and the Wind/U Windows API library
7. Debugging your application to fix nonportable code and testing all functionality
8. Shipping the UNIX version of your application

Wind/U Components

Wind/U consists of the following components:

- The Wind/U runtime libraries
- The Microsoft foundation class libraries

- The Wind/U resource compiler
- Xprinter
- HyperHelp
- Other porting utilities

Wind/U Runtime Libraries

The core technology for Wind/U resides in the Wind/U shared libraries. These libraries provide a Microsoft Windows API to the application, thus allowing you to compile a Windows application on a UNIX system, link the application to the Wind/U libraries, and run it in a standard Motif/X Window System environment.

The libraries provide Windows functionality by translating standard Windows functions into equivalent X Window System and Motif function calls. This translation allows you to maintain a common set of source code that you can compile to create both a Windows and UNIX/Motif version of an application. Wind/U provides both optimized and debug versions of the Wind/U libraries.

Microsoft Foundation Class Libraries

The Wind/U MFC library provides the same application framework technology that MFC provides on other platforms. The Wind/U MFC framework and prebuilt components provide additional portability to your application by providing transparent access to operating system dependent areas. For example, while pathnames are operating system dependent, using the MFC document/view classes eliminates all pathname code from your application. Your application is called only after the user has selected a file and the framework has opened it for reading or writing.

Wind/U Resource Compiler

The Wind/U resource compiler uses existing Windows resource files to specify the layouts for menus and dialogs. You can also use the resource compiler to specify icon, bitmap, and cursor resources.

Xprinter

Graphical UNIX does not have a standard printing mechanism. Xprinter works along with the GDI layer to provide transparent access to the display and to any

PostScript- or PCL-compatible printer. Xprinter is a PostScript and PCL printer library with a common graphics programming interface.

HyperHelp

The Wind/U HyperHelp feature uses existing Microsoft RTF input files to provide full-featured on-line help for Motif applications. HyperHelp allows you to use the Help source files for the Windows version of your application for the UNIX version as well. It provides the same features available in Microsoft Windows Help, including hypertext branching, definition boxes, graphics, keyword searches, browsing, and macro support. The same API you use to invoke WinHelp in you Windows application invokes HyperHelp in the UNIX version.

Other Porting Utilities

Wind/U also provides utilities that perform the following tasks:

- Examine your application source code for potential portability problems and automatically correct many of the most common problems.
- Create a skeleton makefile for your to compile and link your application.

Wind/U Architecture

The Wind/U architecture consists of the following layers: User, Graphical Device Interface (GDI), Kernel, and Microsoft C runtime library.

Figure 3.2 shows the relationships among the Wind/U components, as well as their relationships to other components in the system.

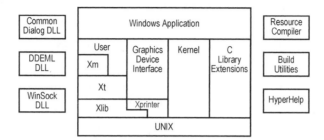

Figure 3.2 Wind/U architecture.

User Layer

The user layer provides the application with window management function APIs. It is equivalent to the Window Manager Interface (WMI) layer in Windows). It contains logic for creating, manipulating, and destroying windows. The Wind/U user layer translates Windows classes into equivalent Motif widgets.

Wind/U implements all standard Windows controls as Motif widgets. When possible, Wind/U maps Windows controls directly to equivalent Motif widgets. When no equivalent Motif widget is available, Wind/U implements custom widgets to provide the same Windows functionality.

GDI Layer

The GDI layer provides graphics operation on both the display and the printer. In most respects it is similar to the graphics routines of Xlib in the X Window System. It provides basic routines for line drawing, text and font handling, tiling, shading, etc. However, GDI also provides the following key functionality not present in the X Window System:

- **Logical coordinate mapping:** GDI allows the application to choose the coordinate system used for GDI graphics operations. Xlib supports only a simple pixel-oriented Cartesian coordinate system. Wind/U provides the logical mapping functionality found in the GDI layer. This logic affects virtually every GDI function. Windows GDI functions can also draw on a Windows metafile (a very popular mechanism for data interchange in the Windows environment). Wind/U GDI provides support for writing to metafiles in all graphics functions, as well as the logic necessary to decode and replay Windows metafiles.

- **Printer support**: Wind/U supports both PostScript and PCL printers through Xprinter.
- **Logical palettes**: GDI's logical palettes are much more flexible and device-independent than X Window System colormaps.
- **Logical font mapping**: GDI allows applications to depend less on the actual fonts available in the X server. WYSIWYG support is therefore simpler.
- **Simplified painting model**: GDI automatically handles multi-region exposure optimization (BeginPaint/EndPaint).
- **Device-independent bitmaps**: GDI allows a device-independent bitmap's external definition to be applied to any device.

Kernel Layer

The kernel layer provides all non-GUI APIs in the Windows environment (similar to the Windows System Services Interface (SSI) layer). These APIs include file I/O, memory management, module management, communications, and a variety of other functionality.

DDEML DLL

The Wind/U Dynamic Data Exchange management Library (DDEML) Dynamic Link Library (DLL) provides the same functionality as the Windows DDEML DLL. The Wind/U DDEML DLL allows Wind/U applications to share data.

Common Dialog DLL

Wind/U provides full support for common dialogs with all of the functionality of Windows common dialogs.

WinSock DLL

Wind/U provides full support for Windows sockets, which provide networking capabilities to Windows applications.

How to Use Wind/U

The first step in using Wind/U for cross-platform development is to set up your Wind/U environment. When you use Wind/U for cross-platform development, every Wind/U user must have a **$HOME/.WindU** file. This file is comparable to the Windows **win.ini** file. To create this file for a user, copy the file **WindU** from the directory where Wind/U is installed (**$WUHOME**) to the user's home directory as **.WindU**. Note that the preceding period is required.

The .WindU File

The **.WindU** file is the functional equivalent to the **win.ini** file in Microsoft Windows. The **.WindU** file contains the current printer setup, font mappings, and other Wind/U tunable parameters. All of the sections in the **win.ini** file are supported in the **.WindU** file, including:

- The [windows] section, which contains the default printer setup.
- The [devices] section, which contains all currently configured devices.
- The [ports] section, which contains all currently configured spool commands.

In addition, it contains a number of Wind/U-specific sections.

This configuration requirement, while a little different from Microsoft Windows, provides for different configurations for each user on the system, since each user has a private copy of the **.WindU** file in their local directory.

If you wish to store the **.WindU** file in a different location, or if you want to use a different name (for example, when you distribute your application), you can set the WINDU environment variable to the location of the **.WindU** file.

The [windows] Section

The [windows] section of the **.WindU** file contains the default printer and dialog font information as follows:

```
[windows]
device=HP 3SI523,PostScript,netprinter:
MinDlgFontSize=12
DlgFontWeight=400
```

The `device` parameter specifies the default printer setup for the user. In this example, the default printer is configured to a Hewlett Packard LaserJet IIIsi printer in PostScript mode. The printer port is given as `netprinter:`. (Refer to "The [`ports`] Section" below for more details on printer port configurations.)

The `MinDlgFontSize` parameter specifies the minimum font size allowed in a dialog template. Applications created with Visual C++ tend to use an 8-point font in dialogs, which is hard to read on most high resolution UNIX displays. Values ranging from 10 to 12 are most common. The default value is 10.

The `DlgFontWeight` parameter specifies the weight field for the default dialog font. The default value is **FW_NORMAL** (400).

The [devices] Section

The [`devices`] section of the **.WindU** file contains a list of all currently configured printers. The keyword in each line of the section is a user-defined alias for the printer. This alias is customarily used by applications to provide meaningful descriptions of the printer setup, as in the following example. You can use any alias you like.

The argument (located on the right side) for each keyword consists of three parts: the printer model, the printer mode (PCL5 or PostScript), and the port to which the printer is connected (from the [ports] section). The printer model is the name of the PPD file (less the .PPD extension) to use when printing to this printer. Obtain valid entries from the **$WUHOME/xprinter/PPDS/FILENAME.MAP** file. As the following example shows, a space separates the printer model and the printer mode; a comma separates the mode and the port.

```
[devices]
HP LaserJet SI PCL5=HP3SI PCL5,Chester
HP LaserJet III SI PostScript=HP3SI PostScript,netprinter:
HP LaserJet II PostScript=HPIIP PostScript,FILE:
```

The [ports] Section

The [`ports`] section of the **.WindU** file is similar to the same section in **win.ini**, except that UNIX does not have the same concept of a port. Because the [`ports`] section in **.WindU** is much more flexible, it can take advantage of UNIX networking capabilities and sophisticated print spoolers.

```
[ports]
netprinter:=lp -d ps -o nobanner
chester=rsh chester lp -d ps -Tpostscript -o nobanner
```

Each line of the [ports] section in the **.WindU** file contains a user-defined port name and an associated command. Unlike Microsoft Windows, the standard DOS port names (lpt1:, prn:, com1:, etc.) have no special meaning in the Wind/U environment. When the user selects to print to a port, the command string associated with the port name is used to spool the output file. The command string should expect the printer data as stdin.

In the [ports] example, three printer ports are configured and may be selected by the user. The first, netprinter:, uses the UNIX lp spooler to print the file on the ps device.

The second port, chester, prints the file by executing an rsh command to the system chester where the UNIX lp spooler is used to print the file. Note that trailing colons in Wind/U port names are treated like any other character in the name. For example, port chester: is NOT equivalent to port chester.

The port name FILE: is the only reserved port; this port causes a print file for the specified printer to be printed to a file. The user specifies the file name in a dialog.

.WindU-Specific Sections

The **.WindU** file has some Wind/U-specific sections for handling printer setup information and font substitution tables. These sections are not normally accessed directly by an application. They are used internally by Wind/U to resolve differences between the X Window System and Microsoft Windows environments, and to store printer configuration information that is used by the Xprinter subsystem.

The **win.ini** file has similar sections where the format is defined by device drivers and is not typically accessed by applications.

The [FontSubstitutes (...)] Sections

The [FontSubstitutes (...)] sections map groups of font name aliases to groups of font names that are known to exist in almost all X servers and printers. Microsoft Windows 3.1 has a similar section called

[FontSubstitutes] that provides a mapping from Windows 3.0 bitmap fonts to 3.1 TrueType fonts.

There are three [FontSubstitutes] sections, one each for the X Window System display, PostScript printers, and PCL printers. The [FontSubstitutes (XDisplay)] section defines the alias-to-real name mapping when the X display is the current device. The [FontSubstitutes (PCL)] section defines the alias-to-real name mapping when a PCL printer is the current device. The [FontSubstitutes (PostScript)] section defines the alias-to-real name mapping when a PostScript printer is the current device.

The following example shows the default values for the [FontSubstitutes] sections:

```
[FontSubstitutes (XDisplay)]
arial=helvetica
helv=helvetica
courier new=courier
times roman=times
times new roman=times
tms rmn=times
ms serif=times
ms sans serif=helvetica


[FontSubstitutes (PostScript)]
arial=helvetica
helv=helvetica
courier new=courier
times roman=times
times new roman=times
tms rmn=times
ms serif=times
ms sans serif=helvetica


[FontSubstitutes (PCL)]
arial=helvetica
helv=helvetica
courier new=courier
times roman=times
times new roman=times
tms rmn=times
ms serif=times
ms sans serif=helvetica
```

The keyword for each line in the [FontSubstitutes] section is the Microsoft Windows font name. The right side contains the mapped font name that is used when loading the font on the X server or a PostScript or PCL printer. The right side is used as the second field in the **XFLD** font name.

The [WindU-CharSet] Section

The [WindU-CharSet] section specifies the character setup grouping for all X Window System and Xprinter font encoding. Wind/U has six predefined sets of internal mappings, as shown in Table 3.1.

Table 3.1 Wind/U Font Mappings

X Font Registry	Encoding	Microsoft Windows Character Set
iso8859	1	ANSI Character Set
adobe	fontspecific	Symbol Character Set
dec	dectech	ANSI Character Set
jisx0201	1976	Kanji Character Set
jisx0208	1976	Kanji Character Set
jisx0208	1983	Kanji Character Set

The keyword for each line in the [WindU-CharSet] section contains the encoding information as provided by the X Window System. The argument for the keyword (right side) contains the Microsoft Windows character set. The numbers used for this mapping are obtained from the **windows.h** file. The keyword is the last two fields in the **XFLD** name. The ANSI Character Set is chosen as the default character set for any X font with unknown mapping. The following example shows the default character mapping.

```
[WindU-CharSet]
-symbol=2
-dingbats =2
dec-decmath_extension=2
dec-decmath_italic=2
dec-decmath_symbol=2
hp-roman8=0
ibm-850=0
ibm-special=2
```

```
ibm-udcjp=128
iso8859-2=0
iso8859-3=0
iso8859-4=0
iso8859-5=0
iso8859-7=0
iso8859-9=0
iso8859-adobe=0
jisx0201.1976-0=128,127
jisx0201.1976-1=128,127
jisx0208.1983-0=127
jisx0208.1983-1=127
ksc5601.1987-0=2
misc-fontspecific=2
sunolcursor-1=2
sunolglyph-1=2
```

The [ScalableFontInfo] Section

The [ScalableFontInfo] section provides a way to disable the use of scalable fonts on the X Window System server. Some X Window System servers use an extremely slow font-scaling algorithm when compared to the Windows TrueType technology, and many applications do not require the availability of scalable fonts. To use scalable fonts, set the value of UseOnDisplay to 1; to disable scalable fonts, set the value to 0. The default value is 0.

```
[ScalableFontInfo]
UseOnDisplay=1
```

The [EnumFonts] Section

Extracting detailed font metric information from the X server is slow, especially when using scalable fonts. To avoid this X server performance problem, Wind/U allows you to specify whether text metrics information should be passed to the EnumFonts callback function. The default value (1) maintains compatibility with Windows and includes the text metric information. Change the value to 0 if you do not need text metric information for every font.

You can also specify whether Wind/U should load only IsoLatin fonts (isolatin-*), only IsoLatin1 fonts (isolatin1-*), or all available fonts. To load only IsoLatin fonts, set the IsoLatinOnly flag to 1. To load only IsoLatin1 fonts, set the IsoLatin1Only flag to 1. To load all available fonts, set both flags to zero. Some other character sets can cause unexpected results when dealing with foreign character sets (for example, French characters). Setting either or both of these flags to 1 ensures that character sets are correct.

The [EnumFonts] section looks like the following:

```
[EnumFonts]
IncludeTextMetrics=1
IsoLatinOnly=1
IsoLatin1Only=0
```

Xprinter Configuration Sections

The printer driver subsystem of Wind/U, Xprinter, maintains device-specific configuration information in the **.WindU** file in the following sections:

```
[Xprinter,PostScript]
Filename=sample2.ps
Scale=1.00
Copies=1
Orientation=Portrait
PageSize=Letter
DPI=300
```

```
[Xprinter,PCL5]
Filename=sample1.pcl
Scale=1.5
Copies=2
Orientation=LandScape
PageSize=Letter
DPI=300
```

```
[HP3SI523,PostScript]
Scale=2.00
Copies=1
PaperTray=Upper
PageSize=Letter
Orientation=LandScape
DPI=300
```

If a section contains a printer device identifier, such as HP3SI523, then that section provides default setup information for that printer configuration. If a section specifies Xprinter as the device identifier, then printer model–independent output is generated as Encapsulated Postscript or Generic PCL4 or PCL5 commands.

The [Ddeml] Section

The [Ddeml] section contains tunable parameters for the Wind/U Dynamic Data Exchange Management Library (DDEML) implementation. (See Chapter 11.)

The first entry, ConnectTimeOut, defines the time interval for DDEML waiting on connection responses from servers when processing a DdeConnect/DdeConnectList call. The default value is 3 seconds (3000 milliseconds).

The second entry, SendMonitorMesg, decides whether DDEML MONITOR type messages should be generated. A value of 1 means monitor messages are to be generated; a value of 0 (the default) means no monitor messages are generated.

The next entry, DataPacketSize, controls the packet size. This parameter is useful when the application is sending data greater than 32 KB. The default packet size is 4000 bytes.

Information regarding each active conversation is stored in a CONVINFO structure. The two fields in the CONVINFO structure, the wConvst field and the wStatus field, contain information regarding the conversation state and status. This structure can be retrieved by calling the DDEML function **DdeQueryConvInfo**. DDEML updates these two fields by sending messages between applications. If an application does not make use of such information, it can disable such message generation by specifying 0 for both the SendConvstMesg and SendStatusMesg entries in the .WindU file. If the application does intend to make use of the information, these entries should be set to 1 (the default) as shown in the following example.

```
[Ddeml]
ConnectTimeOut=3000
SendMonitorMesg=0
DataPacketSize=4000
SendConvstMesg=1
SendStatusMesg=1
```

The [SystemBitmapColor] Section

This section defines the background color to use for the system bitmaps (equivalent to OEM bitmaps in Windows. Wind/U computes the foreground color based on the background color, so that it is visible. In this section you specify a Red, Green, and Blue value. Together, these values make up the RGB value for the system bitmap background, as shown in the following example:

```
[SystemBitmapColor]
Red=0
Green=255
Blue=255
```

The [CommDialog] Section

By default, Wind/U uses the Windows File Open common dialog. If you prefer to use the Motif File Open widget instead of the Windows common dialog, set the MotifFileDialog parameter to 1, as in the following example:

```
[CommDialog]
MotifFileDialog=1
```

If you use Motif style common dialogs, the Help button is disabled by default. To enable the Help button, your application must do the following:

- Enable the flag **OFN_SHOWHELP** for the field pOFN->Flags. (pOFN is an argument to the GetOpenFileName() and GetSaveFileName() calls; it points to the structure OPENFILENAME.)

- Attach a hook function by setting the field pOFN->lpfnHook to this function. The function pOFN->lpfnHook serves as the callback for the Help button. It has the following syntax:

```
UINT (CALLBACK *pHelpHookFunc) (HWND hDlg, UINT msg, WPARAM
wParam, LPARAM lParam)
```

When the hook function is invoked for Help purposes, the arguments passed will have the following values:

```
hDlg == 0;
msg == 0;
wParam == 0;
```

The lParam points to the OPENFILENAME structure passed to GetOpenFileName().

The [Listbox] and [Combobox] Sections

With Wind/U, listboxes and comboboxes do not have a 3-D shadow border by default. To create a border, you must specify the **WS_BORDER** style. However, the drawing rectangle of owner-drawn listboxes or comboboxes starts at (0,0) on the upper-left corner; that is, it overwrites the 3-D border of the listbox.

You can change the default behavior by setting the OwnerDrawnShadowOffset parameter in the [Listbox] or [Combobox] section as follows:

```
[Listbox]
OwnerDrawnShadowOffset=1

[Combobox]
OwnerDrawnShadowOffset=1
```

Setting this parameter value to 1 causes Wind/U to return a drawing rectangle that excludes the left and right border. Preventing the application from overwritting the motif Border.

Transferring Your Source Code to the UNIX System

Once your Wind/U environment is configured with the **.WindU** file, the next step in porting your application to UNIX is to copy your Visual C++ source files and resource files (created with AppStudio) to your UNIX workstation. In this step, you simply need to create a directory for your application and copy the files to it. For example, if you were porting the Scribble3 sample application, you would enter the following commands:

```
$ cd $HOME
$ mkdir scribble3
```

```
$ cp $WUHOME/mfc/samples/scribble3.dos/* scribble3
$ cd scribble3
```

To make sure you have copied the files correctly, list them with and see if your output is correct. For Scribble3, the output would be as follows:

```
$ls
README                    pendlg.h         scribble.def    scribdoc.h
stadfx.h                  mainfrm.cpp      res             scribble.h
scribvw.cppmainfrm.h      resource.h       scribble.rc
scribvw.h                 pendlg.cpp       scribble.cpp
stdafx.cpp
```

Converting the Files to UNIX Format

The Wind/U utility **prepare_source** converts your files from DOS format to UNIX format. This utility processes all files in the current directory that end with **.cpp**, **.h**, **.dlg**, and **.rc** filename extensions. It makes the following changes to the files it processes:

- Changes all **.cpp** file name extensions to **.C**, which is the UNIX convention for C++ files
- Creates a subdirectory called **ORIGINAL** and places a copy of each original source file in it
- Replaces all DOS end-of-line and end-of-file characters (^J, ^M and ^Z) with a UNIX end-of-line character
- Converts file names specified within `rcinclude` and `#include` directives to lowercase and changes all backslash characters to forward slash characters
- Scans the source code for possible problems related to use with Wind/U and records all potential problems in a text file named **WARNINGS**

Enter the following command to convert the DOS Scribble3 files to UNIX:

```
$ prepare_source
```

Creating a UNIX Makefile

DOS makefiles and UNIX makefiles are different enough to make it difficult to use a single makefile in both environments. The Wind/U make_windumakefile utility creates a skeleton UNIX makefile. You can then modify this makefile as necessary to work with your application. In addition to being a UNIX makefile, the generated makefile is a Wind/U Architecture Independent Makefile (AIM).

AIMS allow you to build multiple architectures at the same time without collisions. AIMs achieve this by storing architecture dependent objects and resource files in subdirectories.

To create a UNIX makefile, enter the following command:

```
$ make_windumakefile scribble3>Makefile
```

The generated makefile looks like the following:

```
#
#
#
#           This makefile generated by make_windumakefile
#
#           This Architecture independent makefile made for
#           target scribble on Thu Oct 13 21:58:58 edt 1994 by
#           scot
#
#



# This includes your architecture description file...
include $(WUHOME)/arch/$(ARCH)

# Append application specific defines after CCFLAGS and RCCFLAGS
CFLAGS=$(CCFLAGS)
RCFLAGS=$(RCCFLAGS)
```

```
# Definition of objects in the executable.

OBJS = \
    $(ARCH)/mainfrm.o \
    $(ARCH)/pendlg.o \
    $(ARCH)/scribble.o \
    $(ARCH)/scribdoc.o \
    $(ARCH)/scribvw.o \
    $(ARCH)/stdafx.o \
    $(ARCH)/scribble_rc.o\
    $(ARCH)/def.o

#  Target info

all:: $(ARCH) $(ARCH)/scribble

clean::
    rm -rf $(ARCH)/scribble $(ARCH)/*.dll $(ARCH)/*.o $(ARCH)/*.c

# Make the architecture directory
$(ARCH):
    mkdir $(ARCH)

# The target
$(ARCH)/scribble: $(OBJS)
    $(CC_PLUSPLUS) $(CPPLINKFLAGS) $(CFLAGS) $(WUEXPORTS) -o
$(ARCH)/scribble $(WINCRT0) $(OBJS) $(COMMDLGLIB) $(OLELIB)
$(ODBCLIB) $(MFCLIBS) $(LIBS)

#  Normal objects
$(ARCH)/def.o: def.C
    $(CC_PLUSPLUS) -c $(CFLAGS) $(MFCFLAGS) -o $@ $?
    test ! -s $(@F) || mv $(@F) $(ARCH)/$(@F)

$(ARCH)/mainfrm.o: mainfrm.C
```

```
        $(CC_PLUSPLUS) -c $(CFLAGS) $(MFCFLAGS) -o $@ $?
        test ! -s $(@F) || mv $(@F) $(ARCH)/$(@F)


$(ARCH)/pendlg.o: pendlg.C
        $(CC_PLUSPLUS) -c $(CFLAGS) $(MFCFLAGS) -o $@ $?
        test ! -s $(@F) || mv $(@F) $(ARCH)/$(@F)


$(ARCH)/scribble.o: scribble.C
        $(CC_PLUSPLUS) -c $(CFLAGS) $(MFCFLAGS) -o $@ $?
        test ! -s $(@F) || mv $(@F) $(ARCH)/$(@F)


$(ARCH)/scribdoc.o: scribdoc.C
        $(CC_PLUSPLUS) -c $(CFLAGS) $(MFCFLAGS) -o $@ $?
        test ! -s $(@F) || mv $(@F) $(ARCH)/$(@F)


$(ARCH)/scribvw.o: scribvw.C
        $(CC_PLUSPLUS) -c $(CFLAGS) $(MFCFLAGS) -o $@ $?
        test ! -s $(@F) || mv $(@F) $(ARCH)/$(@F)


$(ARCH)/stdafx.o: stdafx.C
        $(CC_PLUSPLUS) -c $(CFLAGS) $(MFCFLAGS) -o $@ $?
        test ! -s $(@F) || mv $(@F) $(ARCH)/$(@F)


#   Resource objects
$(ARCH)/scribble_rc.o: $(ARCH)/scribble_rc.c
    $(CC_PLUSPLUS) -I. -c $(CFLAGS) -I$(ARCH) -o
$(ARCH)/scribble_rc.o $(ARCH)/scribble_rc.c
        test ! -s $(@F) || mv $(@F) $(ARCH)/$(@F)


# Resource .c files (Invoke the resource compiler)
${ARCH}/scribble_rc.c: scribble.rc
    rc -D_STYPES $(RCFLAGS) $(MFCFLAGS) -o $(ARCH)/scribble_rc.c
scribble.rc


# End of makefile
```

This makefile is architecture-independent; you can use it to build your application on any of the UNIX platforms that Wind/U supports. This feature makes it easy to build your application for multiple architectures at the same time without collisions. To achieve this architecture independence, the makefile includes an architecture description file (ADF) in line 2 of the generated makefile. The ADF looks like the following example (for the Sun SPARC running SunOS):

```
# Sun Running Solaris 2.x (a.k.a SunOS 5.x) (X11R5,Motif1.2)
CC          = cc -O
CC_PLUSPLUS = CC -O -w
CCFLAGS     = -Dsol2 -DWU_APP -DX_USEBFUNCS -I$(WUHOME)/include\
    -I/usr/openwin/include -I/usr/include/Motif1.2
COMMDLGLIB  = -L$(WUHOME)/lib.sol2 -lcommdlg
DDEMLLIB    = -L$(WUHOME)/lib.sol2 -lddeml
DLLCFLAG    = -KPIC
DLLCPPFLAG  = -PIC
LIBS        = -L$(WUHOME)/lib.sol2 -luser -lkernel -lgdi -lprnt \
    -L/usr/openwin/lib -L/usr/lib/Motif1.2 \
    -lXm -lXt -lgen -lXmu -lX11 -lm -ldl
CCLINKFLAGS = -Wl,-t
CPPLINKFLAGS = -Qoption ld -t
MFCFLAGS    = -DMFC -I$(WUHOME)/mfc/include -DWINVER=0x030a \
    -D_WINDOWS -DNO_VBX_SUPPORT -D_PORTABLE
MFCLIBS     = -L$(WUHOME)/lib.sol2 -lmfc
ODBCLIB     = -L$(WUHOME)/lib.sol2 -lodbc
OLELIB      = -L$(WUHOME)/lib.sol2 -lole
RCCFLAGS    = -DWU_APP -Dsparc -Dsol2
WINCRT0     = $(WUHOME)/lib.sol2/wincrt0.o
WINSOCK     = -L$(WUHOME)/lib.sol2 -lwinsock
```

Table 3.2 describes each flag in the ADF.

Table 3.2 ADF Flags

Flag	Meaning
CC	The C compiler on your system.
CC_PLUSPLUS	The C++ Compiler on your system. Required when using MFC.
CCFLAGS	Flags needed for your platform. Wind/U requires that **WU_APP** be defined.

Table 3.2 ADF Flags (continued)

Flag	Meaning
COMMDLGLIB	Special libraries used for common dialogs.
DDEMLLIB	Special libraries used for DDEML.
DLLCFLAG	Special compile flags needed by your system to compile Wind/U DLLs.
LIBS	System Libraries and DLLs used by the application. You may need to change the location of the Motif, Xt, and X libraries for your system.
CCLINKFLAGS	C compiler link flags. The ADF files for the hp700 platform now include the -Wl,-z flag in the CCLINKFLAG macro. This option causes a SEGV if a null pointer is dereferenced, making run-time behavior of the HP more consistent with other platforms.
CPPLINKFLAGS	C++ compiler link flags. Required for sol2 and hp700 only
MFCFLAGS	MFC specific flags needed for your platform.
MFCLIBS	MFC specific libraries used by the application.
ODBCLIB	ODBC specific libraries used by the application.
OLELIB	OLE specific libraries used by the application.
RCCFLAGS	Flags used by the Wind/U Resource Compiler.
WINCRT0	Location of the wincrt0.o object module.
WINSOCK	Location of the winsock DLL.

In addition to generating a makefile, **make_windumakefile** creates a **def.C** file for your application, which contains the definition of **main()**.

Since **make_windumakefile** only includes those source files in the current directory in the makefile, you must modify the makefile if the source is in multiple directories. This utility also does not create dependencies in the generated makefile. That is, editing a header (**.h**) file will not trigger automatic rebuilds of the appropriate source files. If all of your application source (**.C**) files, header (**.h**) files, or resource (**.rc**) files are not in the directory where you run **make_windumakefile**, you must edit the makefile for your build environment.

Building Your Application

Once you have created a makefile for your application, enter the following command to build your application:

```
$ make
```

The **make** utility does the following:

- Creates your architecture directory based on the **all** dependency line in your makefile
- Makes the executable objects
- Compiles **def.C** and your other .C files and places them in the architecture directory
- Invokes the Wind/U resource compiler to create the resource file
- Compiles the resource file
- Links the application and places it in the architecture directory

Since your makefile is architecture-independent, you can use the same makefile to build your application for other platform architectures. By default, the **make** utility builds your application for the platform on which you are currently running. However, you can specify a different platform with the **ARCH** command line option. For example, suppose you are running on a Sun Solaris workstation, but you want to build for an HP workstation as well. To build for the HP, enter the following command:

```
$ make ARCH=hp700
```

You would then have two subdirectories—sol2 and hp700—each containing the executable for that platform. Using traditional makefile, you would have to create one set of objects, change the makefile, delete the objects, recompile, etc., for each different platform architecture.

By default, the make utility builds a non-debug version of your application. When you're testing and debugging your application, however, you'll probably want to use a debug version. Wind/U also provides debug versions of all Wind/U libraries as well as the architecture description files. To build a debug version of your application, simply add -g to your **ARCH**. For example, to build a debug version of your application for the Sun Solaris platform, enter the following command:

```
$ make ARCH=sol2-g
```

Unlike the nondebug version, you must specify the **WUARCH** option, even if you are building for the same platform on which you're currently working.

Testing and Debugging

Once you build your application, your're ready for the most complicated aspect of porting your application: testing and debugging the UNIX version. Wind/U provides a number of tools to help you debug your application.

Prepare_source Warnings

The prepare_source utility looks for potential portability problems in your source code. If it finds any, it creates a file called WARNINGS, which it writes warning messages to. The following is an example WARNINGS file generated by prepare_source:

```
The following source lines may have incorrect casts. Change
to:LocalFree((HLOCAL)...);

dib.c:317: LocalFree((HANDLE)pPal);

dib.c:347: LocalFree((HANDLE)pPal);

------------------------------------------------------

The following source lines have constructs which may not be
portable:


dc.c:105: *((DWORD *) &dcv.windowOrg) = GetWindowOrg(hdc);

dc.c:106: *((DWORD *) &dcv.windowExt) = GetWindowExt(hdc);

dc.c:107: *((DWORD *) &dcv.viewportOrg = GetViewportOrg(hdc);

dc.c:108: *((DWORD *) &dcv.viewportExt) = GetViewportExt(hdc);

dc.c:110: *((DWORD *) &dcv.penpos) = GetCurrentPosition(hdc);

dc.c:111: *((DWORD *) &dcv.brushOrg) = GetBrushOrg (hdc);

dc.c:278: *((DWORD *) &dcv.penpos) = GetCurrentPosition(hdc);

dib.c:248: * lpbi = I(LLPBITMAPINFOHEADER) GlobalLock (hbi);
```

dib.c;433: bc = * (BITMAPCOREHEADER *) &bi;

```
------------------------------------------------------

The following source lines may have incorrect file directory
separators under UNIX.


dialogs.c:89: while(p>path && *p != '\\' && *p != ':' )
```

```
--------------------------------------------------------
```

The following source lines may cause errors on some UNIX implementations (particularly Solaris). Mixing the flags OF_CREATE and OF_READWRITE causes inconsistent results. Try changing OF_READWRITE to OF_WRITE.

```
dib.c:208: fh=OpenFile(szFile,&of,OF_CREATE|
OF_READWRITE);
```

First, let's look at the lines causing the incorrect casts warning:

```
279 LOGPALETTE *pPal;
...
310 for (i=0;i<nNumColors;i++){
311       pPal->palPalEntry[i].peRed=pRgb[i].rgb.Red;
312       pPal->palPalEntry[i].peGreen=pRgb[i].rgb.Green
313       pPal->palPalEntry[i].peBlue=pRgb[i].rgb.Blue
314       pPal->palPalEntry[i].peFlags=(BYTE)0;
315          }
316 hpal=CreatePalette(pPal);
317 LocalFree((HANDLE)pPal);
318 }
```

The problem with this code is that pointers in Wind/U are 32 bits, while handles are 16 bits. Wind/U defines a special 32-bit handle type (HLOCAL) to be used in situations where handles must be 32 bits (like the example here). To fix this portability problem, change the (HANDLE) cast in line 317 to an (HLOCAL) cast.

Next, let's examine the lines causing the OpenFile warning:

```
205 if(!hdib)
206       return FALSE;
207
208 fh=OpenFile(szFile,&of,OF_CREATE|OF_READWRITE);
209 if(fh==-1)
210       return FALSE;
```

```
211
212 lpbi=(VOID FAR *)GlobalLock(hdib);
```

The problem with this code is that on some UNIX workstations, mixing reading and creating attributes may produce inconsistent results. Use OF_CREATE|OF_WRITE in line 208.

```
Next, look at the lines causing the construct warning:
105 *((DWORD *) &dcv.windowOrg) = GetWindowOrg(hdc);
106 *((DWORD *) &dcv.windowExt) = GetWindowExt(hdc);
107 *((DWORD *) &dcv.viewportOrg = GetViewportOrg(hdc);
108 *((DWORD *) &dcv.viewportExt) = GetViewportExt(hdc);
109
110 *((DWORD *) &dcv.penpos) = GetCurrentPosition(hdc);
111 *((DWORD *) &dcv.brushOrg) = GetBrushOrg (hdc);
```

The left side of line 105 defines a 32-bit pointer. The right side defines a 64-bit struct. This conflict causes a bus error, since the 64-bit value returned from GetWindowOrg overflows the bounds of the pointer.

One way to fix this error is to put the result from GetWindowOrg into a temporary variable. Use the HIWORD and LOWORD macros to retrieve the fields of the returned value in a portable way. Or you can use the portable APIs for Windows 3.1 and Windows NT. The following example shows how to fix the code with the portable APIs:

```
105 GetWindowOrgEx(hdc, &dcv.windowOrg);
106 GetWindowExtEx(hdc, &dcv.windowExt);
107 GetViewportOrgEx(hdc, &dcv.viewportOrg);
108 GetViewportExtEx(hdc, &dcv.viewportExt);
109
110 GetCurrentPositionEx(hdc, &dcv.penPos);
111 GetBrushOrgEx(hdc, &dcv.brushOrg);
```

This fix is valid for UNIX, Windows 3.1, and Windows NT.

Finally, look at the code causing the final error:

```
89 while(p>path && *p != '\\' && *p != ':' )
```

To correct this problem, simply change the DOS \\ to the UNIX /.

Compiler Warnings

When you use the make command to build your application, the C++ compiler may also generate warning messages. The following example warning message might be generated when an application is compiled:

```
"dc.c", line 206: warning: argument is incompatible with
prototype: arg #1
```

This message does not indicate a bug in the software. Line 239 in dc.c contains the following code:

```
dcv.brush.lbHatch=(short)MakePatternBitmap(dcv.patChecks);
```

In this case, the function prototype for MakePatternBitmap is not correct. It should have a BYTE array instead of a char array. Change the code to use a BYTE array as follows:

```
HBITMAP MakePatternBitmap(BYTE checks[64])
```

Wind/U Runtime Warnings

When you run your application (linked to the debug libraries) you might see Wind/U warnings, as in the following example:

```
Wind/U Warning (129): Function SetDlgItemText, could not find
specified control id: 322
```

Wind/U warnings may or may not indicate a problem with your application. The debug version of Wind/U watches for potential errors, such as incorrect handles, bad file names, invalid memory pointers, etc. If a potential error is found, the Wind/U debug library generates a run-time warnaing. It is up to you to decide if the warning indicates a problem or an anticipated response. The non-debug version of Wind/U behaves exactly the same way as the debug version, except it does not print out the warnings as they occur.

Once you find a potential problem from a Wind/U debug warning, the fastest way to find the problem is to set a break point at the function as follows:

```
---> wuDebugWarning()
```

Breaking here gives you a stack trace with arguments of what has caused the problem.

It is also important to note that you can mix and match debug and shipping DLLs. For example, if you know your messages are GDI-specific, you can just use the debug version of the GDI DLL (gdi-g.dll) and the non-debug versions of all other DLLs. To mix debug and non-debug versions of the libraries, you must edit your Architecture Description File (ADF).

Wind/U Command Line Options

When you start your application, you can use a number of Wind/U flags to help in debugging. The **-spy** option allows you to use the Wind/U Spy tool to monitor messages sent to an application window and to examine the values of message parameters. Once you've started your application with the **-spy** option, enter the command **spy** to start Wind/U Spy. Figure 3-3 shows Spy in action. You can specify which types of messages you want to monitor, which output device to send messages to, and whether to send output synchronously or asynchronously.

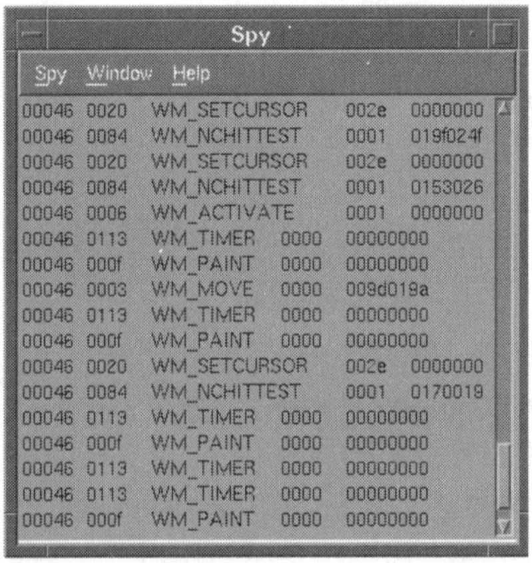

Figure 3.3 Wind/U Spy.

Another Wind/U command line option that you'll find useful for debugging graphics problems or X server errors/warnings is the **-sync** option. This option puts your X server in synchronous mode. Each client X operation will block until the server has executed the operation. This technique eliminates many timing issues and provides a more accurate stack trace.

Another Wind/U command line option you may want to use is **-dlltrace**. Because this option shows detailed information about how your application loads DLLs, you'll find it particularly helpful in debugging DLL problems.

Finally, the **-showleaks** option finds memory handles that are not freed when your application exits. When the application exits, it creates a file called **HANDLES.***n*, where *n* is the process ID. This file contains leak information about your application.

Third-Party Tools

In addition to these Wind/U debugging tools, you may also want to use third-party tools to help you debug your UNIX application. For example, a tool for identifying memory leaks in your application is Purify from Pure Software. Wind/U has been tested thoroughly with Purify, using many sample programs. Though Purify may still report some problems, Wind/U is relatively free of significant memory access errors or memory leaks. If you use Purify with your application, keep the following in mind:

- Most C library implementations of `malloc()` under UNIX never return memory to the operating system. Thus, the amount of memory used by the program as shown by utilities such as ps will never shrink. An increasing amount of memory consumption as shown by ps does not, in and of itself, indicate a memory leak.

- Use Purify's Memory In Use (MIU) reporting with care. For example, calling **purify_new_inuse**() within the function **do_something**() will always report 1000 new bytes; this is not a cause for concern, hower, since the memory is always released.

```
while(/*some condition */) {
    void *ptr = malloc(1000);
    do_something(pt);
    free(ptr);
}
```

For this reason, calling **purify_new_inuse**() from within your application is probably not useful.

- The X/Xt/Motif libraries on some systems generate a number of Purify warnings. You may wish to suppress some or all of these messages; consult your Purify documentation for details.

Another third-party tool you may want to use is XRunner from Mercury Interactive. Mercury Interactive's WinRunner and XRunner products are automated testing tools that you can use without any changes to your application. You can use WinRunner to test the Windows version of your application and XRunner to test the UNIX version. To use XRunner, you need only make sure it is included in your LD_LIBRARY_PATH, SHLIB_PATH, or LIBPATH environment variable.

Other Debugging Hints

Here are a few other hints that will help you identify problems unique to the UNIX version of your application.

- Make sure that both the Windows and UNIX versions of your application compiles cleanly with the strictest warning level set.
- If you are having a problem with PostMessage, instead use SendMessage for debugging. SendMessage bypasses the message queue and gives you a direct stack trace. It also eliminates any timing issues resulting from a client/server environment.
- Use a small sample to isolate problems quickly.
- Vary your configuration. For example, if you are running the OpenLook Window Manager, see if the problem also occurs with the Motif Window Manager. Also try setting your DISPLAY to a different server to see if that server has the same problem (this is particularly helpful for X errors).

Common Problem Areas

When porting your Windows application to UNIX, you'll find that most of the problems you encounter are in a few general areas. These areas are compiler differences, operating system differences, and architecture differences.

Compiler Differences

UNIX C++ compilers are usually based on the AT&T CFront 3.0 implementation, and most Windows C++ compilers are CFront 3.0 compatible. The Microsoft Visual C++ compiler is very compatible with the C++ 3.0 compilers supplied by HP, IBM, and Sun. This section lists some minor differences you may encounter.

Semicolons in Class Definitions

Visual C++ allows an extra semicolon at the end of class definitions, as in the following example:

```
DECLARE_DYNAMIC(ClassName);
```

To make this statement portable to UNIX, leave off the trailing semicolon, as follows:

```
DECLARE_DYNAMIC(ClassName)
```

Access to Base Class Private Members

Visual C++ allows derived classes to access base class private members, as in the following example:

```
class base
{
private:
    int some_member
}...
```

To make this code portable to UNIX, allow access to the member by making it protected in the base class, as follows:

```
class base
{
protected:
    int some_member
}...
```

Type Casting

Visual C++ allows type casting using function call syntax, as in the following example:

```
date.d_Day=unsigned char (i)
```

UNIX C++ compilers only support the C syntax for type casting, as in the following example:

```
date.d_Day=(unsigned char)i;
```

Interchanging Types

Visual C++ allows you to interchange int and BOOL types, as in the following example:

```
BOOL WinCalApp::ExitInstance()
```

With UNIX C++ compilers, these are different types and the return value must match the base class return value type, as follows:

```
int WinCalApp::ExitInstance()
```

Variable Declarations

Visual C++ allows variable declarations in switch statement cases without requiring a new scope, as in the following example:

```
default:
// a real day
int real_day=d_CellType[cell];
Doit(real_day)
```

To make this code portable, enclose the statements in a pair of braces to define explicitly the scope of the new variable, as follows:

```
default:
{
    // a real day
    int     real_day=d_CellType[cell];
    Doit(real_day)
}
```

Pragmas

MFC uses Visual C++ compiler #pragma warning (**disable:4xxx**) directives to eliminate warning messages during compiles. These pragmas are not portable to UNIX C++ compilers. Therefore, you can ignore warnings such as the following that reference MFC include files:

```
"afxwin.h", line 1694: warning: CStatic::Create() hides virtual
CWnd::Create()
```

Constructor Calls

Visual C++ allows complex statements in constructor calls, as in the following example:

```
//Constructor
CRecorderRecord(RecordID rid=NullRID, WORD monitorID=0, long
counter=0, CProcess &process=CProcess());
```

Make this statement more portable by reducing the functionality and not allowing a default for the CProcess argument. The calling code must create the CProcess object before the constructor call.

```
//Constructor
CRecorderRecord(RecordID rid=NullRID, WORD monitorID=0, long
counter=0, CProcess &process);
```

Inline Functions

Visual C++ allows complex inline functions with multiple return points. For UNIX C++ compilers, you must rewrite inline functions to remove multiple return points, or remove the inline keyword.

New and Delete Operators

As a general rule, if you use [ ] when you call new, you must use [ ] when you call delete to make your code more portable and safe. In MFC, if the delete object is not a derived class from CObject, cast the object to a void pointer and make sure you call a global delete operator. For example:

```
struct CRowColInfo {
    .
    .
    .
} *m_pRowInfo;

::delete [] (char *)m_pRowInfo;
```

Anonymous Unions

Visual C++ allows anonymous, or unnamed, unions, as in the following example, which you would access as **struct_name.fred**:

```
struct{
    union{
            char fred[10].
            struct{
                    }jim
    }
}
```

Many UNIX C and C++ compilers do not allow anonymous unions. Instead, you must name the union, as in the following example. You would then use struct_name.tony.jim.

```
struct{
    union{
            char fred[10].
            struct{
                    }jim
    }tony
}
```

Operating System Differences

The biggest difference between UNIX and Windows is that Win16 uses a 16-bit word instead of the 32-bit word used by most UNIX variants. Windows 95 and Windows NT both use the Win32 API, which uses a 32-bit word, just as UNIX does. But if you are porting applications developed with the Win16 API, this difference may cause problems in your application. Wind/U handles most 16/32-bit issues for you automatically. However, it is important to understand the differences between UNIX and Win16 word sizes and the impact they have on other data types.

Table 3.3 shows the sizes of the basic types in Wind/U.

Table 3.3 Basic Data Type Sizes in Wind/U

Data Type	Wind/U	Win16	Win32
char, unsigned char	1	1	1
short, unsigned short	2	2	2
int, unsigned int	4	2	2
pointer, address	4	2	4
long, unsigned long	4	4	4
float	4	4	4
double	8	8	8

Table 3.4 shows the sizes of the Windows types in Wind/U.

Table 3.4 Windows Type Sizes in Wind/U

Data Type	Wind/U (16-bit)	Windows	Wind/U 32-bit
WORD	2	2	2
DWORD	4	4	4
HANDLE	2	2	4
LPCSTR	4	4	4
BOOL	4	2	4
HLOCAL	4	2	4
UINT	4	2	4

Table 3.4 Windows Type Sizes in Wind/U (continued)

Data Type	Wind/U (16-bit)	Windows	Wind/U 32-bit
FARPROC	4	4	4
UPARAM	2	2	4
LPARAM	4	4	4

The following example shows 16-bit Windows code that works fine, but is not portable to a 32-bit environment:

```
typedef unsigned short WORD;
    int function()
    {
            WORD wTwo;
            int nOne;
            ...
            wTwo=(WORD)nOne;
            ...
    }
```

Porting this code to NT or UNIX would cause problems if the value of nOne was ever greater than 65,535 because it would suddenly become too large to fit into wTwo (which is only 16 bits wide); the wTwo variable would wrap and start back at zero. Normally, strong type checking in C++ does not allow code like this to survive, so 16/32-bit problems are not common in C++ unless type casting is used.

Another common 16/32-bit problem is structure packing. On 16-bit systems, compilers pack structures based on 16-bit boundaries by default. On 32-bit systems, the compilers use 32- or 64-bit boundaries (they waste a byte here and there to ensure that the elements of a structure are aligned properly). The end result is that the size of the operator returns different results in 16-bit and 32-bit environments. Structure packing can cause problems if you read structures to and from binary files.

In DOS and Windows, lines in text files are terminated by a combination of a Line Feed and Carriage Return. UNIX uses just a Line Feed to denote the end of a line. Many applications depend on the Line Feed/Carriage Return combination to work properly. Some applications may have to modify code to work the same in both environments.

Another example of Line Feed/Carriage Return incompatibilities is Edit Controls. The text retrieved from an edit control will not have the Line Feed/Carriage Return, only the UNIX style Line Feed.

Another major difference between Windows files and UNIX files is that UNIX uses the forward slash (/) as a directory separator, while Windows uses backslash (\) characters. UNIX filenames are also case sensitive and much larger (256 characters) than Windows filenames. You may have to change some applications to handle these differences.

UNIX also does not have any concept of drive letters. Applications should not depend on **a:\filename**-style filenames.

To avoid differences among fonts, controls, and focus highlights between Windows and Motif dialog boxes, Wind/U uses the same ratios as Windows. To minimize problems when porting dialogs, follow these guidelines:

- Avoid using `Layout->Size to Content`. Always create the control about 20 percent wider than produced by `Size to Content`, to ensure that the strings fit cleanly inside your controls with the X fonts, which are slightly different from Windows default fonts.
- Always keep controls about 12 dialog units from the dialog edges. App Studio partially enforces this guideline, since it does not allow you to place a control closer than 10 dialog units to the edge.
- Always leave about 10 dialog units between controls.

Architecture Differences

Certain architectural differences between UNIX and Windows warrant discussion, since they may impact certain types of applications.

Storage Order and Alignment

Because Wind/U runs on a variety of architectures, it is important to make your code as portable as possible. The following example illustrates how storage order can affect your program. In the example, a structure is cast to type `long` because the programmer knew the order in which the particular architecture stored data.

```
/* Nonportable code */
struct time
```

```
{
    char hour;
    char minute;
    char second;
};
...
struct time now, alarm_time;
...
if ( *(long *)&now >= *(long *)&alarm_time)
{
  /* sound alarm */
}
```

The code in this example makes the nonportable assumption that the data for hour will be stored in a higher-order position than minute and second. This may work on an Intel microprocessor–based machine, but the alarm may never sound on a SPARCStation because the code is not portable.

To make the program in the example portable, you can break the comparison between the two long integers into a component-by-component comparison as follows:

```
/* Portable code */

struct time
{
    char hour;
    char minute;
    char second;
}


...
struct time now, alarm_time;
...
if (time_cmp(now,alarm_time) >=0)
{
/* sound alarm */
}
int time_cmp(struct time t1, struct time t2)
{
    if (t1.hour != t2.hour)
      return (t2.hour - t1.hour);
    if (t1.minute != t2.minute)
      return (t2.minute - t1.minute);
```

```
    if (t1.second != t2.second)
      return (t2.second - t1.second);
    return 1;
}
```

As a general rule, you should always use the fields of a structure instead of making assumptions about their location or size in the structure.

Byte/Word Ordering

The ordering of bytes can vary among machines. Code assuming an internal order is not portable, as is shown by the following example:

```
/* Notportable */

struct tag_int_bytes
{
    char lobyte;
    char hibyte;
};
```

Instead of assuming that the first part is always stored in the low byte, use the **HIBYTE, LOBYTE, HIWORD,** and **LOWORD** macros. Wind/U automatically changes these macros to match the current architecture.

Wind/U provides the following byte-swapping macros and extension functions as portability helpers. These are low-level functions used to swap Intel binary data into a format compatible with RISC computers. Use them if your UNIX application on a RISC-based system must read or write a binary data base that is written or read by an Intel-based system.

- **wuSWAP16()**
  Converts a signed or unsigned 16-bit integer value.

- **wuSWAP32()**
  Converts a signed or unsigned 32-bit integer value.

- **wuSwapBitmapInfoHeader(BITMAPINFOHEADER *lpBmih)**
  Converts a DIB info header read from a binary file and performs the necessary byte swapping.

- **wuReadBitmapInfoHeaderFromFile(HFILE hFile,
  BITMAPINFOHEADER *lpBmi)**

Reads a DIB info header from a binary file and performs the necessary byte swapping.

- **wuWriteBitmapInfoHeaderToFile(HFILE hFile, BITMAPINFOHEADER *lpBmi)**
  Writes a DIB info header to a binary file, performing the necessary byte swapping.

- **wuSwapBitmapFileHeader(char *original, BITMAPFILEHEADER *lpBfh)**
  Converts a DIB file header read from a binary file and performs the necessary byte swapping.

- **wuReadBitmapFileHeaderFromFile(HFILE hFile, BITMAPFILEHEADER *lpBfh)**
  Reads a DIB file header from a binary file and performs the necessary byte swapping.

- **wuWriteBitmapFileHeaderToFile(HFILE hFile, BITMAPFILEHEADER *lpBfh)**
  Writes a DIB file header to a binary file, performing the necessary byte swapping.

- **wuBitmapSwapCoreHeader(char *original, BITMAPCOREHEADER *lpBmc)**
  Converts a DIB core header read from a binary file and performs the necessary byte swapping.

- **wuBitmapReadCoreHeaderFromFile(HFILE hFile, BITMAPCOREHEADER *lpBmc)**
  Reads a DIB core header from a binary file and performs the necessary byte swapping.

- **wuBitmapWriteCoreHeaderToFile(HFILE hFile, BITMAPCOREHEADER *lpBmc)**
  Writes a DIB core header to a binary file, performing the necessary byte swapping.

The following code fragments demonstrate the functionality of these helpers:

```
/**************************************************************
****
Purpose: Load a DIB from binary file on Intel or UNIX platform
```

```
******************************************************************
***/
HBITMAP LoadBitmapFromFile(char *szFile)
{
    OFSTRUCT            ofs;
    BITMAPFILEHEADER    bmf;
    BITMAPINFOHEADER    bmi;
    DWORD               dwSize;
    BYTE_huge *         lpDib;
    HDC                 hdc;
    HBITMAP             hBitmap;
    HANDLE              hDib;
    int                 sFile;
    WORD                wBytes;
    DWORD               dwBytes, dwOffset;

/* open the bitmap file */
if ((sFile=OpenFile(szFile, &ofs, OF_READ))==-1
    return 0;

/* read bitmap file header */
#ifdef WU_APP
    if(!wuReadBitmapFileHeaderFromFile(sFile, &bmf)) {
    _lclose(sFile);
    return 0;
}
#else
    wBytes=_lread(sFile, (LPSTR) &bmf, sizeof(BITMAPFILEHEADER));
    if(wBytes != sizeof(BITMAPFILEHEADER)) {
            _lclose(sFile);
            return 0;
    }
#endif

/* make sure file is a bitmap file! */
if(bmf.bjType != 0x4D42) {
    _lclose(sFile);
    return 0;
}
/* read bitmap info header */
#ifdef WU_APP
    if(!wuReadBitmapInfoHeaderFromFile(sFile, &bmi)) {
            _lclose(sFile);
            return 0;
```

```
        }
#else
    wBytes=_lread(sFile), (LPSTR) &bmi, sizeof(DWORD));
    if(wBytes != sizeof(DWORD) {
            _lclose(sFile);
            return 0;
    }
    wBytes=_lread(sFile, (LPSTR) &bmi+sizeof(DWORD),
            (WORD bmi.biSize-sizeof(DWORD));
    if(wBytes != bmi.biSize-sizeof(DWORD)) {
            _lclose(sFile);
            return 0;
    }
#endif
/* don't handle biBitCount==24 */
if(bmi.biBitCount==24) {
    _lclose(sFile);
    return 0;
}
/* calculate size of bitmap and size of color table */
dwSize=(((bmi.biWidth *bmi.biBitCount+31)&~31)>>3)*bmi.biHeight;
dwOffset=bmi.biSize;
if(bmi.biSize==sizeof(BITMAPCOREHEADER))
    dwOffset+=(1<<bmi.biBitCount)*sizeof(RGBTRIPLE);
else if (bmi.biClrUsed != 0)
    dwOffset+=bmi.biClrUsed*sizeof(RGBQUAD);
else
    dwOffset+=(1<<bmi.biBitCount)*sizeof(RGBQUAD);
    dwSize+=dwOffset;
/* allocate memory for rest of the information */
if(!(hDib=GlobalAlloc(GMEM_MOVEABLE, dwSize))) {
    _lclose(sFile);
    return 0;
}
lpDib=(BYTE *) GlobalLock(hDib);
memcpy(lpDib, &bmi, (WORD)bmi.biSize);
dwBytes=_lread(sFile, (void *)(lpDib+bmi.biSize),dwSize-
bmi.biSize);
if(dwBytes != dwSize-bmi.biSize) {
    _lclose(sFile);
    GlobalUnlock(hDib);
    GlobalFree(hDib);
    return 0;
}
```

```
    _lclose(sFile);
    /* create the bitmap */
    hdc=CreateDC("DISPLAY", 0, 0, 0);
    hBitmap=CreateDIBitmap(hdc,
            (LPBITMAPINFOHEADERO lpDib,
            CBM_INIT,
            lpDib+dwOffset,
            (LPBITMAPINFO) lpDib,
            DIB_RGB_COLORS);
    DeleteDC(hdc);
    GlobalUnlock(hDib);
    GlobalFree(hDib);
    return hBitmap;
}
```

Shared Memory Model

As with Windows NT, all instance data in UNIX is private to the application and cannot be accessed from other modules (for example, **GetInstanceData** is not supported).

Application Message Queues

Like Windows NT, each Wind/U application has its own message queue that is inaccessible to other applications. A module instance handle is unique only to the modules that comprise the application. Other applications executing on the system may have the same instance handle. Likewise, each application contains its own handle table, so that handles are not system-unique. For these reasons, interapplication message passing is currently unsupported by Wind/U. However, Wind/U supports interapplication message passing via DDEML.

Preemptive Multitasking

In some instances, the UNIX preemptive multitasking scheduler may require files to be locked (for example, to prevent race conditions between different applications that access common files). A Wind/U-ported application must not assume that it has indefinite control of the CPU until it returns to the message loop (for example, GetMessage, WaitMessage, Yield). The application may be time-sliced at any time.

## CHAPTER 4

Using MFC Application Framework

The Microsoft Foundation Class (MFC) library provides you with a set of reusable, prebuilt C++ components that provide a portable framework for creating world class applications. MFC components encapsulate common functionality that end users expect in any Windows application, such as toolbars and status bars, form and edit views, print and print preview, OLE visual editing and OLE automation, multiple-document interface, splitter and scroller windows, dialog data exchange and validation, dialog boxes, database access and context sensitive help. By using these prebuilt, pretested, components, you can quickly create professional applications. Simply put, using MFC will save you time!

This chapter categorizes and describes the classes in MFC version 3.1. The sections are grouped as follows:

- Visual C++
- MFC History and Evolution
- Summary of MFC Classes
- Application Architecture Classes
- Visual Object Classes
- General-Purpose Classes
- Database Classes
- OLE Classes
  - Miscellaneous Classes
- Wizards

Visual C++

Visual C++ is a Windows host integrated development environment (IDE) that lets you design, develop and debug and MFC application. While some of the tools you need are separate executables, this IDE seamlessly integrates everything together. The major Visual C++ components are:

- Source code editor—color
- Resource editors—accelerator, bitmap, cursor, dialog, icon, menu, string table and version editors
- Resource compiler
- Source browser—view graphics of inheritance, calling relations, definitions,
- C/C++ optimizing compiler—generate small fast executables
- Incremental linker—link time linear to code changed, not size of application
- Debugger—integrated with source code editor
- Project build tools—project viewer, project dependencies, make
- AppWizard—generates initial MFC based application
- ClassWizard—for creating and modifying classes
- Runtime profiler—for finding performance problems in your application
- Extensive on-line document—1000's of pages on the CD ROM or your hard disk
- Utilities—dumpbin, editbin, DDESpy, PView, ZoomIn, WinDiff,

The Visual C++ IDE eliminates a lot of the traditional application development drudgery, allowing you to spend your time adding value to your application. So what's the catch? To leverage the environment and framework, you must take time to thoroughly learn them.

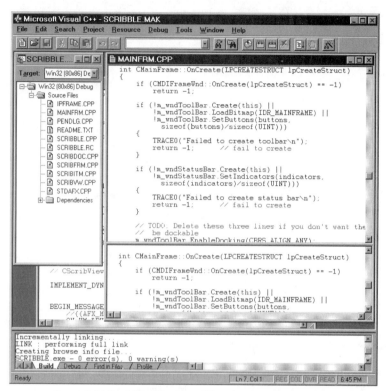

Figure 4-1. Visual C++ Integrated Development Environment

MFC History and Evolution

The MFC framework has grew from a set of C++ wrappers to a full fledged application framework with MFC 3. Microsoft continues to dedicate substantial resources to MFC to make it a growing and evolving library. As the WinAPI under MFC grows, e.g. Win32, OLE, ODBC and new user interface components become standard, e.g. property sheets, toolbars, status bars, MFC will be there to support them. Throughout its evolution MFC has continued to offer the following:

- A C++ API to the underlying Windows C API
- Uses only a sane subset of C++
- Portable to many compilers and operating systems

- Open and licensed to other compiler/tool vendors
- Tuned for small/fast executables

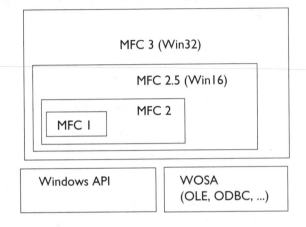

Figure 4-2. Microsoft Foundation Class Library Evolution

MFC 1.0

MFC 1 was released in April 1992 as part of the Microsoft C/C++ Version 7. At that time MFC consistent of a set of general purpose classes and a set of class wrappers for GUI features. Also, MFC 1 was supported on pre-releases of the Win32 SDK in late 1992.

The general purpose classes were the following:

- Collection classes—C*Array, C*List, CMap*
- Exception Handling—CMemoryException, CFileException, CArchiveException, ...
- Files—CStdioFile, CMemFile
- Object persistence—CArchive
- Run-time type information—CRuntimeClass
- Strings—CString
- Time and Date—CTime, CTimeSpan

The Windows-related classes were the following:

- Application startup and other applications services—CWinApp
- Window management—CWnd, CFrameWindow, ...
- Graphics—CDC, CPaintDC, CGdiObject, ...
- Multiple-Document Interface—CMDIFrameWnd, CMDIChildWnd, ...
- Menus - CMenu
- Dialog Boxes—CDialog, CModalDialog
- Controls,—CStatic, CButton, CListBox, CComboBox, ...
- Common dialogs—CFileDialog, CColorDialog, CFontDialog, ...
- OLE 1

MFC 2.0

MFC 2 was released in February 1993 as part of Visual C++ 1.0, Microsoft's first Windows hosted IDE. MFC 2 added to the core features of MFC 1, adding architectural classes to help organize and structure application programs as well as high-level abstractions for prebuilt functionality. Now MFC is a full-fledged application framework, delivering more functionality that is much larger than a set of C++ wrappers around a C API. Also, in August 1992, as part of Visual C++ 1.0 32-bit edition on Windows NT a 32-bit version of MFC 2.0 shipped.

The architectural classes were the following:

- Commands—CCmdTarget
- Context sensitive help, F1 and Shift+F1
- Dialog data exchange and validation (DDX/DDV)
- Documents and views, CDoc, CView, ...
- Printing and print preview

The high-level abstractions were the following:

- Form view—CFormView
- Edit view—CEditView
- Scrolling view—CScrollView
- Splitter window—CSplitterWnd
- Toolbars, status and dialog bars—CToolBar, CStatusBar, CDialogBar

- VBX 1.0 controls (for 16-bit only)

MFC 2.5

MFC 2.5 was released in December of 1993 as part of Visual C++ 1.5. MFC 2.5 added support for database, giving developers access any data source through ODBC and full support for the many features of OLE 2. MFC 2.5 only supports 16-bit development.

The database classes were the following:

- Database engine classes
- Record field exchange (RFX)

- Record view—CRecordView

The OLE 2 classes were the following:

- Visual editing servers—COleServerDoc
- Visual editing containers—COleDocument
- Structured storage—COleStreamFile
- OLE automation servers—COleServerItem
- OLE automation clients—COleClientItem

A 32-bit MFC 2.5 was never shipped in a 32-bit version, instead Microsoft added functionality to MFC 2.5 and introduced MFC 3.0.

MFC 3.0

MFC 3 was released in September of 1994 as part of Visual C++ 2.0. MFC 3.0 only supports 32-bit development. MFC 3 supports all of the new features added to MFC 2.5 and more prebuilt user interface components, more support for Win32 as well as some work for OLE controls (OCXs).

The new user-interface classes are the following:

- Enhanced toolbars—support hints and docking
- Miniframe windows—CMiniFrameWnd
- Property pages (tabbed dialogs)—CPropertyPage, CPropertySheet

The new support for Win32 consists of the following:

- Multithreading—CWinThread
- Unicode support
- Shared 32-bit DLLs

The new language syntax support includes the following:

C++ templates—CArray, CList, CMap, CTypedPtr*

C++ exceptions—CException

MFC 3.1

MFC 3.1 was released in March of 1995 as part of Visual C++ 2.1. MFC 3.1 only supports 32-bit development. The following functionality was added to MFC 3.1:

- Support for the Win32 Windows Common Controls

Class	Definition
CAnimateCtrl	A window that displays successive frames of an Audio Video Interleaved (AVI) clip during a lengthy operation.
CHeaderCtrl	A resizable button that appears above a column of text, allowing the user to display more or less information in the column.
CHotkeyCtrl	A window that enables the user to create a hot key. A "hot key" is a key combination that the user can press to perform an action quickly.
CImageList	A collection of images used to efficiently manage large sets of icons or bitmaps.
CListCtrl	A window that displays a collection of items each consisting of an icon and a label.
CProgressCtrl	(Also known as a "progress bar control.") A window that an application can use to indicate the progress of a lengthy operation.
CSliderCtrl	(Also known as a "trackbar.") A window containing a slider and optional tick marks that

	sends notification messages to indicate changes in its position.
CSpinButtonCtrl	(Also known as an "up-down control.") A pair of arrow buttons that the user can click to increment or decrement a value, such as a scroll position or a number displayed in a companion control.
CStatusBarCtrl	A horizontal window in a parent window in which an application can display various kinds of status information. This control resembles the MFC CStatusBar class.
CTabCtrl	Analogous to the dividers in a notebook or the labels in a file cabinet. By using a tab control, an application can define multiple pages for the same area of a window or dialog box. (See also MFC class CPropertySheet.)
CToolBarCtrl	A window that contains one or more command-generating buttons. This control resembles the MFC CToolBar class.
CToolTipCtrl	A small pop-up window that displays a single line of text describing the purpose of a toolbar button or other tool in an application.
CTreeCtrl	(Also known as a "tree view control.") A window that displays a hierarchical list of items, such as the headings in a document, the entries in an index, or the files and directories on a disk. Each item consists of a label and an optional bitmapped image, and each item can have a list of subitems associated with it.

- A subset of MAPI functionality was added to the CDocument class
- Windows Sockets, the network-independent API for network communications programming under Microsoft Windows and Microsoft Windows NT. Class CAsyncSocket encapsulates the Windows Sockets API. Class CSocket, derived from CAsyncSocket, additionally provides a

simple programming model that lets you serialize data from one socket application to another via a CArchive object, using a CSocketFile object.

- Additonal ODBC drivers, ODBC bulk add optimizations, and support for ODBC classes in OCX controls.

MFC 4

Work on MFC 4 is underway and may already be shipping. MFC 4 is targeted at new user-interface classes and new APIs in Windows 95. MFC 4 will also support additional OLE control functionality and allow OLE controls in dialogs. MFC 4 will replace the custom property pages, toolbar and status bar controls with the Windows common control implementations. And, of course other nifty functionality that make your applications better.

Summary of MFC Classes

Application Architecture Classes	Definition	Mac	UNIX
Windows Application Class			
CWinApp	Encapsulates the code to initialize, run, and terminate the application.	Yes	Yes
Command-Related Classes			
CCmdTarget	Serves as the base class for all classes of objects that can receive and respond to messages.	Yes	Yes
CCmdUI	Provides a programmable interface for updating user-interface objects such as menu items or control-bar buttons. The command target object enables, disables, checks, and/or unchecks the user-interface object via this proxy object.	Yes	Yes
Document/View Classes			
CDocTemplate	Base class for document templates. A document template coordinates the creation of document, view, and frame window objects.	Yes	Yes

Summary of MFC Classes (continued)

Application Architecture Classes	Definition	Mac	UNIX
CSingleDoc Template	Template for documents in the single document interface (SDI). SDI applications have only one open document at a time.	Yes	Yes
CMultiDoc Template	Template for documents in the multiple document interface (MDI). MDIapplications can have multiple documents open at a time.	Yes	Yes
CDocument	Base class for application-specific documents. Derive your document class(es) from CDocument.	Yes	Yes
CView	Base class for application-specific views of a documents data. Views display data and take user input to edit or select the data. Derive your view class(es) from CView.	Yes	Yes
CPrintInfo	Structure containing information about a print or print preview job. Used by CView's printing architecture.	Yes	Yes
CCreateContext	A structure passed by a document template to window-creation functions to coordinate the creation of document, view, and frame window objects.	Yes	Yes

Threading Base Class

CWinThread	The base class for all threads. Use directly, or derive a class from CWinThread if your thread performs user-interface functions. CWinApp is derived from CWinThread	No	Yes

Visual Object Classes
Window Classes

CWnd	Base class for all windows. Use the derived classes below, or derive your own window classes directly from CWnd.	Yes	Yes
CFrameWnd	Base class for a single document interface (SDI) application's main frame window.	Yes	Yes

Summary of MFC Classes (continued)

Application Architecture Classes	Definition	Mac	UNIX
CMDIFrameWnd	Base class for a multiple document interface (MDI) application's main frame window.	Yes	Yes
CMDIChildWnd	Base class for an MDI application's document frame windows.	Yes	Yes
CMiniFrameWnd	A half-height frame window typically seen around floating toolbars.	Yes	Yes

View Classes

	Definition	Mac	UNIX
CView	Base class for application-specific views of a documents data. Views display data and take user input to edit or select the data. Derive your view class(es) from CView or use CScrollView for automatic scrolling.	Yes	Yes
CScrollView	Base class for views with scrolling capabilities. Derive your view class from CScrollView for automatic scrolling.	Yes	Ye
CFormView	A scroll view whose layout is defined in a dialog r esource. Derive classes from CFormView to quickly implement user interfaces based on dialog resources.	Yes	Yes
CEditView	View with text-editing, searching, replacing, and scrolling capabilities. Use this class to provide a text-based user interface to a document.	Yes	Yes

Dialog Classes

	Definition	Mac	UNIX
CDialog	Base class for all dialog boxes, both modal and modeless.	Yes	Yes
CDataExchange	Supplies initialization and validation information for dialog boxes.	Yes	Yes
CFileDialog	Provides a standard dialog box for opening or saving a file.	Yes	Yes
CPrintDialog	Provides a standard dialog box for printing a file.	Yes	Yes
CFontDialog	Provides a standard dialog box for selecting a font.	Yes	Yes

Summary of MFC Classes (continued)

Application Architecture Classes	Definition	Mac	UNIX
CColorDialog	Provides a standard dialog box for selecting a color. CColorDialog is not supported by Wind/U 1.3.	Yes	Yes
CFindReplaceDialog	Provides a standard dialog box for a search-and-replace operation.	Yes	Yes

Property Sheet Classes

CPropertySheet	Provides the frame for multiple property pages. Derive your property sheet class from CPropertySheet to implement your property sheets quickly.	Yes	Yes
CPropertyPage	Provides the individual pages within a property sheet. Derive a class from CPropertyPage for each page to be added to your property sheet.	Yes	Yes

Control Classes

CStatic	A static text control window. Static controls are used to label, box, or separate other controls in a dialog box or window.	Yes	Yes
CButton	A button control window. The class provides a programmatic interface to a pushbutton, check box, or radio button in a dialog box or window.	Yes	Yes
CEdit	An editable text control window. Edit controls are used to take textual input from the user.	Yes	Yes
CScrollBar	A scroll-bar control window. The class provides the functionality of a scroll bar for use as a control in a dialog box or window through which the user can specify a position within a range.	Yes	Yes
CListBox	A list-box control window. A list box displays a list of items that the user can view and select.	Yes	Yes
CComboBox	A combo-box control window. A combo box consists of an edit control plus a list box.	Yes	Yes
CHEdit	A Windows for Pen edit control in which the user can enter and modify text using standard pen editing gestures.	Obsolete	Obsolete

Summary of MFC Classes (continued)

Application Architecture Classes	Definition	Mac	UNIX
CBEdit	A Windows for Pen edit control in which the user can enter and modify text using standard pen editing gestures. This control differs from CHEdit in that it provides boxes to guide text entry.	Obsolete	Obsolete
CControlBar	A window aligned to the top or bottom of a frame window that contains HWND-based child controls or controls not based on an HWND, such as toolbar buttons. The base class for control bars such as toolbars and status bars.	Yes	Yes
CStatusBar	Base class for status-bar control windows.	Yes	Yes
CToolBar	Toolbar control windows that contain bitmap command buttons not based on an HWND.	Yes	Yes
CDialogBar	A modeless dialog box in the form of a control bar.	Yes	Yes
CBitmapButton	A button with a bitmap rather than a text caption.	Yes	Yes
CVBControl	A window whose implementation is a VBX control.	Obsolete	Obsolete
CSplitterWnd	A window that the user can split into multiple panes.	Yes	Yes

Menu Class

	Definition	Mac	UNIX
CMenu	Encapsulates an HMENU handle to the application's menu bar and popup menus.	Yes	Yes

Device Context Classes

	Definition	Mac	UNIX
CDC	Base class for device contexts; used directly for accessing the whole display and for accessing nondisplay contexts such as printers.	Yes	Yes
CPaintDC	Display context used in OnPaint member functions of windows and OnDraw member functions of views. Automatically calls BeginPaint on construction and EndPaint on destruction.	Yes	Yes
CClientDC	Display context for client areas of windows. Used, for example, to draw in immediate response to mouse events.	Yes	Yes

Summary of MFC Classes (continued)

Application Architecture Classes	Definition	Mac	UNIX
CWindowDC	Display context for entire windows, including both the client and frame areas.	Yes	Yes
CMetaFileDC	Device context for Windows metafiles. A Windows metafile contains a sequence of GDI commands that can be replayed to create an image. Calls made to the member functions of a CMetaFileDC are recorded in a metafile.	Yes	Yes

Drawing Object Classes

CGdiObject	Base class for GDI drawing tools.	Yes	Yes
CBitMap	Encapsulates a GDI bitmap, providing an interface for manipulating bitmaps.	Yes	Yes
CBrush	Encapsulates a GDI brush that can be selected as the current brush in a device context.	Yes	Yes
CFont	Encapsulates a GDI font that can be selected as the current font in a device context.	Yes	Yes
CPalette	Encapsulates a GDI color palette for use as an interface between the application and a color output device such as a display.	Yes	Yes
CPen	Encapsulates a GDI pen that can be selected as the current pen in a device context.	Yes	Yes
CRgn	Encapsulates a GDI region for manipulating an elliptical or polygonal area within a window. Used in conjunction with the clipping member functions in class CDC.		

Table 4.xxx General Purpose Classes
Root Class

CObject	The ultimate base class of nearly all other classes. Supports serializing data and obtaining run-time information about a class.	Yes	Yes

Summary of MFC Classes (continued)

Application Architecture Classes	Definition	Mac	UNIX
File Classes			
CFile	Provides a programmatic interface to binary disk files.	Yes	Yes
CMemFile	Provides a programmatic interface to in-memory files.	Yes	Yes
CStdioFile	Provides a programmatic interface to buffered stream disk files, usually in text mode.	Yes	Yes
CArchive	Cooperates with a CFile object to implement persistent storage for objects through serialization. The data files created by CArchive are architecture dependent due to byte ordering and integer size differences.	Yes	Yes
Diagnostics			
CDumpContext	Provides a destination for diagnostic dumps.	Yes	Yes
CMemoryState	Provides snapshots of memory use. The class is also used to compare earlier and later snapshots.	Yes	Yes
CRuntimeClass	Used to determine the exact class of an object at run time.	Yes	Yes
Exceptions			
CException	Base class for exceptions.	Yes	Yes
CArchiveException	An archive exception.	Yes	Yes
CFileException	A file-oriented exception.	Yes	Yes
CMemoryException	An out-of-memory exception.	Yes	Yes
CNotSupported Exception	An exception resulting from the invocation of an unsupported feature.	Yes	Yes
CResource Exception	An exception resulting from a failure to load a Windows resource.	Yes	Yes
COleException	An exception resulting from failures in OLE processing. This class is used by both clients and servers.	Yes	Yes

Summary of MFC Classes (continued)

Application Architecture Classes	Definition	Mac	UNIX
COleDispatch Exception	An exception resulting from a failure in OLE processing. This class is used by both containers and servers.	Yes	Yes
CUserException	An exception used to stop a user-initiated operation. The user has typically been notified of the problem before this exception is thrown.	Yes	Yes

Collections - Arrays

CByteArray	Stores elements of type BYTE in an array.	Yes	Yes
CDWordArray	Stores elements of type doubleword in an array.	Yes	Yes
CObArray	Stores pointers to objects of class CObject or of classes derived from CObject in an array.	Yes	Yes
CPtrArray	Stores pointers to void (generic pointers) in an array.	Yes	Yes
CStringArray	Stores CString objects in an array.	Yes	Yes
CWordArray	Stores elements of type WORD in an array.	Yes	Yes
CUIntArray	Stores elements of type UINT in an array.	Yes	Yes

Collections - Lists

CObList	Stores pointers to objects of class CObject or of classes derived from CObject in a linked list.	Yes	Yes
CPtrList	Stores pointers to void (generic pointers) in a linked list.	Yes	Yes
CStringList	Stores CString objects in a linked list.	Yes	Yes

Collections - Maps

CMapPtrToWord	Maps void pointers to WORDs. Uses void pointers as keys for finding WORDs.	Yes	Yes
CMapPtrToPtr	Maps void pointers to void pointers. Uses void pointers as keys for finding other void pointers.	Yes	Yes

Summary of MFC Classes (continued)

Application Architecture Classes	Definition	Mac	UNIX
CMapStringToOb	Maps CString objects to CObject pointers. Uses CStrings as keys for finding CObject pointers.	Yes	Yes
CMapStringToPtr	Maps CString objects to void pointers. Uses CStrings as keys for finding void pointers.	Yes	Yes
CMapStringToString	Maps CString objects to CString objects. Uses CStrings as keys for finding other CStrings.	Yes	Yes
CMapWordToOb	Maps WORDs to CObject pointers. Uses WORDs for finding CObject pointers.	Yes	Yes
CMapWordToPtr	Maps WORDs to void pointers. Uses WORDs for finding void pointers.	Yes	Yes

Collections - Templates

CArray	Stores elements in an array.	Yes	Yes
CMap	Maps keys to values.	Yes	Yes
CList	Stores elements in a linked list.	Yes	Yes
CTypedPtrList	Type-safe collection that stores pointers to objects in a linked list.	Yes	Yes
CTypedPtrArray	Type-safe collection that stores pointers to objects in an array.	Yes	Yes
CTypedPtrMap	Type-safe collection that maps keys to values; both keys and values are pointers.	Yes	Yes

Miscellaneous Support Classes

CString	Holds character strings.	Yes	Yes
CTime	Holds absolute time and date values.	Yes	Yes
CTimeSpan	Holds relative time and date values.	Yes	Yes
CPoint	Holds coordinate (x, y) pairs.	Yes	Yes
CRect	Holds rectangular areas.	Yes	Yes
CSize	Holds distance, relative positions, or paired values.	Yes	Yes

Summary of MFC Classes (continued)

Application Architecture Classes	Definition	Mac	UNIX
CRectTracker	Displays and handles user interface for resizing and moving rectangular objects.	Yes	Yes

OLE Classes

OLE Base Classes

COleDocument	Abstract base class of COleClientDoc and COleServerDoc classes. A COleDocument is the container for CDocItems. A COleClientDoc contains COleClientItems while a COleServerDoc contains COleServerItems.	Yes	Yes
CDocItem	An item that is part of a document. Abstract base class of COleClientItem and COleServerItem.	Yes	Yes
COleDispatch Driver	Used to call automation servers from your automation client. ClassWizard uses this class to c reate type-safe classes for automation servers that provide a type library.	Yes	Yes

OLE Visual Editing Container Classes

COleLinkingDoc	A class derived from COleDocument which provides the infrastructure for linking. You should derive the document classes for your container applications from this class instead of from COleDocument if you want them to support links to embedded objects.	Yes	Yes
COleClientItem	A client item class that represents the client's side of the connection to an embedded or linked OLE item. You must derive your client items from this class.	Yes	Yes

OLE Visual Editing Server Classes

COleObjectFactory	Used to create items when requested from other OLE containers. This class serves as the base class for more specific types of factories, including COleTemplateServer.	Yes	Yes

Summary of MFC Classes (continued)

Application Architecture Classes	Definition	Mac	UNIX
COleTemplate Server	Used to create documents using the framework's document/view architecture. A COleTemplateServer object delegates most of its work to an associated CDocTemplate object.	Yes	Yes
COleIPFrameWnd	Provides the frame window for a view when a server document is being edited in place.	Yes	Yes
COleResizeBar	Provides the standard user interface for in-place resizing. Objects of this class are always used in conjunction with COleIPFrameWnd objects.	Yes	Yes
COleServerDoc	A server document class that creates and manages server items. You must derive your server documents from this class instead of CDocument.	Yes	Yes
COleServerItem	A server item class that represents the server's side of the connection to an embedded or linked OLE item. You must derive your server items from this class.	Yes	Yes

OLE Data Transfer Classes

COleDropSource	Controls the drag-and-drop operation from start to finish. This class determines when the drag operation starts and when it ends. It also displays cursor feedback during the drag-and-drop operation.	Yes	Yes
COleDropTarget	Represents the target of a drag-and-drop operation. A COleDropTarget object corresponds to a window on screen. It determines whether to accept any data dropped onto it and implements the actual drop operation.	Yes	Yes
COleDataSource	Used when an application provides data for a data transfer. COleDataSource could be viewed as an object-oriented clipboard object.	Yes	Yes
COleDataObject	Used as the client side to COleDataSource. COleDataObject objects provide access to the data contained in a COleDataSource object.	Yes	Yes

Summary of MFC Classes (continued)

Application Architecture Classes	Definition	Mac	UNIX
OLE Dialog Box Classes			
COleDialog	Used by the framework to contain common implementations for all OLE dialog boxes. All dialog box classes in the user-interface category are derived from this base class. Cannot be used directly.	Yes	Yes
COleInsertDialog	Displays the Insert Object dialog box, the standard user interface for inserting new OLE linked or embedded items.	Yes	Yes
COleConvertDialog	Displays the Convert dialog box, the standard user interface for converting OLE items from one type to another.	Yes	Yes
COleChangeIcon Dialog	Displays the Change Icon dialog box, the standard user interface for changing the icon associated with an OLE embedded or linked item.	Yes	Yes
COlePasteSpecial Dialog	Displays the Paste Special dialog box, the standard user interface for implementing the Edit Paste Special command.	Yes	Yes
COleLinksDialog	Displays the Edit Links dialog box, the standard user interface for modifying information about linked items.	Yes	Yes
COleUpdateDialog	Displays the Update dialog box, the standard user interface for updating all links in a document. The dialog box contains a progress indicator to indicate how close the update procedure is to completion.	Yes	Yes
COleBusyDialog	Displays the Server Busy and Server Not Responding dialog boxes, the standard user interface for handling calls to busy applications. Usually displayed automatically by the COleMessageFilter implementation.	Yes	Yes
Miscellaneous OLE Classes			
COleStreamFile	Uses the OLE 2 IStream interface to provide CFile access to compound files. This class (derived from CFile) enables MFC serialization to use OLE 2 structured storage.	Yes	Yes

Summary of MFC Classes (continued)

Application Architecture Classes	Definition	Mac	UNIX
COleMessageFilter	Used to manage concurrency with OLE Lightweight Remote Procedure Calls (LRPC).	Yes	Yes

Database Classes

Class	Definition	Mac	UNIX
CDatabase	Encapsulates a connection to a data source, through which you can operate on the data source.	Partial	Partial
CRecordset	Encapsulates a set of records selected from a data source. Recordsets enable scrolling from record to record, updating records (adding, editing, and deleting records), qualifying the selection with a filter, sorting the selection, and parameterizing the selection with information obtained or calculated at run time.	Partial	Partial
CRecordView	Provides a form view directly connected to a recordset object. The DDX mechanism exchanges data between the recordset and the controls of the record view. Like all form views, a record view is based on a dialog template resource. Record views also support moving from record to record in the recordset, updating records, and closing the associated recordset when the record view closes.	Partial	Partial
CFieldExchange	Supplies context information to support record field exchange (RFX), which exchanges data between the field data members and parameter data members of a recordset object and the corresponding table columns on the data source. Analogous to class CDataExchange, used similarly for dialog data exchange (DDX).	Partial	Partial
CLongBinary	Encapsulates a handle to storage for a binary large object (or BLOB), such as a bitmap. CLongBinary objects are used to manage large data objects stored in database tables.	Partial	Partial

Summary of MFC Classes (continued)

Application Architecture Classes	Definition	Mac	UNIX
CDBException	An exception resulting from failures in data access processing. This class serves the same purpose as other exception classes in the exception-handling mechanism of the class library.	Partial	Partial

Application Architecture Classes

- Application Class
- Command-Related Classes
- Document/View Classes
- Threading Base Class

A key benefit of an application framework is that it not only provides a large body of prebuilt functionality, but it also needs to offers an extensible architecture for you to add new functionality. A framework ony provides just that, a framework that your specific application code must be added to. A good architecture is one that gives developers a logical and obvious location to add application-specific code when implementing features in their applications. For example, you need to leverage the same drawing code for on screen, printing, print preview and clipboard support. MFC knows this an addresses it, and is flexible enough to handle other needs you might need to add next year. MFC addresses these types of issues with a group of highly integrated classes collectively knows as the application architecture classes. These classes provide support for the important areas common to most applications, commands, documents, views, priting, online help and dialog processing. Normally, you leverage this functionality by deriving your classes from the architecture classes, overriding existing member functions and sometimes added new member functions. The principle application architecture objects are:

- CWinApp—class your application object is derived from
- CDocument—class your document objects are derived from, usually associated with persistent storage

- CView—class your view objects are derived from, usually associated with a window and attached to a document

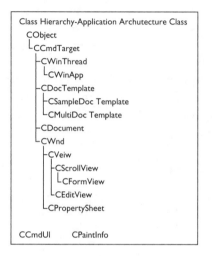

```
Class Hierarchy-Application Archutecture Class
  CObject
    └CCmdTarget
      ├CWinThread
      │  └CWinApp
      ├CDocTemplate
      │  ├CSampleDoc Template
      │  └CMultiDoc Template
      ├CDocument
      └CWnd
        ├CVeiw
        │  ├CScrollView
        │  │  └CFormView
        │  └CEditView
        └CPropertySheet

  CCmdUI        CPaintInfo
```

Figure 4.3. Application Architecture Classes

Commands

Menu items, keyboard accelerators, toolbar buttons and OLE are the most common sources of commands in an application. A command is an instruction to an application to execute a specific action. In Windows, and most GUI operating systems, a command is a message that is routed to various command targets, normally windows, to carry out the action. In MFC command targets are objects derived from the CCmdTarget class. These objects include the application itself (CWinApp), windows (CWnd), views (CView), comand state (CCmdUI) and documents (CDocument).

This command architecture ensures that any user-interface action, such as clicking on a toolbar button or selecting menu item, get routed to the appropriate command handler. This command routing can also be used to update the visual state of menu items and toolbar buttons. For example, the Edit Cut command might have both a menu item and a toolbar button that can be enabled or disabled. Using this command architecture, a single line of code in a single location is used to visually enable or disable the state of both te menu item and the toolbar button.

The integral part of this command architecture is the message map. A message map provides a type-safe mechanism for directing any windows message, control notification, or command to a C++ member function of the appropriate class. Every command target has a message map, and it contains entries that map each command ID defined in the Visual C++ resource editor to a C++ member function. Since there can be a large number of commands, windows messages and notifications handled by each command target, ClassWizard is usually used to create classes and to maintain a class's message maps and message-handler functions. To support OLE automation the ClassWizard, and resulting message maps, are used to expose member variables and member functions as OLE automation properties and methods.

Context-Sensitive Help

Today, support of online and context-sensitive help is required for most applications. MFC provides an architecture that makes it easy to incorporate the most common types of help into your application. MFC help support includes the following:

- F1 Help—displays context based on the currently active object
- Shift+F1 Help—invokes a special "help mode" where the cursor changes to a Help cursor
- Menu item for Help Index—displays the help index for the application
- Menu item for Using Help—displays help on using the on-line help tool
- One line description of all menu items—display in status bar when menu or toolbar item is active
- Toobar hint text—displayed next to toolbar bitmap
- Quitting Help—notify the help viewer that the application is shutting down

For F1 Help, MFC automatically processes the keystroke as a help request for the current command target. For example, the CDialog class processes the help request by calling WinHelp() on the help topic for the currently displayed dialog. If no help context is defined for the current command target, then the application framework automatically launches the default help. The CFrameWnd, CMDIFrameWnd and CDialog classes all provide handler functions for help support. You can add support to any class that is a command target.

When a user presses SHIFT+F1, MFC captures the mouse and changes the cursor into the standard context-sensitive help cursor (arrow + question mark). With this cursor displayed, clicking a user-interface object tells the application framework to invoke the help viewer with the correct help context based on the selected object. Visual C++ creates a the help-context for every user interface element created in the resource editors. In addition, AppWizard provides much of the standard WinHelp-format file with prewritten information on all of the standard commands. All that is needed is an editor capable of editing Rich Text Format (RTF) text, such as Microsoft Word, to add application-specific information. In this way, MFC, AppWizard and the Visual C++ development environment work together to provide programmers most of their applications' help features automatically.

Dialog Data Exchange and Validation (DDX/DDV)

Whenever you create a dialog you need a way to initialize the controls and gather the results from the user. Dialog data exchange (DDX) provides an extensible mechanism for this initialization and results. The associated dialog data validation (DDV) provides for the validation of the dialog control data. In MFC this is accomplished by the DoDataExchange member function, which is called automatically by the application framework when data must be transferred or validated.

Since there are so many possibilites for exchange and validataion (for example, the use of custom controls or the need for application-specific validation schemes), the DDX/DDV architecture is fully extensible.

MFC supplies DDX functions for the following pre-defined control types:

Table 4.1   DDX Variable Types

Control	Variable Type
Edit box	CString, int, UINT, long, DWORD, float, double
Normal check box	BOOL
Three-state check box	int
Radio button (first in group)	int
Nonsorted list box	CString, int
Drop list combo box	CString, int
All other list box and combo box types	CString

MFC supplies default DDV fuctions for the following variable types:

Table 4.2   DDV Variable Types

Variable Type	Data Validation
CString	Maximum length
Numeric (int, UINT, long, DWORD, float, double)	Minimum value, maximum value

With these predefined types it is a trival task with the ClassWizard to initialize, validate and get the results of a users interaction with a dialog. In the following figure the ClassWizard is used to tag an edit box as a UINT value in the range 1 to 20.

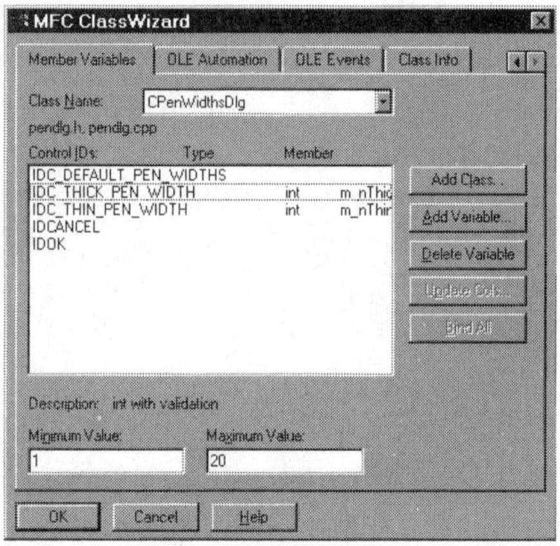

Figure 4-4. Using ClassWizard for DDX/DDV

The DDX mechanism works with any CWnd derived objects, including dialogs, data-bound record views and simple form views. The DDX/DDV architecture is tightly integrated with ClassWizard. This allows you to define all of the necessary member variables and DDX/DDV associations without needing to write any code.

Documents and Views

The document/view architecture supporting in MFC since release 2 is the basis for managing the storage and display of your applications data. The

CDocument class provides support for managing an applications's data, and an application will typically derive a new class from CDocument for each document type. A key feature in CDocument is the ability to save an object and a file for later use. To implement this persistent in your application you override the Serialize member function, which saves and loads the application-specific data to and from storage. Once Serialize is implemented MFC automatically supports high-level commands such as File New..., File Save..., File Save As..., and File Open. MFC does all of the work of displaying a dialog to gather information from the user and managing the disk file. In general, most documents you create will be associated with a file, but the CDocument architecture is flexible enough to allow manipulation of data stored in other ways. For example, your application data may be stored in a database file or in OLE structured storage. Also, CDocument can be used for data without any kind of stored representation.

Each document in an application is attached to one or more views on that document. Views control the graphical display of the applications's data on the screen. Normally, applications derive from the CView class and implement the display code. A view represents the main area of a window on the screen and is a simple child window derived from CWnd. This allows you to use CWnd member functions to manipulate the view. The key member function to override is OnDraw to display the data from a CDocument that should be visible in the CView derived window. Once OnDraw is implemented, your application automatically supports printing and print preview. The best place to handle commands that graphically manipulate the data in the MFC document/view architecture is usually te CView derived class. Using this architecture it is easy to support many views on the some document, where these views may or may not be of the save CView derived class. For example, with a CAD application you may have several views all with a different perspective on the drawing and yet another view showing a parts list.

To coordiante the documents and views, MFC use the helper class CDocTemplate. You usually create one or more document templates in the implementation of your application's InitInstance function. A document template defines the relationships among three types of classes: The following figure illustrates the document/view architecure within the Scribble sample appliction. In this example, one Scribble document is visible in five views, four using splitter windows and the last view in a separate window:

Figure 4.5 Scribble Document/View Architecture

- A document class, which you derive from CDocument
- A view class, which you derive from CView, CScrollView, CFormView, or CEditView
- A frame window class, which contains the view. For an SDI application, you derive from CFrameWnd. For a MDI application, you derive from CMDIChildWnd.

One document template object is created for each document type that you need to support. Each document template is responsible ofr createing and managing all of the documents of its types. The document template stores pointers to the CRuntimeClass objects for the document, view, and frame window classes. These CRuntimeClass objects are specified when constructing a document template. The document template contains the ID of the resources used with the document type (such as menu, icon, or accelerator table resources). The document template also has strings containing additional information about its document type. These include the name of the document type (for example, "Worksheet") and the file extension (for example, ".xls"). Optionally, it can contain other strings used by the application's user interface, the Windows File Manager, and Object Linking and Embedding (OLE) support. If your application is an OLE container and/or server, the document template also defines the ID of the menu used during in-place activation. If your application is an OLE server, the document template defines the ID of the toolbar and menu used during in-place activation.

Printing and Print Preview

Printing and pring preview are a great example of leveraging the MFC framework to provide powerful application features with little application specific code. This is because MFC provides a device-independent printing model via the OnDraw member function. This means, that the same code written for OnDraw in the CView derived class can be used to draw on the screen and on the printer. When your application needs to respond to a print command, for example the File Print command, the framework calls the OnDraw member function with a special device context that is aware of the current printer and knows how to translate the screen display into appropriate printed output. The framework also provides support for all the common printing user-interface dialogs.

In combination with the printing and document/view architectures, the MFC framework supports print preview functionality, which shows a reduced image of either one or two pages of a document as they would appear when printed. The MFC implementation provides the standard user interface for navigating between pages, toggling between one and two page viewing, and zooming the display in and out to different levels of magnification.

Figure 4.5. Scribble Application Print Preview Window

This ability to support print preview is another example of the level of prebuilt functionality and the high level of abstraction in the MFC framework. This print preview feature represents several thousand liens of C++ code in the MFC framework, but like printing above, you only need to handle the display-output code in the OnDraw member fucntion of your CView derived class (and make sure the command is on a menu somewhere) and the framework does the rest.

Threading Base Class

The MFC framework supports multiple threads of execution within an application. All applications have one WinThread derived object, their CWinApp derived object, called the "primary" thread. CWinThread encapsulates a portion of the Win32 operating system's threading capabilities. CWinThread is the base class for all threads. You can use it directly, or derive a class from CWinThread if your thread performs user-interface functions.

Multithreading

MFC 3.0 also is now thread-safe and supports writing multithreaded MFC applications. Threads of execution are encapsulated in the class CWinThread. The main application class, CWinApp, is derived from CWinThread; it represents the main user-interface thread of the application. MFC distinguishes two types of threads: user-interface threads and worker threads. User interface threads are commonly used to handle user input and respond to events and messages generated by the user. Worker threads are commonly used to complete tasks that do not require user input, such as recalculation. MFC handles user-interface threads specially by supplying a message pump for events in the user interface. CWinApp is an example of a user-interface thread object, since it derives from CWinThread and handles events and messages generated by the user. Developers can create additional threads in their applications if they wish, creating new objects of the class CWinThread or a class derived from CWinThread. In most situations, the developer doesn't even have to create these objects explicitly and can instead call the framework helper function AfxBeginThread, which creates the CWinThread object. Of course, even with the multithread enabling of MFC 3.0, writing and debugging multithreaded applications is an inherently complicated and tricky undertaking, because the developer must ensure that a given object is not accessed by more than one thread at a time.

Visual Object Classes

The first version of MFC did not provide enough high-level abstractions to reduce programming time. With MFC 2.0 and later, this issue is addressed with a set of classes that support the most common user-interface idioms and provide capabilities for taking advantage of other prebuilt functionality. These classes, collectively called the high-level abstractions, are designed to be used as supplied by MFC and can result in a dramatic reduction in programming time. In a few lines of code, programmers can build a text-processing window that integrates seamlessly with other MDI windows, or change the base class to turn a view into a scrolling view. In addition to this power, all of these high-level classes are designed to be easily modified using C++ inheritance.

```
Class Hierarchy - Visual Object Classes
CObject ──────────
    ┌ CDC                    └ CGdiObject          └ CMenu
    │   ┌ CClientDC              ┌ CPen
    │   ┌ CWindowDC              ┌ CBrush
    │   ┌ CPaintDC               ┌ CFont
    │   └ CMetaFileDC            ┌ CBitmap
    └ CCmdTarget                 ┌ CPalette
        │                        └ CRgn
        └ CWnd ──────────────────────────────
            ┌ CFrameWnd          ┌ CView              ┌ CStatic
            │   ┌ CMDIChildWnd        ┌ CScrollView        ┌ CButton
            │   ┌ CMDIFrameWnd        └ CFormView          └ CBitmapButton
            │   └ CMiniFrameWnd   └ CEditView          ┌ CListBox
            └ CDialog            └ CControlBar         ┌ CComboBox
                ┌ CFileDialog        ┌ CToolBar        ┌ CScrollBar
                ┌ CColorDialog       ┌ CStatusBar      └ CEdit
                ┌ CFontDialog        └ CDialogBar
                ┌ CPrintDialog
                ┌ CFindReplaceDialog
                └ CPropertyPage
        CCreateContext    CDataExchange
```

Figure 4.7. Visual Object Classes

Control Bars

CToolBar, CStatusBar and CDialogBar all derive from the common base class CControlBar. The CControlBar abstraction enables the MFC implementation to reuse code among these classes. CControlBar provides the functionality for automatic layout within the parent frame window of the derived classes. CControlBar demonstrates the power of a base class that provides a partial implementation that is completed in a series of closely related derived classes. The CStatusBar class implements a row of text output panes, or indicators. The output panes are commonly used as message lines and status indicators. Examples include the menu help- message lines that briefly describe the selected menu command and the indicators for the keyboard states of Num Lock, Scroll Lock and Caps Lock. The CStatusBar class supports any number of panes and automatically lays them out based on the width of the contents. Each pane can have a customized style, including three-dimensional borders, pop-out text, disabled, and stretchy. The MFC command architecture supports automatic menu prompt strings, and when using the Visual C++ menu editor to edit menus for MFC applications, programmers can also define the prompt string for the menu item. When creating a new application with AppWizard, developers can specify whether or not the application will provide a status bar. The CDialogBar class is like a modeless dialog in that it easily supports any combination of Windows controls and is created from a dialog template edited with the Visual C++ dialog editor. Dialog bars support tabbing among controls and can be aligned to the top, bottom, left or right edge of the enclosing frame window. The most common example of a dialog bar is the print preview user interface.

Edit View

CEditView is a simple, plain text-editor view that has all the functionality of the standard Windows edit control. In addition, however, CEditView supports high-level functionality such as printing, find and replace, cut, copy, paste, and undo, as well as the standard File commands (Open, Save, Save As). Of course, since CEditView is derived from CView, all of the architectural benefits described above apply. From a simple AppWizard-created application, programmers can use CEditView by simply creating a document template that uses CEditView; applications can have an MDI text editor without the programmers having to derive their own view classes.

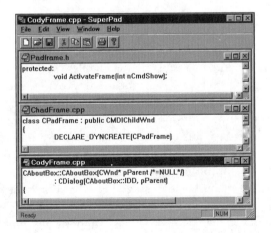

Figure 4.8 Superpad Sample with Multiple CEditView Windows

Enhanced Toolbars

One of the most commonly requested user-interface elements is the toolbar. A toolbar is a row of buttons represented by bitmaps and optional separators. These bitmap buttons can behave like push buttons, check-box buttons, or radio group buttons. The MFC class CToolBar supports the standard toolbar look. All the toolbar buttons are normally taken from a single bitmap image, which is edited using the Visual C++ bitmap editor and contains one image for each button. Storing all the images in one bitmap reduces the amount of system resources used by an application.

One of the key advantages of the MFC CToolBar class is that by using commands, programmers can enable and disable the various buttons in the toolbar in conjunction with any menu items for those same commands. This is important because toolbar buttons almost always duplicate menu items, allowing the programmers to write the command handler once and drive it from either a menu item or a toolbar button.

MFC 3.0 adds a new capability to existing toolbar support: dockable toolbars. A dockable toolbar can be attached or "docked" to any side of its parent window, or it can be "floated" in its own miniframe window (using CMiniFrameWnd). Programmers who use AppWizard to generate the skeleton of your application are asked to choose whether or not they want dockable toolbars. By default, AppWizard creates code to enable docking toolbars. CToolBar and CFrameWnd member functions are available to customize the behavior of the docking toolbar and to programatically dock or float a toolbar.

MFC 3.0 also adds support for "tool tips." When the user moves the mouse over a toolbar button, a small box is shown on top of the button to describe the action that would be performed. Also supported are "fly-by" tool tips that provide a more detailed description of the command on the status bar. This saves the user from having to press a toolbar button to find out what the command does.

MFC 3.0 also allows for the persistence of toolbar configurations. Like many professional applications, MFC allows users to save the entire state of a given frame window's toolbar configuration, including each toolbar's current position and visible and floating states. The CToolBar class can easily support additional standard Windows controls, such as drop-down list boxes or edit controls, on the toolbar. In addition, CToolBar provides programmatic APIs for dynamically changing the buttons on the toolbar, customizing docking behavior, and highly customizing user interfaces in other ways.

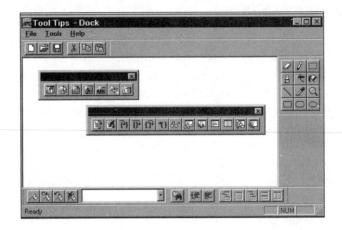

Figure 4.9 Docking Toolbar Sample

Form View

The functionality of CRecordView is built upon the CFormView high-level abstraction introduced in MFC 2.0. CFormView supports many features that true form-processing applications require but which are not available in the native Windows dialog manager, such as scrolling, multiple forms for the same data, synchronous update, and printing. A CFormView provides a view (a class derived from CView) based on a dialog resource that can be edited with the Visual C++ dialog editor. This view can be used to create form views with arbitrary Windows controls. The user can scroll the form view and tab among controls. The benefit of CFormView over standard dialogs is that CFormView objects integrate with the entire application framework architecture, providing automatic support for command handling and document management. A form view can also be an MDI child window.

Scrolling View

Most applications can only show a portion of their data files on the screen at a single time. The CScrollView class, which is another high-level view class derived from CView, supports views that scroll and views that are automatically scaled to the size of the frame window that displays them. By deriving from CScrollView, developers can add the ability to scroll or scale to their view classes. CScrollView manages window sizes and mapping mode for graphics, manages special modes needed for OLE in-place editing, and handles the automatic scrolling in response to user-interface actions such as clicking the scroll bar.

Splitter Window

In a splitter window, the window can be split into two or more separately scrollable panes. A splitter control in the window frame next to the scroll bars allows the user to adjust the relative sizes of the panes. Each pane is a different view on the same document. This type of user interface is useful, for example, when a user wishes to view both the beginning and end of a very long document on a single screen. MFC provides the high-level class CSplitterWnd to support this user-interface model. The CSplitterWnd class also supports the two most common types of splitters: dynamic and static. With dynamic splitters, the user can add or remove arbitrary split panes; static splitters have a predefined number of panes. Each of the splitter pane's views can be the same class, or each can be a different derived CView class. In all cases, the application framework automatically manages all aspects of the user-interface and standard Windows messages.

Controls

Controls are windows that are drawn in the client area of frame windows or as controls in a dialog box. MFC provides classes for all of the standard controls: static text, buttons, edit control, list boxes, combo boxes, scroll bars, handwriting controls and user-defined child windows. MFC makes it easy for developers to derive their own child windows (including deriving from the standard Windows controls) and to customize the behavior of the windows.

Dialogs

MFC makes it easier to use dialogs within an application. The application framework manages many of the intricate details of Windows-based system-oriented dialogs automatically, including the handling of dialog-specific messages. Dialogs are handled with the CDialog class, which supports both modal and modeless dialogs. Programmers simply derive from a dialog class and customize it by overriding member functions and message handlers. This customization model is exactly like every other CWnd-derived class, which provides good programming consistency.

MFC includes classes for all of the common dialogs, CFileDialog, CColorDialog, CFontDialog, CPrintDialog, and CFindReplaceDialog

Frame Windows

Along with an application object, most programs will use a standard frame window. MFC provides support for both the single-document interface and the multiple-document interface (MDI). Many of the common MDI commands and user-interface functionality, such as changing the menu bar that is based on the active window, are provided as prebuilt functionality by the framework. In addition, error-prone areas of programming for Windows such as keyboard accelerators and implementation of default behavior are handled in a seamless manner by the application framework. Frame windows are managed by the document-template class in applications that take advantage of the document/view architecture. A view is contained within a frame window (usually a CFrameWnd or a CMDIChildWnd).

Graphics Device Interface (GDI)

The MFC 1.0 device-context class, CDC, provided a simple Windows API wrapper. MFC 2.0 extended the CDC implementation to allow polymorphic implementations of device- context output functions. This enables a virtual-display context that allows MFC applications to use the same drawing code to send output to the screen, a printer, a metafile or a print-preview view. MFC provides a complete set of classes for drawing graphical objects and managing device contexts. These graphical object classes include all of the standard Windows objects, including pens, brushes, bit maps, fonts, regions and palettes. Several device-context classes are also supplied to make the handling of common Windows idioms (such as window repainting) simpler and less error-prone. The graphical objects are designed to free system resources automatically when they are no longer needed, which simplifies common object-ownership problems and enables an application to run safely in a resource-constrained environment.

Miniframe Windows

Miniframe windows are frame windows with thin caption bars, like those used in the Visual C++ property windows. The MFC class CMiniFrameWnd, derived from CFrameWnd, provides an alternative user interface for floating palettes and toolbars. In fact, the CToolBar implementation of tear-off toolbars uses the CMiniFrameWnd class to hold the torn-off toolbar. A CMiniFrameWnd object represents a half-height frame window typically seen around floating toolbars. These miniframe windows behave like normal frame windows, except that they do not have minimize/maximize buttons or menus, and the user only has to single-click the system menu to dismiss them.

Property Sheets

MFC 3 introduced support for property sheets, also known as "tabbed dialog boxes." A property sheet is a special kind of dialog box that is generally used to modify the attributes of some external object, such as the current selection in a view. The property sheet has three main parts: the containing dialog box, one or more property pages shown one at a time, and a tab at the top of each page that the user clicks to select that page. Property sheets are useful when a number of similar groups of settings or options need to be changed. An example of a property sheet is the Project Settings dialog box in Visual C++. In this case, a number of different groups of options need to be set. The property sheet allows a large amount of information to be grouped in an easily understood fashion. This support is provided in two classes: a class to contain all the pages, CPropertySheet, with one tab per page; and a class that each property page is derived from, CPropertyPage. To create a property sheet with several pages, first create a dialog template resource for each property page using the Visual C++ dialog editor, then use ClassWizard to create a CPropertyPage-derived class corresponding to each property-page dialog template. For each of these new classes, use ClassWizard to create member variables to hold the values for the property page. The process for adding member variables to a property page is exactly the same as adding member variables to a dialog box, since a property page is a specialized dialog box. Creating the property sheet at run time is easy to do either by using the CPropertySheet class directly or by deriving a more specialized property sheet from it. using C++ inheritance and message maps.

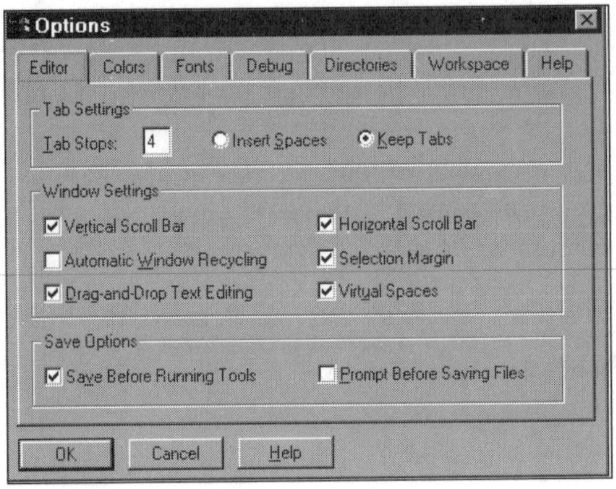

Figure 4.10 Property Sheet with Several Property Pages

Menus

The CMenu class is an encapsulation of the Windows HMENU. It provides member functions for creating, tracking, updating, and destroying a menu. Again, the MFC framework provides a controlled typesafe access to all aspects of interacting with menus, include working with owner-drawn menus. The following table is an example of this complete encapsulation by MFC:

Table 4.3 CMenu Initialization Functions

Attach	Attaches a Windows menu handle to a CMenu object.
Detach	Detaches a Windows menu handle from a CMenu object and returns the handle.
FromHandle	Returns a pointer to a CMenu object given a Windows menu handle.
GetSafeHmenu	Returns the m_hMenu wrapped by this CMenu object.
DeleteTempMap	Deletes any temporary CMenu objects created by the FromHandle member function.
CreateMenu	Creates an empty menu and attaches it to a CMenu object.
CreatePopupMenu	Creates an empty pop-up menu and attaches it to a CMenu object.
LoadMenu	Loads a menu resource from the executable file and attaches it to a CMenu object.

Table 4.3 CMenu Initialization Functions (continued)

LoadMenuIndirect	Loads a menu from a menu template in memory and attaches it to a CMenu object.
DestroyMenu	Destroys the menu attached to a CMenu object and frees any memory that the menu occupied.

Table 4.4 CMenu Operations

DeleteMenu	Deletes a specified item from the menu. If the menu item has an associated pop-up menu, destroys the handle to the pop-up menu and frees the memory used by it.
TrackPopupMenu	Displays a floating pop-up menu at the specified location and tracks the selection of items on the pop-up menu.

Table 4.5 CMenu Item Operations

AppendMenu	Appends a new item to the end of this menu.
CheckMenuItem	Places check marks next to or removes check marks from menu items in the pop-up menu.
EnableMenuItem	Enables, disables, or dims (grays) a menu item.
GetMenuItemCount	Determines the number of items in a pop-up or top-level menu.
GetMenuItemID	Obtains the menu-item identifier for a menu item located at the specified position.
GetMenuState	Returns the status of the specified menu item or the number of items in a pop-up menu.
GetMenuString	Retrieves the label of the specified menu item.
GetSubMenu	Retrieves a pointer to a pop-up menu.
InsertMenu	Inserts a new menu item at the specified position, moving other items down the menu.
ModifyMenu	Changes an existing menu item at the specified position.
RemoveMenu	Deletes a menu item with an associated pop-up menu from the specified menu.
SetMenuItemBitmaps	Associates the specified check-mark bitmaps with a menu item.

Table 4.6 CMenu Overridables For Owner-drawn Menu Items

DrawItem	Called by the framework when a visual aspect of an owner-drawn menu changes.
MeasureItem	Called by the framework to determine menu dimensions when an owner-drawn menu is created.

General-Purpose Classes

- Collections
- Diagnostics
- Exceptions
- File Classes
- Miscellaneous Support Classes
- Template Collections

The general-purpose classes give programmers a wide range of functionality designed to take advantage of the powerful features of C++. These classes are available for programmers to develop the nongraphical portion of the application. In many respects, the general-purpose classes, together with the Windows API classes, are the building blocks for the entire application framework and provide fundamental functionality to those classes as well as programmer-defined classes.

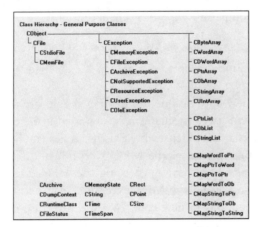

Figure 4.11. General Purpose Classes

Collection Classes

MFC excels in the efficiency of standard data structures. The provided collection classes, a standard component of any C++ class library, are well-tested, well-coded and highly reusable. The MFC collection classes include double-linked list classes, map (dictionary) classes, and dynamic (growable) array classes. All of these have been implemented using the proposed ANSI template syntax for type-safe usage. For example, the list class is supplied with variants supporting UINT, BYTE, WORD, DWORD, void*, CObject* and CString elements. The map and array classes have similar sets of variants. In all, MFC supplies 17 collection classes. For users who wish to take advantage of the template syntax to generate a type-safe variant of a supplied implementation (or write their own templates), a template- expansion tool written using MFC is provided as a sample application.

Exceptions

In MFC, exceptions are used to signal abnormal execution, including situations in which conditions outside the program's control are influencing the outcome of the function, such as low memory or I/O errors. Abnormal situations are handled by catching and throwing exceptions, rather than using return codes that are often overlooked and so result in inefficient code. The MFC exception syntax is a clean and efficient mechanism for abnormal conditions.

MFC provides two compatible ways of using exceptions:

- C++ exceptions, available in MFC version 3.0 and later.
- The MFC exception macros, available in MFC versions 1.0 and later

Developers writing new applications using MFC should use the C++ exceptions mechanism. The macro-based mechanism can be used if the existing application already uses that mechanism extensively. Existing codes can be converted readily to use C++ exceptions instead of the MFC exception macros, if desired. If an application has already been developed using the MFC exception macros, the developer can continue using the MFC exception macros in the existing code while using C++ exceptions in new code. Whether they use the C++ exceptions directly or use the MFC exception macros, developers will use CException or CException-derived objects that may be thrown by the framework or by the application. MFC provides several predefined exceptions classes to handle everything from out-of-memory to OLE dispatch exceptions.

MFC supplies exceptions for the following pre-defined error conditions:

Table 4.7 Execption Classes

CMemoryException	Out-of-memory exception
CNotSupportedException	Request for an unsupported operation
CArchiveException	Archive-specific exceptions
CFileException	File-specific exceptions
CResourceException	Windows resource not found or not createable
COleException	OLE operation exception
CDBException	Database classes exception condition
CUserException	Application-specific exception thrown to stop an end-user operation

The exception macros defined by MFC are listed in Table 4.8.

Table 4.8 Execption Macros

TRY	Designates a block of code for exception processing.
CATCH	Designates a block of code for catching an exception from the preceding TRY block.

Table 4.8 Execption Macros (continued)

AND_CATCH	Designates a block of code for catching additional exception types from the preceding TRY block.
END_CATCH	Ends the last CATCH or AND_CATCH code block.
THROW	Throws a specified exception.
THROW_LAST	Throws the currently handled exception to the next outer handler.

Often, the easies way to throw an exception is to use one of the following predefined MFC exception throwing functions.

Table 4.9 Exception Throwing Functions

AfxThrowArchiveException	Throws an archive exception.
AfxThrowFileException	Throws a file exception.
AfxThrowMemoryException	Throws a memory exception.
AfxThrowNotSupportedException	Throws a not-supported exception.
AfxThrowResourceException	Throws a Windows resource-not-found exception.
AfxThrowUserException	Throws an exception in a user-initiated program action.
AfxThrowOleDispatchException	Throws an exception within an OLE automation function.
AfxThrowOleException	Throws an OLE exception.
AfxThrowDBException	Throws a CDBException from your own code when an exceptional condition occurs during database processing.

Files

MFC offers three general-purpose file classes: CFile and its two derived classes, CStdioFile and CMemFile. CFile supports low-level binary file I/O (read, write and seek). CStdioFile provides buffered file I/O similar to the standard I/O run-time libraries. CMemFile supports file semantics in RAM-resident files for managing Clipboard data as well as other forms of interapplication communication. The polymorphism provided by the three file classes (CFile, CStdioFile and CMemFile) allows the same code to be used for sending data to a variety of destinations using the CFile interface. MFC 2.5 and MFC 3.0 extend the use of the file classes to include compatibility with OLE structure storage (IStream and IStorage). CFile acan also be used to get status information about a file. The following information is returned in the CFileStatus structure:

Table 4.10 CFileStatus Information

CTime m_ctime	The date and time the file was created
CTime m_mtime	The date and time the file was last modified
CTime m_atime	The date and time the file was last accessed for reading
LONG m_size	The logical size of the file in bytes, as reported by the DIR command
BYTE m_attribute	The attribute byte of the file
char m_szFullName[_MAX_PATH]	The absolute filename in the Windows character set.

Object Persistence

Persistence is the ability of any object to save its state to a persistent storage medium, such as a disk. For example, if a collection is made persistent, then all members of that collection are made persistent. The CArchive class is used to support object persistence and allows type-safe retrieval of object data. To use persistence, a class implementor must override the Serialize member function, call the base class' Serialize function, and then implement the data-storage routines for member data that is specific to a derived class. Entire networks of objects, with references to other objects, including both multiple and circular references, can be saved with a single line of code. As with dynamic type checking, the use of persistence is optional.

Points, Rectangles and Sizes

MFC provides highly optimized classes for create and manipulating the basic Windows POINT, RECT and SIZE structures. Most of the member functions for these classes, CPoint, CRect and CSize are implemented as inline functions. While, these are simple structures, they are ubiquitous in Windows applications and need must be lightweight and powerful. MFC delivers both. The following table demonstrations the power of the simple CRect object.

Table 4.11 CRect Operations

Width	Calculates the width of CRect.
Height	Calculates the height of CRect.
Size	Calculates the size of CRect.
TopLeft	Returns a reference to the top-left point of CRect.
BottomRight	Returns a reference to the bottom-right point of CRect.
IsRectEmpty	Determines whether CRect is empty. CRect is empty if the width and/or height are 0.
IsRectNull	Determines whether the top, bottom, left, and right member variables are all equal to 0.
PtInRect	Determines whether the specified point lies within CRect.
SetRect	Sets the dimensions of CRect.
SetRectEmpty	Sets CRect to an empty rectangle (all coordinates equal to 0).
CopyRect	Copies the dimensions of a source rectangle to CRect.
EqualRect	Determines whether CRect is equal to the given rectangle.
InflateRect	Increases or decreases the width and height of CRect.
NormalizeRect	Standardizes the height and width of CRect.
OffsetRect	Moves CRect by the specified offsets.
SubtractRect	Subtracts one rectangle from another.
IntersectRect	Sets CRect equal to the intersection of two rectangles.
UnionRect	Sets CRect equal to the union of two rectangles.

Table 4.12 CRect Operators

Operators	
operator LPCRECT	Converts a CRect to an LPCRECT.
operator LPRECT	Converts a CRect to an LPRECT.
operator =	Copies the dimensions of a rectangle to CRect.
operator ==	Determines whether CRect is equal to a rectangle.
operator !=	Determines whether CRect is not equal to a rectangle.
operator +=	Adds the specified offsets to CRect.
operator -=	Subtracts the specified offsets from CRect.

Table 4.12 CRect Operators (continued)

operator &=	Sets CRect equal to the intersection of CRect and a rectangle.
operator |=	Sets CRect equal to the union of CRect and a rectangle.
operator +	Adds the given offsets to CRect and returns the resulting CRect.
operator -	Subtracts the given offsets from CRect and returns the resulting CRect.
operator &	Creates the intersection of CRect and a rectangle and returns the resulting CRect.
operator |	Creates the union of CRect and a rectangle and returns the resulting CRect.

Run-Time Type Information

Most MFC classes are derived either directly or indirectly from the class CObject, which provides the most basic object-oriented features of the framework. CObject supports dynamic type checking, which allows the type of an object to be queried at run time. This feature provides programmers with a type-safe means to cast down a pointer from a base class to a derived class. Without dynamic type checking, this cast can be a source of errors and can break the type safety of C++. Most programmers find this feature useful, but since it incurs a very small run-time overhead (approximately 24 bytes per class), its use is optional.

Strings

The CString class supports a very fast string implementation that is compatible with standard C "char*" pointers. This class allows strings to be manipulated with syntax similar to the Basic language that includes concatenation operators and functions such as Mid, Left and Right. CString also provides its own memory management, freeing the programmer from having to allocate and free string memory.

Templates

MFC 3.0 provides collection classes based on C++ templates, which makes it easier to derive one's own type-safe collection classes. MFC 3.0 provides two types of collection classes to manage groups of objects:

- Collection classes created from C++ templates

- Collection classes not created from templates

The nontemplate collection classes are the same as those provided by MFC in versions 1.0 and later. Developers whose code already uses these classes can continue to use them. Developers who write new type-safe collection classes for their own data types should consider using the newer template-based classes. A collection class is characterized by its "shape" and by the types of its elements. The shape refers to the way the objects are organized and stored by the collection. MFC provides three basic collection shapes: lists, arrays and maps (also known as dictionaries), which provideeasy-to-understand yet powerful building blocks for the rest of the application. Developers can pick the collection shape most suited to their particular programming problems. List. The list class provides an ordered, nonindexed list of elements, implemented as a doubly linked list. A list has a "head" and a "tail," and adding or removing elements from the head or tail, or inserting or deleting elements in the middle is very fast. Array. The array class provides a dynamically sized, ordered, and integer-indexed array of objects. Map. A map is a collection that associates a key object with a value object. The easiest way to implement a type-safe collection that contains objects of any type is to use one of the MFC template-based classes.

Collection contents

- Arrays
- Lists
- Maps
- Collections of objects of any type
- CArray
- CList
- CMap
- Collections of pointers to objects of any type
- CTypedPtrArray
- CTypedPtrList
- CTypedPtrMap

For example, to create a dynamically sized array of "doubles," use C++ template syntax:

```
CArray<double, double> myArray;
```

If the application already uses MFC nontemplate classes, developers can continue to use them, but they should consider using the template-based classes for new collections.

Time and Date

In addition to the standard time and date functions, a class is provided to conveniently support time-and-date arithmetic using overloaded operators. Binary time values are automatically formatted into human-readable form as needed.

Database Classes

Visual C++ provides integrated support in AppWizard, ClassWizard and the Visual C++ dialog editor for building database applications. New classes in MFC 3 provide database engine functionality. Also, a new mechanism is provided to provide data-bound controls using ClassWizard, which makes it easy for the developer to build forms that view and edit fields in a database without having to write any C++ code. These database classes provide easy access to any database for which an Open Database Connectivity (ODBC) driver is available. Also provided with Visual C++ are portions of the ODBC SDK, the ODBC driver manager and the Microsoft SQL Server ODBC driver.

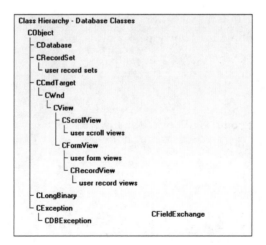

Figure 4.12. Database Classes

Database Engine Classes

Two main classes provide the encapsulation of data sources: CDatabase and CRecordset. These classes are modeled after the high-level database abstractions used in the Visual Basic® programming system and the Microsoft Access® database management system. The MFC versions of these abstractions are provided as type-safe C++ classes that allow programmers to access data in an easy and comfortable way without requiring them to give up the performance and compile-time checking that C++ provides. The class CDatabase represents a connection to a data source through which developers can operate on the data source. The database engine classes are smart enough to allocate and open a new CDatabase connection as needed by the program. Developers who want to manage their database connections manually or to optimize performance or control transactions will want to use the CDatabase class. The class CRecordset encapsulates a set of records selected from a data source. Recordsets enable scrolling from record to record, updating of records (adding, editing and deleting records), qualifying the selection with a filter, sorting the selection, and "parameterizing" the selection with information obtained or calculated at run time. Programmers will normally derive their own custom classes from CRecordset to add type- safe member variables to the class that will be bound to specific columns of a data source. The process of creating a new C++ class and managing the binding of columns to member variables is performed by ClassWizard. The process of moving data between the database and the member variables of the class is called Record Field Exchange (RFX). This technique is similar to the Dialog Data Exchange (DDX) mechanism introduced in MFC 2.0 (see below). Data values obtained from an ODBC data source are turned into C++ and MFC data types such as short, long, float and CString. For large binary data, a class CLongBinary is provided for efficient management of large data values.

Record View

One of the most common types of Windows-based applications is form processing. A form is like a dialog that the user can interact with to fill in edit controls, select options from list boxes and radio groups, and work with other dialog controls. For example, an order-entry database application would probably use forms to allow customer-service representatives to enter order information. MFC 2.0 introduced the high-level abstraction of a form view. MFC 3.0 has a class called CRecordView, derived from CFormView, that provides a form directly connected to a recordset object. Using the same mechanism used for dialogs and simple form views, a record view uses the MFC Dialog Data Exchange (DDX) mechanism to exchange data values between the recordset and the controls of the record view. Like all form views, a record view is based on a dialog template resource. Record views also support moving from record to record in the recordset, updating records, and closing the associated recordset when the record view closes. Like any form view, a record view automatically supports many features, such as scrolling, synchronous update, support for VBX Custom Controls, support for standard Windows controls, and the ability to place a form view in any window, including MDI child windows.

OLE Classes

- OLE Base Classes
- OLE Visual Editing Container Classes
- OLE Visual Editing Server Classes
- OLE Data Transfer Classes
- OLE Dialog Box Classes
- Miscellaneous OLE Classes

OLE 2.0 provides many attractive features to the end user of OLE-capable applications. For the developer, OLE 2.0 provides a lot of functionality in many APIs but adds the burden of many design decisions and a lot of implementation work. The MFC support for OLE 2.0 provides C++ classes integrated with the MFC framework that make developing OLE-capable applications easy. AppWizard has been extended to make it easy to start developing OLE applications. ClassWizard has been extended to make it easier to support OLE Automation in programs. The MFC support for OLE encapsulates much of the complexity of the OLE API in a small set of C++ classes that provide a higher-level interface to OLE. Of course, following the MFC design philosophy, developers can call the underlying C-language OLE API functions directly wherever the OLE classes don't meet their needs. Also provided with Visual C++ is the OLE 2.0 SDK as well as a number of tools and sample applications to help developers test their OLE applications. Online documentation includes overview material, tutorials, an encyclopedia and a class reference. This paper divides the features of OLE into two main categories: features for supporting OLE Visual Editing and features for OLE Automation. Also, the development work involved depends on whether the application is trying to provide these services (i.e., be a server) or to use or consume these services (i.e., be a client or a container).

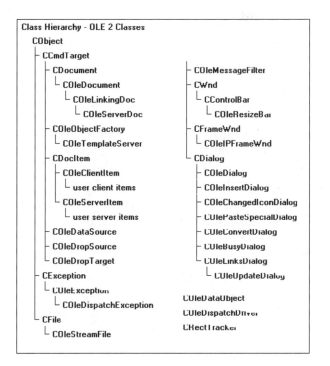

Figure 4.13. Object Linking and Embedding Classes

OLE Overview

OLE is a mechanism that allows users to create and edit documents containing data created by multiple applications. These OLE documents seamlessly integrate various types of data, called items. Sound clips, spreadsheets and bit maps are typical examples of items found in OLE documents. Supporting OLE in an application allows the user to work with OLE documents without worrying about switching back and forth between the different applications; OLE does the switching. A container application is used to create OLE documents, and a server application is used to create the items within the container application. Any application may be a container, a server or both.

OLE incorporates many concepts that all work toward the goal of seamless interaction between applications. These areas include the following:

Linking and Embedding.

Linking and embedding are the two ways used for storing items inside an OLE document that were created in another application.

In-Place Activation.

Activating an embedded or linked item in the context of the container application is called in-place activation. The interface of the container application changes to incorporate the features of the application that created the embedded or linked item. Uniform Data Transfer. Uniform Data Transfer (UDT) is a set of interfaces that allows data to be sent and received in a standard fashion, regardless of the actual method chosen to transfer the data. UDT forms the basis for data transfers using the Clipboard and drag and drop.

Drag and Drop.

Drag and drop is an easy-to-use, direct-manipulation technique to transfer data between applications, between windows within an application, or even within a single window in an application. The data to be transferred is simply selected and dragged to the desired destination.

Compound Files.

Compound files provide a standard file format that simplifies structured storing of OLE documents for OLE applications. Within a compound file, "storages" have many features of directories, and "streams" have many features of files.

Automation.

OLE Automation allows one application to drive another application. The driving application is known as an automation client, and the application being driven is known as an automation server.

Component Object Model.

The OLE Component Object Model (COM) provides the infrastructure used when OLE objects communicate with each other. The Microsoft Foundation Class Library OLE classes simplify OLE COM for the programmer.

Visual Editing

Support for Visual Editing includes in-place activation and editing, drag and drop, and OLE document (structured) storage. Two sets of MFC classes support this. One set of classes is designed for helping developers build OLE servers, the software components that can be embedded or linked inside other applications. This server support lets developers visually export the components in their applications. The other set of classes is designed for helping developers build OLE containers that allow the components from other applications to be visually embedded or linked in OLE documents.

Compound Files (Structured Storage)

Compound files are an integral part of OLE. They are used to facilitate data transfer and OLE-document storage. Compound files are an implementation of the structured-storage model. MFC supports using both compound files and normal flat files for an application's file storage. The code the developer writes is the same. Using the CArchive abstraction, MFC is able to hide the differences between these two file formats while offering the benefits of each. These benefits include support for serialization to a storage (using the OLE IStorage interface), a stream (using the OLE IStream interface), or to a normal or flat file where the developer has complete control over the file format.

Drag and Drop

Drag and drop is an easy-to-use, direct-manipulation technique to transfer data between applications, between windows within an application, or even within a single window in an application. The data to be transferred is simply selected and dragged to the desired destination. One application provides the data for copying, and another application accepts the data for pasting. Each side of the transfer needs to perform different operations on the data for the transfer to succeed. The MFC library provides full support to represent each side of this transfer. Data sources represent the source side of the data transfer. They are created by the source application when data is provided for a drag-and-drop operation. Data objects represent the destination side of the data transfer. They are created when the destination application has data dropped into it.

OLE Automation Clients

An OLE Automation client manipulates components implemented in other applications. The application being manipulated, the OLE Automation server, exposes programmable components and allows clients to automate certain procedures by directly accessing the server components, along with their properties and methods. By creating an OLE Automation client, MFC makes it easy to drive other applications, allowing developers to build an application using C++ language to drive the objects exposed by large applications such as Microsoft Excel, Microsoft Word, or any other OLE Automation server that has a type library. ClassWizard will read the type library provided by the OLE Automation server and create new custom C++ classes for the IDispatch interfaces exposed by that server. MFC provides the glue to connect these dynamic OLE (IDispatch) interfaces into type-safe C++ classes. Therefore, most OLE Automation clients written in C++ do not have to deal with the dynamic nature of IDispatch.

OLE Automation Servers

An OLE Automation server exposes programmable software components, along with their properties and methods, to other applications. These driving applications are called OLE Automation clients. Exposing objects in this way is beneficial when applications provide functionality that is useful for other applications. For example, a word processor might expose its spelling-check functionality so that other programs can use it. Exposure of objects thus enables vendors to improve the functionality of their applications by using the ready-made functionality of other applications. ClassWizard, AppWizard and the framework all provide extensive support for OLE Automation servers. They handle much of the overhead involved in creating an OLE Automation server so that developers can focus their efforts on the functionality of their applications. MFC along with ClassWizard support makes it extremely easy to expose member variables and member functions from type-safe C++ classes as OLE

Automation properties and methods. This allows your application's objects to be driven by an external macro language such as Visual Basic. New to MFC 3.0 and the Visual C++ 2.0 wizards is direct support for creating type libraries. Type libraries are useful for exporting OLE Automation servers to other C++ client applications. The new AppWizard will automatically create a .ODL file, and ClassWizard will automatically maintain the .ODL source file used to create the type library.

OLE Controls

Microsoft recently announced the OLE Control architecture, which merges the popular VBX Custom Control architecture with the open, standard architecture of OLE. OLE Controls make component-based development a reality by allowing developers to easily use existing bodies of functional code encapsulated as OLE Controls. An OLE Control is a custom control, implemented as an OLE object with Visual Editing and OLE Automation support. An OLE Control has additional capabilities beyond those of ordinary OLE components, such as the ability to fire events. OLE Controls will be supported in the future by many development tools, including a future version of Visual C++. Most OLE objects require a substantial amount of implementation effort. Fortunately, the OLE Control Developer's Kit (CDK) — an add-on to Visual C++ 2.0 — provides most of the required implementation, so developers only have to fill in details that are specific to the OLE Control. The OLE Control CDK classes themselves are based on MFC base classes (that is, COleControl derives from CWnd). This makes it easier for developers who are experienced with MFC to create OLE Controls. It also makes it easier to use existing MFC code inside the implementation of new OLE Controls. MFC 3.0 includes support for enabling 32-bit OLE Controls. Developers still need to install the 32-bit version of the OLE Control CDK to get the additional MFC classes, headers, libraries and tools. MFC 3.0 along with the CDK provides support for creating and testing OLE Controls and limited support for using pre-existing OLE Controls. Future versions of MFC will improve the ease of using the new controls.

Visual Editing Containers

A Visual Editing container application can incorporate embedded or linked items into its own documents. The documents managed by a container application must be able to store and display OLE items as well as the data created by the application itself. A container application allows users to insert new items or edit existing items by activating server applications when needed. Container applications will launch and contain a server application. Communication between containers and servers is achieved through the OLE system DLLs. These OLE system DLLs provide functions that containers and servers call, and the containers and servers provide call-back functions that the DLLs call. Using this means of communication, a container doesn't need to know the implementation details of the server application. A container can accept items created by any server without having to define the types of servers with which the container can work. As a result, the user of a container application can take advantage of future applications and data formats. As long as these new applications are OLE servers, an OLE document will be able to incorporate items created by those applications.

Visual Editing Servers

A Visual Editing server application can create OLE items for use by other applications, which have the appropriate OLE support to contain these items (for information on container applications, see the following section, called Visual Editing Containers). Server applications usually support copying their data to the Clipboard or by drag and drop so that container applications can paste the data as an embedded or linked item. A miniserver is a special type of server application that can be launched only by a container. The Microsoft Draw and Microsoft Graph servers are examples of miniservers. A miniserver does not store its own data as files on disk; instead, it reads its documents from and writes them to items in documents belonging to containers. As a result, a miniserver can only support embedding, not linking. A full-server can either be run as a standalone application or be launched by a container application. A full-server can store documents as files on disk. It can support embedding only, both embedding and linking, or only linking. The user of a container application creates an embedded item by choosing the Cut or Copy command in the server and the Paste command in the container. A linked item is created by choosing the Copy command in the server and the Paste Link command in the container. When a server application is launched by a container application and is in place, MFC handles all of the toolbar and menu negotiation to allow the server's menus and toolbar to display in place of the menus and toolbar of the container. Even advanced user-interface features such as docking toolbars are supported when a server is in-place activated; in this case, the toolbars are docked to the container's frame window. MFC handles all the negotiation with the container for the tool space, including showing correct feedback when the toolbar is being dragged.

Miscellaneous

Debugging and Diagnostic Support

An area overlooked by many class libraries is the inclusion of sophisticated diagnostic and debugging facilities. Incorporated directly into the fabric of MFC is a backbone of diagnostic code that is supported in the debug version of the framework. Applications written with MFC and compiled for debugging can be up to twice as large as their nondebug counterparts — an indication of the extensive diagnostic support within the application framework. Programmers can add debug code anywhere in an application that will print out all currently allocated heap objects. This capability is invaluable for the detection of serious memory leaks that are often impossible to track by other means. A memory leak is a slow depletion of system resources that can go undetected for several days until all resources are consumed. For all heap-allocated objects, a record is kept of the size, source file and line number of the allocation. After a debug version of an MFC application terminates, the application framework automatically displays all heap objects the programmer failed to free. Other debug support includes functions that are able to validate any pointer and determine if it refers to a genuine C++ CObject-derived object. The framework also provides run-time assertions and class invariants, which were popularized by the Eiffel programming language. Every class in MFC implements a member function that checks the current state of the object and causes a debug assert if the object is not in a proper state. Library member functions validate parameters to functions in the debug version of the framework. There are more than 3,900 ASSERT statements within the implementation of MFC, each of which checks the condition of the internal state of a class or parameters passed into an API. If a programmer erroneously causes the application framework to enter an unpredictable state, the application will immediately break into the debugger (if it is running), or an alerting message box will be displayed. ASSERT statements catch errors much earlier and can save hours of development time. All major Microsoft applications use assertion statements extensively. In the release (nondebug) version of an MFC application, ASSERT statements are not executed and generate no code (they are designed for testing purposes only), and thus they incur no cost to the application's end users. The ASSERT mechanism is provided for users of MFC as well, and programmers are encouraged to take advantage of it within their own code. MFC also provides TRACE statements, which are formatted information messages. As with ASSERT statements, TRACE statements are executed only in the debug version of an application. The

TRACE statements in the application framework display possible misuse of a feature, low-memory conditions, rarely executed boundary conditions, and full message and command tracing. Since the output can be verbose (there are nearly 300 TRACE statements in MFC 3.0), it is easy to select which categories of messages are reported using the TRACER.EXE tool. For example, developers who are only interested in information about OLE can filter out all the other TRACE output. The TRACE facility can also be used by programmers within their own codes. MFC 3.0 has enhanced support for OLE memory diagnostics. Not only will MFC's debug allocator check a program's allocations for overwrites and memory leaks, but it will also check memory allocations done by the OLE DLLs themselves as well as any OLE servers the application may use.

Unicode Support

Some international markets use languages that have large character sets, such as Japanese and Chinese. To support programming for these markets, the MFC library is enabled for two different approaches to handling large character sets:

- Unicode
- Double Byte Character Sets (DBCS)

DBCS is supported on all platforms. Unicode is supported on all Windows NT platforms. The MFC library is designed to support either option. A special version of the MFC library must be linked in when building a Unicode application. MFC 3.0 is provided in a version that directly supports Unicode characters and strings. In particular, class CString is Unicode-enabled. CString is based on the TCHAR data type. If the symbol _UNICODE is defined for a build of the program, TCHAR is defined as type wchar_t, a 16-bit character encoding type; otherwise, it is defined as char, the normal 8-bit character encoding. As a result, under Unicode, CStrings are composed of 16-bit characters; without Unicode, they are composed of characters of type char. CString also supplies Unicode-aware constructors, assignment operators and comparison operators. If Unicode is not specified, the class library defaults to supporting the ANSI character set with support specifically for DBCS. Under the DBCS scheme, a character can be either one or two bytes wide. If it is two bytes wide, its first byte is a special "lead" byte, chosen from a particular range depending on which code page is in use. Taken together, the lead and "trail" bytes specify a unique character encoding. In either case, CString conversion operators and constructors make it easy to convert ANSI and Unicode strings to a CString object, in the case that program deals with both ANSI and Unicode characters. Note that Unicode string serialization in MFC can read both Unicode and DBCS strings, regardless of which version of the application is running. Because of this, data files are portable between Unicode and DBCS versions of the program.

Wizards

Visual C++ contains two very powerful wizards: AppWizard and ClassWizard. The AppWizard is used to generate a skeleton of a new C++ application. The ClassWizard is used browse and edit classes and hooking up class members to user interface components.

AppWizard

The AppWizard lets you configure the skeleton of a new C++ application that uses MFC. The first step is to answer all of the AppWizard's questions. To run AppWizard, choose the New command from the File menu in Visual C++. In the New dialog box, select the file type "Project." In the New Project dialog box, choose MFC AppWizard (exe) in the Project-type drop-down list.

Start - New Project Dialog Box:

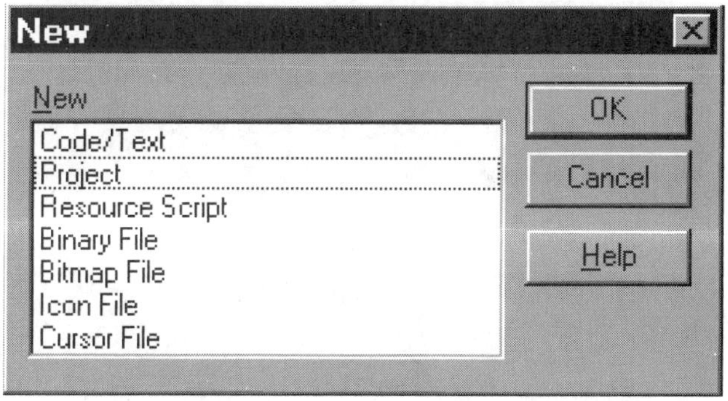

Figure 4.14. New Object Dialog Box

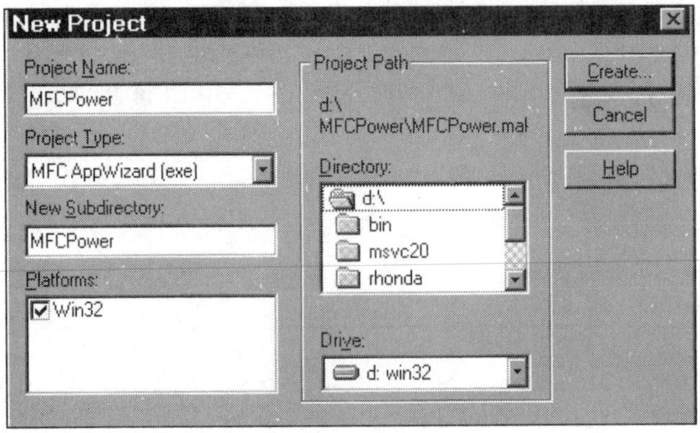

Figure 4.15 New Project Dialog Box

AppWizard lets you configure the skeleton application with the following options in 6 steps:

Step 1 Choose Application Interface Type

- Specify an application type: single document interface (SDI), multiple document interface (MDI), or dialog-based. The new dialog-based option lets you easily use a dialog box as your application's user interface.

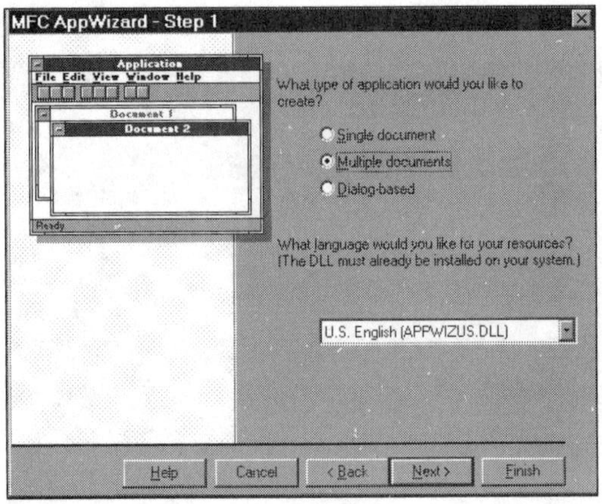

Figure 4.16 AppWizard Document Interface Type

Step 2 - Specify database options. You can:

- Specify minimal support by including the correct header files and link libraries, or you can derive your view class from CRecordView for a form-based application.

- Provide a user interface for opening and saving disk files in addition to accessing a database from the same application.

- Specify a data source to connect to and which table and columns you want to access.

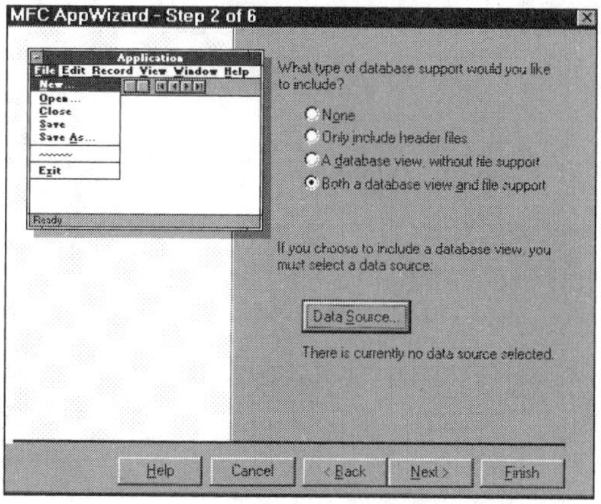

Figure 4.17. AppWizard Database Options

Step 3 - Specify OLE options. You can:specify that your application should be:

- a container,
- a mini-server,
- a full server,
- or both a container and a server,
- and it can have OLE Automation support.

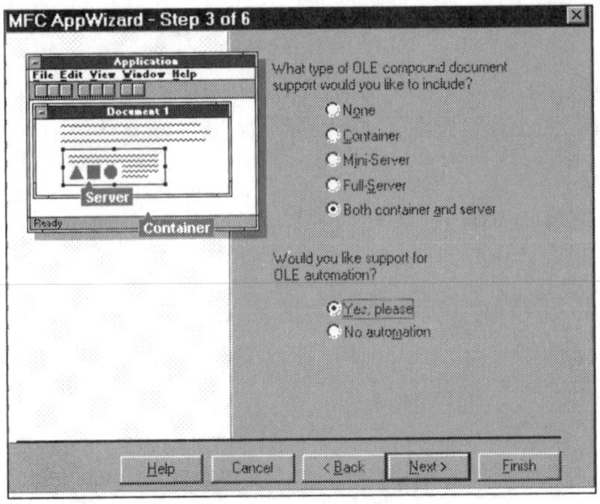

Figure 4.18 AppWizard OLE Options

Step 4 - Applications Options. You can specify that your application should have:

- Specify whether you want a toolbar or a status bar. By default, the toolbar is an MFC "dockable" toolbar, a new feature in MFC version 3.0.
- Specify whether you want an About dialog box (in dialog-based applications).
- Specify support for printing and print preview or context-sensitive help.
- Specify which styles and captions you want for the main frame and child window.
- Specify whether you want splitter window support.
- Specify the number of files listed in the most-recently-used (MRU) file list on the File menu.
- Specify Winsock or MAPI support

Use the Advanced.. dialog

- Document names and OLE short names,
- Document file extensions,
- Registry Information, and
- Styles for your main frame and MDI frame windows.

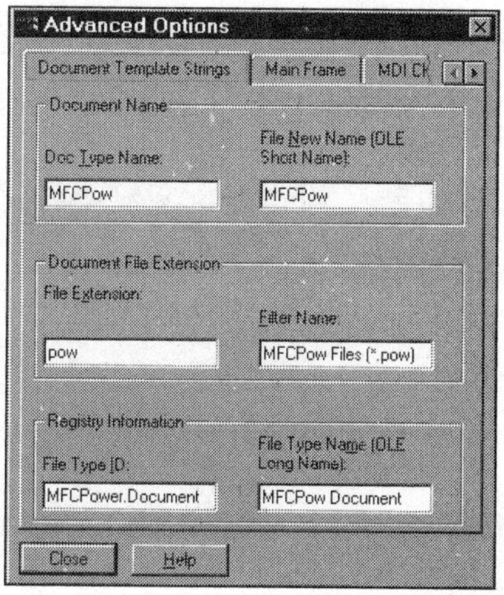

Figure 4.19 AppWizard Application Options

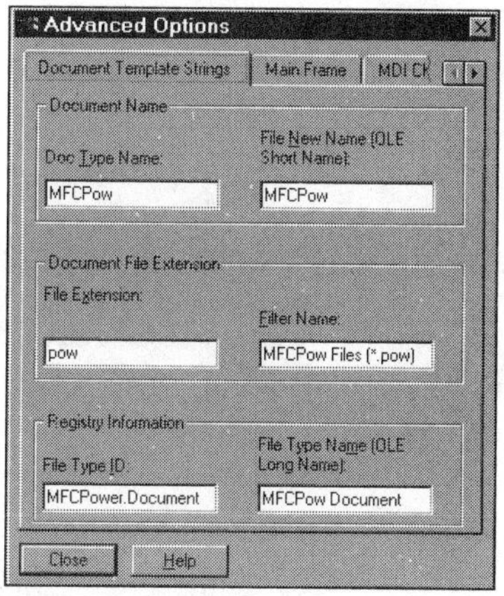

Figure 4.20 AppWizard Advanced Application Options

Step 5 - Build Options. You can specify that your application should have:

- Specify if comments should be included in the generated code.
- Specify whether you want to link with the MFC libraries statically or dynamically. Linking dynamically with AFXDLL (MFC in a DLL) reduces the size of your executable file and lets several applications share a single copy of MFC at run time. By default, AppWizard provides the dynamic linking support.

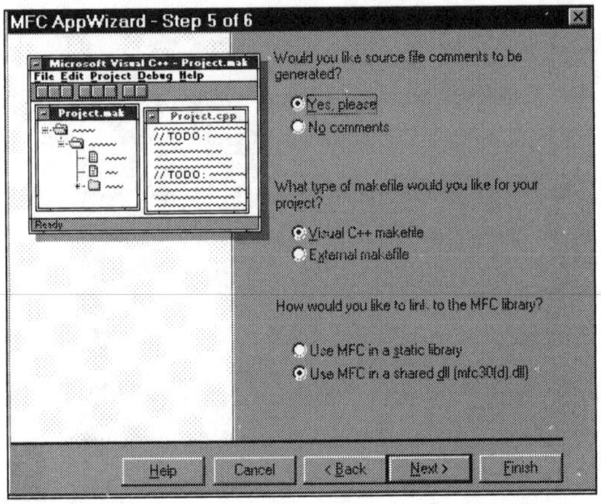

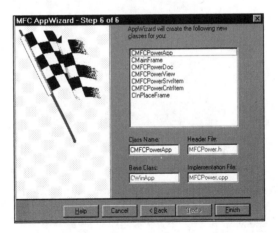

Figure 4.21 AppWizard Build Options

Step 6 - Class Name Options. You can specify that your application should have:

- Specify the names of your application's classes and what class you derive your view class from.

Figure 4.22 AppWizard Class Names and File Names

After completed the previous six steps, the AppWizard display the type of application that will be created.

Figure 4.23 AppWizard New Project Information

ClassWizard

ClassWizard helps you create additional classes beyond those you create with AppWizard.

ClassWizard also lets you browse and edit your classes.

To run ClassWizard, choose the ClassWizard command from the Project menu in Visual

C++. ClassWizard supports the following features:

- Support for creating and managing new classes derived from most of the MFC classes. For example, ClassWizard makes it easy to create classes for your owner-draw list boxes and other controls.
- Support for message maps. You can use ClassWizard to:
- Map Windows messages to message-handler functions in your classes.
- Map command messages from menu items, toolbar buttons, and accelerators to handler functions in your classes.
- Map control-notification messages from dialog controls to your classes.
- Provide "update handlers" to enable or disable user-interface objects, such as menus and toolbar buttons.
- Jump from ClassWizard to the handler function for a particular message or command.

- Specify a "filter" that determines which categories of Windows messages
- Support for mapping dialog controls to class member variables. This helps you enable dialog data exchange (DDX) and dialog data validation (DDV) for
- the controls in your dialog boxes. DDX exchanges data between dialog controls and
- their corresponding member variables in a dialog class. DDV validates this data.
- Add classes that support OLE Automation.
- Add properties and methods to your classes that support OLE Automation.
- Create a C++ class for an existing OLE Automation object on your system, such as Microsoft Excel.
- Specify properties and methods for OLE Controls.
- Specify the events your OLE Control can fire.
- Create classes derived from CRecordset.
- Specify a data source, table, and columns for a recordset.
- Create database form classes derived from CRecordView.
- Map controls of a record view database form to the fields of a recordset object.
- Browse virtual functions provided by MFC and choose the ones you want to override, then jump to the code for editing.

Modifying a class with ClassWizard

A application created by the AppWizard, while containing an impressive GUI, doesn't really do anyting. Using the ClassWizard you can add functionality. For a very simple example, using the ClassWizard to modify the OnDraw the output a string. In the following figure the OnDraw member function of CMFCPowerView is being created.

Add the following 2 lines of code to OnDraw, will draw a randomly colored string in the window.

```
pDC->SetTextColor(RGB(rand() % 255,rand() % 255, rand() % 255));
pDC->TextOut(10,50,"Use MFC to generate powerful applications
quickly.");
```

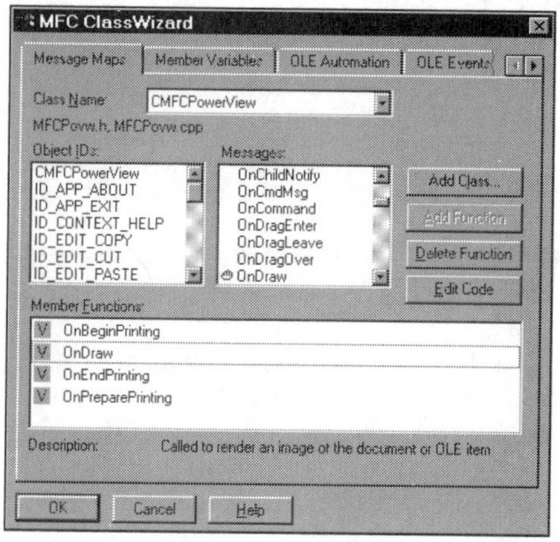

Figure 4.24 Using the ClassWizard To Modify the CMFCPowerView Class

A simple application in just a few minutes

Using Visual C++ for just a few minutes allows you to an application with the basics for a world class GUI application. This simple application, MFCPower, contains the following features:

- Dockable toolbar, with hints
- Status bar
- Multiple documents and views, with splitters
- Menus
- Dialogs - well at least an About box
- Online context sensitive help

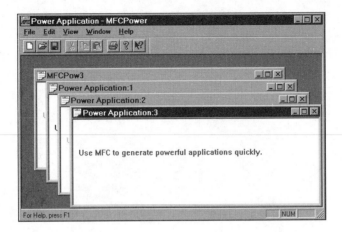

Figure 4.25 MFCPower Showing The Power of MFC

## CHAPTER 5

Implementing Data Persistence

One of the key decisions any cross-platform developer needs to consider is how to create a portable application database. Users of the application should not be burdened with what platform the application database was created on. Instead, they should assume that an application database created on any platform can be read on any other platform. This chapter explains how to use the serialization mechanism provided in the Microsoft Foundation Class Library (MFC) to allow objects to persist between runs of the program in a cross-platform environment. Although the MFC serialization mechanism was not designed to support cross-platform development, it has been extended to support a wide variety of non-Intel platforms by Microsoft and other WinAPI/MFC suppliers.

What is Serialization?

Serialization is the process of writing or reading one or more objects to or from a persistent storage medium, such as a disk file. In general, this disk file is referred to as the *application database*, or simply *database*. MFC supplies built-in support for serialization in the class CObject. Thus, all classes derived from CObject can take advantage of CObject's serialization protocol. Not all of the MFC serialization methods are cross-platform aware and some cannot be made cross-platform safe. That is, simply using the MFC serialization methods does not guarantee a cross-platform compatible application database. However, with minimal work you can use the MFC serialization architecture to create cross-platform compatible application databases.

The basic idea of serialization is that an object should be able to write its current state, usually indicated by the value of its member variables, to persistent storage. Later, the object can be re-created by reading, or deserializing, the object's state from the storage. Serialization handles all the details of object pointers and circular references to objects that are used when you serialize an object. A key point is that the object itself is responsible for reading and writing its own state; thus the object is responsible for implementing some of the cross-platform portability. Therefore, for a class to be serializable, it must implement the basic serialization operations. How to add serialization to a CObject derived class is discussed later in this chapter.

MFC uses an object of the CArchive class as an intermediary between the object to be serialized and the storage medium. This object is always associated with a CFile object, from which it obtains the necessary information for serialization, including the filename and whether the requested operation is a read or write. The object that performs a serialization operation can use the CArchive object without regard to the nature of the storage medium. A CArchive object uses overloaded *insertion* (<<) and *extraction* (>>) operators to perform writing and reading operations.

Cross-Platform Issues

When designing a cross-platform application database the key problem is byte-ordering differences among the operating systems and CPUs. There are two byte-ordering techniques, "little-endian" and "big-endian." Because some new CPUs allow the byte ordering to be specified by the operating system, never assume a byte-ordering method based only on the CPU. The MIPS CPU is an example: when running NT, the byte ordering matches the Intel x86 style; when running UNIX the byte ordering is swapped. Table 5.1 lists the processors that Win32 is available on and their byte ordering.

Table 5.1 Byte Ordering

Processor	OS	Order
Alpha	All	little-endian
HP-PA	NT	little-endian
HP-PA	UNIX	big-endian
Intel x86	All	little-endian

Table 5.1 Byte Ordering (continued)

Processor	OS	Order
Motorola 680x0	All	big-endian
MIPS	NT	little-endian
MIPS	UNIX	big-endian
PowerPC	NT	little-endian
PowerPC	non-NT	big-endian
RS/6000	UNIX	big-endian
SPARC	UNIX	big-endian

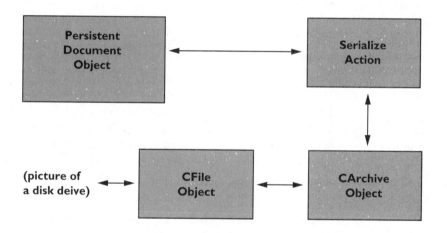

Figure 5.1 The Serialization Process.

The little-endian byte order places the least significant byte first and the most significant byte last. The following code shows the bit and byte layout for 4 bytes of data.

```
bits: [  7  6  5  4  3  2  1  0 ]  Byte 0   < Address
bits: [ 15 14 13 12 11 10  9  8 ]  Byte 1
bits: [ 23 22 21 20 19 18 17 16 ]  Byte 2
bits: [ 31 30 29 28 27 26 25 24 ]  Byte 3
```

For example, a pointer to a 4-byte integer contains the address of the least significant byte of that integer (bits 0–7). Adding 1 to the pointer value causes it to point to the next higher byte of the value (bits 8–15), and so forth.

The big-endian byte ordering places the most significant byte first, followed by the next most significant byte, and so on, with the least significant byte last. The following code shows this big-endian layout:

```
bits: [ 31 30 29 28 27 26 25 24 ]  Byte 0    < Address
bits: [ 23 22 21 20 19 18 17 16 ]  Byte 1
bits: [ 15 14 13 12 11 10  9  8 ]  Byte 2
bits: [  7  6  5  4  3  2  1  0 ]  Byte 3
```

In this ordering, a pointer to an integer value contains the address of the integer's most significant byte. The individual ordering of bits within each byte does not differ among processors. Therefore, writing a single byte of data will be the same on each machine; but writing a larger object, such as a 4-byte integer, will have the bytes swapped.

Why are some CPUs big-endian and some little-endian? The debate goes back for decades about which architecture delivers a better solution. Today, the advantages or disadvantages of one over the other is marginal, if any exist at all. Since hardware companies create CPUs that support both byte orderings, like HP-PA, DEC Alpha, and MIPS, software companies need to create software that can read or write data in both formats.

There are several ways to overcome this byte-ordering issue, from writing ASCII data to tagged streams where every item is marked with type, size, and byte-ordering information. Another option is to convert the binary data to an architecture-neutral format in the application database. Then, convert the data to an architecture-specific format in the application. In an MFC application a variation of this architecture-neutral format can be used in which the neutral format is little-endian byte ordering. This way, no additional code is needed for Windows NT or Windows 95 applications, but UNIX or Mac applications rely on MFC to byte-swap data that is being read or written.

MFC Objects that Support Serialization

MFC supports serialization of CObject-derived objects as well as some MFC objects not derived from CObject and the most native C++ types. Table 5.2 lists the MFC objects that support serialization.

Table 5.2 MFC Objects that Support Serialization

Object	Win32	Macintosh	UNIX
BYTE (unsigned char)	Yes	Yes	Yes
double	Yes	Yes	Yes
DWORD (unsigned long)	Yes	Yes	Yes
float	Yes	Yes	Yes
LONG (long)	Yes	Yes	Yes
WORD (unsigned short)	Yes	Yes	Yes
nt	No	No	No
CObject	Yes	Yes	Yes
CPoint	Yes	Partial	Yes

Table 5.2 MFC Objects that Support Serialization (continued)

Object	Win32	Macintosh	UNIX
iCRect	Yes	Partial	Yes
CSize	Yes	Partial	Yes
CString	Yes	Yes	Yes
CTime	Yes	Yes	Yes
CTimeSpan	Yes	Yes	Yes

N O T E

Early versions of MFC 3 for the Macintosh do not support byte-swapping in the `CPoint`, `CRect`, or `CSize` serialization functions. This support is planned for MFC 4.

Making a Serializable Class

Before dropping inside MFC serialization, here are the five main steps required to make a class serializable:

1. Derive the class from CObject (or from some class derived from CObject).
2. Insert generic serialization members into the class declaration using the DECLARE_SERIAL macro
3. Override and implement the Serialize member function.
4. Define a constructor that takes no arguments.
5. Implement the generic serialization members using the IMPLEMENT_SERIAL macro in the class implementation source file.

Derive the Class from CObject

The basic serialization protocol and functionality are defined in the CObject class. By deriving the class from CObject, or from a class derived from CObject you gain access to the serialization protocol and functionality of CObject. In Scribble the principle object archived is the CStroke object. The CStroke object is derived directly from CObject as follows:

```
///////////////////////////////////////////////////////////////////
///////////
// class CStroke
//
// A stroke is a series of connected points in the scribble
drawing.
// A scribble document may have multiple strokes.

class CStroke : public CObject
{
public:
    CStroke(UINT nPenWidth);
    ...
```

Add the DECLARE_SERIAL **Macro**

The DECLARE_SERIAL macro generates the C++ header code necessary for a CObject-derived class that can be serialized. Insert the DECLARE_SERIAL macro in the .H file for the class, then include that module in all .CPP files that need access to objects of the class. The DECLARE_SERIAL macro includes all the functionality of DECLARE_DYNAMIC and DECLARE_DYNCREATE. DECLARE_DYNAMIC adds the ability to access run-time type information about an object. DECLARE_DYNCREATE enables objects to be created dynamically at run time. The DECLARE_SERIAL macro requires the name of the class (not enclosed in quotation marks). The following code segment illustrates the use of DECLARE_SERIAL in the Scribble CStroke class:

```
/////////////////////////////////////////////////////////////////////
///////////
// class CStroke
//
// A stroke is a series of connected points in the scribble
drawing.
// A scribble document may have multiple strokes.
class CStroke : public CObject
{
public:
    CStroke(UINT nPenWidth);

protected:
    CStroke();
    DECLARE_SERIAL(CStroke)
...
```

When the compiler processes DECLARE_SERIAL, and in turn DECLARE_DYNAMIC and DECLARE_DYNCREATE, the following code is inserted into the CStroke class:

```
protected:
    static CRuntimeClass* __stdcall _GetBaseClass();
```

```
public:
    static  CRuntimeClass classCStroke;
    virtual CRuntimeClass* GetRuntimeClass() const;
    static void __stdcall Construct(void* p);
    friend CArchive& __stdcall operator>>(CArchive& ar, CStroke*
&pOb);
```

Override the Serialize **Member Function**

The Serialize member function, which is defined in the CObject base class, is responsible for the actual serializing of the data necessary to capture an object's current state. The Serialize function has a CArchive argument that it uses to read and write the object data. The CArchive object has a member function, IsStoring, which indicates whether Serialize is storing (writing data) or loading (reading data). Using the results of IsStoring as a guide, you either insert the object's data in the CArchive object with the insertion operator (<<) or extract data with the extraction operator (>>). Again, the CStroke class declaration includes the necessary code to support serialization. In this case the Serialize() member function is shown in the following code segment:

```
class CStroke : public CObject
{
...
// Attributes
    UINT                    m_nPenWidth;    // one pen width
                                            applies to entire
                                            stroke
    CArray<CPoint,CPoint>  m_pointArray;   // series of connected
                                            points
    CRect                   m_rectBounding; // smallest rect
...
public:
    virtual void Serialize(CArchive& ar);
...
```

The above code segment also includes the member variables that must be serialized, the pen width m_nPenWidth, the bounding rectangle m_rectBounding, and the point array m_pointArray. The following code segment shows the actual implementation of the CStroke Serialize() member function:

```
void CStroke::Serialize(CArchive& ar)
{
    CObject::Serialize(ar);  // call parent class serialize
    if (ar.IsStoring())
    {
        ar << m_rectBounding;
        ar << (WORD)m_nPenWidth;
        m_pointArray.Serialize(ar);
    }
    else
    {
        ar >> m_rectBounding;
        WORD w;
        ar >> w;
        m_nPenWidth = w;
        m_pointArray.Serialize(ar);
    }
}
```

Whether reading or writing, the Serialize function serializes the data in the same order. Before serializing any data in the CStroke object, the Serialize function must call the Serialize member of the immediate base class to serialize the inherited portion of the object.

The CObject::Serialize function in MFC 3 is implemented as an empty function. Therefore, calling it does not impact MFC 3 archives.

NOTE

Then the bounding rectangle is serialized, then the pen width, and finally the array of points. The array of points is serialized using the Serialize() member function in the CArray template class. The pen width is serialized as a UINT since CArchive does not support serializing UINT variables. MFC does not support serializing UINT variables since Win16 uses 16-bit UINTs and Win32 uses 32-bit UINTs. Forcing the user to state explicitly the size of the integer to be serialized helps maintain compatibility between Win16 and Win32 archives. For CStroke, the pen size is saved and restored as a WORD (a signed 16-bit number).

This implementation does not use the CArchive::Read and CArchive::Write member functions. Since these Read and Write functions deal with untyped data, archives created with them may not be cross-platform compatible. For example, using Read and Write to serialize the rectangle, as shown below, would create a byte-order-dependent archive.

```
ar.Write(&rect, sizeof(RECT));  // write 16 bytes of data
ar.Read(&rect, sizeof(RECT));   // read 16 bytes of data
```

Instead, CStroke relies on MFC to correctly generate a platform-independent archive.

Create a Constructor with No Arguments

The next major step is to create a constructor that MFC can use when it re-creates the objects as they are deserialized (loaded from disk.) The deserialization process fills all member variables with the values required to re-create the object. This constructor can be declared public, protected, or private. If you make it protected or private, you ensure that it will only be used by the serialization functions. To handle exceptions correctly, this constructor must put the object in a state that allows it to be safely deleted if necessary.

N O T E   If you forget to define a constructor with no arguments in a class that uses the DECLARE_SERIAL and IMPLEMENT_SERIAL macros, you will get a "no default constructor available" compiler warning on the line where the IMPLEMENT_SERIAL macro is used.

```
///////////////////////////////////////////////////////////////
///////////
// class CStroke
//
```

```
// A stroke is a series of connected points in the scribble
drawing.
// A scribble document may have multiple strokes.

class CStroke : public CObject
{
public:
    CStroke(UINT nPenWidth);  // normal constructor for new
                                 strokes

protected:
    CStroke(); // no argument constructor for serialization
    DECLARE_SERIAL(CStroke)
```

For CStroke, this default constructor does not perform any initialization; it is only used in deserialization to allocate memory. Also, to prevent nonserialization classes from creating uninitialized CStroke objects, the function is declared as a protected member.

The `CStroke::CStroke()` implementation looks like this:

```
CStroke::CStroke()
{
    // This empty constructor should be used by serialization only
}
```

Insert the IMPLEMENT_SERIAL **Macro**

The last step to create serializable class is to insert the IMPLEMENT_SERIAL macro in the implementation file. The IMPLEMENT_SERIAL macro is used to define the various functions needed when deriving serializable class from CObject. You use this macro in the implementation file (.**CPP**) for the class. The first two arguments to the macro are the name of the class and the name of its immediate base class. The third argument to this macro is a schema number. The schema number is essentially a version number for objects of the class. Use an integer greater than or equal to 0 for the schema number. The MFC serialization code checks the schema number when reading objects into memory. If the schema number of the object on disk does not match the schema number of the class in memory, the library will throw a CArchiveException, preventing the program from reading an incorrect version of the object.

To support the ability to read *multiple archive versions*, that is, files written with different versions of the application, you bitwise **OR** the value VERSIONABLE_SCHEMA with your schema number.

For CStroke the following is used:

```
IMPLEMENT_SERIAL(CStroke, CObject, 10)
```

This IMPLEMENT_SERIAL macro generates the following member functions for CStroke:

```
void __stdcall CStroke::Construct(void* p)
{
    new(p) CStroke;
}


CRuntimeClass* __stdcall CStroke::_GetBaseClass()
{
    return (&CObject::classCObject);
}


CRuntimeClass CStroke::classCStroke = {
    "CStroke",
    sizeof(CStroke),
    10,
    CStroke::Construct,
    &CStroke::_GetBaseClass,
    0
    };


static const AFX_CLASSINIT _init_CStroke(&CStroke::classCStroke);


CRuntimeClass* CStroke::GetRuntimeClass() const
```

```
    {
        return &CStroke::classCStroke;
    }


    CArchive& __stdcall operator>>(CArchive& ar, CStroke* &pOb)
    {
        pOb = (CStroke) ar.ReadObject((&CStroke::classCStroke));
        return ar;
    }
```

These member functions implement the nuts and bolts of the serialization protocol. The internals of MFC use these functions to identify what objects are contained in an archive.

Serializing an Object Using CArchive

The above sections discussed how to make a class serializable. Once you have a serializable class, you can serialize objects of that class to and from storage via a CArchive object. This section discusses what a CArchive object is, how to create one and how to move data in and out of the archive after it is created. Normally, the MFC framework creates the archive for the serializable document, but your can explicitly create the CArchive object. You can transfer the application data between a file and the serializable object by using the C++ input operator, << or the C++ output operator, >>, for CArchive. Also, the Serialize function for CObject-derived classes and the SerializeElements function for MFC collection classes are used to transfer data to and from the CArchive object.

What is a CArchive Object?

A CArchive object provides a type-safe buffering mechanism for writing or reading serializable objects to or from a CFile object. Usually the CFile object represents a disk file; however, it can also be a memory file (CMemFile object), perhaps representing the Clipboard or an OLE storage mechanism. A given CArchive object either stores (writes, serializes) data or loads (reads, deserializes) data, but never both. The life of a CArchive object is limited to one pass through writing objects to a file or reading objects from a file. Thus, two successively created CArchive objects are required to serialize data to a file and then deserialize it back from the file. When an archive stores objects to a file, the archive attaches the CRuntimeClass name to the objects. This CRuntimeClass name is the name first argument specified in the IMPLEMENT_SERIAL macro.

The name specified in the IMPLEMENT_SERIAL macro must be unique from all objects in the archive.

N O T E

To reduce overhead and increase performance CArchive only stores the name in the archive the first time a new object type is encountered. Later, a 15-bit identifier for the object is used. Thus, the MFC implementation imposes a limit of 32766 object types per archive. Then, when another archive loads objects from a file to memory, the CObject-derived objects are dynamically reconstructed based on the CRuntimeClass of the objects. A given object may be referenced more than once as it is written to the file by the storing archive. The loading archive, however, will reconstruct the object only once. As data is serialized to an archive, the archive accumulates the data until its buffer is full. Then the archive writes its buffer to the CFile object pointed to by the CArchive object. Similarly, as you read data from an archive, it reads data from the file to its buffer and then from the buffer to the deserialized object. This buffering reduces the number of times a hard disk is physically read, thus improving the application's performance. The default buffer size is 512 bytes. For increased performance on large archive files, a larger buffer may be specified when the CArchive object is created.

Creating a CArchive Object

There are two main ways to create a CArchive object:

1. Implicit creation of a CArchive object via the MFC framework
2. Explicit creation of a CArchive object

Implicit Creation of a CArchive Object via the Framework

The most common, and easiest, way is to let the MFC framework create a CArchive object for the document on behalf of the **Save**, **Save As**, and **Open** commands on the File menu. For example, here is what MFC does when the user of the application issues the **Save As** command from the File menu:

1. Presents the File Save As dialog box and gets the filename from the user.
2. Opens the file named by the user as a CFile object.
3. Creates a CArchive object that points to this CFile object. In creating the CArchive object, the framework:

    -   sets the mode to "store" (write, serialize), as opposed to "load" (read, deserialize) and
    -   sets the mode to "no byte swap" on little-endian architectures.

Calls the `Serialize` function defined in the CDocument-derived class, passing it a reference to the CArchive object. The document's `Serialize` function then writes data to the CArchive object, as explained below. Upon return from the `Serialize` function, the framework destroys the CArchive object and then the CFile object. Thus, if you let the framework create the CArchive object for the document, all you have to do is implement the document's `Serialize` function that writes and reads to and from the archive. You also have to implement `Serialize` for any CObject-derived objects that the document's `Serialize` function in turn serializes directly or indirectly. The following code segment shows how the Scribble CDocument-derived class, CScribDoc uses the framework-created CArchive:

```
//////////////////////////////////////////////////////////////////
///////////
// CScribDoc serialization

void CScribDoc::Serialize(CArchive& ar)
{
    if (ar.IsStoring())
    {
        ar << m_sizeDoc;  // CSize object containing the number of
                          pixels in scribble sheet
    }
    else
    {
```

```
        ar >> m_sizeDoc;
    }
    m_strokeList.Serialize(ar);
}
```

With implicit creation, the framework is responsible for validating the pathname and opening the file. With the syntax and semantics of hierarchical pathnames different across platforms, implicit creation increases the portability of your application. Once again, leverage the portability of the framework to create your cross-platform application.

Explicit Creation of a CArchive Object

Besides serializing a document via the framework, there are other occasions when you may need a CArchive object. For example, you might want to serialize data to and from the Clipboard, represented by a CMemFile object. Or, you may want to use a user interface for saving a file that is different from the one offered by the framework. In this case, you can explicitly create a CArchive object. You do this the same way the framework does, using the following procedure.

To explicitly create a CArchive object

1. Construct a CFile object or an object derived from CFile.
2. Pass the CFile object to the constructor for CArchive, as shown in the following example:

   ```
   CMemFile theClipboardData;
   CArchive archive(&theClipboardData, CArchive::store |
   CArchive::bNoByteSwap);
   ```

The second argument to the CArchive constructor is an enumerated value that specifies whether the archive will be used for storing or loading data to or from the file and byte swapping information on this computer architecture. The Serialize function of an object checks this state by calling the IsStoring function for the archive object. When you have finished storing or loading data to or from the CArchive object, close it. Although the CArchive (and CFile) objects will automatically close the archive (and file), it is good practice to do so explicitly, since it makes recovery from errors easier. The following example illustrates how to close the CArchive object:

```
archive.Close();
theClipboardData.Close();
```

Byte-Swapping in Archives

On the Macintosh and UNIX RISC systems, MFC archives are byte-swapped by default. Byte-swapped archives are always kept in the little-endian order that is used on x86-based computers. Byte-swapping is performed whenever a **WORD**, **DWORD, LONG**, float, or double is read from or written to an archive, unless the Read or Write member functions are used. The Read and Write member functions never byte swap. To prevent archives from being byte swapped, use the bNoByteSwap mode flag when creating the archive, as shown in the following example:

```
CArchive ar(pfile, CArchive::store | CArchive::bNoByteSwap);
```

Using the above code on UNIX or the Macintosh creates an archive that stores data in the big-endian byte order that is native to the Macintosh and UNIX RISC implementations, rather than swapping bytes and storing them in the little-endian order native to x86-based computers or Windows NT RISC implementations.

Using the CArchive << and >> Operators

CArchive provides << and >> operators for writing and reading simple data types as well as CObjects to and from a file. The DECLARE_SERIAL and IMPLEMENT_SERIAL macros discussed above declare and implement these operators. The following example shows how to store an object in a file via an archive:

```
CArchive    archive(&orderFile, CArchive::store);
double      dItemCost;
LONG        nItemQuantity

...

archive << dItemCost;
archive << nItemQuantify

...
```

The following example shows how to load an object from a value previously stored in an archive:

```
CArchive archive(&orderFile, CArchive::load);
double     dItemCost;
LONG       nItemQuantity
...
archive >> dItemCost;
archive >> nItemQuantify
...
```

Usually, you store and load data to and from a file via an archive in the Serialize functions of CObject-derived classes, which you must have declared with the DECLARE_SERIALIZE macro. A reference to a CArchive object is passed to the Serialize function. You call the IsStoring function of the CArchive object to determine whether the Serialize function has been called to load data from the file or store data to the file. The Serialize function of a serializable CObject-derived class typically has the following form:

```
void CSomeObject::Serialize(CArchive& ar)
{
    CObject::Serialize(ar); // always call the parent serialize
                               function
    if (ar.IsStoring())
    {
        // TODO:  add storing code here
    }
    else
    {
        // TODO:  add loading code here
    }
}
```

The above code template is exactly the same as the one AppWizard creates for the Serialize function of the document (a class derived from CDocument). This code template helps you write code that is easier to review, because the storing code and the loading code should always be parallel, as in the following example from Scribble:

```
/////////////////////////////////////////////////////////////////
///////////
// CScribDoc serialization

void CScribDoc::Serialize(CArchive& ar)
{
    if (ar.IsStoring())
    {
        ar << m_sizeDoc;
    }
    else
    {
        ar >> m_sizeDoc;
    }
    m_strokeList.Serialize(ar);
}
```

The CArchive << and >> operators always return a reference to the CArchive object, which is the first operand. This enables you to chain the operators, as illustrated by the rewrite of a previous example:

```
CArchive    archive(&orderFile, CArchive::store);
double      dItemCost;
LONG        nItemQuantity
...
archive << dItemCost << nItemQuantify;
...
```

Storing and Loading CObjects via an Archive

Storing and loading CObjects via an archive requires extra consideration. In certain cases, you should call the Serialize function of the object, where the CArchive object is a parameter of the Serialize call, as opposed to using the <<

or >> operator of the CArchive. The important fact to keep in mind is that the CArchive >> operator constructs the CObject in memory based on CRuntimeClass information previously written to the file by the storing archive. Therefore, whether you use the CArchive << and >> operators, versus calling Serialize, depends on whether you need the loading archive to dynamically reconstruct the object based on previously stored CRuntimeClass information. Use the Serialize function in the following cases:

- When deserializing the object, if you know the exact class of the object beforehand.
- When deserializing the object, if you already have memory allocated for it.

If you load the object using the Serialize function, you must also store the object using the Serialize function. Don't store using the CArchive << operator and then load using the Serialize function, or store using the Serialize function and then load using CArchive >> operator. In summary, if the serializable class defines an embedded CObject as a member, you should not use the CArchive << and >> operators for that object, but should call the Serialize function instead. Also, if the serializable class defines a pointer to a CObject (or an object derived from CObject) as a member, but constructs this other object in its own constructor, you should also call Serialize.

Inside MFC Serialization

Understanding more about how MFC implements serialization allows you to see examples of cross-platform persistent storage and learn what areas are portable. See MFC Technical Note 2: Persistent Object Data Format for information on the structure of an archive.

This section examines the details inside MFC serialization in order to demonstrate how to create portable serializable objects and shows areas to avoid when creating a cross-platform application database.

Fundamental Types

On little-endian architectures the serialization functions for the fundamental types are implemented as inline functions in **afx.inl**. For big-endian architectures most serialization functions are implemented in **arccore.cpp**. First, the code from **afx.inl**:

```
_AFX_INLINE CArchive& CArchive::operator<<(BYTE by)
    { if (m_lpBufCur + sizeof(BYTE) > m_lpBufMax) Flush();
        *(UNALIGNED BYTE*)m_lpBufCur = by; m_lpBufCur +=
        sizeof(BYTE); return *this; }
#ifndef _MAC || _WU_BIG_ENDIAN
_AFX_INLINE CArchive& CArchive::operator<<(WORD w)
    { if (m_lpBufCur + sizeof(WORD) > m_lpBufMax) Flush();
        *(UNALIGNED WORD*)m_lpBufCur = w; m_lpBufCur +=
        sizeof(WORD); return *this; }
_AFX_INLINE CArchive& CArchive::operator<<(LONG l)
    { if (m_lpBufCur + sizeof(LONG) > m_lpBufMax) Flush();
        *(UNALIGNED LONG*)m_lpBufCur = l; m_lpBufCur +=
        sizeof(LONG); return *this; }
_AFX_INLINE CArchive& CArchive::operator<<(DWORD dw)
    { if (m_lpBufCur + sizeof(DWORD) > m_lpBufMax) Flush();
        *(UNALIGNED DWORD*)m_lpBufCur = dw; m_lpBufCur +=
        sizeof(DWORD); return *this; }
_AFX_INLINE CArchive& CArchive::operator<<(float f)
    { if (m_lpBufCur + sizeof(float) > m_lpBufMax) Flush();
        *(UNALIGNED _AFX_FLOAT*)m_lpBufCur = *(_AFX_FLOAT*)&f;
        m_lpBufCur += sizeof(float); return *this;
    }
_AFX_INLINE CArchive& CArchive::operator<<(double d)
    { if (m_lpBufCur + sizeof(double) > m_lpBufMax) Flush();
        *(UNALIGNED _AFX_DOUBLE*)m_lpBufCur = *(_AFX_DOUBLE*)&d;
        m_lpBufCur += sizeof(double); return *this; }
#endif
_AFX_INLINE CArchive& CArchive::operator>>(BYTE& by)
    { if (m_lpBufCur + sizeof(BYTE) > m_lpBufMax)
            FillBuffer(sizeof(BYTE) - (UINT)(m_lpBufMax -
            m_lpBufCur));
        by = *(UNALIGNED BYTE*)m_lpBufCur; m_lpBufCur +=
        sizeof(BYTE); return *this; }
#ifndef _MAC || WU_BIG_ENDIAN
```

```
_AFX_INLINE CArchive& CArchive::operator>>(WORD& w)
    { if (m_lpBufCur + sizeof(WORD) > m_lpBufMax)
            FillBuffer(sizeof(WORD) - (UINT)(m_lpBufMax -
            m_lpBufCur));
        w = *(UNALIGNED WORD*)m_lpBufCur; m_lpBufCur +=
sizeof(WORD); return *this; }
_AFX_INLINE CArchive& CArchive::operator>>(DWORD& dw)
    { if (m_lpBufCur + sizeof(DWORD) > m_lpBufMax)
            FillBuffer(sizeof(DWORD) - (UINT)(m_lpBufMax -
            m_lpBufCur));
        dw = *(UNALIGNED DWORD*)m_lpBufCur; m_lpBufCur +=
sizeof(DWORD); return *this; }
_AFX_INLINE CArchive& CArchive::operator>>(float& f)
    { if (m_lpBufCur + sizeof(float) > m_lpBufMax)
            FillBuffer(sizeof(float) - (UINT)(m_lpBufMax -
            m_lpBufCur));
        *(_AFX_FLOAT*)&f = *(UNALIGNED _AFX_FLOAT*)m_lpBufCur;
m_lpBufCur += sizeof(float); return *this; }
_AFX_INLINE CArchive& CArchive::operator>>(double& d)
    { if (m_lpBufCur + sizeof(double) > m_lpBufMax)
            FillBuffer(sizeof(double) - (UINT)(m_lpBufMax -
            m_lpBufCur));
        *(_AFX_DOUBLE*)&d = *(UNALIGNED _AFX_DOUBLE*)m_lpBufCur;
m_lpBufCur += sizeof(double); return *this; }
_AFX_INLINE CArchive& CArchive::operator>>(LONG& l)
    { if (m_lpBufCur + sizeof(LONG) > m_lpBufMax)
            FillBuffer(sizeof(LONG) - (UINT)(m_lpBufMax -
            m_lpBufCur));
        l = *(UNALIGNED LONG*)m_lpBufCur; m_lpBufCur +=
        sizeof(LONG); return *this; }
#endif
```

Thus, on little-endian architectures the bytes for the fundamental types are efficiently inserted or extracted into the archive buffer. Since BYTE data is not impacted by the architecture, it is always inlined.

On big-endian architectures, the bytes must be swapped *before* the data is inserted into the archive buffer and swapped *after* the data is extracted from the archive buffer. To improve efficiency and readability, there are static arrays defined at the top of **arccore.cpp** to serve as temporary storage for the swapped bytes. The following code segment illustrates these static structures:

```
#ifdef _MAC || WU_BIG_ENDIAN
struct _AFXWORD
{
    BYTE WordBits[sizeof(WORD)];
};
struct _AFXDWORD
{
    BYTE DwordBits[sizeof(DWORD)];
};

struct _AFXFLOAT
{
    BYTE FloatBits[sizeof(float)];
};
struct _AFXDOUBLE
{
    BYTE DoubleBits[sizeof(double)];
};
```

Byte-swapping of the 16-bit WORD type is implemented using the following two functions:

```
CArchive& CArchive::operator<<(WORD w)
{
    if (m_lpBufCur + sizeof(WORD) > m_lpBufMax)
        Flush();

    if (!(m_nMode & bNoByteSwap))
    {
        _AFXWORD wAfx;
        *(WORD*)&wAfx = w;
        ASSERT(sizeof(WORD) == 2);
```

```
        BYTE* pb = m_lpBufCur;
        *pb++ = wAfx.WordBits[1];
        *pb = wAfx.WordBits[0];
    }
    else
    {
        *(WORD FAR*)m_lpBufCur = w;
    }


    m_lpBufCur += sizeof(WORD);
    return *this;
}


CArchive& CArchive::operator>>(WORD& w)
{
    if (m_lpBufCur + sizeof(WORD) > m_lpBufMax)
        FillBuffer(sizeof(WORD) - (UINT)(m_lpBufMax -
        m_lpBufCur));

    w = *(WORD FAR*)m_lpBufCur;
    m_lpBufCur += sizeof(WORD);

    if (!(m_nMode & bNoByteSwap))
    {
        _AFXWORD wAfx;
        *(WORD*)&wAfx = w;

        ASSERT(sizeof(WORD) == 2);
        (*(_AFXWORD*)&w).WordBits[0] = wAfx.WordBits[1];
        (*(_AFXWORD*)&w).WordBits[1] = wAfx.WordBits[0];
    }

    return *this;
}
```

In both functions, the statement *(WORD*)&wAfx = w; is used to fill the static structure with the unswapped bytes. Then the bytes are swapped one at a time using WordBits array within the static structure.

Byte-swapping of the 32-bit LONG type is implemented using the following two functions:

```
CArchive& CArchive::operator<<(LONG l)
{
    ASSERT(sizeof(LONG) == sizeof(DWORD));
    return operator<<((DWORD) l);
}
CArchive& CArchive::operator>>(LONG& l)
{
    ASSERT(sizeof(LONG) == sizeof(DWORD));
    return operator>>((DWORD&) l);
}
```

In both functions, the DWORD CArchive operator is called, since the DWORD is also a 32-bit integer.

Byte-swapping of the 32- bit DWORD type is implemented using the following two functions:

```
CArchive& CArchive::operator<<(DWORD dw)
{
    if (m_lpBufCur + sizeof(DWORD) > m_lpBufMax)
        Flush();

    if (!(m_nMode & bNoByteSwap))
    {
        _AFXDWORD dwAfx;
        *(DWORD*)&dwAfx = dw;

        ASSERT(sizeof(DWORD) == 4);

        BYTE* pb = m_lpBufCur;
```

```
            *pb++ = dwAfx.DwordBits[3];
            *pb++ = dwAfx.DwordBits[2];
            *pb++ = dwAfx.DwordBits[1];
            *pb = dwAfx.DwordBits[0];
        }
        else
        {
            *(DWORD FAR*)m_lpBufCur = dw;
        }

        m_lpBufCur += sizeof(DWORD);
        return *this;
    }
    CArchive& CArchive::operator>>(DWORD& dw)
    {
        if (m_lpBufCur + sizeof(DWORD) > m_lpBufMax)
            FillBuffer(sizeof(DWORD) - (UINT)(m_lpBufMax -
            m_lpBufCur));

        dw = *(DWORD FAR*)m_lpBufCur;
        m_lpBufCur += sizeof(DWORD);

        if (!(m_nMode & bNoByteSwap))
        {
            _AFXDWORD dwAfx;
            *(DWORD*)&dwAfx = dw;

            ASSERT(sizeof(DWORD) == 4);

            (*(_AFXDWORD*)&dw).DwordBits[0] = dwAfx.DwordBits[3];
            (*(_AFXDWORD*)&dw).DwordBits[1] = dwAfx.DwordBits[2];
            (*(_AFXDWORD*)&dw).DwordBits[2] = dwAfx.DwordBits[1];
            (*(_AFXDWORD*)&dw).DwordBits[3] = dwAfx.DwordBits[0];
        }
```

```
        return *this;
    }
```

Like the WORD implementations, the statement *(DWORD*)&dwAfx = dw; is used to fill the static structure with the 4 unswapped bytes. Then the bytes are swapped one at a time using DwordBits array within the static structure.

Byte-swapping of the 32-bit float type is implemented using the following two functions:

```
CArchive& CArchive::operator<<(float f)
{
    if (m_lpBufCur + sizeof(float) > m_lpBufMax)
        Flush();

    if (!(m_nMode & bNoByteSwap))
    {
        _AFXFLOAT fAfx;
        *(float*)&fAfx = f;

        ASSERT(sizeof(float) == 4);

        BYTE* pb = m_lpBufCur;
        *pb++ = fAfx.FloatBits[3];
        *pb++ = fAfx.FloatBits[2];
        *pb++ = fAfx.FloatBits[1];
        *pb = fAfx.FloatBits[0];
    }
    else
    {
        *(_AFXFLOAT FAR*)m_lpBufCur = *(_AFXFLOAT FAR*)&f;
    }

    m_lpBufCur += sizeof(float);
    return *this;
}
```

```
CArchive& CArchive::operator>>(float& f)
{
    if (m_lpBufCur + sizeof(float) > m_lpBufMax)
        FillBuffer(sizeof(float) - (UINT)(m_lpBufMax -
        m_lpBufCur));

    *(_AFXFLOAT FAR*)&f = *(_AFXFLOAT FAR*)m_lpBufCur;
    m_lpBufCur += sizeof(float);

    if (!(m_nMode & bNoByteSwap))
    {
        _AFXFLOAT fAfx;
        *(float*)&fAfx = f;

        ASSERT(sizeof(float) == 4);

        (*(_AFXFLOAT*)&f).FloatBits[0] = fAfx.FloatBits[3];
        (*(_AFXFLOAT*)&f).FloatBits[1] = fAfx.FloatBits[2];
        (*(_AFXFLOAT*)&f).FloatBits[2] = fAfx.FloatBits[1];
        (*(_AFXFLOAT*)&f).FloatBits[3] = fAfx.FloatBits[0];
    }

    return *this;
}
```

Like the DWORD implementations, the statement *(float*)&fAfx = f; is used to fill the static structure with the 4 unswapped bytes. Then the bytes are swapped one at a time using FloatBits array within the static structure.

Byte-swapping of the 64-bit double type is implemented using the following two functions:

```
CArchive& CArchive::operator<<(double d)
{
    if (m_lpBufCur + sizeof(double) > m_lpBufMax)
        Flush();
```

```
    if (!(m_nMode & bNoByteSwap))
    {
        _AFXDOUBLE dAfx;
        *(double*)&dAfx = d;

        ASSERT(sizeof(double) == 8);

        BYTE* pb = m_lpBufCur;
        *pb++ = dAfx.DoubleBits[7];
        *pb++ = dAfx.DoubleBits[6];
        *pb++ = dAfx.DoubleBits[5];
        *pb++ = dAfx.DoubleBits[4];
        *pb++ = dAfx.DoubleBits[3];
        *pb++ = dAfx.DoubleBits[2];
        *pb++ = dAfx.DoubleBits[1];
        *pb = dAfx.DoubleBits[0];
    }
    else
    {
        *(_AFXDOUBLE FAR*)m_lpBufCur = *(_AFXDOUBLE FAR*)&d;
    }

    m_lpBufCur += sizeof(double);
    return *this;
}
CArchive& CArchive::operator>>(double& d)
{
    if (m_lpBufCur + sizeof(double) > m_lpBufMax)
        FillBuffer(sizeof(double) - (UINT)(m_lpBufMax -
        m_lpBufCur));

    *(_AFXDOUBLE FAR*)&d = *(_AFXDOUBLE FAR*)m_lpBufCur;
    m_lpBufCur += sizeof(double);
```

```
        if (!(m_nMode & bNoByteSwap))
        {
            _AFXDOUBLE dAfx;
            *(double*)&dAfx = d;

            ASSERT(sizeof(double) == 8);

            (*(_AFXDOUBLE*)&d).DoubleBits[0] = dAfx.DoubleBits[7];
            (*(_AFXDOUBLE*)&d).DoubleBits[1] = dAfx.DoubleBits[6];
            (*(_AFXDOUBLE*)&d).DoubleBits[2] = dAfx.DoubleBits[5];
            (*(_AFXDOUBLE*)&d).DoubleBits[3] = dAfx.DoubleBits[4];
            (*(_AFXDOUBLE*)&d).DoubleBits[4] = dAfx.DoubleBits[3];
            (*(_AFXDOUBLE*)&d).DoubleBits[5] = dAfx.DoubleBits[2];
            (*(_AFXDOUBLE*)&d).DoubleBits[6] = dAfx.DoubleBits[1];
            (*(_AFXDOUBLE*)&d).DoubleBits[7] = dAfx.DoubleBits[0];
        }

        return *this;
    }
```

Again, like the other implementations, the statement `*(double*)&dAfx = d;` is used to fill the static structure with the unswapped bytes. Then the bytes are swapped one at a time using the `DoubleBits` array within the static structure. This code allows you to create cross platform with the major fundamental data types, WORD, LONG, DWORD, float, and double.

MFC Simple Value Types

Along with the fundamental data types above, most framework applications will use several of the simple value types supplied by MFC. These simple value types are:

- `CPoint`—encapsulates the Window `POINT` structure, which contains x and y coordinates
- `CRect`—encapsulates the Window `RECT` structure, which contains left, top, right, and bottom coordinates

- CSize—encapsulates the Window SIZE structure, which contains a relative coordinate or position
- CString—a variable-length sequence of characters, the characters are of type **TCHAR,** which is a 16-bit character for UNICODE and an 8-bit character for normal ASCII applications
- CTime—represents an absolute time and date
- CTimeSpan—represents a relative time span of approximately ±68 years

To archive these simple value types, the framework builds on the byte-swapped fundamental types covered in the last section. This layering on top of the fundamental types is the key to serializing your own objects in a cross-platform application database.

Version 3 of MFC for the Macintosh does not support byte-swapped CPoint, CRect, and CSize objects.m Support is planned for MFC 4.

NOTE

The CPoint class is derived from the POINT structure and the archive operators are implemented for the Windows C POINT structure. Since CPoint objects are derived from POINT structures, CPoint objects are archived using the POINT operators. The following code segment contains the portable POINT input and output operators:

```
_AFXWIN_INLINE CArchive& AFXAPI operator<<(CArchive& ar, POINT
point)
{
#ifndef _MAC || WU_BIG_ENDIAN
    ar.Write(&point, sizeof(POINT));
#else
    ar << point.x << point.y;
#endif
    return ar;
}
_AFXWIN_INLINE CArchive& AFXAPI operator>>(CArchive& ar, POINT&
point)
```

```
{
#ifndef _MAC || WU_BIG_ENDIAN
    ar.Read(&point, sizeof(POINT));
#else
    ar >> point.x >> point.y;
#endif
    return ar;
}
```

The portable version of these operators simply serializes two 4-byte LONG types, x and y, instead of directly serializing 8 bytes of untyped data using the CArchive Read and Write members. The implementations of RECT and SIZE are similar to POINT, as illustrated in the next code segment:

```
_AFXWIN_INLINE CArchive& AFXAPI operator<<(CArchive& ar, RECT
rect)
{
#ifndef _MAC || WU_BIG_ENDIAN
    ar.Write(&rect, sizeof(RECT));
#else
    ar << rect.left << rect.top << rect.right << rect.bottom;
#endif
    return ar;
}
_AFXWIN_INLINE CArchive& AFXAPI operator>>(CArchive& ar, RECT&
rect)
{
#ifndef _MAC || WU_BIG_ENDIAN
    ar.Read(&rect, sizeof(RECT));
#else
    ar >> rect.left >> rect.top >> rect.right >> rect.bottom;
#endif
    return ar;
}
_AFXWIN_INLINE CArchive& AFXAPI operator<<(CArchive& ar, SIZE
size)
```

```
{
#ifndef _MAC || WU_BIG_ENDIAN
    ar.Write(&size, sizeof(SIZE));
#else
    ar << size.cx << size.cy;
#endif
    return ar;
}
_AFXWIN_INLINE CArchive& AFXAPI operator>>(CArchive& ar, size&
SIZE)
{
#ifndef _MAC || WU_BIG_ENDIAN
    ar.Read(&size, sizeof(SIZE));
#else
    ar >> size.cx >> size.cy;
#endif
    return ar;
}
```

The portable version for RECT structures simply serializes four 4-byte LONG types; the nonportable version serializes 16 bytes of untyped data. Similarly, the portable version of SIZE serializes two 4-byte LONG types; the nonportable version serializes 8 bytes of untyped data.

At first glance, CString objects seem inherently portable, but the object contains a length that needs to be byte-swapped, and serialization must deal with the interoperability of ANSI and UNICODE strings. The following code segment from **arccore.c** illustrates this complexity:

```
CArchive& AFXAPI operator<<(CArchive& ar, const CString& string)
{
    // special signature to recognize unicode strings
#ifdef _UNICODE
    ar << (BYTE)0xff;
    ar << (WORD)0xfffe;
#endif
```

```
    if (string.m_nDataLength < 255)
    {
        ar << (BYTE)string.m_nDataLength;
    }
    else if (string.m_nDataLength < 0xfffe)
    {
        ar << (BYTE)0xff;
        ar << (WORD)string.m_nDataLength;
    }
    else
    {
        ar << (BYTE)0xff;
        ar << (WORD)0xffff;
        ar << (DWORD)string.m_nDataLength;
    }
    ar.Write(string.m_pchData,
string.m_nDataLength*sizeof(TCHAR));
    return ar;
}
// return string length or -1 if UNICODE string is found in the
   archive
static UINT AFXAPI ReadStringLength(CArchive& ar)
{
    DWORD nNewLen;

    // attempt BYTE length first
    BYTE bLen;
    ar >> bLen;

    if (bLen < 0xff)
        return bLen;

    // attempt WORD length
    WORD wLen;
```

```
        ar >> wLen;
        if (wLen == 0xfffe)
        {
            // UNICODE string prefix (length will follow)
            return (UINT)-1;
        }
        else if (wLen == 0xffff)
        {
            // read DWORD of length
            ar >> nNewLen;
            return (UINT)nNewLen;
        }
        else
            return wLen;
    }
CArchive& AFXAPI operator>>(CArchive& ar, CString& string)
{
#ifdef _UNICODE
    int nConvert = 1;   // if we get ANSI, convert
#else
    int nConvert = 0;   // if we get UNICODE, convert
#endif

    UINT nNewLen = ReadStringLength(ar);
    if (nNewLen == (UINT)-1)
    {
        nConvert = 1 - nConvert;
        nNewLen = ReadStringLength(ar);
        ASSERT(nNewLen != -1);
    }

    // set length of string to new length
    UINT nByteLen = nNewLen;
#ifdef _UNICODE
```

```
    string.GetBufferSetLength((int)nNewLen);
    nByteLen += nByteLen * (1 - nConvert);  // bytes to read
#else
    nByteLen += nByteLen * nConvert;     // bytes to read
    string.GetBufferSetLength((int)nByteLen);
#endif

    // read in the characters
    if (nNewLen != 0)
    {
        ASSERT(nByteLen != 0);

        // read new data
        if (ar.Read(string.m_pchData, nByteLen) != nByteLen)

AfxThrowArchiveException(CArchiveException::endOfFile);

#ifndef _MAC
        // convert the data if as necessary
        if (nConvert != 0)
        {
#ifdef _UNICODE
            LPSTR pszData = (LPSTR)string.m_pchData;
#else
            LPWSTR pszData = (LPWSTR)string.m_pchData;
#endif
            ASSERT((LPTSTR)pszData != &afxChNil);
            pszData[nNewLen] = '\0';    // must be NUL terminated
            string.m_pchData = &afxChNil;   // don't delete the
                                                data
            string.Empty();
            string = pszData;   // convert with operator=(LPWCSTR)
            delete[] (LPTSTR)pszData;
        }
#endif
```

```
    }
    return ar;
}
```

The header in a serialized CString contains information on both the length of the string and the type of the string, ANSI or UNICODE. This information is encoded in the first few bytes' archive as follows:

String length	Encoding
Less than 255	Byte 1 contains string length
Less than 65535	Byte 1 = 0xFF, bytes 2 and 3 are a WORD containing the string length
Greater than 65534	Byte 1 = 0xFF, bytes 2 and 3 = 0xFFFF, bytes 4, 5, 6, and 7 are a DWORD containing the string length

UNICODE strings contain a leading 0xFF, 0xFFFe before the length information. In general, UNICODE is not supported on all architectures and should not be used in the cross-platform application.

The CTime and CTimeSpan objects contain the time component as a time_t type. The time_t type in turn is defined as a LONG. Thus, serializing these time objects is as easy as casting the time component to a portable fundamental data type. The following code segment illustrates serializing these time components using portable DWORDs:

```
CArchive& AFXAPI operator <<(CArchive& ar, CTime time)
{
    return ar << (DWORD) time.m_time;
}

CArchive& AFXAPI operator >>(CArchive& ar, CTime& rtime)
{
    return ar >> (DWORD&) rtime.m_time;
}
CArchive& AFXAPI operator <<(CArchive& ar, CTimeSpan timeSpan)
{
    return ar << (DWORD) timeSpan.m_timeSpan;
```

```
}

CArchive& AFXAPI operator >>(CArchive& ar, CTimeSpan& rtimeSpan)
{
    return ar >> (DWORD&) rtimeSpan.m_timeSpan;
}
```

When serializing these MFC simple-value types, the application database remains cross-platform compatible. As an application developer, you will find that any required byte swapping is handled by the framework, hidden from you.

MFC Collection Classes

The MFC collection classes are used throughout the implementation of MFC—including serialization—and by most developers using MFC. MFC has a wide variety of collection classes—arrays, lists, and maps—in both template-based implementations (new for MFC 3) and nontemplate-based implementations. The cross-platform serialization portability of these classes varies. The next few sections enumerates the template classes and discusses if they should be used for architecture-independent application databases.

All MFC 3 collection classes cast the integer number of elements in the collection, m_nSize, to a 16-bit unsigned short (WORD) when archiving. Therefore, serialization of collections that contain more than 64K items will fail.

WARNING

Arrays

CByteArray

The CByteArray class supports dynamic arrays of bytes. The serialize function: void CByteArray::Serialize(CArchive& ar) simply reads/writes the byte array bits. Since the data is bytes it should not need to be byte-swapped; therefore, the CByteArray serialization is portable.

```
void CByteArray::Serialize(CArchive& ar)
{
    ASSERT_VALID(this);
```

```
    CObject::Serialize(ar);

    if (ar.IsStoring())
    {
        ar << (WORD) m_nSize;
        ar.Write(m_pData, m_nSize * sizeof(BYTE));
    }
    else
    {
        WORD nOldSize;
        ar >> nOldSize;
        SetSize(nOldSize);
        ar.Read(m_pData, m_nSize * sizeof(BYTE));
    }
}
```

CDWordArray

The CDWordArray class supports arrays of 32-bit doublewords. The serialization function, void CDWordArray::Serialize(CArchive& ar), simply reads/writes the DWORD array bits. Since the DWORD storage is architecture-dependent, the data must be byte-swapped. Therefore the CDWordArray serialization is not portable.

NOTE

Check latest production documentation: MFC 3 on the Macintosh did not byte-swap, Support is planned for MFC 4 for the Macintosh.

```
void CDWordArray::Serialize(CArchive& ar)
{
    ASSERT_VALID(this);

    CObject::Serialize(ar);
```

```
    if (ar.IsStoring())
    {
        ar << (WORD) m_nSize;
        ar.Write(m_pData, m_nSize * sizeof(DWORD));
    }
    else
    {
        WORD nOldSize;
        ar >> nOldSize;
        SetSize(nOldSize);
        ar.Read(m_pData, m_nSize * sizeof(DWORD));
    }
}
```

CObArray

The CObArray class supports arrays of CObject pointers. The serialization function, void CObArray::Serialize(CArchive& ar), loops through all objects in the array serialization each object in turn. Therefore, CObArray is portable, but the serialization of the object itself must also be portable.

```
void CObArray::Serialize(CArchive& ar)
{
    ASSERT_VALID(this);

    CObject::Serialize(ar);

    if (ar.IsStoring())
    {
        ar << (WORD) m_nSize;
        for (int i = 0; i < m_nSize; i++)
            ar << m_pData[i];
    }
    else
    {
```

```
    WORD nOldSize;
    ar >> nOldSize;
    SetSize(nOldSize);
    for (int i = 0; i < m_nSize; i++)
        ar >> m_pData[i];
    }
}
```

CPtrArray

The CPtrArray class supports arrays of void pointers. The CPtrArray class does not support serialization.

CStringArray

The CStringArray class supports arrays of CString pointers. The serialization function, `void CStringArray::Serialize(CArchive& ar)`, loops through all CString objects in the array, serializing each object in turn. Therefore, CStringArray is completely portable, since the serialization of the CString object is portable.

```
void CStringArray::Serialize(CArchive& ar)
{
    ASSERT_VALID(this);

    CObject::Serialize(ar);

    if (ar.IsStoring())
    {
        ar << (WORD) m_nSize;
        for (int i = 0; i < m_nSize; i++)
            ar << m_pData[i];
    }
    else
    {
        WORD nOldSize;
```

```
    ar >> nOldSize;
    SetSize(nOldSize);
    for (int i = 0; i < m_nSize; i++)
        ar >> m_pData[i];
    }
}
```

CWordArray

The CDWordArray class supports arrays of 16-bit unsigned words. The serialization function, void CWordArray::Serialize(CArchive& ar), like CDWordArray, simply reads/writes the WORD array bits. Since the WORD storage is architecture-dependent, the data must be byte-swapped. Therefore, the CWordArray serialization may not be portable.

NOTE

Check latest product documentation: MFC 3 on the Macintosh did not byte-swap. Support is planned for MFC 4 for the Macintosh.

```
void CWordArray::Serialize(CArchive& ar)
{
    ASSERT_VALID(this);

    CObject::Serialize(ar);

    if (ar.IsStoring())
    {
        ar << (WORD) m_nSize;
        ar.Write(m_pData, m_nSize * sizeof(WORD));
    }
    else
    {
        WORD nOldSize;
        ar >> nOldSize;
```

```
        SetSize(nOldSize);
        ar.Read(m_pData, m_nSize * sizeof(WORD));
    }
}
```

CUIntArray

The CUIntArray class supports arrays of unsigned integers. The CUIntArray class does not support serialization.

Lists

MFC supplies predefined list classes for CString objects, CObject pointers, and void pointers. A *list* is an ordered grouping of elements. New elements can be added at the head or tail of the list, or before or after a specified element. The list can be traversed in forward or reverse sequence, and elements can be retrieved or removed during the traversal. The lists are implemented using a doubly linked list data structure.

CObList

The CObList class supports ordered lists of nonunique CObject pointers accessible sequentially or by pointer value. The serialization function, void CObList::Serialize(CArchive& ar), iterates over all CObject pointers in the list, serializing each object in turn. Therefore, CObList can be made portable, since the serialization of the CObject-derived object is responsible for portability.

```
    void CObList::Serialize(CArchive& ar)
    {
        ASSERT_VALID(this);

        CObject::Serialize(ar);
        if (ar.IsStoring())
        {
            ar << (WORD) m_nCount;
            for (CNode* pNode = m_pNodeHead; pNode != NULL; pNode =
            pNode->pNext)
```

```
            {
                ASSERT(AfxIsValidAddress(pNode, sizeof(CNode)));
                ar << pNode->data;
            }
        }
        else
        {
            WORD nNewCount;
            ar >> nNewCount;

            CObject* newData;
            while (nNewCount--)
            {
                ar >> newData;
                AddTail(newData);
            }
        }
    }
```

CStringList

The CObList class supports ordered lists of nonunique CObject pointers accessible sequentially or by pointer value. The serialization function, `void CObList::Serialize(CArchive& ar)`, iterates over all CObject pointers in the list, serializing each object in turn. Therefore, CObList can be made portable, since the serialization of the CObject-derived object is responsible for portability.

```
    void CStringList::Serialize(CArchive& ar)
    {
        ASSERT_VALID(this);

        CObject::Serialize(ar);

        if (ar.IsStoring())
        {
            ar << (WORD) m_nCount;
```

```
        for (CNode* pNode = m_pNodeHead; pNode != NULL; pNode =
        pNode->pNext)
        {
            ASSERT(AfxIsValidAddress(pNode, sizeof(CNode)));
            ar << pNode->data;
        }
    }
    else
    {
        WORD nNewCount;
        ar >> nNewCount;

        CString newData;
        while (nNewCount--)
        {
            ar >> newData;
            AddTail(newData);
        }
    }
}
```

CPtrList

The CPtrList class supports lists of untyped pointers. The CPtrList class does not support serialization.

Maps

In MFC, *maps* are dictionaries that map keys to values. MFC supplies predefined map classes that support CString objects, WORDs, CObject pointers, and void pointers.

CMapPtrToPtr

The CMapPtrToPtr class supports maps of void pointers keyed by void pointers. The CMapPtrToPtr class does not support serialization.

CMapPtrToWord

The CMapPtrToWord class supports maps of 16-bit words keyed by void pointers. The CMapPtrToWord class does not support serialization.

CMapStringToOb

CMapStringToOb is a dictionary collection class that maps unique CString objects to CObject pointers. The CMapStringToOb class supports portable serialization by iterating over all elements in the map, serializing each one individually. The CString key object is completely portable and the CObject value object relies on the object's serialization to the portable.

```
void CMapStringToOb::Serialize(CArchive& ar)
{
    ASSERT_VALID(this);

    CObject::Serialize(ar);

    if (ar.IsStoring())
    {
        ar << (WORD) m_nCount;
        if (m_nCount == 0)
            return;  // nothing more to do

        ASSERT(m_pHashTable != NULL);
        for (UINT nHash = 0; nHash < m_nHashTableSize; nHash++)
        {
            CAssoc* pAssoc;
            for (pAssoc = m_pHashTable[nHash]; pAssoc != NULL;
              pAssoc = pAssoc->pNext)
            {
                ar << pAssoc->key;
                ar << pAssoc->value;
            }
        }
    }
```

```
    }
    else
    {
        WORD wNewCount;
        ar >> wNewCount;

        CString newKey;
        CObject* newValue;
        while (wNewCount--)
        {
            ar >> newKey;
            ar >> newValue;
            SetAt(newKey, newValue);
        }
    }
}
```

CMapStringToPtr

The CMapStringToPtr class supports maps of void pointers keyed by CString objects. The CMapStringToPtr class does not support serialization.

CMapStringToString

The CMapStringToString class supports maps of CString objects keyed by CString objects. The CMapStringToString class supports completely portable serialization by iterating over all elements in the map, serializing each one individually. The CString key and value objects are completely portable.

```
void CMapStringToString::Serialize(CArchive& ar)
{
    ASSERT_VALID(this);

    CObject::Serialize(ar);

    if (ar.IsStoring())
```

```
    {
        ar << (WORD) m_nCount;
        if (m_nCount == 0)
            return;  // nothing more to do

        ASSERT(m_pHashTable != NULL);
        for (UINT nHash = 0; nHash < m_nHashTableSize; nHash++)
        {
            CAssoc* pAssoc;
            for (pAssoc = m_pHashTable[nHash]; pAssoc != NULL;
              pAssoc = pAssoc->pNext)
            {
                ar << pAssoc->key;
                ar << pAssoc->value;
            }
        }
    }
    else
    {
        WORD wNewCount;
        ar >> wNewCount;

        CString newKey;
        CString newValue;
        while (wNewCount--)
        {
            ar >> newKey;
            ar >> newValue;
            SetAt(newKey, newValue);
        }
    }
}
```

CMapWordToOb

The CMapWordToOb class supports maps of CObject pointers keyed by 16-bit words. The CMapWordToOb class supports portable serialization by iterating over all elements in the map, serializing each one individually. The WORD key object is completely portable and the CObject value object relies on the object's serialization to the portable.

```
void CMapWordToOb::Serialize(CArchive& ar)
{
    ASSERT_VALID(this);

    CObject::Serialize(ar);

    if (ar.IsStoring())
    {
        ar << (WORD) m_nCount;
        if (m_nCount == 0)
            return;  // nothing more to do

        ASSERT(m_pHashTable != NULL);
        for (UINT nHash = 0; nHash < m_nHashTableSize; nHash++)
        {
            CAssoc* pAssoc;
            for (pAssoc = m_pHashTable[nHash]; pAssoc != NULL;
              pAssoc = pAssoc->pNext)
            {
                ar << pAssoc->key;
                ar << pAssoc->value;
            }
        }
    }
    else
    {
```

```
        WORD wNewCount;
        ar >> wNewCount;
        WORD newKey;
        CObject* newValue;
        while (wNewCount--)
        {
            ar >> newKey;
            ar >> newValue;
            SetAt(newKey, newValue);
        }
    }
}
```

CMapWordToPtr

The CMapWordToPtr class supports maps of void pointers keyed by 16-bit words. The CMapWordToPtr class does not support serialization.

Template Collection Classes

The template-based collection classes were introduced with MFC 3. These template collection classes, like the collection classes above, can hold a variety of objects in arrays, lists, and maps. These collection classes are templates whose parameters determine the types of the objects stored in the aggregates. To make these classes serializable, the Serialize and SerializeElements helper functions have been incorporated into the template implementations.

Collection	Type
CArray	Stores elements in an array.
CMap	Maps keys to values.
CList	Stores elements in a linked list.
CTypedPtrList	Type-safe collection that stores pointers to objects in a linked list.
CTypedPtrArray	Type-safe collection that stores pointers to objects in an array.
CTypedPtrMap	Type-safe collection that maps keys to values; both keys and values are pointers.

The CArray, CList, and CMap classes call `SerializeElements` to store collection elements to or read them from an archive. The default implementation of the `SerializeElements` helper function is not portable and does a bitwise write from the objects to the archive, or a bitwise read from the archive to the objects, depending on whether the objects are being stored in or retrieved from the archive. For a cross platform application database you must override `SerializeElements`. The following is the default nonportable `SerializeElements` function from **afxtempl.h**:

```
template<class TYPE>
void AFXAPI SerializeElements(CArchive& ar, TYPE* pElements, int
nCount)
{
    ASSERT(AfxIsValidAddress(pElements, nCount * sizeof(TYPE)));

    // default is bit-wise read/write
    if (ar.IsStoring())
        ar.Write((void*)pElements, nCount * sizeof(TYPE));  //
        untyped write
    else
        ar.Read((void*)pElements, nCount * sizeof(TYPE)); //
        untyped read
}
```

To serialize CObject-derived objects that have IMPLEMENT_SERIAL included, an implementation modeled after the following will keep your database portable:

```
CStroke : public CObject { . . . };
CArray< CMyKidsObject, CMyKidsObject& > kidsArray;

void SerializeElements( CArchive& ar, CMyKidsObject* pKids, int
nCount )
{
    for ( int i = 0; i < nCount; i++, pKids++ )
    {
        // Serialize each CMyKidsObject object
        if ( ar.IsStoring() )
```

```
            ar << pKids;
        else
            ar >> pKids;
    }
}
```

In the above SerializeElements, instead of a single untyped **ar.Read** or **ar.Write**, each object is serialized using its own serialization ability. In this case, for each object in the array, the overridden input or output operator is used to create a portable database. While the above code makes sense for CArray template collections, where pKids is the head of the array, it is not obvious how this could work for CList or CMap collections where there is no array of elements. But, it does work! The implementations of CArray, CList, and CMap Serialize are good examples of creating portable Serialize functions. Taking a closer look will explain how SerializeElements can work for CList and CMap and will demonstrate portable Serialize functions. First, void CArray::Serialize:

```
template<class TYPE, class ARG_TYPE>
void CArray<TYPE, ARG_TYPE>::Serialize(CArchive& ar)
{
    ASSERT_VALID(this);

    CObject::Serialize(ar);
    if (ar.IsStoring())
    {
        ar << (WORD) m_nSize;
    }
    else
    {
        WORD nOldSize;
        ar >> nOldSize;
        SetSize(nOldSize);
    }
    SerializeElements(ar, m_pData, m_nSize);
}
```

There are three basic steps in `CArray::Serialize`:

1. Serialize the parent class, CObject for CArray.
2. Serialize local member data, the array size m_nSize.
3. Serialize the element data, using SerializeElements.

Now, looking at the `CList Serialize` function:

```
template<class TYPE, class ARG_TYPE>
void CList<TYPE, ARG_TYPE>::Serialize(CArchive& ar)
{
    ASSERT_VALID(this);

    CObject::Serialize(ar);

    if (ar.IsStoring())
    {
        ar << (WORD) m_nCount;
        for (CNode* pNode = m_pNodeHead; pNode != NULL; pNode =
        pNode->pNext)
        {
            ASSERT(AfxIsValidAddress(pNode, sizeof(CNode)));
            SerializeElements(ar, &pNode->data, 1);
        }
    }
    else
    {
        WORD nNewCount;
        ar >> nNewCount;

        TYPE newData;
        while (nNewCount--)
        {
            SerializeElements(ar, &newData, 1);
            AddTail(newData);
```

```
        }
    }
}
```

Again, you can break CList Serialize into the same three steps:

1. Serialize the parent class, CObject for CList.
2. Serialize local member data, the number of nodes in the list, m_nCount.
3. Serialize the element data node by node, using SerializeElements.

For CList collections, SerializeElements is called for every node in the list, with an item count of 1. In CArray, SerializeElements is called once; in CList, SerializeElements is called for every element in the list.

Lastly, CMap builds on this concept as follows:

```
template<class KEY, class ARG_KEY, class VALUE, class ARG_VALUE>
void CMap<KEY, ARG_KEY, VALUE, ARG_VALUE>::Serialize(CArchive& ar)
{
    ASSERT_VALID(this);

    CObject::Serialize(ar);

    if (ar.IsStoring())
    {
        ar << (WORD) m_nCount;
        if (m_nCount == 0)
            return;   // nothing more to do

        ASSERT(m_pHashTable != NULL);
        for (UINT nHash = 0; nHash < m_nHashTableSize; nHash++)
        {
            CAssoc* pAssoc;
            for (pAssoc = m_pHashTable[nHash]; pAssoc != NULL;
              pAssoc = pAssoc->pNext)
```

```
            {
                SerializeElements(ar, &pAssoc->key, 1);
                SerializeElements(ar, &pAssoc->value, 1);
            }
        }
    }
    else
    {
        WORD wNewCount;
        ar >> wNewCount;

        KEY newKey;
        VALUE newValue;
        while (wNewCount--)
        {
            SerializeElements(ar, &newKey, 1);
            SerializeElements(ar, &newValue, 1);
            SetAt(newKey, newValue);
        }
    }
}
```

Again, you can break CMap Serialize into the same three steps:

1. Serialize the parent class, CObject for CMap.
2. Serialize local member data, the number of map entries, m_nCount.
3. Serialize the entry data node by node, using SerializeElements.

For CMap collections SerializeElements is called twice for every entry in the map, each time with an item count of 1. While SerializeElements is called a different number of times for each collection type—CArray = once, CList = the number of items, CMap = twice the number of items—the purpose is the same: to allow the developer to control what is archived. Thus, a cross-platform database can be created using the MFC template-based collections.

MFC Architecture Classes

While MFC collections handle mostly the low-level serializations, the architecture class contains a thread of serialization logic to help manage the serialization process. For example, `void CDocItem::Serialize(CArchive& ar)` defines the serialization process, but does not actually serialize any data. Where MFC has implemented serialization in a view, in CEditView, the serialization is portable and can be used in a cross-platform database. For CEditView the following member functions are used:

`void CEditView::Serialize (CArchive& ar)`	Serialize number of characters (not bytes) using a DWORD
`void CEditView:: ReadFrom-Archive (CArchive& ar, UINT nLen)`	Read a number of characters
`void CEditView:: WriteToArchive (CArchive& ar)`	Write a number of characters
`void CEditView:: SerializeRaw (CArchive& ar)`	Read/write simple text files without DWORD header

For CDocItem, the OLE classes COleClientItem and COleDocument are used to encapsulate the serialization logic. Only CollectItem is used to store data directly into the archive. The data stored by COleClientItem is completely portable

Other MFC Classes

There are a few additional MFC classes involved in serialization process. The CRuntimeClass has `Load` and `Store` functions that deal with an object's name and schema. This information is serialized in a portable format. The schema is stored as a WORD and the class name is stored in two parts, the length as a WORD and string bytes. The only other MFC class that directly serializes data is the docking toolbar class introduced in MFC 3. If you use the built-in ability to serialize the toolbar state using `CDockState::Serialize`, the information serialized by _AFX_BARINFO is not portable in the initial released of MFC 3 on Macintosh. Check the latest product documentation. The initial release of MFC 3 serialized an array of intergers as a byte stream, not allowing for the byte-swapping of individaul elements.

Changing Scribble for Cross-Platform Serialization

This section discusses the changes required to the Scribble sample application, as defined in samples/mfc/scribble/step6. Since Scribble uses the MFC serialization, architecture is mostly portable. The main change required is overridding the SerializeElements helper function for the CArray<CPoint, CPoint> template array.

The following call stack is from the nonportable version of Scribble. The call to CArchive::Write to save the array of CPoints as untyped data creates the nonportable database. The locations in the CPoint structures need to be byte-swapped.

```
CArchive::Write(void * 0x0076314c, unsigned int 0) line 647

SerializeElements(CArchive & {...}, CPoint * 0x0076304c, int 32)
line 62

CArray<CPoint,CPoint>::Serialize(CArchive & {...}) line 414 + 23
bytes

CStroke::Serialize(CArchive & {...}) line 160

CArchive::WriteObject(const CObject * 0x00762964) line 107

operator<<(CArchive & {...}, const CObject * 0x00762964) line 347
+ 18 bytes

CObList::Serialize(CArchive & {...}) line 356

CScribDoc::Serialize(CArchive & {...}) line 74

CDocument::OnSaveDocument(char * 0x00764c18) line 628

CDocument::DoSave(char * 0x00000000, int 1) line 344 + 20 bytes

CDocument::DoFileSave() line 279 + 15 bytes

CDocument::OnFileSave() line 265

DispatchCmdMsg(CCmdTarget * 0x007618e4, unsigned int 57603, int 0,
void (void)* 0x5f82a36c CDocument::OnFileSave(void), void *
0x00000000, unsigned int 10, AFX_CMDHANDLERINFO * 0x00000000) line
96

CCmdTarget::OnCmdMsg(unsigned int 57603, int 0, void * 0x00000000,
AFX_CMDHANDLERINFO * 0x00000000) line 235 + 39 bytes

CDocument::OnCmdMsg(unsigned int 57603, int 0, void * 0x00000000,
AFX_CMDHANDLERINFO * 0x00000000) line 816 + 24 bytes
```

```
CView::OnCmdMsg(unsigned int 57603, int 0, void * 0x00000000,
AFX_CMDHANDLERINFO * 0x00000000) line 164 + 33 bytes
CFrameWnd::OnCmdMsg(unsigned int 57603, int 0, void * 0x00000000,
AFX_CMDHANDLERINFO * 0x00000000) line 808 + 37 bytes
CWnd::OnCommand(unsigned int 57603, long 0) line 1714 + 23 bytes
CFrameWnd::OnCommand(unsigned int 57603, long 0) line 302 + 16
bytes
CWnd::WindowProc(unsigned int 273, unsigned int 57603, long 0)
line 1341 + 25 bytes
AfxCallWndProc(CWnd * 0x00761a54, HWND__ * 0x00000c38, unsigned
int 273, unsigned int 57603, long 0) line 217 + 23 bytes
CMDIFrameWnd::OnCommand(unsigned int 57603, long 0) line 57 + 39
bytes
CWnd::WindowProc(unsigned int 273, unsigned int 57603, long 0)
line 1341 + 25 bytes
AfxCallWndProc(CWnd * 0x00760a8c, HWND__ * 0x00000c18, unsigned
int 273, unsigned int 57603, long 0) line 217 + 23 bytes
AfxWndProc(HWND__ * 0x00000c18, unsigned int 273, unsigned int
57603, long 0) line 316 + 25 bytes
USER32! bff23419()
97700003()
```

Creating the following `SerializeElements` function to serialize the CPoint array point by point allows for the opportunity to perform byte-swapping. While this function has no direct dependencies to Scribble, it can be added to the bottom of **scribdoc.cpp**.

```
void SerializeElements( CArchive& ar, CPoint* pPoints, int nCount
)
{
    for ( int i = 0; i < nCount; i++, pPoints++ )
    {
        // Serialize each CPoint object
        if ( ar.IsStoring() )
            ar << pPoints;
```

```
        else
            ar >> pPoints;
    }
}
```

With the above function, the call stack becomes:

With minimal changes, only the addition of one function, Scribble's application database has become a cross-platform database. Now, Scribbles created on Windows 95, Windows NT, Macintosh, and UNIX share a common database format—a format that the Windows versions have already been writing and a format that requires no changes in the MFC DLL shipped with Visual C++.

Summary

Creating a cross-platform application database has always been a tedious task and full of trade-offs. As you have seen, using the MFC serialization functions and creating a compact binary database with little-endian byte ordering has never been as easy. You have already been creating this portable database with MFC serialization on Windows, and now with a few changes to your source code, UNIX and Macintosh applications can read and write the same database.

CHAPTER 6

Using Dialogs

Dialog boxes are one of the key user-interface components of your application, and can have a significant impact on the usability of your product. This chapter discusses the following issues that you should be aware of when planning dialogs for your cross-platform application:

- Differences between Windows and Macintosh dialog boxes
- Differences between Windows and OSF/Motif dialog boxes
- The use of custom controls in ported dialogs
- The use of common dialogs in cross-platform applications
- Support status for all dialog box APIs

Dialog Overview

Virtually all Windows applications use dialogs to interact with the user. Some applications use simple dialogs to open files, provide status information, and configure options. Others use dialogs more extensively to provide data input forms. With Visual C++ and MFC, dialogs become especially powerful and easy to develop for the following reasons:

- Visual C++ provides a very friendly dialog designer in AppStudio.
- MFC provides powerful data validation and dialog handling functionality.

In the past, dialogs have been some of the more difficult components to develop for Windows applications. Now, with Visual C++ and MFC, they are among the most straightforward components to develop.

Just as Visual C++ and MFC make Windows dialogs easy to create, the Visual C++ Extensions for Macintosh and Wind/U make porting dialogs to Macintosh and UNIX easy. Both of these cross-platform environments support virtually all of the dialog APIs and MFC classes.

Macintosh Dialog Box Overview

Differences between the standard dialog box interfaces for the Macintosh and Windows can introduce significant incompatibilities. By default, dialog boxes managed by the Windows Portability Library follow Macintosh conventions, which are different from Windows dialog boxes in the following ways:

- Macintosh dialog boxes allow focus to go only to edit controls and list boxes; in Windows, focus can go to any control, including pushbuttons, radio buttons, and checkboxes.

- In Macintosh dialogs, pressing the **Tab** key or sending the **WM_NEXTDLGCTL** message moves the focus to the next control that accepts keystrokes, instead of to the next control that has the tabstop style bit set. By default, the only controls that accept keystrokes are edit controls, list boxes, and nondropdown-list combo boxes. However, the user can still use Command-Tab to move the focus to the next control with the tabstop style bit set.

- Showing the selection when an edit control does not have the focus is not common practice on the Macintosh. Therefore, the **ES_HIDESEL** style bit is not turned on in the edit control created by combo box controls.

- A pushbutton does not become the default button when clicked, as it does in Windows.

- A Macintosh list box with the focus draws a bold border around itself.

- Clicking on the scrollbar of a Macintosh list box causes the focus to move to that list box.

In addition to the standard Macintosh dialog box, the Windows Portability Library also implements a dialog box interface consistent with Windows, using the **DS_WINDOWSUI** style. You can include this style flag when you create dialog boxes (usually in the **STYLE** section of your .RC file). This capability is important if your users expect to see a consistent user interface among all versions of your application. In most cases, however, your users will probably expect a user interface similar to native applications for each platform.

Unless you use the **DS_WINDOWSUI** style, your dialog boxes will follow Macintosh conventions by default. Because of the differences above, you need to test your dialog boxes carefully to ensure that these differences do not interfere with their usability.

Unix Dialog Box Overview

We have seen that there are significant differences between Macintosh and Windows dialog boxes. For most Windows dialogs, the Windows Portability Library and the Macintosh version of MFC handle these differences transparently to your application. You need only be concerned about how these differences might affect the usability of your user interface.

In the UNIX environment, dialog box look-and-feel is much more compatible with Windows, primarily because of the common background of the OSF/Motif and Microsoft Windows graphical user interfaces. In particular, the focus policies and tab traversal are close enough between Windows and OSF/Motif for any differences to be relatively insignificant to your application. The Wind/U portability toolkit handles any such slight differences.

While the functionality and look-and-feel are very similar for both Windows and OSF/Motif dialog boxes, dialog performance can be tricky in the OSF/Motif environment. Because of the distributed architecture of the X Window System (on which OSF/Motif is based), window creation and redraws can be slower. As we will see later in this chapter, Wind/U provides enhancements that can significantly increase dialog performance in the X Window System environment.

Mapping Windows Controls to Motif Widgets

OSF/Motif and Windows share some common heritage in the early OS/2 Presentation Manager design work done by Microsoft and IBM. Over the years, however, there has been a divergence in design of these two graphical user-interface environments.

The most significant difference is the set of controls (known as "widgets" in the OSF/Motif world) that each environment supports. For instance, until very recently, OSF/Motif did not support a control equivalent to the Windows combo box control. Where there are analogous OSF/Motif and Windows controls, the Windows controls in general provide many features not available in the OSF/Motif widgets.

Some of these advanced features are the owner-drawn listbox and combo box, tabbed lists, sorted lists, and user-defined word breaks in edit controls. To provide Windows-compatible controls in the OSF/Motif environment, Wind/U enhances many of the standard Motif widgets to provide these missing advanced features. By subclassing the standard OSF/Motif widgets to provide these enhancements (as opposed to rewritting or emulating them), Wind/U is able to provide Windows compatibility and also maintain complete consistency with OSF/Motif look and feel.

Table 6.1 shows the underlying widget hiearchy used by Wind/U to implement Windows-compatible controls in the OSF/Motif environment:

Table 6.1 Windows Controls to Motif Widgets

Windows Control	Motif Widget
Listbox	XmList subclassed for tabs and ownerdrawn
Scrollbar	XmScroll
Button (radio, check, etc.)	XmToggle, XmRadio
Edit	XmText
Static	XmLabel
Groupbox	XmFrame

Dialog Box Controls

The most significant difference between Windows and Windows Portability Library controls is that the following classes are implemented using native Macintosh controls:

- Button, edit, and scroll bar window classes
- Dropdown and dropdown-list combo box window classes

This difference has several consequences:

- Mouse tracking for these controls occurs during the first **WM_MOUSEMOVE** after a mouse-down in the control. Therefore, tracking is completely modal and takes place entirely inside the Macintosh system software. Neither your message loop nor the control's **wndproc** will receive **WM_MOUSEMOVE** messages during mouse tracking.

- QuickDraw does not support some font attributes, such as *strikethrough*. Instead, the Windows Portability Library GDI synthesizes them. Since QuickDraw draws the the titles of these controls, if you use the **WM_SETFONT** message to change the font of the control, only those font attributes supported directly by QuickDraw are displayed.

- In Windows it is possible to print a control by sending a **WM_PAINT** message to the control, with the wParam of the message being a printer HDC. This method does not generally work for those Windows Portability Library controls that are based on native Macintosh controls.

For UNIX applications, Wind/U implements all Windows control classes as OSF/Motif widgets. Some consequences of this design are listed below:

- Unlike the Windows Portability Library for Macintosh, Wind/U controls provides mouse tracking consistent with Windows.

- Some attributes of a font, such as strikethrough, are not supported by OSF/Motif and are synthesized by the Wind/U GDI instead. Since OSF/Motif draws the the titles of these controls, if you use the **WM_SETFONT** message to change the font of the control, only those font attributes supported directly by OSF/Motif are displayed.

- In Windows it is possible to print a control by sending a **WM_PAINT** message to the control, with the wParam of the message being a printer HDC. This method does not generally work Wind/U controls that are based on native OSF/Motif controls.

Buttons

Since the Windows Portability Library implements button window classes with native Macintosh controls, there are differences in buttons on the Macintosh and in Windows. These differences affect tri-state checkboxes and button size.

In Windows, the third state of a tri-state checkbox is a gray-filled square. Because the Windows Portability Library follows the Macintosh standard, the default appearance of the third state of a tri-state checkbox is a checkbox-sized square with a dash in the middle. If a tri-state checkbox has the **WS_EX_WINDOWSUI** style bit added to its extended style flags, its third state has the Windows appearance of a gray-filled square.

On the Macintosh, the client area of a pushbutton control includes a four-pixel space on all sides for a bold border. Therefore, the button itself is smaller on the Macintosh than it is on Windows. You may need to edit your dialog box resources to increase the size of your buttons. The **BS_USERBUTTON** style is not supported.

On UNIX systems, Wind/U maps the Windows button class to a variety of different OSF/Motif widgets, depending on the style of the button. The **BS_PUSHBUTTON** (and **BS_DEFPUSHBUTTON**) are mapped to the XmPushButton widget, while the **BS_CHECKBOX, BS_RADIOBUTTON,** and **BS_3STATE** styles are mapped to XmToggleButton widgets.

The other significant button style, **BS_GROUPBOX**, is mapped to custom logic inside of Wind/U, rather than to an OSF/Motif widget. In the Wind/U environment, group boxes do not have an associated X Window, and therefore cannot be directly rendered on with GDI calls. Also, groupboxes do not receive input events from the mouse or keyboard under any circumstances.

OSF/Motif does not support the Windows concept of *button state*, and subsequently the Windows messages **BM_SETSTATE** and **BM_GETSTATE** not supported. In Windows, button state only effects the appearance of a button, not its functionality. Therefore, the lack of support in Wind/U woud rarely affect the usability of your ported applications.

Table 6.2 shows the current support status of all button messages and styles in Wind/U, Windows NT, Windows 95, and on the Macintosh. Note that in the OSF/Motif environment, the **BS_HOLLOW** style is only supported for ellipse APIs.

Table 6.2 Button Messages and Styles

Message or Style	Wind/U	Windows NT	Windows 95	Macintosh
BM_GETBITMAP	No	No	Yes	No
BM_GETCHECK	Yes	Yes	Yes	Yes
BM_GETICON	No	No	Yes	No

Table 6.2 Button Messages and Styles (continued)

Message or Style	Wind/U	Windows NT	Windows 95	Macintosh
BM_GETIMAGE	No	No	Yes	No
BM_GETSTATE	No	Yes	Yes	Yes
BM_SETBITMAP	No	No	Yes	No
BM_SETCHECK	Yes	Yes	Yes	Yes
BM_SETICON	No	No	Yes	No
BM_SETIMAGE	No	No	Yes	No
BM_SETSTATE	No	Yes	Yes	Yes
BM_SETSTYLE	Yes	Yes	Yes	Yes
BN_CLICKED	Yes	Yes	Yes	Yes
BN_DISABLE	No	Yes	Yes	Yes
BN_DOUBLECLICKED	No	Yes	Yes	Yes
BN_HILITE	No	Yes	Yes	Yes
BN_PAINT	No	Yes	Yes	Yes
BN_UNHILITE	No	Yes	Yes	Yes
BS_CHECKBOX	Yes	Yes	Yes	Yes
BS_DEFPUSHBUTTON	Yes	Yes	Yes	Yes
BS_DIBPATTERN	No	Yes	Yes	No
BS_DIBPATTERN8X8	No	Yes	Yes	No
BS_DIBPATTERNPT	No	Yes	Yes	No
BS_GROUPBOX	Yes	Yes	Yes	Yes
BS_HATCHED	Yes	Yes	Yes	No
BS_HOLLOW	Partial	Yes	Yes	No
BS_INDEXED	No	Yes	Yes	No
BS_LEFT	No	No	Yes	Yes
BS_LEFTTEXT	Yes	No	No	Yes
BS_MULTILINE	No	No	Yes	No
BS_NOTIFY	No	No	Yes	No
BS_NULL	Yes	Yes	Yes	No

Table 6.2 Button Messages and Styles (continued)

Message or Style	Wind/U	Windows NT	Windows 95	Macintosh
BS_OWNERDRAW	Yes	Yes	Yes	Yes
BS_PATTERN	Yes	Yes	Yes	No
BS_PATTERN8X8	No	Yes	Yes	No
BS_PUSHBOX	No	No	Yes	No
BS_PUSHBUTTON	Yes	Yes	Yes	Yes
BS_PUSHLIKE	No	No	Yes	No
BS_RADIOBUTTON	Yes	Yes	Yes	Yes
BS_RIGHT	No	No	Yes	No
BS_RIGHTBUTTON	No	No	Yes	No
BS_SOLID	Yes	Yes	Yes	No
BS_TOP	No	No	Yes	No
BS_USERBUTTON	No	No	No	No
BS_VCENTER	No	No	Yes	No

List Boxes

Listbox differences between the Macintosh and Windows affect the position of user interface elements and the beavior of certain keys on the keyboard.

If a listbox has the **WS_TABSTOP** style bit set, and there is at least one other sibling window that is a tab stop, then the listbox is drawn with a bold border around the outside when the listbox has the focus, to indicate that it is the target of keystrokes. If any user-interface elements conflict with the border, you may have to move them. To eliminate this border, add the **WS_EX_WINDOWSUI** style bit to the extended style flags of the listbox.

By default, listboxes use Macintosh conventions for the behavior of the **Home, End, Page Up,** and **Page Down** keys. When pressed, these keys all scroll the listbox but none of them moves the selection, unlike Windows. You can make these keys move the selection as they scroll the listbox by adding the **WS_EX_WINDOWSUI** style bit to the extended style flags of the listbox.

When a listbox receives keyboard input under Windows, it changes the listbox selection to be the first item after the current selection that begins with the input character. Windows Portability Library listboxes that do not have the **LBS_SORT** style behave the same way. Sorted list boxes, however, follow the Macintosh convention of accumulating input characters into a string and selecting the first item greater than or equal to the string. After an interval has elapsed without keyboard input, the contents of the string are reset to nothing. The interval is based on the keyboard repeat threshold.

Finally, listboxes do not support the extended-selection Add mode provided by Windows listboxes.

Under UNIX, the Wind/U listbox is based on the OSF/Motif listbox, but with extensive changes to support the following Windows listbox features:

- Sorted lists
- Ownerdrawn lists
- Tabbed lists
- User data

Table 6.3 shows the current support status of all listbox messages and styles in Wind/U, Windows NT, Windows 95, and on the Macintosh.

Table 6.3 List Box Messages and Styles

Message or Style	Wind/U	Windows NT	Windows 95	Macintosh
LB_ADDSTRING	Yes	Yes	Yes	Yes
LB_DELETESTRING	Yes	Yes	Yes	Yes
LB_DIR	Yes	Yes	Yes	Yes
LB_FINDSTRING	Yes	Yes	Yes	Yes
LB_FINDSTRINGEXACT	Yes	Yes	Yes	Yes
LB_GETANCHORINDEX	No	No	Yes	No
LB_GETCARETINDEX	Yes	Yes	Yes	Yes
LB_GETCOUNT	Yes	Yes	Yes	Yes

Table 6.3 List Box Messages and Styles (continued)

Message or Style	Wind/U	Windows NT	Windows 95	Macintosh
LB_GETCURSEL	Yes	Yes	Yes	Yes
LB_GETHORIZONTALEXTENT	Yes	Yes	Yes	Yes
LB_GETITEMDATA	Yes	Yes	Yes	Yes
LB_GETITEMHEIGHT	No	Yes	Yes	Yes
LB_GETITEMRECT	No	Yes	Yes	Yes
LB_GETLOCALE	No	Yes	Yes	No
LB_GETSEL	Yes	Yes	Yes	Yes
LB_GETSELCOUNT	Yes	Yes	Yes	Yes
LB_GETSELITEMS	Yes	Yes	Yes	Yes
LB_GETTEXT	Yes	Yes	Yes	Yes
LB_GETTEXTLEN	Yes	Yes	Yes	Yes
LB_GETTOPINDEX	Yes	Yes	Yes	Yes
LB_INITSTORAGE	No	No	Yes	No
LB_INSERTSTRING	Yes	Yes	Yes	Yes
LB_ITEMFROMPOINT	No	No	Yes	No
LB_MSGMAX	No	Yes	Yes	Yes
LB_RESETCONTENT	Yes	Yes	Yes	Yes
LB_SELECTSTRING	Yes	Yes	Yes	Yes
LB_SELITEMRANGE	Yes	Yes	Yes	Yes
LB_SETANCHORINDEX	No	No	Yes	No
LB_SETCARETINDEX	Yes	Yes	Yes	Yes
LB_SETCOLUMNWIDTH	No	Yes	Yes	No
LB_SETCURSEL	Yes	Yes	Yes	Yes
LB_SETHORIZONTALEXTENT	Yes	Yes	Yes	Yes
LB_SETITEMDATA	Yes	Yes	Yes	Yes
LB_SETITEMHEIGHT	Yes	Yes	Yes	Yes
LB_SETLOCALE	No	Yes	Yes	Yes
LB_SETSEL	Yes	Yes	Yes	Yes

Table 6.3 List Box Messages and Styles (continued)

Message or Style	Wind/U	Windows NT	Windows 95	Macintosh
LB_SETTABSTOPS	Yes	Yes	Yes	Yes
LB_SETTOPINDEX	Yes	Yes	Yes	Yes
LBN_DBLCLK	Yes	Yes	Yes	Yes
LBN_ERRSPACE	No	Yes	Yes	Yes
LBN_KILLFOCUS	Yes	Yes	Yes	Yes
LBN_SELCANCEL	No	Yes	Yes	Yes
LBN_SELCHANGE	Yes	Yes	Yes	Yes
LBN_SETFOCUS	Yes	Yes	Yes	Yes
LBS_DISABLENOSCROLL	Partial	Yes	Yes	No
LBS_EXTENDEDSEL	Yes	Yes	Yes	Yes
LBS_HASSTRINGS	Yes	Yes	Yes	Yes
LBS_MULTICOLUMN	Yes	Yes	Yes	Yes
LBS_MULTIPLESEL	Yes	Yes	Yes	Yes
LBS_NODATA	No	Yes	Yes	No
LBS_NOINTEGRALHEIGHT	Yes	Yes	Yes	Yes
LBS_NOREDRAW	No	Yes	Yes	Yes
LBS_NOTIFY	Yes	Yes	Yes	Yes
LBS_OWNERDRAWFIXED	Yes	Yes	Yes	Yes
LBS_OWNERDRAWVARIABLE	Yes	Yes	Yes	Yes
LBS_SORT	Yes	Yes	Yes	Yes
LBS_STANDARD	Yes	Yes	Yes	Yes
LBS_USETABSTOPS	Yes	Yes	Yes	Yes
LBS_WANTKEYBOARDINPUT	Yes	Yes	Yes	Yes

In OSF/Motif the three-dimensional shadow around the listbox is considered part of the widget. Thus, for an owner-drawn list, when Wind/U sends out a **WM_DRAWITEM** message, the rectangle for the item is in general shrinked to take this border into account. Thus the left edge is generally *greater* than zero.

Yet some Windows applications assume that the left edge of an owner-drawn listbox item is zero. These applications use this as a criterion to determine if the given window is a listbox control.

Thus Wind/U allows the user to switch between the two modes through two extension functions:

- BOOL wuODListboxSetShadowOffset(HWND hWnd, BOOL nMode) If nMode == 1, the listbox shadow is considered when the rectangle coordinate is computed. If nMode == 0, the left edge is always at 0.

- BOOLwuODListboxGetShadowOffset(HWNDhWnd) This function returns the current mode.

Wind/U also provides the user the ability to specify the overall behavior of all listboxes in an application by adjusting the following entry in the **.WindU** file:

```
[Listbox]
OwnerDrawnShadowOffset=1
```

The dynamic functions always override the default **.WindU** values though. If you do not specify a value, either with the function or in the **.WindU** file, the default value is 1. Figure 6.1 shows the effect of using the wuODListboxSet ShadowOffset() function. The listbox on the right has an nMode value of 1; the listbox on the left has an nMode value of 0.

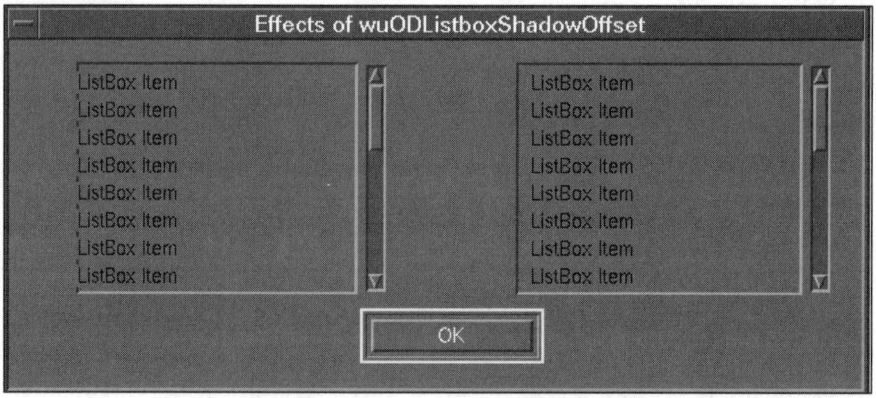

Figure 6.1 Effects of wuODListboxSetShadowOffset()

Combo Boxes

Combo box differences between the Macintosh and Windows environments include the appearance of the dropdown area, the types of combo boxes supported, mouse tracking in combo boxes, scroll bar appearance, and notifications.

By default, the Windows Portability Library draws the dropdown area for combo boxes with the **CBS_DROPDOWNLIST** using Macintosh conventions (a white rectangle with a downward-pointing arrow and a drop shadow). Also, combo boxes of this style place the popup menu over the dropdown area, again following Macintosh conventions. Adding the **WS_EX_WINDOWSUI** style bit to the extended style flags of a **CBS_DROPDOWNLIST** combo box causes the dropdown area to be drawn to look for like a Windows combo box (with a gray background and chiseled edges). This style also causes the popup menu to be placed underneath the static text and dropdown area.

Differences between Macintosh and Windows combo boxes mean that some types of combo boxes are not supported by the Windows Portability Library. For example, multiple selection combo boxes are not supported. **CB_DIR** directory combo boxes are also not supported. However, **CBS_SIMPLE** combo boxes work like Windows combo boxes. The list box is implemented using a Windows Portability Library list box. CBS_SIMPLE comboxes should be entirely compatible with Windows code.

CBS_DROPDOWN and **CBS_DROPDOWNLIST** combo boxes, however, are implemented quite differently than in Windows, and are incompatible with their Windows counterparts in several ways. Windows Portability Library dropdown combo boxes look like Macintosh popup menus. Note that the size of the dropdown is not determined by the size of the window rectangle you give in CreateWindow, but rather by the amount of data in the combo box.

The Windows Portability Library also tries to position the dropdown so that the current combo box selection is always under the mouse when the list box drops down. As a result, instead of the listbox dropping down directly below the combo box edit control, Macintosh combo listboxes popup directly under the mouse pointer. To retain the Windows-style positioning instead, create the combo box with the **WS_EX_WINDOWSUI extended style.**

Mouse tracking in Macintosh combo boxes is modal: The dropdown item collapses when the user lifts up on the mouse. This is a significant change to the way Windows applications interact with combo boxes. When the

CB_SHOWDROPDOWN message is sent to force the combo box to drop down, control is not returned until the list box collapses.

Unlike Windows combo boxes, Macintosh combo box dropdowns do not contain scrollbars. Instead, they use the Macintosh convention of scroll arrows at the top and/or bottom of the dropdown. This implementation makes combo boxes inappropriate for very large dropdown lists.

On the Macintosh, the **CBN_SELENDOK** and **CBN_SELENDCANCEL** notifications are sent to the combo box's owner only after the list box has been hidden. Under Windows, these notifications are sent after the user has completed the selection, but before Windows hides the list box (this only applies to combo boxes with the **CBS_DROPDOWN** and **CBS_DROPDOWNLIST** styles, since a combo box with the **CBS_SIMPLE** style never hides its list box). Therefore, your application cannot assume that the list box is still visible when it receives either of these notifications.

The Wind/U combo box for UNIX applications is a custom OSF/Motif composite widget. It includes the subclassed Wind/U listbox widget, as well as various other widgets for the edit field, dropdown arrow button, and static fields. The Windows combo box control has most of the advanced features of the list box control, and these features are supported by the Wind/U combo box widget through its use of the list box widget.

Table 6.4 shows the current support status of all combo box messages and styles in Wind/U, Windows NT, Windows 95, and on the Macintosh.

Table 6.4 Combo Box Messages and Styles

Message or Style	Wind/U	Windows NT	Macintosh	Windows 95
CB_ADDSTRING	Yes	Yes	Yes	Yes
CB_DELETESTRING	Yes	Yes	Yes	Yes
CB_DIR	Yes	Yes	Yes	Yes
CB_FINDSTRING	Yes	Yes	Yes	Yes
CB_FINDSTRINGEXACT	Yes	No	Yes	No
CB_GETCOUNT	Yes	Yes	Yes	Yes
CB_GETCURSEL	Yes	Yes	Yes	Yes
CB_GETDROPPEDCONTROLRECT	Yes	Yes	Yes	Yes

Table 6.4 Combo Box Messages and Styles (continued)

Message or Style	Wind/U	Windows NT	Macintosh	Windows 95
CB_GETDROPPEDSTATE	Yes	Yes	Yes	Yes
CB_GETDROPPEDWIDTH	No	No	No	Yes
CB_GETEDITSEL	Yes	Yes	Yes	Yes
CB_GETEXTENDEDUI	No	Yes	Yes	Yes
CB_GETHORIZONTALEXTENT	No	No	No	Yes
CB_GETITEMDATA	Yes	Yes	Yes	Yes
CB_GETITEMHEIGHT	Yes	Yes	Yes	Yes
CB_GETLBTEXT	Yes	Yes	Yes	Yes
CB_GETLBTEXTLEN	Yes	Yes	Yes	Yes
CB_GETTOPINDEX	No	No	No	Yes
CB_INITSTORAGE	No	No	No	Yes
CB_INSERTSTRING	Yes	Yes	Yes	Yes
CB_LIMITTEXT	Yes	Yes	Yes	Yes
CB_MSGMAX	No	Yes	Yes	Yes
CB_RESETCONTENT	Yes	Yes	Yes	Yes
CB_SELECTSTRING	Yes	Yes	Yes	Yes
CB_SETCURSEL	Yes	Yes	Yes	Yes
CB_SETDROPPEDWIDTH	No	No	No	Yes
CB_SETEDITSEL	Yes	Yes	Yes	Yes
CB_SETEXTENDEDUI	No	Yes	Yes	Yes
CB_SETHORIZONTALEXTENT	No	No	No	Yes
CB_SETITEMDATA	Yes	Yes	Yes	Yes
CB_SETITEMHEIGHT	Yes	Yes	Yes	Yes
CB_SETTOPINDEX	No	No	No	Yes
CB_SHOWDROPDOWN	Yes	Yes	Yes	Yes
CBN_CLOSEUP	Yes	Yes	Yes	Yes
CBN_DBLCLK	Yes	Yes	Yes	Yes
CBN_DROPDOWN	Yes	Yes	Yes	Yes

Table 6.4 Combo Box Messages and Styles (continued)

Message or Style	Wind/U	Windows NT	Macintosh	Windows 95
CBN_EDITCHANGE	Yes	Yes		Yes
CBN_EDITUPDATE	Yes	Yes		Yes
CBN_ERRSPACE	No	Yes		Yes
CBN_KILLFOCUS	Yes	Yes		Yes
CBN_SELCHANGE	Yes	Yes		Yes
CBN_SELENDCANCEL	No	No		No
CBN_SELENDOK	No	No		No
CBN_SETFOCUS	Yes	Yes		Yes
CBS_AUTOHSCROLL	No	Yes		Yes
CBS_DISABLENOSCROLL	No	Yes		Yes
CBS_DROPDOWN	Yes	Yes		Yes
CBS_DROPDOWNLIST	Yes	Yes		Yes
CBS_HASSTRINGS	Yes	Yes		Yes
CBS_LOWERCASE	No	No		Yes
CBS_NOINTEGRALHEIGHT	Yes	Yes		Yes
CBS_OEMCONVERT	No	Yes		Yes
CBS_OWNERDRAWFIXED	Yes	Yes		Yes
CBS_OWNERDRAWVARIABLE	Yes	Yes		Yes
CBS_SIMPLE	Yes	Yes		Yes
CBS_SORT	Yes	Yes		Yes
CBS_UPPERCASE	No	No		Yes

In OSF/Motif the three-dimensional shadow around the combo box is considered part of the widget. Thus, for an owner-drawn combo box, when Wind/U sends out a **WM_DRAWITEM** message, the rectangle for the item is in general shrinked to take this border into account. Thus the left edge is generally greater than zero.

Yet some Windows applications assume that the left edge of an ownerdrawn combo box item is zero. These applications use this as a criterion to determine if the given window is a combo box control.

Thus Wind/U allows the user to switch between the two modes through two extension functions:

- BOOL wuODComboboxSetShadowOffset(HWND hWnd, BOOL nMode) If nMode == 1, the combo box shadow is considered when the rectangle coordinate is computed. If nMode == 0, the left edge is always at 0.

- BOOLwuODComboboxGetShadowOffset(HWNDhWnd) This function returns the current mode.

Wind/U also provides the user the ability to specify the overall behavior of all combo boxes in an application by adjusting the following entry in the **.WindU** file:

```
[Combobox]
OwnerDrawnShadowOffset=1
```

The dynamic functions always override the default **.WindU** values, though. If you do not specify a value, either with the function or in the **.WindU** file, the default value is 1. Figure 6.2 shows the effect of using the wuODListboxSetShadow Offset() function. The listbox on the right has an nMode value of 1; the listbox on the left has an nMode value of 0.

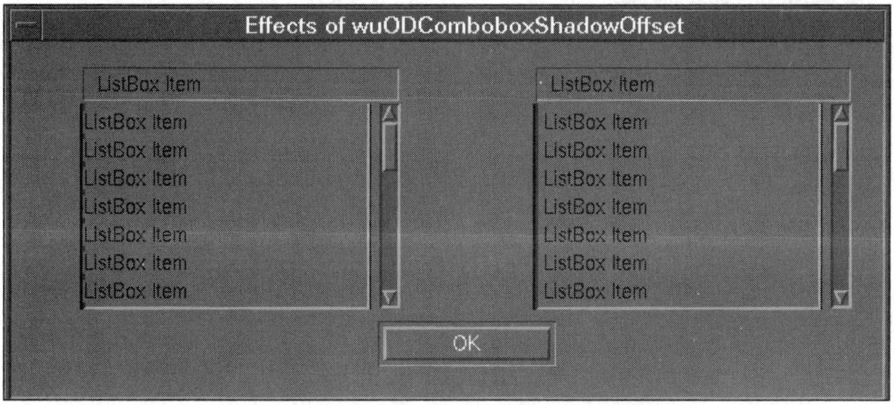

Figure 6.2 Effects of wuODComboboxSetShadowOffset()

Edit Controls

Differences between Macintosh and Windows edit controls include character limits, selection appearance and tracking, and a number of differences at the programming level.

Since edit controls are implemented using Macintosh TextEdit, they have many of the same restrictions as TextEdit. In particular, there is a 32,767 character limit on the length of text.

Edit control selections look different than in Windows. For example, a caret is only visible for zero-width selections. When the selection contains the last character of a line, the selected region extends to the right edge of the control. Under Windows, only a few pixels to the right of the edge of the text are selected.

Unlike Windows, selection tracking in edit controls (by clicking the mouse and dragging) is modal. The application's message pump is not executed while the mouse is moving. If your applications depend on seeing **WM_MOUSEMOVE** messages while tracking the edit control selection changes, you can expect to have compatability problems.

In addition to the user interface differences, there are a number of specific differences on the programming level:

- **ES_OEMCONVERT** is not supported. The Windows Portability Library assumes that all fonts are in the OEM character set.

- **ES_NOHIDESEL** edit controls display their selection with a dotted outline when they are inactive. Windows leaves the entire selection highlighted.

- The Windows Portability Library does not support tabs; **EM_SETTABSTOPS** is not supported.

- The Windows Portability Library does not support Undo; **EM_CAN UNDO, EM_EMPTYUNDOBUFFER,** and **EM_UNDO** are not supported.

- The Windows Portability Library does not support custom word breaks, so that **EM_GETWORDBREAKPROC** and **EM_SETWORDBREAK PROC** are not implemented.

- The **EM_FMTLINES** message is not supported. The soft line break character sequence (**CR CR LF**) is never inserted into an edit control's text.

- Use the handle returned by **EM_GETHANDLE** with care. While you have this handle locked, the underlying TextEdit record is in an illegal state, and certain edit control operations can cause your display to be corrupted.

In UNIX applications, Wind/U maps the Windows edit control to the OSF/Motif XmText widget. Advanced styles such as **ES_PASSWORD, ES_UPPERCASE, ES_LOWERCASE, ES_READONLY,** and **ES_WANTRETURN** are implemented with subclassing to the XmText widget.

The following capabilities of the Windows edit control are not supported by Wind/U:

- application-customized word breaks (**EM_SETWORDBREAKPROC**),
- application-supplied tab stops (**EM_SETTABSTOPS**),
- and Undo (**EM_CANUNDO**).

Table 6.5 shows the current support status of all edit control messages and styles in Wind/U, Windows NT, Windows 95, and on the Macintosh. Note that in the OSF/Motif environment, the **EM_EMPTYUNDOBUFFER** message is part of the **EM_UNDO** task. Also, **EM_CANUNDO** always returns a value of false.

Table 6.5 Edit Control Messages and Styles

Message or Style	Wind/U	Windows NT	Macintosh	Windows 95
EM_CANUNDO	Partial	Yes	Yes	Yes
EM_CHARFROMPOS	No	No	No	Yes
EM_EMPTYUNDOBUFFER	No	Yes	Yes	Yes
EM_FMTLINES	No	Yes	Yes	Yes
EM_GETFIRSTVISIBLELINE	Yes	Yes	Yes	Yes
EM_GETHANDLE	Yes	Yes	Yes	Yes
EM_GETLIMITTEXT	No	No	No	Yes
EM_GETLINE	Yes	Yes	Yes	Yes
EM_GETLINECOUNT	Yes	Yes	Yes	Yes
EM_GETMARGINS	No	No	No	Yes

Table 6.5 Edit Control Messages and Styles (continued)

Message or Style	Wind/U	Windows NT	Macintosh	Windows 95
EM_GETMODIFY	Yes	Yes	Yes	Yes
EM_GETPASSWORDCHAR	Yes	No	No	No
EM_GETRECT	No	Yes	Yes	Yes
EM_GETSEL	Yes	Yes	Yes	Yes
EM_GETTHUMB	No	Yes	Yes	Yes
EM_GETWORDBREAKPROC	No	No	No	No
EM_LIMITTEXT	Yes	Yes	Yes	Yes
EM_LINEFROMCHAR	Yes	Yes	Yes	Yes
EM_LINEINDEX	Yes	Yes	Yes	Yes
EM_LINELENGTH	Yes	Yes	Yes	Yes
EM_LINESCROLL	Yes	Yes	Yes	Yes
EM_POSFROMCHAR	No	No	No	Yes
EM_REPLACESEL	Yes	Yes	Yes	Yes
EM_SCROLL	No	Yes	Yes	Yes
EM_SETHANDLE	Yes	Yes	Yes	Yes
EM_SETLIMITTEXT	No	No	No	Yes
EM_SETMARGINS	No	No	No	Yes
EM_SETMODIFY	Yes	Yes	Yes	Yes
EM_SETPASSWORDCHAR	Yes	Yes	Yes	Yes
EM_SETREADONLY	Yes	Yes	Yes	Yes
EM_SETRECT	No	Yes	Yes	Yes
EM_SETRECTNP	No	Yes	Yes	Yes
EM_SETSEL	Yes	Yes	Yes	Yes
EM_SETTABSTOPS	No	Yes	Yes	Yes
EM_SETWORDBREAK	No	Yes	Yes	Yes
EM_SETWORDBREAKPROC	No	No	No	No
EM_UNDO	No	Yes	Yes	Yes

Table 6.5 Edit Control Messages and Styles (continued)

Message or Style	Wind/U	Windows NT	Macintosh	Windows 95
EN_CHANGE	Yes	Yes	Yes	Yes
EN_ERRSPACE	No	Yes	Yes	Yes
EN_HSCROLL	No	Yes	Yes	Yes
EN_KILLFOCUS	Yes	Yes	Yes	Yes
EN_MAXTEXT	No	Yes	Yes	Yes
EN_SETFOCUS	Yes	Yes	Yes	Yes
EN_UPDATE	Yes	Yes	Yes	Yes
EN_VSCROLL	No	Yes	Yes	Yes
ES_AUTOHSCROLL	Yes	Yes	Yes	Yes
ES_AUTOVSCROLL	Yes	Yes	Yes	Yes
ES_CENTER	No	Yes	Yes	Yes
ES_LEFT	Yes	Yes	Yes	Yes
ES_LOWERCASE	Yes	Yes	Yes	Yes
ES_MULTILINE	Yes	Yes	Yes	Yes
ES_NOHIDESEL	No	Yes	Yes	Yes
ES_OEMCONVERT	No	Yes	Yes	Yes
ES_PASSWORD	Yes	Yes	Yes	Yes
ES_READONLY	Yes	Yes	Yes	Yes
ES_RIGHT	No	Yes	Yes	Yes
ES_UPPERCASE	Yes	Yes	Yes	Yes
ES_WANTRETURN	No	Yes	Yes	Yes

Scroll Bars

Because of differences between Macintosh and Windows dialogs, the Windows Portability Library does not support the keyboard interface for scroll bars.

Scrollbars support only the **ESB_ENABLEBOTH** and **ESB_DISABLEBOTH** parameters to EnableScrollBar. Disabling just one arrow of a scroll bar is not supported. The Macintosh scroll bar control does not attempt to keep a fixed-width arrow area when the scroll bar is wider or narrower than 16 pixels, but rather scales the arrow area to match the width of the scroll bar. Therefore, it is generally not useful to create scroll bar controls that are not 16 pixels wide. Also, if the length of the scroll bar is insufficient to draw the scroll bar thumb, the Windows Portability Library removes the thumb and just draws the arrow areas. If there is not enough room to even draw the arrows, the Windows Portability Library fills the control window with gray instead of drawing the scroll bar.

A convention of the Macintosh user interface is that scroll bars in inactive windows are hidden. This is generally not true under Windows. If you find that your scroll bars are being hidden by the Windows Portability Library when you do not want them to be, you can send the top-level window containing the hidden scroll bars a **WM_NCACTIVATE** message to force the window to be active. This makes the scroll bar visible.

As is the case under Windows 3.x and Win32s, the "range" value for Windows Portability Library scrollbars is limited to 16 bits in size, not 32 bits.

In UNIX applications, Wind/U maps the Windows scrollbar class to the OSF/Motif XmScrollbar widget.

Table 6.6 shows the current support status of all scroll bar messages and styles in Wind/U, Windows NT, Windows 95, and on the Macintosh.

Table 6.6 Scroll Bar Messages and Styles

Message or Style	Wind/U	Windows NT	Macintosh	Windows 95
SB_BOTTOM	Yes	Yes	Yes	Yes
SB_ENDSCROLL	Yes	Yes	Yes	Yes
SB_GETBORDERS	No	Yes	Yes	Yes
SB_GETPARTS	No	Yes	Yes	Yes
SB_GETTEXT	No	Yes	Yes	Yes
SB_GETTEXTLENGTH	No	Yes	Yes	Yes
SB_LINEDOWN	Yes	Yes	Yes	Yes
SB_LINEUP	Yes	Yes	Yes	Yes
SB_PAGEDOWN	Yes	Yes	Yes	Yes

Table 6.6 Scroll Bar Messages and Styles (continued)

Message or Style	Wind/U	Windows NT	Macintosh	Windows 95
SB_PAGEUP	Yes	Yes	Yes	Yes
SB_SETBORDERS	No	No	No	Yes
SB_SETMINHEIGHT	No	No	No	Yes
SB_SETPARTS	No	No	No	Yes
SB_SETTEXT	No	No	No	Yes
SB_SIMPLE	No	No	No	Yes
SB_THUMBPOSITION	Yes	Yes	No	Yes
SB_THUMBTRACK	Yes	Yes	Yes	Yes
SB_TOP	Yes	Yes	Yes	Yes
SBM_ENABLE_ARROWS	No	No	No	Yes
SBM_GETPOS	No	Yes	Yes	Yes
SBM_GETRANGE	No	Yes	Yes	Yes
SBM_GETSCROLLINFO	No	No	No	Yes
SBM_SETPOS	No	Yes	Yes	Yes
SBM_SETRANGE	No	Yes	Yes	Yes
SBM_SETRANGEREDRAW	No	Yes	Yes	Yes
SBM_SETSCROLLINFO	No	No	No	Yes
SBS_BOTTOMALIGN	No	Yes	Yes	Yes
SBS_HORZ	Yes	Yes	Yes	Yes
SBS_LEFTALIGN	No	Yes	Yes	Yes
SBS_RIGHTALIGN	No	Yes	Yes	Yes
SBS_SIZEBOX	No	Yes	Yes	Yes
SBS_SIZEBOXBOTTOMRIGHTALIGN	No	Yes	Yes	Yes
SBS_SIZEBOXTOPLEFTALIGN	No	Yes	Yes	Yes
SBS_TOPALIGN	No	Yes	Yes	Yes
SBS_VERT	Yes	Yes	Yes	Yes

Porting Visual C++ Dialog Boxes to Macintosh

Macintosh Look-and-Feel Issues

Where differences exist between the look-and-feel on the Macintosh and Windows, the Windows Portability Library follows the Macintosh conventions by default. The look-and-feel diffferences between the Macintosh and Windows dialogs are generally in three areas.

First, the *focus policy* in the Macintosh is less flexible than in Microsoft Windows. On the Macintosh, focus can only go to edit or listbox controls. On Windows, however, focus can go to any control, including pushbuttons, radio buttons, and checkboxes.

This fundamental difference in user interface design is a result of the Common User Access (CUA) compliance requirements fullfilled by Microsoft Windows. To be CUA-compliant, Windows (and any application written for Windows) should be fully functional with the keyboard alone. Windows does not require a mouse or other pointing device, whereas much of the user interface of the Macintosh assumes that a mouse is present on the system.

The next major area of look and feel incompatibility is in the concept of *tab traversal*. In Macintosh dialogs, pressing the **Tab** key (or sending the **WM_NEXTDLGCTL** message) moves the focus to the next control that can accept keystrokes instead of the next control that has the tabstop (**WS_TABSTOP**) style bit set. The Windows Portability Library follows this Macintosh convention by default, so if your dialogs are particularly sensitive to tab traversal order, you may have problems in this area. Note, however, that the user can still use the Command-**Tab** key sequence to move the focus to the next control with the tabstop style bit set.

On the Macintosh, a pushbutton does not become the default button when clicked with the mouse. This minor point should not normally be an issue to your application.

The Windows Portability Library assumes that you want your *dialog interfaces* to be consistent with the standard dialog interfaces on the Macintosh. However, in some rare instances, developers require that the user interface be consistent with Windows. The Windows Portability Library also implements a dialog box interface consisten with Windows, using the **DS_WINDOWSUI** style in the dialog-style field of your .**RC** file. This capability is important if your users expect to see a consistent user interface among all versions of your application.

Macintosh Dialog Extensions

The Windows Portability Library provides several extension functions for accessing the underlying Macintosh windowing structures from within the Windows API context. The CheckoutHandle(), CheckinHandle(), WrapHandle(), and UnwrapHandle() APIs provide mechanisms for accessing the native Macintosh window constructs that are normally hidden by the Windows local and global allocation scheme.

The CheckoutHandle() function retrieves the Macintosh handle corresponding to the specified local or global allocation. The Macintosh handle returned can then be passed to the Macintosh operating system or Macintosh Toolbox, thereby providing a means to integrate native Macintosh code into your ported Win32 application. When you are finished with the Macintosh handle, check it back in with CheckinHandle().

Where the CheckoutHandle() and CheckinHandle() APIs provide a means of translating from Windows handles to Macintosh handles, WrapHandle() and UnwrapHandle() provide a translation from Macintosh handles to Windows handles. Use WrapHandle() to convert an allocation created by the Macintosh operating system to a Windows application that can subsequently be used by Win32 APIs. For example, if your application calls out to some native Macintosh code that creates a window using native Macintosh APIs, you can use WrapHandle() to convert the Macintosh window handle to an HWND that can subsequently be used in GDI calls that draw on the window.

For a similar APIs to CheckinHandle() and CheckoutHandle() in the Motif environment, see wuhWndToCanvasWidget(), wuhWndToControlWidget(), and wuhWndToDrawingWidget().

Porting Visual C++ Dialog Boxes to UNIX

As with the Macintosh, when porting Dialog boxes to UNIX you might encounter some problems with look-and-feel issues. However, with minor tuning of your dialog templates, you can come up with a layout that works on all Win32 hosted environments.

Since the look-and-feel of Motif was designed to be very similar to Windows, you will not have the focus, traversal, and other functional differences that you will encounter on the Macintosh. Rather, the issues that you will face in the

Motif environment have more to do with performance, font differences, and Motif dialog layout conventions than with usability problems.

Motif Look and Feel Issues

In most respects, the layout and feel of OSF/Motif dialogs are identical to Windows. There are a few areas, however, where you might want to change the appearance of dialogs to better conform to Motif conventions for dialog layouts.

As an example of look-and-feel incompatibility, consider button placement (see Figure 6.3). OSF/Motif, by convention, puts buttons at the bottom of a dialog horizontally. Windows often puts them on the right side vertically.

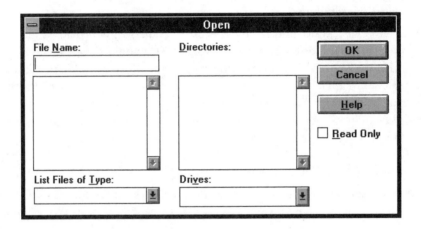

Figure 6.3 Windows Look-and-Feel Dialogs

As one solution to this problem, at least in the case of the file selector, Wind/U allows you to use the standard OSF/Motif XmFileSelection widget instead of the Wind/U implementation of the FileOpen common dialog. However, by mapping the GetOpenFileName and GetSaveFileName API's to the Motif XmFileSelection widget, some advanced functionality—such as custom templates and control subclassing—is lost. Nevertheless, this solution is popular for applications that don't do anything exotic in their file open and save dialogs.

Most developers simply overlook this minor discrepency between OSF/Motif and Windows look-and-feel. (In general, developers are more concerned with a common user interface between their ported applications than with strict compliance with minor GUI conventions.) But if you must solve these types of problems, AppStudio makes it easy to make minor modifications to your dialogs if you choose. To solve this problem, use conditional compilation in the **.rc** file that compiles differents parts of the dialog template based on the environment. The following example changes the position and size of the Exit, Cancel, and Help buttons in the Wind/U environment:

```
WINWHOIS DIALOG DISCARDABLE -6, 18, 320, 154
SYTLE WS_MINIMIZEBOX | WS_POPUP |WS_CAPTION | WS_SYSMENU
CAPTION "WinWhoIs"
MENU EditMenu
BEGIN
    LTEXT       "Name to Query",-1,30,5,98,8,NOT WS_GROUP
    EDITTEXT     IDC_NAMEINPUT,10,14,244,12,WS_GROUP
    DEFPUSHBUTTON "Make Query",IDC_MAKEQUERY,265,14,44,12
    LTEXT       "Responses",-1,30,48,39,8
    EDITTEXT     IDC_RESPONSES,10,38,263,102,ES_MULTILINE |
            ES_AUTOVSCROLL | WS_VSCROLL | WS_HSCROLL
    CTEXT       "Waiting for input...",IDC_STATUS,30,141,124,10,
            NOT WS_GROUP
#ifdef WU_APP
    PUSHBUTTON   "Exit",IDC_EXIT,277,58,32,25
    PUSHBUTTON   "Clear",IDC_CLEAR,277,89,32,25
    PUSHBUTTON   "Help",IDC_HELP,277,120,32,25
#else
    PUSHBUTTON   "Exit",IDC_EXIT,277,51,32,25
    PUSHBUTTON   "Clear",IDC_CLEAR,277,83,32,25
    PUSHBUTTON   "Help",IDC_HELP,277,115,32,25
#endif
```

These minor changes in the **.rc** file will make the dialog be strictly compliant with either target platform's look-and-feel conventions:

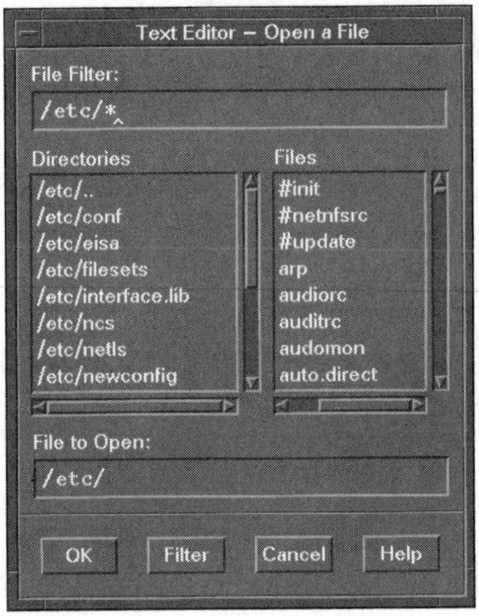

Figure 6.4 Native Dialog Look-and-Feel

Dialog Geometry Based on Fonts

Windows dialog geometry is specified in logical font units. Vertical geometry is specified in 1/8 font-height units, while Horizontal geometry is specified in 1/4 font-width units. The font used to calculate height and width units is the font specified for the dialog in the template from the **.rc** file. Specifying a font in the **.rc** file is not mandatory; if none is specified, the default system font is used.

Since the fonts available on the X Window System are from a different source than the fonts on Windows, it is no surprise that the font geometries are slightly different. As a result, some dialog geometry settings from AppStudio will be slightly off in the OSF/Motif environment. Experience tells us that often the X Window System fonts are slightly wider than their Windows equivalents. The result of this minor incompatibilty is that some Windows dialog controls will be slightly too narrow when compiled in the OSF/Motif environment.

This problem is made somewhat worse by the "Size to Content" option in AppStudio. This option automatically changes the size of a control so that it is the appropriate size for its text caption. Size to Content depends on the exact font geometry from Windows, and therefore can cause slight problems in the OSF/Motif environment.

The solution to this problem is to allow a few extra pixels of space for dialog controls.

Wind/U provides the dlgpreview utility, which you can use to quickly visually inspect your dialogs to see if minor geometry changes are needed. To use dlgpreview, enter the following command:

```
$ dlgpreview dialogs.dll
```

The **dialogs.dll** is a stub-shared library that includes the **.rc** file from your application. To build dialogs.dll, do the following:

1. Create a stub DllMain module like the following:

2. Compile and link to the **_rc.o** output from the Wind/U resource compiler:

```
dllink -CC dialogs.dll .....
```

Dialogs.dll contains ensentially nothing but your dialog resources. The dlgpreview utility goes through each dialog in your **.rc** file and displays it on the screen. Of course, the source code associated with your dialogs through their DialogProcs is not executed. Nevertheless, you can identify and correct most geometry problems with dialog boxes with just a visual inspection.

The dlgpreview utility lets you methodically go through your dialogs and correct geometry problems, rather than searching thru each dialog when running your application in a less methodical manner.

The Wind/U Dialog Cache

Wind/U provides two features for optimizing dialog performance under OSF/Motif. Loading a dialog into memory is an expensive operation in Motif. Preloading a dialog loads it into memory at application startup, so that it displays faster when invoked from the application. To enable preloading, simply specify PRELOAD as an attribute for the dialog. The dialog must also be cached for preloading to take effect.

Caching a dialog causes the dialog to be cached instead of destroyed when the application destroys it. Then, when it is invoked again, the dialog is read from cache instead of recreated. To enable caching, add the following entry to your resource file:

```
WU_INFO name DIALOG WU_CACHEDIALOG
```

The *name* field specifies the name of the dialog to be cached. This statement must appear before the dialog definition in the resource file. The resource compiler issues warnings for unused **WU_INFO** statements. To maintain Windows source compatibility, include **WU_INFO** statements within an #ifdef **WU_APP** block.

Wind/U Dialog Extensions

Every Windows window in Wind/U has two or three Motif widgets associated with it. These widgets are called the canvas, control, and drawing widgets.

Canvas widgets provide containers for their children, the control widget, and the drawing widget. For overlapped windows, the canvas widget is an application shell. For child windows, the canvas widget is a form widget. For popup windows, the canvas widget is a dialog shell.

Control widgets provide the functionality for the window. For overlapped windows, the control widget is a Motif main window. For child windows, such as controls, the control widget is the corresponding Motif widget for the control. For example, Windows Static controls are Motif Labels. For popups, the control widget is a Bulletin Board.

Drawing widgets are only used in cases where two Motif widgets do not suffice for implementing the Windows window. They are usually the widget drawn upon by GDI functions, thus the name Drawing widgets.

For overlapped windows, the drawing widget is a BulletinBoard. For child windows (except for standard controls), the drawing widget is the same as the control widget. For popup windows, the drawing widget is a BulletinBoard widget.

There are Wind/U extension functions that take a HWND and return each of these widgets:

```
Widget wuhWndToCanvasWidget(HWND);
Widget wuhWndToControlWidget(HWND);
Widget wuhWndToDrawingWidget(HWND);
```

The following function takes a dialog handle and shows how to add a Motif button to a dialog using the control widget.

```
void extCreateButton(HWND hDlg)
{
    Arg args[10];
    int ac = 0;
    Widget widCanvas =
            wuhWndToControlWidget(hDlg);
    Widget widButton;      XmString xmstring =
            XmStringCreateLtoR("UNIX",
            XmSTRING_DEFAULT_CHARSET);
    XtSetArg(args[ac],XmNx,50), ac++;
    XtSetArg(args[ac],XmNy,50), ac++;
    XtSetArg(args[ac],XmNwidth,60),ac++;
    XtSetArg(args[ac],XmNheight,40),ac++;
    XtSetArg(args[ac],
            XmNlabelString,xmstring),ac++;
    widButton = XmCreatePushButton(
            widCanvas,"PushButton",args,ac);
    XtAddCallback(widButton,
            XmNactivateCallback,extButtonCB,NULL);
    XtManageChild(widButton);
    XmStringFree(xmstring);
}
```

One of the most powerful uses of these functions is that they give you the ability to add Motif widgets that do not have Windows equivalents to your ported dialogs. For an example, you can use these extensions to add option menus and scale widgets to your dialogs.

Unlike the Windows Portability Library for Macintosh, Wind/U defaults to the Microsoft Windows tabbing scheme rather than using the standard Motif scheme. Most users do not notice this change from Motif tabbing because the tab traversal schemes from Windows and Motif are so similar. However, some applications rely heaviliy on the exact Windows look and feel for tabbing, so Wind/U accomodates these types of applications by implementing the Windows tabbing scheme.

The Wind/U extension API EnableMotifTabbing() has the effect of returning the tabbing scheme back to the normal Motif method rather than using the Wind/U implementation in IsDialogMessage(). Calling this API has the reverse effect of the **DS_WINDOWSUI** style bit in the Windows Portability Library for Macintosh.

Using Native OSF/Motif Widgets in Ported Dialogs

Sometimes you may want to use native OSF/Motif widgets in dialogs in the UNIX version of your application. OSF/Motif contains a few widgets, such as the Motif scale or option menus, which do not have analogous controls in the Windows environment. Enhancing your ported Windows application to use these widgets is fairly straight-forward, but does require some knowledge of OSF/Motif programming.

Using Custom Controls in Ported Dialogs

Using custom controls in both the Macintosh and OSF/Motif environments is exactly the same as in Windows. You just link in the custom control, initialize it prior to creating a dialog that uses it, and make the dialog template refer to this new class.

Macintosh Common Dialog Boxes

For common operations, such as opening or printing, it is likely that your application uses common dialogs. Most of these dialog classes are supported in both the Macintosh and OSF/Motif environments, although there are some slight differences in both environments.

The ChooseFont dialog box is generally compatible with the Windows ChooseFont dialog. However, there are several minor cosmetic changes which make it look a little more like a standard Macintosh font picker. If you use a ChooseFont template, you can change it in your Macintosh application to more closely approximate the Windows convention. The template that the Windows Portability Library provides is the **FONT.DLG** file. This file is located in the **\M68K\INCLUDE** subdirectory, and you can use it as a base for your modifications.

The PrintDlg API brings up the standard printer Print Job dialog box for the currently installed printer. Since this dialog box is implemented completely at the discretion of the printer driver, the Windows Portability Library does not support templates for this dialog box. You should bring up this standard print job dialog box in your application's Print command.

Because the functionality of PrintDlg's **PD_PRINTSETUP** dialog box is implemented in the Macintosh Chooser, the Windows Portability Library has not implemented a separate printer-setup dialog box . This is a case where the menus of most applications will differ in the Windows and Macintosh versions.

Unlike Windows, the Macintosh has a standard printer-specific "Document Setup" (also known as Print Style) dialog box. On the Macintosh, PrintDlg brings up this printer-specific style dialog box whenever the **PD_PRINTSETUP** bit is set in the **PRINTDLG** Flag field. To adhere to Macintosh user-interface conventions, your application should have a Document Setup command that brings up this **PD_PRINTSETUP** dialog box. As with the print job dialog box, templates for the print style dialog box are not supported on the Macintosh.

Dialog Box Hooks and Templates

The GetOpenFileName, GetSaveFileName, ChooseColor, and PrintDlg dialog boxes are all implemented with standard Macintosh dialog boxes. As a result, the ChooseColor and PrintDlg dialog boxes do not support dialog box hooks or the ENABLEHOOK flag, and the GetOpenFileName and GetSaveFileName dialog boxes provide only limited support for the dialog box hook. If the **OFN_ENABLEHOOK** flag is set for the file dialog boxes, the dialog box hook receives the **SHAREVISTRING** registered window message and the FILEOKSTRING registered window message. The dialog box hook does not receive any of the normal input or notification messages that it would receive under Windows, and the dialog box window handle passed to the dialog box hook is always NULL. Furthermore, none of these dialog boxes supports the custom dialog box template feature of Windows common dialog boxes. The ENABLETEMPLATE and ENABLETEMPLATEHANDLE flags for these dialog boxes are all ignored.

However, you can supply your own Macintosh DLOG and DITL resources for the file common dialog boxes. The Windows Portability Library uses the resource IDs in Table 6.7 for its customized file dialog box resources.

Table 6.7 Common Dialog Resource IDs

Resource ID	Common dialog (DLOG and DITL)
17,000	GetSaveFileName
17,001	GetOpenFileName

You can make a copy of the appropriate Windows Portability Library resource and customize it as necessary. The original Windows Portability Library DLOG and DITL resources are located in the **FILEOPEN.R** file in the \M68K\INCLUDE subdirectory. In your Macintosh resource .R file, include lines like the following to instruct MRC to delete the originals:

```
include "commdlg.rsc";
delete 'DLOG' (1700x);
delete 'DITL' (1700x);
```

Then, include your customized version. You may also want to use the **WHM_DIALOGHOOK** Windows hook to manage any additional controls that you add to the dialog box.

UNIX Common Dialog Boxes

Wind/U implements all Windows common dialogs in the OSF/Motif environment. As in the Macintosh environment, however, there are some small differences you should be aware of.

One difference is the ChooseColor common dialog. OSF/Motif does not support dithered colors; therefore, this dialog box can only show a maximum of 256 distinct colors in the OSF/Motif environment.

ChooseFont does not currently support the **CF_USESTYLE** flag.

The PrintDlg common dialog does not support the **PS_ENABLESETUP HOOK** or **PS_NOWARNING** flags. The functionality of the PrintDlg **PD_PRINTERSETUP** dialog box is implemented in Xprinter, from Bristol Technology. As in the Macintosh environment, the Printer Setup dialog box is one aspect of your application that will be different for the OSF/Motif environment. The reason for this difference is that the Xlib interface, which OSF/Motif uses for graphics support, only directs output to an X Window display; it does not provide any mechanism for directing output to a printer. The Xprinter Printer Setup widget allows users to specify a default printer, configure new printers, and set printer-specific options such as resolution, page size, and choice of paper tray to use.

Wind/U supports the CreateFile common dialog function for creating, opening, or truncating files. In the OSF/Motif environment, the following flags are ignored:

- Security attributes
- File sharing
- File attributes
- The hTemplateFile used to specify extended attributes

Wind/U provides the OpenFile common dialog, except for the following `fuMode` values:

- OF_CANCEL
- OF_SHARE_COMPAT
- OF_SHARE_DENY_NONE
- OF_SHARE_DENY_READ
- OF_SHARE_DENY_WRITE
- OF_SHARE_EXCLUSIVE
- OF_SHARE_VERIFY

Dialog Box Hooks and Templates

The Windows common dialogs are laid out in typical Windows style with buttons along the right side of the dialog. It is possible to make them more compatible with OSF/Motif by overriding the default templates with a layout that is more consistent with OSF/Motif dialogs.

Dialog Box APIs

Table 6.8 shows the support status of Windows dialog box APIs on the Win32 hosted systems.

Table 6.8 Windows Dialog Box API Support Status

API	Windows 95	Windows NT	Macintosh	Unix
CreateDialog	Yes	Yes	Yes	Yes
CreateDialogIndirect	Yes	Yes	Yes	Yes
CreateDialogIndirectParam	Yes	Yes	Yes	Yes

Table 6.8 Windows Dialog Box API Support Status (continued)

API	Windows 95	Windows NT	Macintosh	Unix
CreateDialogParam	Yes	Yes	Yes	Yes
DefDlgProc	Yes	Yes	Yes	Yes
DialogBox	Yes	Yes	Yes	Yes
DialogBoxIndirect	Yes	Yes	Yes	Yes
DialogBoxIndirectParam	Yes	Yes	Yes	Yes
DialogBoxParam	Yes	Yes	Yes	Yes
DialogProc	Yes	Yes	Yes	Yes
EndDialog	Yes	Yes	Yes	Yes
GetDialogBaseUnits	Yes	Yes	Yes	Yes
GetDlgCtrlID	Yes	Yes	Yes	Yes
GetDlgItem	Yes	Yes	Yes	Yes
GetDlgItemInt	Yes	Yes	Yes	Yes
GetDlgItemText	Yes	Yes	Yes	Yes
GetNextDlgGroupItem	Yes	Yes	Yes	Yes
GetNextDlgTabItem	Yes	Yes	With restrictions	Yes
IsDialogMessage	Yes	Yes	Yes	Yes
MapDialogRect	Yes	Yes	Yes	Yes
MessageBox	Yes	Yes	Yes	Yes
MessageBoxEx	Yes	Yes	Yes	Yes
SendDlgItemMessage	Yes	Yes	Yes	Yes
SetDlgItemInt	Yes	Yes	Yes	Yes
SetDlgItemText	Yes	Yes	Yes	Yes

Summary

Dialog boxes are one of the most important aspects of your application's user interface. While both the Macintosh and UNIX environments provide the same Dialog Box functionality as the Windows environment, there are certain differences you should be aware of. In general, your cross-platform development tools will make these differences transparent to you as a developer, but it is important that you test your dialog boxes thoroughly to ensure that these differences do not affect your application's usability.

In addition to porting your Windows dialogs as they are, Wind/U also provides the ability to take advantage of OSF/Motif widget functionality not available in Windows. While doing so will result in slight differences between the UNIX and Windows versions of your applications, there may be cases when the additional functionality justifies any differences.

CHAPTER 7

System APIs

In Windows, the kernel, or system, library provides system services such as multitasking, memory management, and resource management. This chapter describes cross-platform issues related to the following system services. While the system APIs are not graphical, that is, they don't create menus or draw lines, they are a key area of portability concerns. Always use these system APIs to access the underlying operating system and hardware. This allows the portability layer on the Macintosh and UNIX systems to create a layer between your application and the underlying nonportable operating system calls.

- Error handling
- Internationalization
- Pipe creation
- Resource management
- Process synchronization
- System information
- Tape management
- Time

Atoms

In the Win32 API an atom table is a system-defined table that stores strings and corresponding identifiers. An application places a string in an atom table and receives a 16-bit integer, called an *atom*, that can be used to access the string. A string that has been placed in an atom table is called an *atom name*. Dynamic data exchange (DDE) applications use an atom table to share item-name and topic-name strings with other applications. Instead of passing actual strings, a DDE application passes atoms to its partner application. The partner uses the atoms to obtain the strings from the atom table.

The Windows global atom table is available to all applications. When an application places a string in the global atom table, the system generates an atom that is unique throughout the system. Any application that has the atom can obtain the string it identifies by querying the global atom table. An application that defines a private clipboard-data format or DDE-data format for sharing data with other applications should place the format name in the global atom table. This technique prevents conflicts with the names of formats defined by the system or other applications and makes the identifiers (atoms) for the messages or formats available to the other applications. An application can use a local atom table to efficiently manage a large number of strings used only within the application. An application requiring the same string in a number of structures can reduce memory usage by using a local atom table. Rather than copying the string into each structure, the application can place the string in the atom table and include the resulting atom in the structures. In this way, a string appears only once in memory but can be used many times in the application. Applications can also use local atom tables to save time when they are searching for a particular string. To perform a search, an application need only place the search string in the atom table and compare the resulting atom with the atoms in the relevant structures. Comparing atoms is typically faster than comparing strings. This technique is used internally within Windows, for example, the control class names are stored in an atom table for efficient comparison of class names.

On the Macintosh the global atom table can only be accessed by the application that created it, therefore it cannot be used to share information among applications. The other APIs are available on all platforms, but Macintosh restrictions are indicated in Table 7.1, which shows the support status of all Atom APIs in Windows 95, Windows NT, the Windows Portability Library for the Macintosh, and Wind/U for UNIX.

Table 7.1   Atom APIs

Function	Windows 95	Windows NT	Macintosh	UNIX
AddAtom	Yes	Yes	Yes	Yes
DeleteAtom	Yes	Yes	Yes	Yes
FindAtom	Yes	Yes	Yes	Yes
GetAtomName	Yes	Yes	Yes	Yes
GlobalAddAtom	Yes	Yes	Partial	Yes
GlobalDeleteAtom	Yes	Yes	Partial	Yes
GlobalFindAtom	Yes	Yes	Partial	Yes
GlobalGetAtomName	Yes	Yes	Partial	Yes
InitAtomTable	Yes	Yes	Yes	Yes

Communication

A communications resource is a physical or logical device that provides a single bidirectional, asynchronous data stream. Serial ports, parallel ports, fax machines, and modems are examples of communications resources. For each communications resource, there is a service provider consisting of a library or driver, which enables applications to access the resource.

In Win32 the file input and output (I/O) functions (`CreateFile`, `CloseHandle`, `ReadFile`, `ReadFileEx`, `WriteFile`, and `WriteFileEx`) provide the basic interface for opening and closing a communications resource handle and for performing read and write operations.

This communication access method is only available on Windows NT; it should not be used in applications that need to support Windows 95, Macintosh, or UNIX. Table 7.2 shows the support status of all communication resource APIs in Windows 95, Windows NT, the Windows Portability Library for the Macintosh, and Wind/U for UNIX.

Table 7.2 Communication APIs

Function	Windows 95	Windows NT	Macintosh	UNIX
BuildCommDCB	Yes	No	No	No
BuildCommDCBAndTimeouts	Yes	No	No	No
ClearCommBreak	Yes	No	No	No
ClearCommError	Yes	No	No	No
EnumCommDevices	Yes	No	No	No
EscapeCommFunction	Yes	No	No	No
GetCommEvent	Yes	No	No	No
GetCommMask	Yes	No	No	No
GetCommModemStatus	Yes	No	No	No
GetCommProperties	Yes	No	No	No
GetCommState	Yes	No	No	No
GetCommTimeouts	Yes	No	No	No
ModemAnswer	Yes	No	No	No
ModemClose	Yes	No	No	No
ModemCommand	Yes	No	No	No
ModemDial	Yes	No	No	No
ModemGetCommand	Yes	No	No	No
ModemHangUp	Yes	No	No	No
ModemOpen	Yes	No	No	No
PurgeComm	Yes	No	No	No
SetCommBreak	Yes	No	No	No
SetCommMask	Yes	No	No	No
SetCommState	Yes	No	No	No
SetCommTimeouts	Yes	No	No	No
SetCommUsage	Yes	No	No	No
SetupComm	Yes	No	No	No
TransmitCommChar	Yes	No	No	No
WaitCommEvent	Yes	No	No	No

Console/Character-Mode

The Win32 API provides consoles that manage input and output (I/O) for character-mode applications (applications that do not provide their own graphical user interface). Consoles provide high-level support for simple character-mode applications that interact with the user by using functions that read from standard input and write to standard output or standard error. Consoles also provide sophisticated low-level support that gives direct access to a console's screen buffer and enables applications to receive extended input information (such as mouse input).

The console APIs are only available on Windows 95 and Windows NT; they should not be used in applications that need to support the Macintosh or UNIX. Table 7.3 shows the support status of all console APIs in Windows 95, Windows NT, the Windows Portability Library for the Macintosh, and Wind/U for UNIX.

Table 7.3 Console APIs

Function	Windows 95	Windows NT	Macintosh	UNIX
AllocConsole	Yes	Yes	No	No
CreateConsoleScreenBuffer	Yes	Yes	No	No
FillConsoleOutputAttribute	Yes	Yes	No	No
FillConsoleOutputCharacter	Yes	Yes	No	No
FlushConsoleInputBuffer	Yes	Yes	No	No
FreeConsole	Yes	Yes	No	No
GenerateConsoleCtrlEvent	Yes	Yes	No	No
GetConsoleCP	No	Yes	No	No
GetConsoleCursorInfo	Yes	Yes	No	No
GetConsoleMode	Yes	Yes	No	No
GetConsoleOutputCP	No	Yes	No	No
GetConsoleScreenBufferInfo	Yes	Yes	No	No
GetConsoleTitle	Yes	Yes	No	No
GetLargestConsoleWindowSize	Yes	Yes	No	No

Table 7.3 Console APIs (continued)

Function	Windows 95	Windows NT	Macintosh	UNIX
GetNumberOfConsoleInputEvents	Yes	Yes	No	No
GetNumberOfConsoleMouseButtons	Yes	Yes	No	No
PeekConsoleInput	Yes	Yes	No	No
ReadConsole	Yes	Yes	No	No
ReadConsoleInput	Yes	Yes	No	No
ReadConsoleOutput	Yes	Yes	No	No
ReadConsoleOutputAttribute	Yes	Yes	No	No
ReadConsoleOutputCharacter	Yes	Yes	No	No
ScrollConsoleScreenBuffer	Yes	Yes	No	No
SetConsoleActiveScreenBuffer	Yes	Yes	No	No
SetConsoleCP	No	Yes	No	No
SetConsoleCtrlHandler	Yes	Yes	No	No
SetConsoleCursorInfo	Yes	Yes	No	No
SetConsoleCursorPosition	Yes	Yes	No	No
SetConsoleMode	Yes	Yes	No	No
SetConsoleOutputCP	No	Yes	No	No
SetConsoleScreenBufferSize	Yes	Yes	No	No
SetConsoleTextAttribute	Yes	Yes	No	No
SetConsoleTitle	Yes	Yes	No	No
SetConsoleWindowInfo	Yes	Yes	No	No
WriteConsole	Yes	Yes	No	No
WriteConsoleInput	Yes	Yes	No	No
WriteConsoleOutput	Yes	Yes	No	No
WriteConsoleOutputAttribute	Yes	Yes	No	No
WriteConsoleOutputCharacter	Yes	Yes	No	No

Debugging

The Win32 API contains set of APIs that can be used to create a basic event-driven debugger and to print diagnostic output. The APIs designed to create debuggers are very operating-system-dependent and are not available on Macintosh or UNIX. A few APIs are available on all platforms, but there are restrictions that you should be aware of if you use these functions. Table 7.4 shows the support status of dynamic-link library APIs in Windows 95, Windows NT, the Windows Portability Library for the Macintosh, and Wind/U for UNIX.

Table 7.4 Debugging APIs

Function	Windows 95	Windows NT	Macintosh	UNIX
ContinueDebugEvent	Yes	Yes	No	No
DebugActiveProcess	Yes	Yes	No	No
DebugBreak	Yes	Yes	Yes	No
FatalAppExit	Yes	Yes	Partial	Partial
FatalExit	Yes	Yes	Partial	Partial
FlushInstructionCache	Yes	Yes	No	No
GetThreadContext	Yes	Yes	No	No
GetThreadSelectorEntry	Yes	Yes	No	No
OutputDebugString	Yes	Yes	Yes	Yes
ReadProcessMemory	Yes	Yes	No	No
SetDebugErrorLevel	Yes	Yes	No	No
SetThreadContext	Yes	Yes	No	No
WaitForDebugEvent	Yes	Yes	No	No
WriteProcessMemory	Yes	Yes	No	No

Device Input and Output

The Win32 API contains an API with set control codes to directly communicate with a device. Again, this functionality is very operating-system-dependent and is not available on Macintosh or UNIX. Table 7.5 shows the support status of device input/output functionality in Windows 95, Windows NT, the Windows Portability Library for the Macintosh, and Wind/U for UNIX.

Table 7.5 Debugging APIs

Function	Windows 95	Windows NT	Macintosh	UNIX
DeviceIoControl	Yes	Yes	No	No
FSCTL_DISMOUNT_VOLUME	Yes	Yes	No	No
FSCTL_LOCK_VOLUME	Yes	Yes	No	No
FSCTL_UNLOCK_VOLUME	Yes	Yes	No	No
IOCTL_DISK_CHECK_VERIFY	Yes	Yes	No	No
IOCTL_DISK_EJECT_MEDIA	Yes	Yes	No	No
IOCTL_DISK_FORMAT_TRACKS	Yes	Yes	No	No
IOCTL_DISK_GET_DRIVE_GEOMETRY	Yes	Yes	No	No
IOCTL_DISK_GET_DRIVE_LAYOUT	Yes	Yes	No	No
IOCTL_DISK_GET_MEDIA_TYPES	Yes	Yes	No	No
IOCTL_DISK_GET_PARTITION_INFO	Yes	Yes	No	No
IOCTL_DISK_LOAD_MEDIA	Yes	Yes	No	No
IOCTL_DISK_MEDIA_REMOVAL	Yes	Yes	No	No
IOCTL_DISK_PERFORMANCE	Yes	Yes	No	No
IOCTL_DISK_REASSIGN_BLOCKS	Yes	Yes	No	No
IOCTL_DISK_SET_DRIVE_LAYOUT	Yes	Yes	No	No
IOCTL_DISK_SET_PARTITION_INFO	Yes	Yes	No	No
IOCTL_DISK_VERIFY	Yes	Yes	No	No
IOCTL_SERIAL_LSRMST_INSERT	Yes	Yes	No	No

Dynamic-Link Library (DLLs) APIs

In Win32, dynamic-link libraries provide a way for a process to call a function that is not part of its executable code. The executable code for the function is located in a dynamic-link library (DLL) containing one or more functions that are compiled, linked, and stored separately from the processes using them. On UNIX and Windows the Win32 API is implemented as a set of dynamic-link libraries.

Dynamic linking allows an executable module (either a library or a program) to include only the information needed at run time to locate the executable code for a DLL function. This type of linking differs from the more familiar static linking, which requires a copy of a library function's executable code in the executable module of each application using it.

There are two methods for calling a function in a DLL:

- Load-time dynamic linking occurs when an application's code makes an explicit call to a DLL function. This type of linking requires that the executable module of the application be built by linking with the DLL's import library, which supplies the information needed to locate the DLL function when the application starts.

- Run-time dynamic linking occurs when a program uses the `LoadLibrary` and `GetProcAddress` functions to get the starting address of a DLL function. This type of linking eliminates the need to link with an import library.

A DLL attaches to a process when the process starts or when one of its threads calls the LoadLibrary function. When a DLL attaches to a process, the operating system maps the DLL module into the address space of the process, making the DLL's executable code available to the process. When a DLL detaches from a process at process termination or as a result of a call to the `FreeLibrary` function, the DLL module is unmapped from the address space of the process. Like any other function, a DLL function is executed in the context of the thread (and the thread's process) that calls it. Therefore, the following conditions apply:

1. The threads of the process that called the DLL can use handles opened by a DLL function. Similarly, handles opened by any thread of the calling process can be used in the DLL function.

2. The DLL uses the user stack of the calling thread and the address space of the calling process.

3. Memory allocated by the DLL is in the address space of the calling process.

4. The threads of the process that called the DLL can read from or write to the globally declared variables in the DLL.

Windows DLLs are fully supported on Windows NT and Windows 95, mostly supported on UNIX and partly supported on Macintosh. Key APIs are available on all platforms, but there are restrictions that you should be aware of if you use these functions. Table 7.6 shows the support status of dynamic-link library APIs in Windows 95, Windows NT, the Windows Portability Library for the Macintosh, and Wind/U for UNIX.

Table 7.6 Dynamic-Link Library APIs

Function	Windows 95	Windows NT	Macintosh	UNIX
DisableThreadLibraryCalls	No	Yes	No	No
DllEntryPoint	Yes	Yes	No	Partial
FreeLibrary	Yes	Yes	No	Yes
FreeModule	Obsolete, use FreeLibrary	Obsolete	Obsolete	Obsolete
FreeProcInstance	Obsolete, not needed in Win32	Obsolete	Obsolete	Obsolete
GetCodeHandle	Obsolete, no handles to code address in Win32	Obsolete	Obsolete	Obsolete
GetInstanceData	Obsolete, protected address space in Win32	Obsolete	Obsolete	Obsolete
GetModuleFileName	Yes	Yes	Partial	Yes
GetModuleHandle	Yes	Yes	No	Yes
GetModuleUsage	Obsolete, protected address space in Win32	Obsolete	Obsolete	Obsolete
GetProcAddress	Yes	Yes	Partial	Partial
LoadLibrary	Yes	Yes	No	Yes
LoadLibraryEx	No	Yes	No	No

Table 7.6 Dynamic-Link Library APIs (continued)

Function	Windows 95	Windows NT	Macintosh	UNIX
LoadModule	Obsolete, use CreateProcess	Obsolete	Obsolete	Obsolete
MakeProcInstance	Obsolete, functions are called directly in Win32	Obsolete	Obsolete	Obsolete

Error Handling

Well-written applications include code that allows them to recover gracefully from unexpected errors. When an error occurs, the application may need to request user intervention, or it may be able to recover without help. In extreme cases, the application may log the user off or shut down the system. When an error occurs, most functions in the Win32 API return an error code, usually FALSE, NULL, 0xFFFFFFFF, or -1. Most functions in the Win32 API also set an internal error code called the last-error code. When a function succeeds, the last-error code is not reset. The error code is maintained separately for each running thread; an error in one thread does not overwrite the last-error code in another thread. An application can retrieve the last-error code by using the GetLastError function; the error code may tell more about what actually occurred to make the function fail. The GetLastError function is portable to all APIs. The SetLastError function sets the error code for the current thread. The SetLastErrorEx function also allows the caller to set an error type indicating the severity of the error. These functions are intended primarily for dynamic-link libraries (DLLs), so they can emulate the behavior of the Win32 API. The Win32 API defines a set of error codes that can be set as last-error codes or returned by these functions. Error codes are 32-bit values (bit 31 is the most significant bit). Bit 29 is reserved for application-defined error codes; no Win32 API error code has this bit set. Developers who define an error code for an application should set this bit to indicate that the error code has been defined by an application and to ensure that the error code does not conflict with any system-defined error codes.

Most error APIs are available on all platforms, but there are restrictions that you should be aware of if you use these functions. Table 7.7 shows the support status of all error APIs in Windows 95, Windows NT, the Windows Portability Library for the Macintosh, and Wind/U for UNIX.

Table 7.7 Error APIs

Function	Windows 95	Windows NT	Macintosh	UNIX
Beep	Yes	Yes	Partial	Partial
CloseSound	Obsolete	Obsolete	Obsolete	Obsolete
CountVoiceNotes	Obsolete	Obsolete	Obsolete	Obsolete
ExitWindows	Yes	Yes	No	No
ExitWindowsEx	Yes	Yes	No	No
FlashWindow	Yes	Yes	Partial	Partial
GetLastError	Yes	Yes	Partial	Yes
GetThresholdEvent	Obsolete	Obsolete	Obsolete	Obsolete
GetThresholdStatus	Obsolete	Obsolete	Obsolete	Obsolete
MessageBeep	Yes	Yes	Yes	Yes
OpenSound	Obsolete	Obsolete	Obsolete	Obsolete
SetErrorMode	Yes	Yes	Partial	Partial
SetLastError	Yes	Yes	Yes	Yes
SetLastErrorEx	Yes	Yes	Yes	Yes
SetSoundNoise	Obsolete	Obsolete	Obsolete	Obsolete
SetVoiceAccent	Obsolete	Obsolete	Obsolete	Obsolete
SetVoiceEnvelope	Obsolete	Obsolete	Obsolete	Obsolete
SetVoiceNote	Obsolete	Obsolete	Obsolete	Obsolete
SetVoiceQueueSize	Obsolete	Obsolete	Obsolete	Obsolete
SetVoiceSound	Obsolete	Obsolete	Obsolete	Obsolete
SetVoiceThreshold	Obsolete	Obsolete	Obsolete	Obsolete
StartSound	Obsolete	Obsolete	Obsolete	Obsolete
StopSound	Obsolete	Obsolete	Obsolete	Obsolete
SyncAllVoices	Obsolete	Obsolete	Obsolete	Obsolete
WaitSoundState	Obsolete	Obsolete	Obsolete	Obsolete

Event Logging

When an error occurs in an application written for Microsoft Windows, Macintosh, or UNIX, the system administrator or support personnel must determine what caused the error, attempt to recover any lost data, and prevent the error from recurring. If applications record important events such as low-memory conditions or excessive disk retries, the record of this information, called an *event log*, can be used to help determine what conditions may have caused the error and the context in which the error occurred. By periodically viewing the event log, the system administrator may be able to identify problems before they cause serious damage.

The style of recording errors varies greatly among operating systems. Also, many applications record errors and events in various proprietary error logs. These proprietary logs have different formats, apply different user interfaces for their display, and cannot be merged to provide a complete report. But all of these logs store similar information and present the logged data in similar ways.

The Win32 API has added a set of functions to provide a standard centralized way for applications to record important software and hardware events. While this concept is widespread the APIs that support it are nonportable at this time. The event-logging APIs are not available on all platforms. Table 7.8 shows the support status of all event-logging APIs in Windows 95, Windows NT, the Windows Portability Library for the Macintosh, and Wind/U for UNIX.

Table 7.8 Event-Logging APIs

Function	Windows 95	Windows NT	Macintosh	UNIX
BackupEventLog	Yes	Yes	No	No
ClearEventLog	Yes	Yes	No	No
CloseEventLog	Yes	Yes	No	No
DeregisterEventSource	Yes	Yes	No	No
GetNumberOfEventLogRecords	Yes	Yes	No	No
GetOldestEventLogRecord	Yes	Yes	No	No
NotifyChangeEventLog	Yes	Yes	No	No
OpenBackupEventLog	Yes	Yes	No	No

Table 7.8 Event-Logging APIs (continued)

Function	Windows 95	Windows NT	Macintosh	UNIX
OpenEventLog	Yes	Yes	No	No
ReadEventLog	Yes	Yes	No	No
RegisterEventSource	Yes	Yes	No	No
ReportEvent	Yes	Yes	No	No

File I/O and File Systems

There are a number of file systems that Win32 applications must run on. On Windows NT there are three file systems: New Technology file system (NTFS), file allocation table (FAT) file system, and high-performance file system (HPFS). On Windows 95 there are the FAT and VFAT (virtual file allocation table) file systems. The Macintosh file system is a breed apart, with create types, file types, directory IDs, and so on. The UNIX file system consist of a large tree with long filenames, which can have other drives or network drives mounted anywhere in the tree.

Standard Windows code that parses and manipulates pathnames will not work on the Macintosh or UNIX. Also, HFILE handles returned by Win32 functions will not work in the normal C run-time library functions. The attributes of the various file systems are listed in Table 7.9.

Table 7.9 File System Attributes

File System	Long Filenames	Separator	Drives	Case-Sensitive
FAT	No	\ or /	A: ... Z:	No
HPFS	Yes	\ or /	A: ... Z:	No, preserves case
NTFS	Yes	\ or /	A: ... Z:	No, preserves case
VFAT	Yes	\ or /	A: ... Z:	No, preserves case
Mac	Yes	/	named objects	Yes
UNIX	Yes	/	named objects	Yes

File systems like NTFS preserve the case that the filename was created in, but all file system comparisons are case-insensitive. Thus, *Word, word,* and *WORD,* all refer to the same file. Yet, even with all of these differences, it is easy to make most MFC applications portable. For example, in the MFC tutorial Scribble, the pathname to the file is almost totally managed by the MFC framework. In the Scribble application, code that deals with the pathname simply passes the string on or prints the string.

```
From: mfc/scribble/step5/scribdoc.cpp
//////////////////////////////////////////////////////////////////////
//////////
// CScribDoc commands

BOOL CScribDoc::OnOpenDocument(LPCTSTR lpszPathName)
{
    if (!CDocument::OnOpenDocument(lpszPathName))
            return FALSE;
    InitDocument();
    return TRUE;
}
```

In the `OnOpenDocument` member function the pathname is forwarded on the parent class CDocument to use. The application code does not parse or examine the pathname in any way.

```
From: mfc/scribble/step5/scribvw.cpp
void CScribView::PrintTitlePage(CDC* pDC, CPrintInfo* pInfo)
{
    // Prepare a font size for displaying the file name
    ...
    // Get the file name, to be displayed on title page
    CString strPageTitle = GetDocument()->GetTitle();

    // Display the file name 1 inch below top of the page,
    // centered horizontally
    pDC->SetTextAlign(TA_CENTER);
```

```
pDC->TextOut(pInfo->m_rectDraw.right/2, -100, strPageTitle);
    ...
}
```

Here the `CDocument::GetTitle()` member function is used to create a `CString` containing the filename. The filename is not parsed or examined: it is simply drawn using `TextOut()`. The MFC libraries, not your application, deal with any platform dependencies.

At times you need to go beyond what is easy to do with high-level MFC classes. If this is the case, use the MFC `CFileDialog` which is built on the Windows common dialog functions, `GetOpenFileName()` and `GetSaveFileName()`. `CFileDialog` can be used to help create a layer between your application code and the various file systems. When using `CFileDialog` to build a file-system-independent layer, start by examining the implementation of `CWinApp::OnFileOpen` and `CDocument::OnFileSave` and related functions in the MFC source code. The following code segment illustrates some differences you will need to deal with between most Windows-based file systems and the Mac file system and how MFC deals with them:

```
From: mfc/src/doccore.cpp
#ifndef _MAC
                  // check for dubious filename
                  int iBad = newName.FindOneOf(_T(" #%;/\\"));
#else
                  int iBad = newName.FindOneOf(_T(":"));
#endif
```

In this example, MFC uses a `#ifndef` to deal with the differences in the set of invalid characters allowed in a pathname. Some types of programs will need to access the file system outside or the MFC class library. When your application needs direct access, start with the Win32 file system APIs and add `#ifdefs` as needed.

Most file APIs are available on all platforms, but there are restrictions that you should be aware of if you use these functions. Table 7.10 shows the support status of all file APIs in Windows 95, Windows NT, the Windows Portability Library for the Macintosh, and Wind/U for UNIX.

Table 7.10 File APIs

Function	Windows 95	Windows NT	Macintosh	UNIX
_hread	Yes	Yes	Yes	Yes
_hwrite	Yes	Yes	Yes	Yes
_lclose	Yes	Yes	Yes	Yes
_lcreat	Yes	Yes	Yes	Yes
_llseek	Yes	Yes	Yes	Yes
_lopen	Yes	Yes	Yes	Yes
_lread	Yes	Yes	Yes	Yes
_lwrite	Yes	Yes	Yes	Yes
AreFileApisANSI	No	Yes	No	No
CloseHandle	Yes	Yes	Partial	Partial
CopyFile	Yes	Yes	Partial	Partial
CreateDirectory	Yes	Yes	No	Yes
CreateDirectoryEx	Yes	Yes	No	Partial
CreateFile	Yes	Yes	Partial	Partial
CreateIoCompletionPort	No	Yes	No	No
DefineDosDevice	Yes	Yes	No	No
DeleteFile	Yes	Yes	Yes	Yes
FileIOCompletionRoutine	No	Yes	No	No
FindClose	Yes	Yes	Yes	Yes
FindCloseChangeNotification	Yes	Yes	No	No
FindFirstChangeNotification	Yes	Yes	No	No
FindFirstFile	Yes	Yes	Partial	Yes
FindNextChangeNotification	Yes	Yes	No	No
FindNextFile	Yes	Yes	No	Yes
FlushFileBuffers	Yes	Yes	Yes	Yes
GetBinaryType	No	Yes	No	No
GetCurrentDirectory	Yes	Yes	No	Yes
GetDiskFreeSpace	Yes	Yes	No	Yes

Table 7.10 File APIs (continued)

Function	Windows 95	Windows NT	Macintosh	UNIX
GetDriveType	Yes	Yes	No	Partial
GetFileAttributes	Yes	Yes	Partial	Partial
GetFileInformationByHandle	Yes	Yes	Partial	Partial
GetFileSize	Yes	Yes	Yes	Yes
GetFileType	Yes	Yes	Partial	Partial
GetFullPathName	Yes	Yes	Yes	Yes
GetLogicalDrives	Yes	Yes	No	No
GetLogicalDriveStrings	Yes	Yes	No	No
GetQueuedCompletionStatus	No	Yes	No	No
GetShortPathName	No	Yes	No	No
GetTempDrive	Obsolete, use GetTempPath	Obsolete	Obsolete	Obsolete
GetTempFileName	Yes	Yes	Partial	Partial
GetTempPath	Yes	Yes	Partial	Partial
GetVolumeInformation	Yes	Yes	No	No
LockFile	Yes	Yes	Partial	Partial
LockFileEx	No	Yes	No	Partial
MoveFile	Yes	Yes	Yes	Yes
MoveFileEx	No	Yes	No	Partial
OpenFile	Yes	Yes	Partial	Partial
QueryDosDevice	Yes	Yes	No	No
ReadFile	Yes	Yes	Partial	Partial
ReadFileEx	No	Yes	No	Partial
RemoveDirectory	Yes	Yes	No	Yes
SearchPath	Yes	Yes	No	Yes
SetCurrentDirectory	Yes	Yes	No	Yes

Table 7.10 File APIs (continued)

Function	Windows 95	Windows NT	Macintosh	UNIX
SetEndOfFile	Yes	Yes	Yes	Yes
SetFileApisToANSI	No	Yes	No	No
SetFileApisToOEM	No	Yes	No	No
SetFileAttributes	Yes	Yes	Partial	Partial
SetFilePointer	Yes	Yes	Yes	Yes
SetHandleCount	Yes	Yes	No	No
SetVolumeLabel	Yes	Yes	No	No
UnlockFile	Yes	Yes	Partial	Partial
UnlockFileEx	No	Yes	No	Partial
WriteFile	Yes	Yes	Partial	Partial
WriteFileEx	No	Yes	No	Partial

File Mapping

File mapping is the copying of a file's contents to a process's virtual address space. The copy of the file's contents is called the *file view*, and the internal structure the operating system uses to maintain the copy is called the *file-mapping object*.

Another process can create an identical file view in its own virtual address space by using the first process's file-mapping object to create the view. This enables the processes to share data. Any process that has the name or a handle of a file-mapping object can create a file view.

No file-mapping API is available on all platforms, but most exist on all platforms expect Macintosh. Table 7.11 shows the support status of all file-mapping APIs in Windows 95, Windows NT, the Windows Portability Library for the Macintosh, and Wind/U for UNIX.

Table 7.11 File-Mapping APIs

Function	Windows 95	Windows NT	Macintosh	UNIX
CreateFileMapping	Yes	Yes	No	Yes
FlushViewOfFile	Yes	Yes	No	Yes
MapViewOfFile	Yes	Yes	No	Yes
MapViewOfFileEx	Yes	Yes	No	Yes
OpenFileMapping	Yes	Yes	No	Yes
UnmapViewOfFile	Yes	Yes	No	Yes

MailSlots

A *mailslot* is a mechanism for one-way interprocess communications (IPC). The owner of the mailslot can retrieve messages that are stored there. These messages are typically sent over a network to either a specified computer or all computers in a specified domain. A *domain* is a group of workstations and servers that share a group name.

A mailslot is a pseudofile; it resides in memory, and standard Windows file functions write to it. Unlike disk files, however, mailslots are temporary. When every handle of a mailslot is closed, the mailslot and all the data it contains are deleted. The data in a mailslot message can be in any form.

A mailslot server is a process that creates and owns a mailslot. When the server creates a mailslot, it receives a mailslot handle. This handle must be used when a process reads messages from the mailslot. Only the process that creates a mailslot (or has obtained the handle by some other mechanism, such as inheritance) can read from the mailslot. A mailslot exists until all server handles to it have been closed or all server processes have exited. All mailslots are local to the process that creates them; a process cannot create a remote mailslot.

The mailslot APIs are limited to Windows operating systems. Table 7.12 shows the support status of all mailslot APIs in Windows 95, Windows NT, the Windows Portability Library for the Macintosh, and Wind/U for UNIX.

Table 7.12 Mailslot APIs

Function	Windows 95	Windows NT	Macintosh	UNIX
CreateMailslot	Yes	Yes	No	No
GetMailslotInfo	Yes	Yes	No	No
SetMailslotInfo	Yes	Yes	No	No

Memory Management

In Win32, MFC, and the C run-time library there are several ways to allocate memory. The most portable memory management technique is to use the functions built into C++, new and delete. When you need more sophisticated memory management, you normally need multiple heaps of memory to minimize heap fragmentation and maximize memory locality. For heap management, you can use the Win32 Heap* APIs or a third-party library, such as SmartHeap from MicroQuill. Third-party libraries offer better performance and more functionality than the Win32 Heap* APIs. The old Windows 3.1 memory APIs Local* and Global* are generally not needed in Win32 applications. They exist to minimize the Win16-to-Win32 porting issues. Although most APIs are available on all platforms, there are restrictions that you should be aware of if you use these functions. Table 7.13 shows the support status of all memory management APIs in Windows 95, Windows NT, the Windows Portability Library for the Macintosh, and Wind/U for UNIX.

Table 7.13 Memory APIs

Function	Windows 95	Windows NT	Macintosh	UNIX
ChangeSelector	Obsolete	Obsolete	Obsolete	Obsolete
CopyMemory	Yes	Yes	Yes	Yes
DefineHandleTable	Obsolete	Obsolete	Obsolete	Obsolete
FillMemory	Yes	Yes	Yes	Yes

Table 7.13 Memory APIs (continued)

Function	Windows 95	Windows NT	Macintosh	UNIX
FreeSelector	Obsolete	Obsolete	Obsolete	Obsolete
GetCodeInfo	Obsolete	Obsolete	Obsolete	Obsolete
GetFreeSpace	Obsolete, use GlobalMemoryStatus	Obsolete	Obsolete	Obsolete
GetProcessHeap	Yes	Yes	No	Yes
GetProcessHeaps	Yes	Yes	No	Yes
GlobalAlloc	Yes	Yes	Partial	Partial
GlobalCompact	Obsolete	Obsolete	Obsolete	Obsolete
GlobalDiscard	Yes	Yes	Partial	Partial
GlobalDosAlloc	Obsolete	Obsolete	Obsolete	Obsolete
GlobalDosFree	Obsolete	Obsolete	Obsolete	Obsolete
GlobalFix	Obsolete	Obsolete	Obsolete	Obsolete
GlobalFlags	Yes	Yes	Partial	Yes
GlobalFree	Yes	Yes	Yes	Partial
GlobalHandle	Yes	Yes	Yes	Yes
GlobalLock	Yes	Yes	Partial	Partial
GlobalLRUNewest	Obsolete	Obsolete	Obsolete	Obsolete
GlobalLRUOldest	Obsolete	Obsolete	Obsolete	Obsolete
GlobalMemoryStatus	Yes	Yes	Partial	Yes
GlobalNotify	Obsolete	Obsolete	Obsolete	Obsolete
GlobalPageLock	Obsolete	Obsolete	Obsolete	Obsolete
GlobalPageUnlock	Obsolete	Obsolete	Obsolete	Obsolete
GlobalReAlloc	Yes	Yes	Partial	Partial
GlobalSize	Yes	Yes	Yes	Yes
GlobalUnfix	Obsolete	Obsolete	Obsolete	Obsolete
GlobalUnlock	Yes	Yes	Yes	Partial
GlobalUnWire	Obsolete	Obsolete	Obsolete	Obsolete
GlobalWire	Obsolete	Obsolete	Obsolete	Obsolete

Table 7.13 Memory APIs (continued)

Function	Windows 95	Windows NT	Macintosh	UNIX
HeapAlloc	Yes	Yes	No	Yes
HeapCompact	Yes	Yes	No	Yes
HeapCreate	Yes	Yes	No	Yes
HeapDestroy	Yes	Yes	No	Yes
HeapFree	Yes	Yes	No	Yes
HeapLock	Yes	Yes	No	Yes
HeapReAlloc	Yes	Yes	No	Yes
HeapSize	Yes	Yes	No	Yes
HeapUnlock	Yes	Yes	No	Yes
HeapValidate	Yes	Yes	No	Yes
HeapWalk	Yes	Yes	No	Yes
IsBadCodePtr	Yes	Yes	No	Yes
IsBadHugeReadPtr	Yes	Yes	No	Yes
IsBadHugeWritePtr	Yes	Yes	No	Yes
IsBadReadPtr	Yes	Yes	No	Yes
IsBadStringPtr	Yes	Yes	No	Yes
IsBadWritePtr	Yes	Yes	No	Yes
LimitEmsPages	Obsolete	Obsolete	Obsolete	Obsolete
LocalAlloc	Yes	Yes	Partial	Partial
LocalCompact	Obsolete	Obsolete	Obsolete	Obsolete
LocalDiscard	Yes	Yes	No	Yes
LocalFlags	Yes	Yes	Yes	Partial
LocalFree	Yes	Yes	Yes	Partial
LocalHandle	Yes	Yes	Yes	Yes
LocalInit	Obsolete	Obsolete	Obsolete	Obsolete
LocalLock	Yes	Yes	Yes	Partial
LocalReAlloc	Yes	Yes	Partial	Partial
LocalShrink	Obsolete	Obsolete	Obsolete	Obsolete

Table 7.13 Memory APIs (continued)

Function	Windows 95	Windows NT	Macintosh	UNIX
LocalSize	Yes	Yes	Yes	Yes
LocalUnlock	Yes	Yes	Yes	Partial
LockSegment	Obsolete	Obsolete	Obsolete	Obsolete
MoveMemory	Yes	Yes		Yes
SetSwapAreaSize	Obsolete	Obsolete	Obsolete	Obsolete
SwitchStackBack	Obsolete	Obsolete	Obsolete	Obsolete
SwitchStackTo	Obsolete	Obsolete	Obsolete	Obsolete
UnlockSegment	Obsolete	Obsolete	Obsolete	Obsolete
VirtualAlloc	Yes	Yes	No	No
VirtualFree	Yes	Yes	No	No
VirtualLock	Yes	Yes	No	No
VirtualProtect	Yes	Yes	No	No
VirtualProtectEx	No	Yes	No	No
VirtualQuery	Yes	Yes	No	No
VirtualQueryEx	No	Yes	No	No
VirtualUnlock	Yes	Yes	No	No
ZeroMemory	Yes	Yes	No	Yes

Network Dynamic Data Exchange (NetDDE)

The Win32 API provides network dynamic data exchange (NetDDE) services. *Dynamic data exchange* lets a process establish data conversations with other processes executing on the same computer. *Network DDE* lets a process establish data conversations with other processes executing on other computers over a network.

The NetDDE APIs are only available on Windows platforms; in most cases the Winsock APIs can be used for more portable network interprocess communication. Table 7.14 shows the support status of all NetDDE APIs in

Windows 95, Windows NT, the Windows Portability Library for the Macintosh, and Wind/U for UNIX.

Table 7.14 Network DDE APIs

Function	Windows 95	Windows NT	Macintosh	UNIX
NDdeGetErrorString	Yes	Yes	No	No
NDdeGetShareSecurity	Yes	Yes	No	No
NDdeGetTrustedShare	Yes	Yes	No	No
NDdeIsValidAppTopicList	Yes	Yes	No	No
NDdeIsValidShareName	Yes	Yes	No	No
NDdeSetShareSecurity	Yes	Yes	No	No
NDdeSetTrustedShare	Yes	Yes	No	No
NDdeShareAdd	Yes	Yes	No	No
NDdeShareDel	Yes	Yes	No	No
NDdeShareEnum	Yes	Yes	No	No
NDdeShareGetInfo	Yes	Yes	No	No
NDdeShareSetInfo	Yes	Yes	No	No
NDdeTrustedShareEnum	Yes	Yes	No	No

Networking

The Win32 API contains functions to implement networking capabilities without making allowances for a particular network provider or physical network implementation. In other words, Win32 network functions are network-independent. Applications can use these functions to add and cancel network connections and to retrieve information about the current configuration of the network. In addition, the Win32 API implements a version of the IBM NetBIOS network interface for applications that require it. In addition to using the network functions, processes can use the Win32 API implementations of mailslots and named pipes to communicate with one another.

The network APIs are currently only available on Windows platforms; in most cases the Winsock APIs can be used for more portable network interprocess communication. Table 7.15 shows the support status of all network APIs in Windows 95, Windows NT, the Windows Portability Library for the Macintosh, and Wind/U for UNIX.

Table 7.15 Network APIs

Function	Windows 95	Windows NT	Macintosh	UNIX
AcsLan	No	Yes	No	No
Netbios	Yes	Yes	No	No
WNetAddConnection	Yes	Yes	No	No
WNetAddConnection2	Yes	Yes	No	No
WNetAddConnection3	Yes	Yes	No	No
WNetCancelConnection	Yes	Yes	No	No
WNetCancelConnection2	Yes	Yes	No	No
WNetCloseEnum	Yes	Yes	No	No
WNetConnectionDialog	Yes	Yes	No	No
WNetDisconnectDialog	Yes	Yes	No	No
WNetEnumResource	Yes	Yes	No	No
WNetGetConnection	Yes	Yes	No	No
WNetGetLastError	Yes	Yes	No	No
WNetGetUniversalName	Yes	Yes	No	No
WNetGetUser	Yes	Yes	No	No
WNetOpenEnum	Yes	Yes	No	No

Driver and Hardware Management

Accessing the hardware at any level can lead to nonportable code. Even, such seemingly common devices as the keyboard can create portability problems. On PCs there are only a few types of keyboards, on UNIX workstations there are a wide variety of keyboards, and on the Macintosh more than one keyboard is allowed. For example, GetKeyState (VK_MBUTTON) and GetKeyState (VK_RBUTTON) always return zero on the Macintosh. Macintosh keyboards have a **caps lock** key that physically locks down, as on a typewriter. As a result, the most significant bit of the return value from GetKeyState (VK_CAPITAL) is never set on the Macintosh. The least significant bit of the return value can be used to determine whether the **caps lock** key is toggled. When multiple keyboards are connected to the Macintosh, GetKeyState returns the current up/down state of the requested virtual key on the keyboard where that virtual key was last pressed or released. As a result, the return value of GetKeyState may not be correct for all keyboards. For example, if the requested virtual key is pressed but not released on Keyboard A, then pressed and released on Keyboard B, GetKeyState reports the key to be up (the correct state on Keyboard B), although the key is still down on Keyboard A. GetAsyncKeyState returns the up/down state of the requested virtual key on the last keyboard to be typed on, regardless of what key was pressed or released there. GetKeyState duplicates this behavior when reporting the toggle state of toggle keys.

Similar problems exist on UNIX, where toggling the **caps lock** key only sends notification to the active process. A few of these APIs are available on all platforms, and there are restrictions that you should be aware of if you use these functions. Table 7.16 shows the support status of all driver and keyboard APIs in Windows 95, Windows NT, the Windows Portability Library for the Macintosh, and Wind/U for UNIX.

Table 7.16 Driver and Hardware APIs

Function	Windows 95	Windows NT	Macintosh	UNIX
EnableHardwareInput	Yes	Yes	No	No
GetDriverInfo	Yes	Yes	No	No
GetDriverModuleHandle	Yes	Yes	No	No
GetInputState	Yes	Yes	No	No
GetKeyboardState	Yes	Yes	Partial	Yes
GetKeyNameText	Yes	Yes	No	Yes
GetKeyState	Yes	Yes	Partial	Yes
GetNextDriver	Yes	Yes	No	No
MapVirtualKey	Yes	Yes	Yes	Yes
OemKeyScan	Yes	Yes	No	No

Table 7.16 Driver and Hardware APIs (continued)

Function	Windows 95	Windows NT	Macintosh	UNIX
SetKeyboardState	Yes	Yes	Partial	No
VkKeyScan	Yes	Yes	Yes	No

Environment Variables

Every process has an environment block that contains a set of environment variables and their values. Programs inherit the environment variables from the application that started them. By default, a child process inherits the environment variables of its parent process. However, you can specify a different environment for the child process by creating a new environment block and passing a pointer to it as a parameter to the CreateProcess function. The GetEnvironmentStrings function returns a pointer to the environment block of the calling process. This should be treated as a read-only block; do not modify it directly. Instead, use the SetEnvironmentVariable function to change an environment variable. The GetEnvironmentVariable function determines whether a specified variable is defined in the environment of the calling process, and, if so, what its value is.

Table 7.17 shows the support status of all Environment APIs in Windows 95, Windows NT, the Windows Portability Library for the Macintosh, and Wind/U for UNIX.

Table 7.17 Environment APIs

Function	Windows 95	Windows NT	Macintosh	UNIX
FreeEnvironmentStrings	No	Yes	No	Yes
GetEnvironmentStrings	Yes	Yes	No	Yes
GetEnvironmentVariable	Yes	Yes	No	Yes
SetEnvironmentVariable	Yes	Yes	No	Yes

Miscellaneous

There are a few other kernel APIs that are not very portable. Table 7.18 shows the support status of all these miscellaneous kernel APIs in Windows 95, Windows NT, the Windows Portability Library for the Macintosh, and Wind/U for UNIX.

Table 7.18 Miscellaneous Kernel APIs

Function	Windows 95	Windows NT	Macintosh	UNIX
CreateIoCompletionPort	No	Yes	No	No
DefineDosDevice	No	Yes	No	No
DeviceIoControl	Yes	Yes	No	No
GetBinaryType	No	Yes	No	No
GetMailslotInfo	Yes	Yes	No	No
GetOverlappedResult	Yes	Yes	No	No
GetPriorityClass	Yes	Yes	No	No
GetQueuedCompletionStatus	No	Yes	No	No
GetStartupInfo	Yes	Yes	No	No
QueryDosDevice	Yes	Yes	No	No
QueryPerformanceCounter	Yes	Yes	No	No
QueryPerformanceFrequency	Yes	Yes	No	No
SetPriorityClass	Yes	Yes	No	No
SetProcessShutdownParameters	No	Yes	No	No
SetStdHandle	Yes	Yes	No	No
SetSystemPowerState	Yes	Future	No	No
SetSystemTimeAdjustment	No	Yes	No	No
SetUnhandledExceptionFilter	Yes	Yes	No	No
SystemTimeToTzSpecificLocalTime	Yes	Yes	No	No
UnhandledExceptionFilter	Yes	Yes	No	No

Performance Monitoring

The following Windows 3.1 profiling APIs are mostly obsolete and are not supported on the Macintosh or UNIX. Profiling tools are provided with Visual C++ for Windows NT, Windows 95, and the Macintosh. On UNIX a wide variety of profiling tools are available.

Table 7.19 shows the support status of all profiling and performance monitoring APIs in Windows 95, Windows NT, the Windows Portability Library for the Macintosh, and Wind/U for UNIX.

Table 7.19 Profile and Performance Monitoring APIs

Function	Windows 95	Windows NT	Macintosh	UNIX
ProfClear	Obsolete	Obsolete	Obsolete	Obsolete
ProfFinish	Obsolete	Obsolete	Obsolete	Obsolete
ProfFlush	Obsolete	Obsolete	Obsolete	Obsolete
ProfInsChk	Obsolete	Obsolete	Obsolete	Obsolete
ProfSampRate	Obsolete	Obsolete	Obsolete	Obsolete
ProfSetup	Obsolete	Obsolete	Obsolete	Obsolete
ProfStart	Obsolete	Obsolete	Obsolete	Obsolete
ProfStop	Obsolete	Obsolete	Obsolete	Obsolete
QueryPerformanceCounter	Yes	Yes	No	No
QueryPerformanceFrequency	Yes	Yes	No	No
RegConnectRegistry	Yes	Yes	No	No
RegQueryValueEx	Yes	Yes	No	No

Pipes

A *pipe* is a communication conduit with two ends: A process with a handle to one end can communicate with a process having a handle to the other end. Pipes can be one-way, where one end is read-only and the other end is write-only, or they can be two-way, where both ends of the pipe can read and write. The Win32 API provides both anonymous (unnamed) pipes and named pipes.

The pipe APIs are limited to Windows operating systems. Table 7.20 shows the support status of all pipe APIs in Windows 95, Windows NT, the Windows Portability Library for the Macintosh, and Wind/U for UNIX.

Table 7.20 Kernel Pipe APIs

Function	Windows 95	Windows NT	Macintosh	UNIX
CallNamedPipe	Yes	Yes	No	No
ConnectNamedPipe	No	Yes	No	No
CreateNamedPipe	No	Yes	No	No
CreatePipe	Yes	Yes	No	No
DisconnectNamedPipe	No	Yes	No	No
GetNamedPipeHandleState	Yes	Yes	No	No
GetNamedPipeInfo	Yes	Yes	No	No
ImpersonateNamedPipeClient	Yes	Yes	No	No
PeekNamedPipe	Yes	Yes	No	No
SetNamedPipeHandleState	Yes	Yes	No	No
TransactNamedPipe	Yes	Yes	No	No
WaitNamedPipe	Yes	Yes	No	No

Processes and Threads

An application written for Windows or UNIX can consist of more than one process, and a process can consist of more than one thread. The Win32 API supports multitasking, which creates the effect of simultaneous execution of multiple processes and threads.

A *process* is a program that is loaded into memory and prepared for execution. Each process has a private virtual address space. A process consists of the code, data, and other system resources such as files, pipes, and synchronization objects that are accessible to the threads of the process. Each process is started with a single thread, but additional independently executing threads can be created.

A *thread* can execute any part of the program's code, including a part executed by another thread. Threads are the basic entity to which the operating system allocates CPU time. Each thread maintains a set of structures for saving its context while waiting to be scheduled for processing time. The context includes the thread's set of machine registers, the kernel stack, a thread environment block, and a user stack in the address space of the thread's process. All threads of a process share the virtual address space and can access the global variables and system resources of the process.

Other APIs are available on all platforms, but there are restrictions that you should be aware of if you use these functions. Table 7.21 shows the support status of all process and threads APIs in Windows 95, Windows NT, the Windows Portability Library for the Macintosh, and Wind/U for UNIX.

Table 7.21 Process and Thread APIs

Function	Windows 95	Windows NT	Macintosh	UNIX
AttachThreadInput	Yes	Yes	No	No
CommandLineToArgvW	Yes	Yes	No	No
CreateProcess	Yes	Yes	No	Yes
CreateRemoteThread	Yes	Yes	No	No
CreateThread	Yes	Yes	No	Yes
DuplicateHandle	Yes	Yes	No	Partial
ExitProcess	Yes	Yes	No	Yes
ExitThread	Yes	Yes	No	Yes
FreeEnvironmentStrings	Yes	Yes	No	Yes
GetCommandLine	Yes	Yes	No	Yes
GetCurrentProcess	Yes	Yes	No	Yes
GetCurrentProcessId	Yes	Yes	No	Yes
GetCurrentThread	Yes	Yes	Yes	Yes
GetCurrentThreadId	Yes	Yes	No	Yes
GetEnvironmentStrings	Yes	Yes	No	Yes

Table 7.21 Process and Thread APIs (continued)

Function	Windows 95	Windows NT	Macintosh	UNIX
GetEnvironmentVariable	Yes	Yes	No	Yes
GetExitCodeProcess	Yes	Yes	No	Yes
GetExitCodeThread	Yes	Yes	No	Yes
GetPriorityClass	Yes	Yes	No	No
GetProcessAffinityMask	Yes	Yes	No	No
GetProcessShutdownParameters	Yes	Yes	No	No
GetProcessTimes	Yes	Yes	No	No
GetProcessWorkingSetSize	Yes	Yes	No	No
GetStartupInfo	Yes	Yes	No	No
GetThreadPriority	Yes	Yes	No	No
GetThreadTimes	Yes	Yes	No	No
OpenProcess	Yes	Yes	No	No
ResumeThread	Yes	Yes	No	No
SetEnvironmentVariable	Yes	Yes	No	Yes
SetPriorityClass	Yes	Yes	No	No
SetProcessShutdownParameters	Yes	Yes	No	No
SetProcessWorkingSetSize	Yes	Yes	No	No
SetThreadAffinityMask	Yes	Yes	No	No
SetThreadPriority	Yes	Yes	No	No
Sleep	Yes	Yes	No	Yes
SleepEx	Yes	Yes	No	Partial
SuspendThread	Yes	Yes	No	No
TerminateProcess	Yes	Yes	No	Yes
TerminateThread	Yes	Yes	No	Yes
TlsAlloc	Yes	Yes	No	Yes
TlsFree	Yes	Yes	No	Yes
TlsGetValue	Yes	Yes	No	Yes
TlsSetValue	Yes	Yes	No	Yes

Table 7.21 Process and Thread APIs (continued)

Function	Windows 95	Windows NT	Macintosh	UNIX
WaitForInputIdle	Yes	Yes	No	No
WinExec	Yes	Yes	No	Yes
WriteProcessMemory	Yes	Yes	No	No
Yield	Obsolete	Obsolete	Obsolete	Obsolete

Registry and Initialization Files

When writing Win32 applications use initialization files to store information that otherwise would be lost when the application closes. These files typically contain such information as user preferences for the configuration of the application. Initialization files, however, have the following inherent limitations:

- Information in initialization files is typically available only to the application that put it there.
- The text format of initialization files allows casual manipulation by potentially naive end users.
- Separate initialization files for many applications can proliferate on a hard disk.
- There is no way to secure initialization files against tampering.
- Initialization files do not support multiple users.
- Initialization files do not support multiple versions of the same application.
- Initialization files are not recoverable.
- Information in initialization files cannot be accessed or administered remotely in any consistent way.

Win32 also includes a registration database. A registration database contains information that supports shell applications (such as Windows File Manager) and applications that use object linking and embedding (OLE). Each piece of information in the database is identified by a key, which may have a value (data) associated with it.

The registry database meets the following goals:

- Provides one source for configuration information, making initialization and configuration files (such as **CONFIG.SYS** and **WIN.INI**) obsolete.

- Enumerates, tracks, and configures the applications, device drivers, and operating system control parameters.

- Enumerates and tracks the hardware on a computer.

- Standardizes the user interface for configuration information through the use of Windows Control Panel.

- Reduces the likelihood of syntactic errors in configuration information.

- Separates user-, application-, and computer-related information so that separate data for multiple users can be maintained on a single computer.

- Provides security for configuration data. This security prevents unauthorized changes to critical data but allows users direct control over matters of personal preference.

- Provides a set of network-independent functions for setting and querying configuration information and enables direct examination of configuration data over a network.

- Provides storage that is recoverable after the system crashes.

- Provides atomicity of edits.

Few APIs are available on all platforms; as OLE is supported on all platforms, the registry APIs will be supported. Table 7.22 shows the support status of all registry APIs in Windows 95, Windows NT, the Windows Portability Library for the Macintosh, and Wind/U for UNIX.

Table 7.22 Registry APIs

Function	Windows 95	Windows NT	Macintosh	UNIX
GetPrivateProfileInt	Yes	Yes	Yes	Yes
GetPrivateProfileSection	Yes	Yes	No	No
GetPrivateProfileString	Yes	Yes	Yes	Yes
GetProfileInt	Yes	Yes	No	Partial

Table 7.22 Registry APIs (continued)

Function	Windows 95	Windows NT	Macintosh	UNIX
GetProfileSection	Yes	Yes	No	No
GetProfileString	Yes	Yes	No	Partial
RegCloseKey	Yes	Yes	No	Yes
RegConnectRegistry	Yes	Yes	No	Yes
RegCreateKey	Yes	Yes	No	Yes
RegCreateKeyEx	Yes	Yes	No	Yes
RegDeleteKey	Yes	Yes	No	Yes
RegDeleteValue	Yes	Yes	No	Yes
RegEnumKey	Yes	Yes	No	Yes
RegEnumKeyEx	Yes	Yes	No	Yes
RegEnumValue	Yes	Yes	No	Yes
RegFlushKey	Yes	Yes	No	Yes
RegGetKeySecurity	No	Yes	No	Yes
RegLoadKey	Yes	Yes	No	Yes
RegNotifyChangeKeyValue	No	Yes	No	Yes
RegOpenKey	Yes	Yes	No	Yes
RegOpenKeyEx	Yes	Yes	No	Yes
RegQueryInfoKey	Yes	Yes	No	Yes
RegQueryValue	Yes	Yes	No	Yes
RegQueryValueEx	Yes	Yes	No	Yes
RegReplaceKey	No	Yes	No	Tes
RegRestoreKey	Yes	Yes	No	Yes
RegSaveKey	Yes	Yes	No	Yes
RegSetKeySecurity	Yes	Yes	No	Yes
RegSetValue	Yes	Yes	No	Yes
RegSetValueEx	Yes	Yes	No	Yes
RegUnloadKey	Yes	Yes	No	Yes
WritePrivateProfileSection	Yes	Yes	No	No

Table 7.22 Registry APIs (continued)

Function	Windows 95	Windows NT	Macintosh	UNIX
WritePrivateProfileString	Yes	Yes	Partial	Partial
WriteProfileSection	Yes	Yes	No	No
WriteProfileString	Yes	Yes	No	Partial

Remote Access

Remote Access Service (RAS) lets remote users work as if they were connected directly to a computer network, accessing one RAS server or thousands of servers. The remote-access functions allow you to establish and terminate remote-access connections under program control. These functions are not portable and should not be used on non-Windows applications.

No remote-access APIs are available on all platforms; only Windows 95 and Windows NT are supported. Table 7.23 shows the support status of all remote-access APIs in Windows 95, Windows NT, the Windows Portability Library for the Macintosh, and Wind/U for UNIX.

Table 7.23 Remote-Access APIs

Function	Windows 95	Windows NT	Macintosh	UNIX
RasDial	Yes	Yes	No	No
RasDialFunc	Yes	Yes	No	No
RasDialFunc1	Yes	Yes	No	No
RasEnumConnections	Yes	Yes	No	No
RasEnumEntries	Yes	Yes	No	No
RasGetConnectStatus	Yes	Yes	No	No
RasGetErrorString	Yes	Yes	No	No
RasGetProjectionInfo	Yes	Yes	No	No
RasHangUp	Yes	Yes	No	No

Resources

A *resource* is binary data that a resource compiler or developer adds to an application's executable file. A resource can be either standard or defined. The data in a standard resource describes an icon, cursor, menu, dialog box, bitmap, font, accelerator table, message-table entry, string-table entry, or version. An application-defined resource, also called a *custom resource*, contains any data required by a specific application. The custom resource binary data is simply passed to the application; the application is responsible for the portability of this binary data. Table 7.24 describes the standard resources in a Win32 application.

Table 7.24 Resource Types

Type	Content
Bitmap	A *bitmap* is a powerful graphics object used to create, manipulate (scale, scroll, rotate, and paint), and store images as files on a disk.
Cursor	A *cursor* is a small bitmap whose location on the screen is controlled by a pointing device, such as a mouse, pen, or trackball.
Dialog box	A *dialog box* is a temporary window an application creates to retrieve user input.
Font	*Fonts* are used to draw text on video displays and other output devices.
Accelerator table	An *accelerator table* consists of an array of keyboard accelerators, keystrokes, or combinations of keystrokes that generates a WM_COMMAND or WM_SYSCOMMAND messages for your application
Icon	An *icon* is a small bitmap that usually represents a minimized application but can also illustrate a warning message or other window.
Menu	*Hierarchical menus* that represent the commands provided by an application.
Message-table entry	A *binary resource* created by the message compiler.
String-table entry	A *string table* is a Windows resource that contains a list of IDs, values, and captions for all the strings of your application.
Version information	*Version information* includes company and product identification, a product release number, and a copyright and trademark notification.

Most of the resource APIs are available on all platforms, but there are some restrictions that you should be aware of if you use these functions. Table 7.25

shows the support status of all resource APIs in Windows 95, Windows NT, the Windows Portability Library for the Macintosh, and Wind/U for UNIX.

Table 7.25 Kernel Resource APIs

Function	Windows 95	Windows NT	Macintosh	UNIX
AccessResource	Obsolete	Obsolete	Obsolete	Obsolete
AllocResource	Obsolete	Obsolete	Obsolete	Obsolete
BeginUpdateResource	No	Yes	No	No
EndUpdateResource	No	Yes	No	No
EnumResLangProc	Yes	Yes	No	No
EnumResNameProc	Yes	Yes	Yes	Yes
EnumResourceLanguages	Yes	Yes	Partial	Partial
EnumResourceNames	Yes	Yes	Partial	Partial
EnumResourceTypes	Yes	Yes	Partial	Partial
EnumResTypeProc	Yes	Yes	Yes	Yes
FindResource	Yes	Yes	Partial	Yes
FindResourceEx	Yes	Yes	No	Partial
FreeResource	Obsolete	Obsolete	Obsolete	Obsolete
LoadResource	Yes	Yes	Partial	Partial
LockResource	Yes	Yes	Yes	Partial
SetResourceHandler	Obsolete	Obsolete	Obsolete	Obsolete
SizeofResource	Yes	Yes	Partial	Yes
UnlockResource	Obsolete	Obsolete	Obsolete	Obsolete
UpdateResource	Yes	Yes	No	No

Security

The Win32 API includes functions to support the security provisions of Windows NT. In general, these APIs are only available to Windows NT–based applications. Since UNIX contains the same level of security, future versions of Win32 on UNIX may contain some security APIs.

The security functions in the Win32 API allow an application to selectively grant and deny access to an object. An application can specify many different kinds of access for particular users and groups of users. The operating system grants or denies access to an object based on a comparison of the security provisions stored with an object with the access rights specified in a token associated with the process or thread requesting the access. These security functions allow an application to query and manipulate the security features of both an object and a process or thread.

The impact of Windows security on most Windows functions is minimal, and a Windows-based application not requiring security functionality usually does not need to incorporate any special code. However, a developer can use the security features of Windows NT to provide a number of services in a Windows-based application. Generally, any application that manipulates a system-wide resource such as the system time must use the security system to gain access to that resource. A security-aware application might allow the user to query the security attributes of a file, provide specialized feedback when access to a secure file is denied, or customize the security attributes of a file or group of files so that only a subset of other users on a network has access to the information.

Windows NT is designed to support C2-level security as defined by the U.S. Department of Defense. Some of the most important requirements of C2-level security are shown in the following list.

- It must be possible to control access to a resource. This access control must include or exclude individual users or named groups of users.

- Memory must be protected so that its contents cannot be read after it is freed by a process.

- Users must identify themselves in a unique manner when they log on. All auditable actions must identify the user performing the action.

- System administrators must be able to audit security-related events. Access to this audit data must be limited to authorized administrators.

- The system must protect itself from external interference or tampering, such as modification of the running system or of system files stored on disk.

Table 7.26 shows the support status of all security APIs in Windows 95, Windows NT, the Windows Portability Library for the Macintosh, and Wind/U for UNIX.

Table 7.26 Security APIs

Function	Windows 95	Windows NT	Macintosh	UNIX
AccessCheck	No	Yes	No	No
AccessCheckAndAuditAlarm	No	Yes	No	No
AddAccessAllowedAce	No	Yes	No	No
AddAccessDeniedAce	No	Yes	No	No
AddAce	No	Yes	No	No
AddAuditAccessAce	No	Yes	No	No
AdjustTokenGroups	No	Yes	No	No
AdjustTokenPrivileges	No	Yes	No	No
AllocateAndInitializeSid	No	Yes	No	No
AllocateLocallyUniqueId	No	Yes	No	No
AreAllAccessesGranted	No	Yes	No	No
AreAnyAccessesGranted	No	Yes	No	No
CopySid	No	Yes	No	No
CreatePrivateObjectSecurity	No	Yes	No	No
DdeImpersonateClient	No	Yes	No	No
DeleteAce	No	Yes	No	No
DestroyPrivateObjectSecurity	No	Yes	No	No
DuplicateToken	No	Yes	No	No
EqualPrefixSid	No	Yes	No	No
EqualSid	No	Yes	No	No
FindFirstFreeAce	No	Yes	No	No
FreeSid	No	Yes	No	No
GetAce	No	Yes	No	No
GetAclInformation	No	Yes	No	No
GetFileSecurity	No	Yes	No	No
GetKernelObjectSecurity	No	Yes	No	No
GetLengthSid	No	Yes	No	No
GetPrivateObjectSecurity	No	Yes	No	No

Table 7.26 Security APIs (continued)

Function	Windows 95	Windows NT	Macintosh	UNIX
GetProcessWindowStation	No	Yes	No	No
GetSecurityDescriptorControl	No	Yes	No	No
GetSecurityDescriptorDacl	No	Yes	No	No
GetSecurityDescriptorGroup	No	Yes	No	No
GetSecurityDescriptorLength	No	Yes	No	No
GetSecurityDescriptorOwner	No	Yes	No	No
GetSecurityDescriptorSacl	No	Yes	No	No
GetSidIdentifierAuthority	No	Yes	No	No
GetSidLengthRequired	No	Yes	No	No
GetSidSubAuthority	No	Yes	No	No
GetSidSubAuthorityCount	No	Yes	No	No
GetThreadDesktop	No	Yes	No	No
GetTokenInformation	No	Yes	No	No
GetUserObjectSecurity	No	Yes	No	No
ImpersonateNamedPipeClient	No	Yes	No	No
ImpersonateSelf	No	Yes	No	No
InitializeAcl	No	Yes	No	No
InitializeSecurityDescriptor	No	Yes	No	No
InitializeSid	No	Yes	No	No
IsValidAcl	No	Yes	No	No
IsValidSecurityDescriptor	No	Yes	No	No
IsValidSid	No	Yes	No	No
LookupAccountName	No	Yes	No	No
LookupAccountSid	No	Yes	No	No
LookupPrivilegeDisplayName	No	Yes	No	No
LookupPrivilegeName	No	Yes	No	No
LookupPrivilegeValue	No	Yes	No	No
MakeAbsoluteSD	No	Yes	No	No

Table 7.26 Security APIs (continued)

Function	Windows 95	Windows NT	Macintosh	UNIX
MakeSelfRelativeSD	No	Yes	No	No
MapGenericMask	No	Yes	No	No
ObjectCloseAuditAlarm	No	Yes	No	No
ObjectOpenAuditAlarm	No	Yes	No	No
ObjectPrivilegeAuditAlarm	No	Yes	No	No
OpenProcessToken	No	Yes	No	No
OpenThreadToken	No	Yes	No	No
PrivilegeCheck	No	Yes	No	No
PrivilegedServiceAuditAlarm	No	Yes	No	No
RevertToSelf	No	Yes	No	No
SetAclInformation	No	Yes	No	No
SetFileSecurity	No	Yes	No	No
SetKernelObjectSecurity	No	Yes	No	No
SetPrivateObjectSecurity	No	Yes	No	No
SetSecurityDescriptorDacl	No	Yes	No	No
SetSecurityDescriptorGroup	No	Yes	No	No
SetSecurityDescriptorOwner	No	Yes	No	No
SetSecurityDescriptorSacl	No	Yes	No	No
SetThreadToken	No	Yes	No	No
SetTokenInformation	No	Yes	No	No
SetUserObjectSecurity	No	Yes	No	No

Service

In the Win32 API, a *service* is an executable object that is installed in a registry database maintained by the service control manager. The services database includes information that determines whether each installed service is started on demand or automatically when the system starts up. The database can also contain logon and security information for a service so that a service can run even though no user is logged on. Services can be divided into these two groups:

- Win32 services that conform to the interface rules of the service control manager, and
- Driver services that conform to the device driver protocols for Windows NT.

Other APIs are available on all platforms, but there are restrictions that you should be aware of if you use these functions. Table 7.27 shows the support status of all service APIs in Windows 95, Windows NT, the Windows Portability Library for the Macintosh, and Wind/U for UNIX.

Table 7.27 Service APIs

Function	Windows 95	Windows NT	Macintosh	UNIX
ChangeServiceConfig	No	Yes	No	No
CloseServiceHandle	No	Yes	No	No
ControlService	No	Yes	No	No
CreateService	No	Yes	No	No
DeleteService	No	Yes	No	No
EnumDependentServices	No	Yes	No	No
EnumServicesStatus	No	Yes	No	No
GetServiceDisplayName	No	Yes	No	No
GetServiceKeyName	No	Yes	No	No
Handler	No	Yes	No	No
LockServiceDatabase	No	Yes	No	No
NotifyBootConfigStatus	No	Yes	No	No
OpenSCManager	No	Yes	No	No
OpenService	No	Yes	No	No
QueryServiceConfig	No	Yes	No	No
QueryServiceLockStatus	No	Yes	No	No
QueryServiceObjectSecurity	No	Yes	No	No

Table 7.27 Service APIs (continued)

Function	Windows 95	Windows NT	Macintosh	UNIX
QueryServiceStatus	No	Yes	No	No
RegisterServiceCtrlHandler	No	Yes	No	No
ServiceMain	No	Yes	No	No
SetServiceBits	No	Yes	No	No
SetServiceObjectSecurity	No	Yes	No	No
SetServiceStatus	No	Yes	No	No
StartService	No	Yes	No	No
StartServiceCtrlDispatcher	No	Yes	No	No
UnlockServiceDatabase	No	Yes	No	No

Shell API

The Win32 API includes features of the shell for the Windows 95 and Windows NT operating systems. The following features are supported by the dynamic-link library **SHELL.DLL:**

- the drag-drop feature
- associations (used) to find and start applications
- extraction of icons from executable files

These features are operating-system-specific and are not available on all platforms. Table 7.28 shows the support status of all shell APIs in Windows 95, Windows NT, the Windows Portability Library for the Macintosh, and Wind/U for UNIX.

Table 7.28 Shell APIs

Function	Windows 95	Windows NT	Macintosh	UNIX
DragAcceptFiles	Yes	Yes	Partial	No
DragFinish	Yes	Yes	Partial	No

Table 7.28 Shell APIs (continued)

Function	Windows 95	Windows NT	Macintosh	UNIX
DragQueryFile	Yes	Yes	Partial	No
DuplicateIcon	Yes	Yes	Partial	No
ExtractAssocIcon	Yes	Yes	No	No
ExtractIcon	Yes	Yes	No	No
FindExecutable	Yes	Yes	No	No
ShellAbout	Yes	Yes	No	No
ShellExecute	Yes	Yes	No	No

Strings and Unicode

An important aspect of developing portable applications for international markets is the adequate representation of local character sets. For portable applications, you must use multibyte charater set (MBCS) encoding. The ASCII character set defines characters in the range 0x00 to 0x7F. There are other character sets, primarily European, that define the characters within the range 0x00 to 0x7F identically to the ASCII character set and define an extended character set from 0x80 to 0xFF. Thus an 8-bit, single-byte character set (SBCS) is sufficient to represent the ASCII character set as well as the character sets for many European languages. However, some non-European character sets, such as Japanese Kanji, include many more characters than can be represented in a single-byte coding scheme and therefore require multibyte-character set encoding. MFC and the C run-time library are enabled in two ways to assist your international programming:

- Unicode support on NT; no Windows 95, Macintosh, or UNIX support
- Multibyte character set (MBCS), no Macintosh support

Unicode is 16-bit character encoding, providing enough encodings for all languages. All ASCII characters are included in Unicode as "widened" characters. MBCS is also called double-byte character set (DBCS) on all platforms, except Macintosh. DBCS characters are composed of one or two bytes. Some ranges of bytes are set aside for use as lead bytes. A *lead byte* specifies that it and the following *trail byte* comprise a single two-byte-wide character. You must keep track of which bytes are lead bytes. In a particular multibyte character set, the lead bytes fall within a certain range, as do the trail bytes. When these ranges overlap, it may be necessary to evaluate the context to determine whether a given byte is functioning as a lead byte or a trail byte. By definition, the ASCII character set is a subset of all multibyte-character sets. In many multibyte character sets, each character in the range 0x00–0x7F is identical to the character that has the same value in the ASCII character set. For example, in both ASCII and MBCS character strings, the one-byte NULL character ('\0') has value 0x00 and indicates the terminating null character. Also, the NULL is never used in the tail bytes of MBCS strings. While the environment you are programming in supplies MBCS, you must be careful to avoid making assumptions about character and string manipulation that do not work well for international applications.

Here are some tips for creating international enabled Win32 applications. Both Unicode and MBCS are enabled by means of portable data types in MFC function parameter lists and return types. These types are conditionally defined in the appropriate ways, depending on whether your build defines the symbol **_UNICODE** or the symbol **_MBCS** (which means DBCS). Since Unicode is limited to Windows NT, always define **_MBCS** for UNIX, Macintosh, and Windows 95 applications.

- Use the same portable run-time functions that make MFC portable under either environment. Browse the MFC source code for the techniques used by Microsoft.
- Make literal strings and characters portable under either environment using the _T macro.
- Take precautions when parsing strings under MBCS.
- Take care if you mix ANSI (8-bit) and Unicode (16-bit) characters in your application. It's possible to use ANSI characters in some parts of your program and Unicode characters in others, but you cannot mix them in the same string.

Making your application MBCS clean is the first step. Using a "locale" to reflect local conventions and language for a particular geographical region is the next step. A given language may be spoken in more than one country; for example,

Spanish is spoken in Mexico and in Spain. Conversely, a country may have more than one official language. For example, Canada has two: English and French. Thus, Canada has two distinct locales: Canadian-English and Canadian-French. Some locale-dependent categories include the formatting of dates and the display format for monetary values. The language determines the text and data formatting conventions, while the country determines the national conventions. Every language has a unique mapping, represented by "code pages" or NLS (native language support) settings which include characters other than those in the alphabet (such as punctuation marks and numbers).

MFC supports MBCS by using "internationalizable" data types and C runtime functions. You should do the same in your code. Under MBCS, characters are encoded in either one or two bytes. In two-byte characters, the first, or lead byte signals that both it and the following byte are to be interpreted as one character. The first byte comes from a range of codes reserved for use as lead bytes. Which ranges of bytes can be lead bytes depends on the code page in use. For example, Japanese code page 932 uses the range 0x81 through 0x9F as lead bytes, but Korean code page 949 uses a different range. Consider the following in your MBCS programming:

1. MBCS characters in the environment: MBCS characters can appear in strings such as file and directory names.

2. Editing operations:

   - Editing operations in MBCS applications should operate on characters, not bytes.

   - The caret should not split a character, the **Right arrow** key should move right one character, and so on.

   - Delete should delete a character; Undo should reinsert it.

3. String handling: In an application that uses MBCS, string handling poses special problems. Characters of both widths are mixed in a single string; therefore you must remember to check for lead bytes.

Using MFC CString is the best way to support internationalized strings. In general, this makes MFC responsible for dealing with the portability issues associated with strings.

The best way to deal with strings is to use the MFC CString objects. This moves the burden of portability to the MFC supplier. If you use the string APIs keep the following in mind, on both Macintosh and UNIX the Char functions, `CharLower`, `CharUpper`, and so on assume that the OEM character set is being used.

Other APIs are available on all platforms, but there are restrictions that you should be aware of if you use these functions. Table 7.29 shows the support status of all string and Unicode APIs in Windows 95, Windows NT, the Windows Portability Library for the Macintosh, and Wind/U for UNIX.

Table 7.29 String and Unicode APIs

Function	Windows 95	Windows NT	Macintosh	UNIX
AnsiLower	Obsolete, use CharLower	Obsolete	Obsolete	Obsolete
AnsiLowerBuff	Obsolete, use CharLowerBuff	Obsolete	Obsolete	Obsolete
AnsiNext	Obsolete, use CharNext	Obsolete	Obsolete	Obsolete
AnsiPrev	Obsolete, use CharPrev	Obsolete	Obsolete	Obsolete
AnsiToOem	Obsolete, use CharToOem	Obsolete	Obsolete	Obsolete
AnsiToOemBuff	Obsolete, use CharToOemBuff	Obsolete	Obsolete	Obsolete
AnsiUpper	Obsolete, use CharUpper	Obsolete	Obsolete	Obsolete
AnsiUpperBuff	Obsolete, use CharUpperBuff	Obsolete	Obsolete	Obsolete
CharLower	Yes	Yes	Partial	Partial
CharLowerBuff	Yes	Yes	Partial	Partial
CharNext	Yes	Yes	Yes	Yes
CharPrev	Yes	Yes	Yes	Yes
CharToOem	Yes	Yes	Partial	Partial
CharToOemBuff	Yes	Yes	Partial	Partial
CharUpper	Yes	Yes	Partial	Partial

Table 7.29 String and Unicode APIs (continued)

Function	Windows 95	Windows NT	Macintosh	UNIX
CharUpperBuff	Yes	Yes	Partial	Partial
CompareStringW	Yes	Yes	No	No
ConvertDefaultLocale	No	Yes	No	No
EnumCalendarInfo	Yes	Yes	Yes	Yes
EnumCalendarInfoProc	Yes	Yes	Yes	Yes
EnumCodePagesProc	Yes	Yes	Yes	Yes
EnumDateFormats	Yes	Yes	Yes	Yes
EnumDateFormatsProc	Yes	Yes	Yes	Yes
EnumLocalesProc	Yes	Yes	Yes	Yes
EnumSystemCodePages	Yes	Yes	Yes	Yes
EnumSystemLocales	Yes	Yes	Yes	Yes
EnumTimeFormats	Yes	Yes	Yes	Yes
EnumTimeFormatsProc	Yes	Yes	Yes	Yes
FoldStringW	Yes	Yes	No	No
FormatMessage	Yes	Yes	No	No
GetACP	Yes	Yes	No	No
GetCPInfo	Yes	Yes	No	No
GetCurrencyFormat	Yes	Yes	No	No
GetDateFormat	Yes	Yes	No	No
GetLocaleInfoW	Yes	Yes	No	No
GetNumberFormat	Yes	Yes	No	No
GetOEMCP	Yes	Yes	No	No
GetStringTypeA	Yes	Yes	No	No
GetStringTypeEx	Yes	Yes	No	No
GetStringTypeW	Yes	Yes	No	No
GetSystemDefaultLangID	Yes	Yes	No	No
GetSystemDefaultLCID	Yes	Yes	No	No
GetThreadLocale	Yes	Yes	No	No

Table 7.29 String and Unicode APIs (continued)

Function	Windows 95	Windows NT	Macintosh	UNIX
GetTimeFormat	Yes	Yes	No	No
GetUserDefaultLangID	Yes	Yes	No	No
GetUserDefaultLCID	Yes	Yes	No	No
IsCharAlpha	Yes	Yes	Yes	Yes
IsCharAlphaNumeric	Yes	Yes	Yes	Yes
IsCharLower	Yes	Yes	Yes	Yes
IsCharUpper	Yes	Yes	Yes	Yes
IsDBCSLeadByte	Yes	Yes	Yes	Yes
IsTextUnicode	Yes	Yes	Yes	Yes
IsValidCodePage	Yes	Yes	No	No
IsValidLocale	Yes	Yes	No	No
LCMapStringW	Yes	Yes	No	No
LoadString	Yes	Yes	Yes	Yes
lstrcat	Yes	Yes	Yes	Yes
lstrcmp	Yes	Yes	Yes	Yes
lstrcmpi	Yes	Yes	Yes	Yes
lstrcpy	Yes	Yes	Yes	Yes
lstrcpyn	Yes	Yes	Yes	Yes
lstrlen	Yes	Yes	Yes	Yes
MultiByteToWideChar	Yes	Yes	No	No
OemKeyScan	Yes	Yes	No	No
OemToAnsi	Obsolete, use OemToChar	Obsolete	Obsolete	Obsolete
OemToAnsiBuff	Obsolete, use OemToCharBuff	Obsolete	Obsolete	Obsolete
OemToChar	Yes	Yes	Yes	Yes
OemToCharBuff	Yes	Yes	Yes	Yes
SetLocaleInfo	Yes	Yes	Yes	Yes

Table 7.29 String and Unicode APIs (continued)

Function	Windows 95	Windows NT	Macintosh	UNIX
SetThreadLocale	Yes	Yes	No	No
ToAscii	Yes	Yes	No	Partial
ToUnicode	No	Yes	No	No
WideCharToMultiByte	Yes	Yes	No	No
wsprintf	Yes	Yes	Yes	Yes
wvsprintf	Yes	Yes	Yes	Yes

Structured Exception Handling (SEH)

An exception is an event that occurs during the execution of a program that requires the execution of software outside the normal flow of control. Hardware exceptions can result from the execution of certain instruction sequences, such as division by zero or an attempt to access an invalid memory address. A software routine can also initiate an exception explicitly.

The Win32 API supports structured exception handling, a mechanism for handling hardware- and software-generated exceptions. Structured exception handling gives programmers complete control over the handling of exceptions, provides support for debuggers, and is usable across all programming languages and machines.

The Win32 API also supports termination handling, which enables programmers to ensure that whenever a guarded body of code is executed, a specified block of termination code is also executed. The termination code is executed regardless of how the flow of control leaves the guarded body. For example, a termination handler can guarantee that clean-up tasks are performed even if an exception or some other error occurs while the guarded body of code is being executed.

Structured exception and termination handling is an integral part of the Win32 system on Windows 95 and Windows NT and it enables a very robust implementation of the system software. It is envisioned that application developers will also use these mechanisms to create consistently robust and reliable applications.

Structured exception handling is made available to application developers primarily through compiler support. For example, most C++ compilers support the `try` keyword that identifies a guarded body of code, and the `except` and `finally` keywords that identify an exception handler and a termination handler, respectively.

The C++ keywords are supported on all platforms, but some Win32 specific APIs are only supported on Windows 95 and Windows NT. Table 7.30 shows the support status of all structured exception handling APIs in Windows 95, Windows NT, the Windows Portability Library for the Macintosh, and Wind/U for UNIX.

Table 7.30 Support Status for Structured Exception Handling APIs

Function	Windows 95	Windows NT	Macintosh	UNIX
AbnormalTermination	Yes	Yes	No	No
Catch	Obsolete	Obsolete	Obsolete	Obsolete
GetExceptionCode	Yes	Yes	No	No
GetExceptionInformation	Yes	Yes	No	No
RaiseException	Yes	Yes	No	No
SetUnhandledExceptionFilter	Yes	Yes	No	No
Throw	Obsolete	Obsolete	Obsolete	Obsolete
UnhandledExceptionFilter	Yes	Yes	No	No

Synchronization

The Win32 API provides a variety of ways to coordinate multiple threads of execution. These functions provide synchronization mechanisms, such as wait functions and synchronization objects, and overlapped input and output (I/O) operations. The synchronization mechanisms also include critical section objects and interlocked variable access.

A synchronization object is an object whose handle can be specified in one of the wait functions to coordinate the execution of multiple threads. The state of a synchronization object is either signaled, which can allow the wait function to return, or nonsignaled, which can prevent the function from returning. More than one process can have a handle of the same synchronization object, making interprocess synchronization possible.

The Win32 API provides the following three object types intended exclusively for synchronization as listed in Table 7.31.

Table 7.31 Synchronization Objects

Type	Description
Event	Notifies one or more waiting threads that an event has occurred.
Mutex	Can be owned by only one thread at a time, enabling threads to coordinate mutually exclusive access to a shared resource.
Semaphore	Maintains a count between zero and some maximum value, limiting the number of threads that are simultaneously accessing a shared resource.

The portability of the synchronization APIs is similar to the thread APIs. Other APIs are available on all platforms, but there are restrictions that you should be aware of if you use these functions. Table 7.32 shows the support status of all synchronization APIs in Windows 95, Windows NT, the Windows Portability Library for the Macintosh, and Wind/U for UNIX.

Table 7.32 Synchronization APIs

Function	Windows 95	Windows NT	Macintosh	UNIX
CreateEvent	Yes	Yes	No	Yes
CreateMutex	Yes	Yes	No	Yes
CreateSemaphore	Yes	Yes	No	Yes
DeleteCriticalSection	Yes	Yes	No	Yes
EnterCriticalSection	Yes	Yes	No	Yes
GetOverlappedResult	No	Yes	No	No
InitializeCriticalSection	Yes	Yes	No	Yes
InterlockedDecrement	Yes	Yes	No	No
InterlockedExchange	Yes	Yes	No	No
InterlockedIncrement	Yes	Yes	No	No

Table 7.32 Synchronization APIs (continued)

Function	Windows 95	Windows NT	Macintosh	UNIX
LeaveCriticalSection	Yes	Yes	No	Yes
MsgWaitForMultipleObjects	No	Yes	No	Yes
OpenEvent	Yes	Yes	No	Yes
OpenMutex	Yes	Yes	No	Yes
OpenSemaphore	Yes	Yes	No	Yes
PulseEvent	Yes	Yes	No	No
ReleaseMutex	Yes	Yes	No	Yes
ReleaseSemaphore	Yes	Yes	No	Yes
ResetEvent	Yes	Yes	No	Yes
SetEvent	Yes	Yes	No	Yes
WaitForMultipleObjects	Yes	Yes	No	Yes
WaitForMultipleObjectsEx	Yes	Yes	No	Yes
WaitForSingleObject	Yes	Yes	No	Yes
WaitForSingleObjectEx	Yes	Yes	No	Yes

System Information

The Win32 API includes functions that describe the current system configuration. These functions retrieve a variety of data, such as the computer name, user name, settings of environment variables, processor type, and system colors. It also includes functions that can change the system configuration, shut down the system, and start the help application.

For portability, examine all areas of your application that use the system information APIs. By their nature they are accessing information that is dependent on the environment. Some of the system information APIs are available on all platforms, but how the results are used is a better indication of portability. Table 7.33 shows the support status of all system information APIs in Windows 95, Windows NT, the Windows Portability Library for the Macintosh, and Wind/U for UNIX.

Table 7.33 System Information APIs

Function	Windows 95	Windows NT	Macintosh	UNIX
AbortSystemShutdown	Yes	Yes	No	No
DOS3Call	Obsolete	Obsolete	Obsolete	Obsolete
ExpandEnvironmentStrings	Yes	Yes	No	No
GetComputerName	Yes	Yes	Partial	Partial
GetCurrentPDB	Obsolete	Obsolete	Obsolete	Obsolete
GetCurrentTask	Obsolete	Obsolete	Obsolete	Obsolete
GetDOSEnvironment	Obsolete	Obsolete	Obsolete	Obsolete
GetKeyboardType	Yes	Yes	No	No
GetSysColor	Yes	Yes	Partial	Partial
GetSystemDirectory	Yes	Yes	No	Partial
GetSystemInfo	Yes	Yes	No	Partial
GetSystemMetrics	Yes	Yes	Partial	Partial
GetThreadDesktop	Yes	Yes	No	No
GetUserName	Yes	Yes	Partial	Partial
GetVersion	Yes	Yes	Yes	Yes
GetVersionEx	Yes	Yes	No	Partial
GetWindowsDirectory	Yes	Yes	No	Partial
GetWinFlags	Obsolete	Obsolete	Obsolete	Obsolete
InitiateSystemShutdown	Yes	Yes	No	No
IsTask	Obsolete	Obsolete	Obsolete	Obsolete
SetComputerName	Yes	Yes	No	No
SetSysColors	Yes	Yes	No	Partial
SystemParametersInfo	Yes	Yes	Partial	Partial
WinHelp	Yes	Yes	Yes	Yes

Tape Backup

The tape backup APIs in Win32 are only needed by a few applications and are not portable. No tape backup APIs are available on all platforms; only Windows 95 and Windows NT are supported. Table 7.34 shows the support status of all tape backup APIs in Windows 95, Windows NT, the Windows Portability Library for the Macintosh, and Wind/U for UNIX.

Table 7.34 Kernel Tape APIs

Function	Windows 95	Windows NT	Macintosh	UNIX
BackupRead	No	Yes	No	No
BackupSeek	No	Yes	No	No
BackupWrite	No	Yes	No	No
CreateTapePartition	No	Yes	No	No
EraseTape	No	Yes	No	No
GetTapeParameters	No	Yes	No	No
GetTapePosition	No	Yes	No	No
GetTapeStatus	No	Yes	No	No
PrepareTape	No	Yes	No	No
SetTapeParameters	No	Yes	No	No
SetTapePosition	No	Yes	No	No
WriteTapemark	No	Yes	No	No

Time

The Win32 API represents time values in two formats. *File time* is a 64-bit value representing the number of 100-nanosecond intervals that have elapsed since January 1, 1601. *System time* is the "real-time" clock format. System time uses a structure containing individual members for the date and time. A few of the

Win32 time APIs are portable. Others APIs have restrictions that you should be aware of if you use these functions. Table 7.35 shows the support status of all time APIs in Windows 95, Windows NT, the Windows Portability Library for the Macintosh, and Wind/U for UNIX.

Table 7.35 Time APIs

Function	Windows 95	Windows NT	Macintosh	UNIX
CompareFileTime	Yes	Yes	Yes	Yes
DosDateTimeToFileTime	Yes	Yes	No	No
FileTimeToDosDateTime	Yes	Yes	No	No
FileTimeToLocalFileTime	Yes	Yes	Yes	Yes
FileTimeToSystemTime	Yes	Yes	Yes	Yes
GetCurrentTime	Yes	Yes	Yes	Yes
GetFileTime	Yes	Yes	Yes	Yes
GetLocalTime	Yes	Yes	Yes	Yes
GetSystemTime	Yes	Yes	Yes	Yes
GetSystemTimeAdjustment	Yes	Yes	No	No
GetTickCount	Yes	Yes	Yes	Partial
GetTimeZoneInformation	No	Yes	No	Partial
LocalFileTimeToFileTime	Yes	Yes	Yes	Yes
SetFileTime	Yes	Yes	Yes	Partial
SetLocalTime	Yes	Yes	No	No
SetSystemTime	Yes	Yes	No	No
SetTimeZoneInformation	No	Yes	No	No
SystemTimeToFileTime	Yes	Yes	Yes	Yes
SystemTimeToTZSpecificLocalTime	Yes	Yes	No	Yes

## CHAPTER 8

Cross-Platform GDI

In Windows, all output to a window is performed by the graphics device interface (GDI). The cross-platform implementations of GDI is one of the most complete among the Win32 components. With the exception of some advanced features—such as paths and Bezier curves—that have recently been introduced in Windows NT, most GDI functionality is supported on all Win32 hosted platforms.

Though the implementations are very complete, there are still issues that must be considered when porting your Win32 MFC code to different platforms. You must consider:

- The capabilities supported on each platform
- GDI performance

Platform-Specific GDI Capabilities

The GDI capabilities for Windows 3.1 with Win32s, Windows 95, and Windows NT are roughly the same, but there are a few major exceptions. The UNIX and Macintosh GDI implementations, however, are implemented on top of the native graphics engines on each platform. Therefore, there are some limitations on these platforms that are not present on the Windows variants. On the other hand, the UNIX and Macintosh native graphics engines also provide some additional capabilities that are also not present in the various Windows implementations.

This section describes the support status of the GDI APIs on all of these target platforms.

Bitmaps

Bitmap handling under the X Window system can be slow because so much data must move between the client application and the X Window Server. In particular, the StretchBlt() API can be particularly slow because it combines bitmap scaling with large data transfers.

Both the Macintosh and UNIX Win32 toolkits support standard Windows bitmap (.BMP) files, as well as icon and cursor files. You can use resources generated by the Visual C ++ AppStudio without any modifications. However, when porting your bitmap or DIB code, you should be aware that not all bitmap APIs are available on all platforms; you should avoid using any APIs that are not available on all your target platforms. Other APIs are available on all platforms, but there are restrictions that you should be aware of if you use these functions. Table 8.1 shows the support status of all bitmap APIs in Windows 95, Windows NT, the Windows Portability Library for the Macintosh, and Wind/U for UNIX.

Table 8.1 Bitmap APIs

Function	Windows 95	Windows NT	Macintosh	UNIX
BitBlt	Yes	Yes	With restrictions	With restrictions
CreateBitmap	Yes	Yes	Yes	Yes
CreateBitmapIndirect	Yes	Yes	Yes	Yes
CreateCompatibleBitmap	Yes	Yes	Yes	Yes
CreateDIBitmap	Yes	Yes	Yes	With restrictions
CreateDiscardableBitmap	Yes	Yes	Yes	Yes
ExtFloodFill	Yes	Yes	No	No
FloodFill	Yes	Yes	No	No
GetBitmapBits	Yes	Yes	Yes	Yes
GetBitmapDimension	No	No	Yes	No
GetBitmapDimensionEx	Yes	Yes	Yes	Yes
GetDIBits	Yes	Yes	With restrictions	Yes

Table 8.1 Bitmap APIs (continued)

Function	Windows 95	Windows NT	Macintosh	UNIX
GetGraphicsMode	With restrictions	Yes	No	No
GetPixel	Yes	Yes	With restrictions	Yes
GetStretchBltMode	Yes	Yes	With restrictions	Yes
LoadBitmap	Yes	Yes	Yes	Yes
MaskBlt	No	Yes	No	No
PatBlt	Yes	Yes	With restrictions	With restrictions
PlgBlt	No	Yes	No	No
SetBitmapBits	Yes	Yes	Yes	With restrictions
SetBitmapDimension	No	No	No	No
SetBitmapDimensionEx	Yes	Yes	Yes	Yes
SetDIBits	Yes	Yes	Yes	With restrictions
SetDIBitsToDevice	Yes	Yes	Yes	With restrictions
SetGraphicsMode	No	Yes	No	No
SetPixel	Yes	Yes	Yes	Yes
SetPixelV	Yes	Yes	No	No
SetStretchBltMode	Yes	Yes	With restrictions	Yes
StretchBlt	Yes	Yes	With restrictions	With restrictions
StretchDIBits	Yes	Yes	With restrictions	With restrictions

The Macintosh allows the screen depth to change while your application is running. If screen-compatible bitmaps are in existence when the screen depth changes, they will no longer be compatible afterwards. Be aware that you may need to re-create your bitmaps in response to a **WM_SYSCOLORCHANGE** message. Be careful about deleting bitmaps that are selected in HDCs. This was illegal under Windows, but did not always cause a General Protection Fault. It will definitely cause such a condition under the Windows Portability Library for the Macintosh.

On the Macintosh, GetDIBits ignores the biCompression field of the BITMAPINFOHEADER. It always returns an uncompressed DIB. SetDIBits does support compression.

Unlike Windows, the Macintosh Windows Portability Library must allocate a good deal of extra memory to provide for drawing on a bitmap. Applications can save this memory by marking a bitmap read-only, using the Windows Portability Library SetBitmapReadOnly API. This is particularly important for applications that use many bitmaps (on the order of 20 or more).

Brushes

As with bitmaps, not all brush APIs are available on all platforms; you should avoid using any APIs that are not available on all your target platforms. Others APIs are available on all platforms, but there are restrictions that you should be aware of if you use these functions. Table 8.2 shows the support status of all brush APIs in Windows 95, Windows NT, the Windows Portability Library for the Macintosh, and Wind/U for UNIX.

Table 8.2 Brush APIs

GDI API	Windows 95	Windows NT	Macintosh	UNIX
CreateBrushIndirect	Yes	Yes	With restrictions	With restrictions
CreateDIBPatternBrush	Yes	Yes	Yes	Yes
CreateDIBPatternBrushPt	No	Yes	No	No
CreateHatchBrush	Yes	Yes	Yes	Yes
CreatePatternBrush	Yes	Yes	Yes	Yes
CreateSolidBrush	Yes	Yes	Yes	Yes
FixBrushOrgEx	No	No	No	No
GetBrushOrg	Yes	Yes	No	Yes
GetBrushOrgEx	Yes	Yes	Yes	Yes
GetStockObject	Yes	Yes	Yes	With restrictions
SetBrushOrg	Yes	Yes	No	Yes
SetBrushOrgEx	Yes	Yes	Yes	No

Clipping

Most of GDI Clipping APIs are supported on all platforms. The most significant issue that you might have to deal with in clipping is that the UNIX implementation does not support elliptical regions. See the Regions section later in the chapter for complete details.

Table 8.3 shows the support status of all clipping APIs in Windows 95, Windows NT, the Windows Portability Library for the Macintosh, and Wind/U for UNIX.

Table 8.3 Clipping APIs

GDI API	Windows 95	Windows NT	Macintosh	UNIX
ExcludeClipRect	Yes	Yes	Yes	With restrictions
ExtSelectClipRgn	Yes	Yes	No	No
GetClipBox	Yes	Yes	Yes	With restrictions
GetClipRgn	Yes	Yes	Yes	No
GetMetaRgn	Yes	Yes	No	No
IntersectClipRect	Yes	Yes	Yes	With restrictions
OffsetClipRgn	Yes	Yes	Yes	With restrictions
PtVisible	Yes	Yes	Yes	Yes
RectVisible	Yes	Yes	Yes	Yes
SelectClipPath	Yes	Yes	No	No
SelectClipRgn	Yes	Yes	Yes	With restrictions
SetMetaRgn	Yes	Yes	No	No

Color and Palettes

Support for color palettes under Windows and Windows NT depends on which graphics card and driver are installed in your system. Generally, any graphics card and driver above standard VGA usually support palettes. Most graphics hardware (either in Windows, the X Window System, or Macintosh) has some limit on the number of colors that may be displayed at any instance in time.

A logical color palette acts as a buffer between color-intensive applications and the system, allowing an application to use as many colors as necessary without interfering with either its own displayed color or with colors displayed by other windows. When a window has the input focus and calls the RealizePalette function, Windows ensures that the window will display all the requested colors (up to the maximum number simultaneously available on the screen) and Windows displays additional colors by matching them to available colors. In addition, Windows matches the colors requested by inactive windows that call RealizePalette as closely as possible to the available colors. This significantly reduces undesirable changes in the colors displayed in inactive windows.

Palettes allow the program to control what colors are available at any given instance. It provides a way for the application with focus to get the most accurate representation of its data, at the potential expense of background applications.

In the Win32 programming paradigm, a palette is a logical object. It is not tied to a particular hardware capability. For example, it is possible to create a palette of 1024 colors and draw on a graphics display that only supports 16 colors. The mapping of the 1024 to 16 is handled by the graphics driver. Obviously, the quality of the representation when mapping from 1024 to 16 is not as good as the same rendering on a 256 color display, but the beauty of this approach is that it allows your program to render graphics without considering the capabilities of the hardware. All mapping is handled by GDI and the display driver.

The X Window System supports a concept called *Colormaps*, which is similar to Windows palettes, except that they are more closely tied to the hardware capabilities. Native X Window applications must query the hardware and adjust its logic to these capabilities dynamically. For instance, the colormap size is always the number of colors that the display adapter is capable of displaying. If the application requires more colors than the display is capable of displaying, it must implement the logic to perform the logical mapping of colors to the hardware's capability.

Since the Wind/U GDI DLL handles this logical mapping for the X Window System for your application, for the most part you don't have to concern yourself with such mapping. However, there are a few things that you should be aware of that are significantly different than in the Windows environment.

In Windows, when the application changes the system palette with the RealizePalette API, Windows sends a **WM_PALETTECHANGED** message to all other top level windows on the screen. When a window receives this message, the most common response is to realize its own logical palette and redraw its client area to ensure that the colors are as correct as possible.

In the X Window System, there is no standardized method for sending a message to applications that do not have window focus. Windows owned by the same application that changes the system palette receive the **WM_PALETTECHANGED** message, but windows owned by other applications do not. As a result, while other windows owned by the same application do update their colors to make them as correct as possible, windows owned by other applications do not. This means that if your application loses focus to another window on the screen, it will not have an opportunity to redraw itself using the new active palette. While this condition can potentially cause the application to look bad, it is a well-known shortcoming of the X Window System. Luckily, this condition is very rare.

In addition to this condition, application performance is better for applications that don't require palette capability, and most applications do not actually require this capability. Therefore, Wind/U does not use palettes by default. If you want to use palettes, you must enable by using wuEnablePalettes(), an initialization extension API, in the *def.c* file:. (See Chapter 3 for more information about the *def.c* file.)

There are also a number of areas in which Macintosh and Windows palette handling is quite different. Below is a list of some of the more commonly encountered porting issues that arise because of these differences:

- Unlike Windows palettes, Macintosh palettes do not support the standard reserved colors. Instead, only black and white are guaranteed to exist in the system palette. As a result, the requirement that the PALETTERGB or PALETTEINDEX macros be used to choose colors outside the reserved color range has been relaxed.

- GetSystemPaletteUse always returns **SYSPAL_NOSTATIC**, and SetSystemPaletteUse is not implemented.

- UpdateColors is implemented by invalidating the window's client area. It does not cause colors to change on screen.

- AnimatePalette is not implemented, and **PC_RESERVED** palette entries (designed for animation) are not supported.

- **PC_EXPLICIT** colors store the palette index in the 16-bit word starting at

PALETTEENTRY.peRed. For example:

```
PALETTEENTRY pe;
pe.peFlags = PC_EXPLICIT;
*(WORD*)&pe.peRed = index;
```

The Windows specification for PC_EXPLICIT entries is vague and does not map well to big-endian processors such as the 680x0. There are several palette sample applications that create invalid **PC_EXPLICIT** palette entries, so you should review your palette code carefully. The above code is portable to all systems.

Table 8.4 shows the support status for all palette APIs on Windows 95, Windows NT, Macintosh, and UNIX platforms. You should avoid using any APIs that are not available on all your target platforms. Others APIs are available on all platforms, but there are restrictions that you should be aware of if you use these functions.

Table 8.4 Palette APIs (continued)

GDI API	Windows 95	Windows NT	Macintosh	UNIX
AnimatePalette	Yes	Yes	No	Yes
CreatePalette	Yes	Yes	Yes	Yes
CreateHalftonePalette	No	Yes	No	No
GetColorAdjustment	No	Yes	No	No
GetNearestColor	Yes	Yes	Yes	Yes
GetNearestPaletteIndex	Yes	Yes	Yes	Yes
GetPaletteEntries	Yes	Yes	Yes	Yes
GetSystemPaletteEntries	Yes	Yes	Yes	Yes
GetSystemPaletteUse	Yes	Yes	With restrictions	No
RealizePalette	Yes	Yes	With restrictions	Yes
ResizePalette	Yes	Yes	Yes	No
SelectPalette	Yes	Yes	With restrictions	Yes
SetColorAdjustment	No	Yes	No	No
SetPaletteEntries	Yes	Yes	With restrictions	Yes

Table 8.4 Palette APIs (continued)

GDI API	Windows 95	Windows NT	Macintosh	UNIX
SetSystemPaletteUse	Yes	Yes	No	No
UnrealizeObject	Yes	Yes	Yes	Yes
UpdateColors	Yes	Yes	With restrictions	Yes

Coordinate Spaces and Transformations

Windows 3.1 and Windows 95 both have a 16-bit implementation of GDI, even though the APIs have been widened to 32 bits. All coordinate spaces in Windows 3.1 and Windows 95 are limited to 16 bits. Windows NT, however, has a true 32-bit GDI implementation. For most applications, this difference won't matter. But for high-end applications with extremely large virtual coordinate spaces (for example, CAD applications), this difference can be a big issue for portability between NT and Windows 95.

Both the Macintosh and Wind/U GDI implementations have a 32-bit coordinate space. With Wind/U, all logical coordinate mapping is done in the Win32 GDI library rather than at the X protocol level. (The X Window System graphics protocol is relatively simple and does not include advanced graphics primitives or logical coordinate mapping.)

Not all coordinate space and transformation APIs are available on all platforms; you should avoid using any APIs that are not available on all your target platforms. Others APIs are available on all platforms, but there are restrictions that you should be aware of if you use these functions. Table 8.5 shows the support status of all coordinate space APIs in Windows 95, Windows NT, the Windows Portability Library for the Macintosh, and Wind/U for UNIX.

Table 8.5 Logical Coordinate APIs

GDI API	Windows 95	Windows NT	Macintosh	UNIX
ClientToScreen	Yes	Yes	Yes	Yes
CombineTransform	No	Yes	No	No

Table 8.5 Logical Coordinate APIs (continued)

GDI API	Windows 95	Windows NT	Macintosh	UNIX
DPtoLP	Yes	Yes	Yes	Yes
GetCurrentPositionEx	Yes	Yes	Yes	Yes
GetMapMode	Yes	Yes	Yes	Yes
GetViewportExtEx	Yes	Yes	Yes	Yes
GetViewportOrgEx	Yes	Yes	Yes	Yes
GetWindowExtEx	Yes	Yes	Yes	Yes
GetWindowOrgEx	Yes	Yes	Yes	Yes
GetWorldTransform	No	Yes	No	No
LPtoDP	Yes	Yes	Yes	Yes
MapWindowPoints	Yes	Yes	Yes	Yes
ModifyWorldTransform	No	Yes	No	No
OffsetViewportOrgEx	Yes	Yes	Yes	Yes
OffsetWindowOrgEx	Yes	Yes	Yes	Yes
ScaleViewportExtEx	Yes	Yes	Yes	Yes
ScaleWindowExtEx	Yes	Yes	Yes	Yes
ScreenToClient	Yes	Yes	Yes	Yes
SetViewportExtEx	Yes	Yes	Yes	Yes
SetViewportOrgEx	Yes	Yes	Yes	Yes
SetWindowExtEx	Yes	Yes	Yes	Yes
SetWindowOrgEx	Yes	Yes	Yes	Yes
SetWorldTransform	No	Yes	No	No

Device Contexts (DC)

Not all device context (DC) APIs are available on all platforms; you should avoid using any APIs that are not available on all your target platforms. Others APIs are available on all platforms, but there are restrictions that you should be aware of if you use these functions. Table 8.6 shows the support status of all DC APIs in Windows 95, Windows NT, the Windows Portability Library for the Macintosh, and Wind/U for UNIX.

Table 8.6 PC APIs

GDI API	Windows 95	Windows NT	Macintosh	UNIX
CancelDC	No	Yes	No	No
CreateCompatibleDC	Yes	Yes	Yes	Yes
CreateDC	Yes	Yes	With restrictions	Yes
CreateIC	Yes	Yes	With restrictions	Yes
DeleteDC	Yes	Yes	Yes	Yes
DeleteObject	Yes	Yes	Yes	Yes
EnumObjects	Yes	Yes	Yes	Yes
EnumObjectsProc	Yes	Yes	Yes	Yes
GetCurrentObject	No	Yes	No	No
GetDC	Yes	Yes	Yes	Yes
GetDCEx	Yes	Yes	Yes	No
GetDCOrgEx	Yes	Yes	Yes	Yes
GetDeviceCaps	Yes	Yes	With restrictions	With restrictions
GetObject	Yes	Yes	Yes	Yes
GetObjectType	No	Yes	Yes	Yes
ReleaseDC	Yes	Yes	Yes	Yes
ResetDC	Yes	Yes	With restrictions	No
RestoreDC	Yes	Yes	Yes	Yes
SaveDC	Yes	Yes	Yes	Yes
SelectObject	Yes	Yes	Yes	Yes

The GetDeviceCaps API, in particular, has significant differences on the Macintosh and UNIX platforms. This API retrieves device-specific information about a given device. On the Macintosh, the following capabilities are implemented:

- ASPECTX (Always has a value of 1)
- CURVECAPS
- NUMCOLORS

- RASTERCAPS
- ASPECTXY (Always has a value of 1)
- HORZSIZE
- NUMFONTS
- SIZEPALETTE
- ASPECTY (Always has a value of 1)
- LINECAPS
- NUMPENS
- TECHNOLOGY (Always RT_RASDISPLAY)
- BITSPIXEL
- LOGPIXELSX
- NUMRESERVED
- TEXTCAPS
- CLIPCAPS
- LOGPIXELSY
- PLANES
- VERTSIZE
- COLORRES
- NUMBRUSHES
- POLYGONALCAPS

The following capabilities are not implemented at all on the Macintosh:

- DRIVERVERSION
- PHYSICALHEIGHT
- PHYSICALWIDTH
- NUMMARKERS
- PHYSICALOFFSETX
- SCALINGFACTORX
- PDEVICESIZE
- PHYSICALOFFSETY
- SCALINGFACTORY

The Windows Portability Library supports the transparent BitBlt extensions from **MMSYSTEM.H** on Color QuickDraw systems. GetDeviceCaps(hdc, CAPS1) returns **C1_TRANSPARENT** if transparent BitBlts work on the current system.

In UNIX, GetDeviceCaps has the following differences:

- This function always returns a value of 1 for the DRIVERVERSION.
- GetDeviceCaps does not support the following values for TECHNOLOGY:
  - DT_PLOTTER
  - DT_RASCAMERA
  - DT_CHARSTREAM
  - DT_METAFILE
  - DT_DISPFILE
- This function always returns a value of 1000 for the following:
  - NUMBRUSHES
  - NUMPENS
  - NUMMARKERS
  - NUMFONTS
- GetDeviceCaps does not support the following values for CLIPCAPS
  - CP_NONE
  - CP_RECTANGLE
- This function always returns a value of 16 for NUMRESERVED.
- GetDevice Caps does not support the following values for RASTERCAPS:
  - RC_BANDING
  - RC_BIGFONT
  - RC_BITMAP64
  - RC_DEVBITS
  - RC_DI_BITMAP
  - RC_FLOODFILL
  - RC_GDI20_OUTPUT
  - RC_GDI20_STATE
  - RC_OP_DX_OUTPUT

- RC_SAVEBITMAP
- RC_SCALING
- This function does not support the LINECAPS value of LC_WIDE.
- GetDeviceCaps does not support the POLYGONALCAPS value of PC_SCANLINE.
- This function does not support the following values for TEXTCAPS :
  - TC_OP_STROKE
  - TC_CP_STROKE
  - TC_CR_90
  - TC_CR_ANY
  - TC_SF_X_YINDEP
  - TC_SA_DOUBLE
  - TC_SA_INTEGER
  - TC_SA_CONTIN
  - TC_EA_DOUBLE
  - TC_IA_ABLE
  - TC_SO_ABLE
  - TC_RA_ABLE
  - TC_VA_ABLE

Filled Shape Drawing

Not all filled-shape drawing APIs are available on all platforms; you should avoid using any APIs that are not available on all your target platforms. Others APIs are available on all platforms, but there are restrictions that you should be aware of if you use these functions. Table 8.7 shows the support status of all these APIs in Windows 95, Windows NT, the Windows Portability Library for the Macintosh, and Wind/U for UNIX.

Table 8.7 Filled-shape Drawing APIs

GDI API	Windows 95	Windows NT	Macintosh	UNIX
Chord	Yes	Yes	No	Yes
Ellipse	Yes	Yes	With restrictions	Yes
FillRect	Yes	Yes	Yes	Yes
FrameRect	Yes	Yes	Yes	Yes
InvertRect	Yes	Yes	Yes	Yes
Pie	Yes	Yes	With restrictions	Yes
Polygon	Yes	Yes	With restrictions	Yes
PolyPolygon	Yes	Yes	No	Yes
Rectangle	Yes	Yes	With restrictions	Yes
RoundRect	Yes	Yes	With restrictions	Yes

Font and Text Drawing

Windows and Windows NT have TrueType fonts built into them, with add-ons like Adobe Type Manager available as well. You must make sure that any application code that talks directly to add-ons like ATM is conditionally compiled on other platforms.

Since the same font name and point size might have slightly different metrics on different platforms, do not hard-code font metrics. You can hard-code the standard TrueType and system fonts from Windows, because UNIX and Macintosh products provide a mapping to a closest-match font. Don't assume that scalable fonts are present, because many X Window servers either don't support scalable fonts or don't have any installed.

On UNIX platforms, Wind/U uses a file called **.WindU**, which is stored in the user's home directory, to configure the user's environment, similar to the **WIN.INI** file in Windows. The [FontSubstitutes (...)] sections of the **.WindU** file map groups of font-name aliases to groups of font names that are known to exist in almost all X Window servers and printers. The Windows 3.1 **WIN.INI** file has a similar section called [FontSubstitutes] that provides a mapping from Windows 3.0 bitmap fonts to 3.1 TrueType fonts.

There are three [FontSubstitutes] sections, one each for the X Window System display, PostScript printers, and PCL printers.

- The [FontSubstitutes (XDisplay)] section defines the alias-to-real name mapping when the X display is the current device.
- The [FontSubstitutes (PCL)] section defines the alias-to-real name mapping when a PCL printer is the current device.
- The [FontSubstitutes (PostScript)] section defines the alias-to-real name mapping when a PostScript printer is the current device.

The following example shows the default values for the [FontSubstitutes] sections.

```
[FontSubstitutes (XDisplay)]
arial=helvetica
helv=helvetica
courier new=courier
times roman=times
times new roman=times
tms rmn=times
ms serif=times
ms sans serif=helvetica

[FontSubstitutes (PostScript)]
arial=helvetica
helv=helvetica
courier new=courier
times roman=times
times new roman=times
tms rmn=times
ms serif=times
ms sans serif=helvetica

[FontSubstitutes (PCL)]
arial=helvetica
helv=helvetica
courier new=courier
times roman=times
times new roman=times
tms rmn=times
ms serif=times
ms sans serif=helvetica
```

The keyword for each line in the [FontSubstitutes] section is the Microsoft Windows font name. The right side contains the mapped font name that is used when loading the font on the X Window server or a PostScript or PCL printer. The right side is used as the second field in the XFLD font name.

Fonts in Windows are complex entities, defined by a dozen or so different parameters. Everything from the face-name and height to the clipping precision and output quality can be used to pick a font. Fonts are also device-specific, in that one device may not support the same set of fonts as another. The process of mapping a logical, device-independent font to a physical, device-dependent font is called font resolution. The *font mapper* is used to find the physical font that most closely matches a requested logical font.

The native Macintosh font model is simpler. An output font is specified by its face name, height, and attributes. The Macintosh font manager can simulate all the font attributes and can scale font heights on all output devices, so the need for a complex font mapper is not as great. With the development of TrueType outline fonts, many of the scaling and font mapping problems in Windows have been simplified as well.

The Windows Portability Library for Macintosh GDI tries to map Windows font names into equivalent Macintosh font names. The name mapping table is kept in the "FTAB" 17000 resource in the application's resource fork, and is used if the Windows Portability Library for Macintosh cannot find the requested face name in the list of installed fonts. The format of the "FTAB" resource and the recommended font mappings can be found in **FTAB.R**, located in the \M68K\INCLUDE\MRC subdirectory. If you do not want face name mappings to occur, simply remove this resource from your application.

More accurate cross-platform font mapping can also occur if font family information can be associated with Macintosh fonts. Font families for several standard Macintosh fonts are also included in **FTAB.R**, as part of the "FFAM" 17000 resource. If this resource is missing, all Macintosh fonts are assumed to be a member of the **FF_DONTCARE** family.

Not all font-related APIs are available on all platforms; you should avoid using any APIs that are not available on all your target platforms. Others APIs are available on all platforms, but there are restrictions that you should be aware of if you use these functions. Table 8.8 shows the support status of all these APIs in Windows 95, Windows NT, the Windows Portability Library for the Macintosh, and Wind/U for UNIX.

Table 8.8 Font APIs

GDI API	Windows 95	Windows NT	Macintosh	UNIX
AddFontResource	Yes	Yes	No	No
CreateFont	Yes	Yes	Yes	With restrictions
CreateFontIndirect	Yes	Yes	Yes	With restrictions
CreateScalableFontResource	Yes	Yes	No	No
DrawText	Yes	Yes	Yes	With restrictions
EnumFontFamilies	Yes	Yes	With restrictions	Yes
EnumFontFamProc	Yes	Yes	Yes	No
EnumFonts	Yes	Yes	With restrictions	Yes
EnumFontsProc	Yes	Yes	Yes	Yes
ExtTextOut	Yes	Yes	With restrictions	Yes
GetAspectRatioFilterEx	Yes	Yes	Yes	Yes
GetCharABCWidths	Yes	Yes	Yes	Yes
GetCharABCWidthsFloat	No	Yes	No	No
GetCharWidth	Yes	Yes	With restrictions	Yes
GetCharWidth32	Yes	Yes	No	No
GetCharWidthFloat	Yes	Yes	No	No
GetFontData	Yes	Yes	Yes	No
GetGlyphOutline	Yes	Yes	No	No
GetKerningPairs	Yes	Yes	No	No
GetOutlineTextMetrics	Yes	Yes	With restrictions	No
GetRasterizerCaps	Yes	Yes	Yes	With restrictions
GetTabbedTextExtent	Yes	Yes	Yes	Yes
GetTextAlign	Yes	Yes	Yes	Yes
GetTextCharacterExtra	Yes	Yes	No	Yes
GetTextColor	Yes	Yes	Yes	Yes
GetTextExtentExPoint	Yes	Yes	No	Yes
GetTextExtentPoint	Yes	Yes	With restrictions	Yes
GetTextExtentPoint32	Yes	Yes	No	No

Table 8.8 Font APIs (continued)

GDI API	Windows 95	Windows NT	Macintosh	UNIX
GetTextFace	Yes	Yes	Yes	Yes
GetTextMetrics	Yes	Yes	With restrictions	Yes
MulDiv	Yes	Yes	Yes	Yes
PolyTextOut	Yes	Yes	No	No
RemoveFontResource	Yes	Yes	With restrictions	No
SetMapperFlags	Yes	Yes	Yes	With restrictions
SetTextAlign	Yes	Yes	Yes	Yes
SetTextCharacterExtra	Yes	Yes	No	Yes
SetTextColor	Yes	Yes	Yes	Yes
SetTextJustification	Yes	Yes	No	Yes
TabbedTextOut	Yes	Yes	With restrictions	With restrictions
TextOut	Yes	Yes	With restrictions	Yes

Line and Curve Drawing

Not all line and curve drawing APIs are available on all platforms; you should avoid using any APIs that are not available on all your target platforms. Others APIs are available on all platforms, but there are restrictions that you should be aware of if you use these functions. Table 8.9 shows the support status of all these APIs in Windows 95, Windows NT, the Windows Portability Library for the Macintosh, and Wind/U for UNIX.

Table 8.9 Line and Curve Drawing APIs

GDI API	Windows 95	Windows NT	Macintosh	UNIX
AngleArc	No	Yes	No	No
Arc	Yes	Yes	With restrictions	Yes
ArcTo	No	Yes	No	No
GetArcDirection	Yes	Yes	No	No

Table 8.9 Line and Curve Drawing APIs (continued)

GDI API	Windows 95	Windows NT	Macintosh	UNIX
LineDDA	Yes	Yes	Yes	Yes
LineDDAProc	Yes	Yes	Yes	Yes
LineTo	Yes	Yes	With restrictions	Yes
MoveToEx	Yes	Yes	Yes	Yes
PolyBezier	Yes	Yes	No	No
PolyBezierTo	Yes	Yes	No	No
PolyDraw	Yes	Yes	No	No
Polyline	Yes	Yes	With restrictions	Yes
PolylineTo	Yes	Yes	No	No
PolyPolyline	Yes	Yes	No	No
SetArcDirection	Yes	Yes	No	No

Painting and Drawing

Not all painting and drawing APIs are available on all platforms; you should avoid using any APIs that are not available on all your target platforms. Others APIs are available on all platforms, but there are restrictions that you should be aware of if you use these functions. Table 8.10 shows the support status of all these APIs in Windows 95, Windows NT, the Windows Portability Library for the Macintosh, and Wind/U for UNIX.

Table 8.10 Painting and Drawing APIs

GDI API	Windows 95	Windows NT	Macintosh	UNIX
BeginPaint	Yes	Yes	Yes	Yes
DrawFocusRect	Yes	Yes	Yes	Yes
EndPaint	Yes	Yes	Yes	Yes
ExcludeUpdateRgn	Yes	Yes	Yes	No

Table 8.10 Painting and Drawing APIs (continued)

GDI API	Windows 95	Windows NT	Macintosh	UNIX
FrameRect	Yes	Yes	Yes	Yes
GdiFlush	No	Yes	No	No
GdiGetBatchLimit	No	Yes	No	No
GdiSetBatchLimit	No	Yes	No	No
GetBkColor	Yes	Yes	Yes	Yes
GetBkMode	Yes	Yes	Yes	Yes
GetBoundsRect	Yes	Yes	No	No
GetROP2	Yes	Yes	With restrictions	Yes
GetUpdateRect	Yes	Yes	Yes	Yes
GetUpdateRgn	Yes	Yes	Yes	Yes
GetWindowDC	Yes	Yes	With restrictions	Yes
GrayString	Yes	Yes	Yes	With restrictions
InvalidateRect	Yes	Yes	Yes	Yes
InvalidateRgn	Yes	Yes	Yes	Yes
LockWindowUpdate	Yes	Yes	No	No
OutputProc	Yes	Yes	No	Yes
RedrawWindow	Yes	Yes	Yes	With restrictions
SetBkColor	Yes	Yes	Yes	Yes
SetBkMode	Yes	Yes	With restrictions	Yes
SetBoundsRect	Yes	Yes	No	No
SetRectRgn	Yes	Yes	Yes	Yes
SetROP2	Yes	Yes	With restrictions	Yes
UpdateWindow	Yes	Yes	Yes	Yes
ValidateRect	Yes	Yes	Yes	Yes
ValidateRgn	Yes	Yes	Yes	Yes
WindowFromDC	Yes	Yes	No	No

Path Drawing

Not all path drawing APIs are available on all platforms; you should avoid using any APIs that are not available on all your target platforms. Others APIs are available on all platforms, but there are restrictions that you should be aware of if you use these functions. Table 8.11 shows the support status of all these APIs in Windows 95, Windows NT, the Windows Portability Library for the Macintosh, and Wind/U for UNIX.

Table 8.11 Path Drawing APIs

GDI API	Windows 95	Windows NT	Macintosh	UNIX
AbortPath	Yes	Yes	No	No
BeginPath	Yes	Yes	No	No
CloseFigure	Yes	Yes	No	No
EndPath	Yes	Yes	No	No
ExtCreatePen	Yes	Yes	No	No
FillPath	Yes	Yes	No	No
FlattenPath	Yes	Yes	No	No
GetMiterLimit	Yes	Yes	No	No
GetPath	Yes	Yes	No	No
PathToRegion	Yes	Yes	No	No
SetMiterLimit	Yes	Yes	No	No
StrokeAndFillPath	Yes	Yes	No	No
StrokePath	Yes	Yes	No	No
WidenPath	Yes	Yes	No	No

Pens

When drawing wide lines, Windows uses a round pen, which results in the endpoints and line joints of wide lines looking round. On the Macintosh, the Windows Portability Library uses a rectangular pen, which results in the endpoints and line joints of wide lines looking square. As a result, applications that rely on end point and line join behavior may not work correctly on the Macintosh.

Similarly, when drawing the outline around a RoundRect, Windows does not maintain a line of constant thickness when tracing the round corners, whereas the Macintosh does. This should be noticeable only with very wide pens.

Not all pen-related APIs are available on all platforms; you should avoid using any APIs that are not available on all your target platforms. Others APIs are available on all platforms, but there are restrictions that you should be aware of if you use these functions. Table 8.12 shows the support status of all these APIs in Windows 95, Windows NT, the Windows Portability Library for the Macintosh, and Wind/U for UNIX.

Table 8.12 Pen APIs

GDI API	Windows 95	Windows NT	Macintosh	UNIX
CreatePen	Yes	Yes	Yes	Yes
CreatePenIndirect	Yes	Yes	Yes	Yes
ExtCreatePen	Yes	Yes	No	No

Rectangles

Not all rectangle drawing APIs are available on all platforms; you should avoid using any APIs that are not available on all your target platforms. Others APIs are available on all platforms, but there are restrictions that you should be aware of if you use these functions. Table 8.13 shows the support status of all these APIs in Windows 95, Windows NT, the Windows Portability Library for the Macintosh, and Wind/U for UNIX.

Table 8.13 Rectangle Drawing APIs

GDI API	Windows 95	Windows NT	Macintosh	UNIX
CopyRect	Yes	Yes	Yes	Yes
EqualRect	Yes	Yes	Yes	Yes
InflateRect	Yes	Yes	Yes	Yes
IntersectRect	Yes	Yes	Yes	Yes
IsRectEmpty	Yes	Yes	Yes	Yes

Table 8.13 Rectangle Drawing APIs (continued)

GDI API	Windows 95	Windows NT	Macintosh	UNIX
OffsetRect	Yes	Yes	Yes	Yes
PtInRect	Yes	Yes	Yes	Yes
SetRect	Yes	Yes	Yes	Yes
SetRectEmpty	Yes	Yes	Yes	Yes
SubtractRect	Yes	Yes	Yes	Yes
UnionRect	Yes	Yes	Yes	Yes

Regions

Support for graphical regions is provided at the protocol level of the X Window system. A significant limitation of the X Window scheme for region handling is its lack of support for elliptical regions. All regions in the X Windows system are composed of rectangular elements only. As a result of this X Window system limitation, Wind/U does not support the elliptical region API's. This is not a significant limitation, however, because the use of elliptical regions in Windows applications is rare.

Table 8.14 shows the support status of all these APIs in Windows 95, Windows NT, the Windows Portability Library for the Macintosh, and Wind/U for UNIX.

Table 8.14 Region APIs

GDI API	Windows 95	Windows NT	Macintosh	UNIX
CombineRgn	Yes	Yes	Yes	With restrictions
CreateEllipticRgn	Yes	Yes	Yes	With restrictions
CreateEllipticRgnIndirect	Yes	Yes	Yes	With restrictions
CreatePolygonRgn	Yes	Yes	With restrictions	Yes
CreatePolyPolygonRgn	Yes	Yes	No	Yes
CreateRectRgn	Yes	Yes	Yes	Yes
CreateRectRgnIndirect	Yes	Yes	Yes	Yes

Table 8.14 Region APIs (continued)

GDI API	Windows 95	Windows NT	Macintosh	UNIX
CreateRoundRectRgn	Yes	Yes	Yes	With restrictions
EqualRgn	Yes	Yes	Yes	Yes
ExtCreateRegion	Yes	Yes	No	No
FillRgn	Yes	Yes	Yes	Yes
FrameRgn	Yes	Yes	Yes	Yes
GetPolyFillMode	Yes	Yes	With restrictions	Yes
GetRegionData	Yes	Yes	No	No
GetRgnBox	Yes	Yes	Yes	With restrictions
InvertRgn	Yes	Yes	Yes	Yes
OffsetRgn	Yes	Yes	Yes	With restrictions
PaintRgn	Yes	Yes	Yes	Yes
PtInRegion	Yes	Yes	Yes	Yes
RectInRegion	Yes	Yes	Yes	Yes
SetPolyFillMode	Yes	Yes	With restrictions	Yes

Printing

Windows and the Macintosh have powerful graphical solutions that are tightly integrated with their graphical subsystems. The Windows Portability Layer components of the Visual C ++ for Macintosh toolkit maps printer API's to the native printer subsystem on the Macintosh.

Since the application can only access one printer on the Macintosh system, a lot of Windows printing setup complexity goes away. There is no need to read the **WIN.INI** file for printer settings. To create a printer device context, simply call `CreateDC`, as follows:

```
hDC = CreateDC("PRINTER", NULL, NULL, NULL);
```

This creates a device context ready for printing. `CreateDC` specifically checks for the string "PRINTER" in order to create a printing device context.

Alternatively, you can use the PrintDlg common dialog API to get a printer device context.

Use the Windows 3.1 APIs for controlling a printer document and for paging it. StartDoc, EndDoc, StartPage, and EndPage are all implemented on both Macintosh and UNIX.

An application may need access to the underlying Macintosh print record to save Macintosh-specific printer settings in its document files. Given a printer DC or IC, you can get at the underlying print record using CheckoutPrint and CheckinPrint. Similarly, if you read in a print record from a document file, you can create a printer DC out of it using WrapPrint.

On UNIX, however, there is no native printer subsystem that is integrated with the X Window System. Since Windows applications ported to UNIX, obviously, must be able to print, the Wind/U cross-platform toolkit includes a complete printer subsystem modeled after the Windows print subsystem.

As indicated in the diagram, the Xprinter component of Wind/U maps graphics calls from GDI to printer commands for either PostScript or PCL printers. This is just one example of how the Windows API solution on UNIX provides significant features that are generally unavailable to natively written applications.

There are several printer APIs that are not supported on the Macintosh and UNIX Win32 implementations. For MFC users, however, these restrictions are not an issue because the MFC application framework does a very good job of hiding these implementation details from your application. Many of the APIs that are not supported are used to access the system print spooler, and therefore often have no meaning on non-Windows systems. The most significant limitation emposed by the printer API support is in the Macintosh environment. It is not possible to provide a user interface that allows the user to select from a list of preconfigured printers as in the Windows environment. The native Macintosh environment also does not provide this capability, so your application will be consistent with what Macintosh users expect.

Table 8.15 shows the support status of all these APIs in Windows 95, Windows NT, the Windows Portability Library for the Macintosh, and Wind/U for UNIX.

Table 8.15 Printing and Spooling APIs

GDI API	Windows 95	Windows NT	Macintosh	UNIX
AbortDoc	Yes	Yes	With restrictions	Yes
AbortPrinter	Yes	Yes	No	No
AddForm	No	Yes	No	No
AddJob	Yes	Yes	No	No
AddMonitor	Yes	Yes	No	No
AddPort	Yes	Yes	No	No
AddPrinter	Yes	Yes	No	No
AddPrinterConnection	Yes	No	No	No
AddPrinterDriver	Yes	Yes	No	No
AddPrintProcessor	Yes	Yes	No	No
AddPrintProvidor	Yes	Yes	No	No
AdvancedDocumentProperties	Yes	Yes	No	No
ClosePrinter	Yes	Yes	No	No
ConfigurePort	Yes	Yes	No	No
ConnectToPrinterDlg	Yes	Yes	No	No
DeleteForm	No	Yes	No	No
DeleteMonitor	Yes	Yes	No	No
DeletePort	Yes	Yes	No	No
DeletePrinter	Yes	Yes	No	No
DeletePrinterConnection	Yes	No	No	No
DeletePrinterDriver	Yes	Yes	No	No
DeletePrintProcessor	Yes	Yes	No	No
DeletePrintProvidor	Yes	Yes	No	No
DeviceCapabilitiesEx	Yes	Yes	No	No
DocumentProperties	Yes	Yes	No	No
EndDoc	Yes	Yes	With restrictions	Yes
EndDocPrinter	Yes	Yes	No	No
EndPage	Yes	Yes	With restrictions	Yes

Table 8.15 Printing and Spooling APIs (continued)

GDI API	Windows 95	Windows NT	Macintosh	UNIX
EndPagePrinter	Yes	Yes	No	No
EnumForms	No	Yes	No	No
EnumJobs	Yes	Yes	No	No
EnumMonitors	Yes	Yes	No	No
EnumPorts	Yes	Yes	No	No
EnumPrinterDrivers	Yes	Yes	No	No
EnumPrinters	Yes	Yes	No	No
EnumPrintProcessors	Yes	Yes	No	No
Escape	Yes	Yes	With restrictions	With restrictions
ExtEscape	Yes	Yes	No	No
GetForm	No	Yes	No	No
GetJob	Yes	Yes	No	No
GetPrinter	Yes	Yes	No	No
GetPrinterData	Yes	Yes	No	No
GetPrinterDriver	Yes	Yes	No	No
GetPrinterDriverDirectory	Yes	Yes	No	No
GetPrintProcessorDirectory	Yes	Yes	No	No
OpenPrinter	Yes	Yes	No	No
PrinterMessageBox	Yes	Yes	No	No
PrinterProperties	Yes	Yes	No	No
ReadPrinter	Yes	Yes	No	No
ResetPrinter	Yes	Yes	No	No
ScheduleJob	Yes	Yes	No	No
SetAbortProc	Yes	Yes	Yes	Yes
SetForm	No	Yes	No	No

Table 8.15 Printing and Spooling APIs (continued)

GDI API	Windows 95	Windows NT	Macintosh	UNIX
SetJob	Yes	Yes	No	No
SetPrinter	Yes	Yes	No	No
SetPrinterData	Yes	Yes	No	No
StartDoc	Yes	Yes	Yes	With restrictions
StartDocPrinter	Yes	Yes	No	No
StartPage	Yes	Yes	Yes	Yes
StartPagePrinter	Yes	Yes	No	No
WaitForPrinterChange	Yes	Yes	No	No
WritePrinter	Yes	Yes	No	No

Binary Raster Operations

Because of limitations of the capabilities of the X Window System protocol, binary and ternary raster operations are limited under the X Window System on UNIX platforms. The Wind/U cross-platform toolkit maps Windows binary raster operations (ROP) functions to X Window System graphics context (GC) functions as shown in Table 8.16.

Table 8.16 Binary Windows ROP Function to X Window GC Function Mapping

Windows ROP Function	X Window GC Function
R2_BLACK	GXclear
R2_NOTMERGEPEN	GXnor
R2_MASKNOTPEN	GXandInverted
R2_NOTCOPYPEN	GXcopyInverted
R2_MASKPENNOT	GXandReverse
R2_NOT	GXinvert
R2_XORPEN	GXxor
R2_NOTMASKPEN	GXnand

Table 8.16 Binary Windows ROP Function to X Window GC Function Mapping (continued)

Windows ROP Function	X Window GC Function
R2_MASKPEN	GXand
R2_NOTXORPEN	GXequiv
R2_NOP	GXnoop
R2_MERGENOTPEN	GXorInverted
R2_COPYPEN	GXcopy
R2_MERGEPENNOT	GXorReverse
R2_MERGEPEN	GXor
R2_WHITE	GXset

The effect of this mapping is that some unusual Windows ROPs might not have the desired result under the X Window System. However, the most commonly used ROPs (such as COPY and XOR) map to corresponding X Window System functions. It is very unlikely that your application will require an unsupported ROP.

On both UNIX and Macintosh platforms, QuickDraw does not support the full range of binary raster operations available under Windows. Windows also supports the concept of background mode, which determines how the white bits in two-color patterns mix with the existing display surface background. The binary raster operation is set with SetROP2, and the background mode is set with SetBkMode.

Table 8.17 shows the mixtures of ROP2 and background mode that are supported on the Macintosh and UNIX platforms.

Table 8.17 ROP2 and Background Mode Mixtures

Raster Operation	Transparent	Opaque
R2_BLACK	Yes	Yes
R2_NOTMERGEPEN	No	No
R2_MASKNOTPEN	Yes	No
R2_NOTCOPYPEN	Yes	No
R2_MASKPENNOT	No	No

Table 8.17 ROP2 and Background Mode Mixtures (continued)

Raster Operation	Transparent	Opaque
R2_NOT	Yes	Yes
R2_XORPEN	Yes	No
R2_NOTMASKPEN	Yes	No
R2_MASKPEN	No	No
R2_NOTXORPEN	Yes	No
R2_NOP	Yes	Yes
R2_MERGENOTPEN	Yes	No
R2_COPYPEN	Yes	Yes
R2_MERGEPENNOT	No	No
R2_MERGEPEN	Yes	No
R2_WHITE	Yes	Yes

Ternary Raster Operations

Windows supports a large number (256) of ternary raster operations in the BitBlt (and related) operations. They allow for arbitrary logical operations combining the source, destination, and current brush pattern.

Although this set of raster operations is comprehensive, many of the operations are never used in practice. Because Apple did not implement so general an interface on the Macintosh, the Windows Portability Library for Macintosh supports only a small subset of the Windows raster operations. Table 8.18 is a list of the operations that are currently implemented. Absence of a Common Name indicates that no common name is assigned.

Table 8.18 Ternary Raster Operations on the Macintosh

Common Name	Operation	Hex Code	Comments
BLACKNESS	0	0x00000042	
DSTINVERT	Dn	0x00550009	(see Note following)
MERGECOPY	PSa	0x00C000CA	
MERGEPAINT	DSno	0x00BB0226	

Table 8.18 Ternary Raster Operations on the Macintosh (continued)

Common Name	Operation	Hex Code	Comments
NOTSRCCOPY	Sn	0x00330008	(see Note following)
NOTSRCERASE	DSon	0x001100A6	(see Note following)
PATCOPY	P	0x00F00021	
PATINVERT	DPx	0x005A0049	(see Note following)
PATPAINT	DPSnoo	0x00FB0A09	
SRCAND	DSa	0x008800C6	
SRCCOPY	S	0x00CC0020	
SRCERASE	SDna	0x00440328	(see Note following)
SRCINVERT	DSx	0x00660046	(see Note following)
SRCPAINT	DSo	0x00EE0086	
WHITENESS	1	0x00FF0062	
	DPon	0x000500A9	
	DPna	0x000A0329	
	Pn	0x000F0001	
	DSna	0x00220326	(see Note following)
	PDna	0x00500325	
	DPan	0x005F00E9	
	DSan	0x007700E6	(see Note following)
	DSxn	0x00990066	
	DPa	0x00A000C9	
	PDxn	0x00A50065	
	D	0x00AA0029	
	DPno	0x00AF0229	
	PSDPxax	0x00B8074A	
	SDno	0x00DD0228	(see Note following)
	DSPDxax	0x00E20746	
	PDno	0x00F50225	
	DPo	0x00FA0089	

The color inversion on the Macintosh may result in some surprising color combinations, and will definitely not be compatible with Windows inverse color mapping. However, if the inverted colors are black or white (or are on a monochrome bitmap), then you should get the same mapping.

The Wind/U cross-platform toolkit maps Windows ternary raster operations (ROP) functions to X Window System graphics context (GC) functions as shown in Table 8.10.

Table 8.19 Ternary Windows ROP Function to X Window GC Function Mapping

Windows ROP Function	X Window GC Function
SRCCOPY	GXcopy
SRCPAINT	GXor
SRCAND	GXand
SRCINVERT	GXxor
SRCERASE	GXandReverse
NOTSRCCOPY	GXcopyInverted
NOTSRCERASE	GXorInverted
MERGECOPY	GXand
MERGEPAINT	GXorReverse
DSTINVERT	GXinvert
BLACKNESS	GXclear
WHITENESS	GXset
0x0990066	GXequiv

Metafiles

Most metafile APIs have been implemented on the Macintosh and UNIX platforms, but with some significant restrictions. Extended metafile APIs are not supported. Metafiles are implemented on the Macintosh using Macintosh Pictures, which works well for rendering graphics to the clipboard, since a Picture is the standard format for data interchange on the Macintosh. Although

Macintosh Pictures and Windows metafiles are similar in concept, they differ significantly in so many details that it is prohibitively expensive to implement many of the Windows metafile APIs completely.

In particular, there are several metafile functions that can be used to directly look at and modify the contents of a Windows-format metafile. Since Macintosh and UNIX metafiles are not stored in Windows format, code that uses these metafile functions will probably need to be rewritten.

For example, GetMetaFileBits and SetMetaFileBits assume a Windows-format metafile, and are therefore not implemented on the Macintosh or UNIX platforms. Also, EnumMetaFile has been implemented on the Macintosh in such a way that it is useful only to allow for interruption of the playback of large metafiles. Under the Windows Portability Library for Macintosh, EnumMetaFile cannot be used to parse out the individual METARECORD structures of a Macintosh metafile. The parameters to the EnumMetaFile callback function do not contain useful information. In fact, EnumMetaFile draws the metafile on the HDC you pass in! No physical drawing is done until the application calls PlayMetaFileRecord from within the callback, but as soon as PlayMetaFileRecord is called once, all the remaining metafile are drawn on the output device context, even if the application never calls PlayMetaFileRecord again.

When recording a metafile, the Windows API behaves in an unexpected manner. Unlike normal device contexts, a Windows metafile does not store any drawing state. This means that any return value that might represent the current (or past) state of a device context is not defined in a metafile. For example, GetTextColor does not work if the HDC is a metafile, and SetTextColor's return value will not contain the old text color. Instead, when recording a metafile, the Windows GDI routines return only failure or success.

On the Macintosh, Windows Portability Library metafiles can store the device context state. This means that the return values of functions dealing with metafiles will be different on the Macintosh than they are under Windows, and that code which works using the Windows Portability Library on the Macintosh may not work under Windows. When recording a metafile, the bounding box of the Macintosh picture is assigned by way of the window origin and window extent (using SetWindowOrgEx and SetWindowExtEx). If no window origin or extent is provided, the bounding box is set to {0,0,256,256}.

Under UNIX, since there is no equivalent to Windows metafiles in the X Window System, Windows metafiles are translated directly to native X Window calls. Once again, this is a significant feature that is not available to native Motif applications.

Avoid using any APIs that are not available on all your target platforms. Some APIs are available on all platforms, but there are restrictions that you should be aware of if you use these functions. Table 8.20 shows the support status of all these APIs in Windows 95, Windows NT, the Windows Portability Library for the Macintosh, and Wind/U for UNIX.

Table 8.20 Metafile APIs

GDI APIs	Windows 95	Windows NT	Macintosh	UNIX
CloseMetaFile	Yes	Yes	Yes	Yes
CopyMetaFile	Yes	Yes	Yes	Yes
CreateMetaFile	Yes	Yes	With restrictions	Yes
DeleteMetaFile	Yes	Yes	Yes	Yes
EnumMetaFile	Yes	Yes	With restrictions	Yes
EnumMetaFileProc	Yes	Yes	Yes	Yes
GetMetaFile	Yes	Yes	With restrictions	Yes
GetMetaFileBitsEx	Yes	Yes	No	No
PlayMetaFile	Yes	Yes	With restrictions	Yes
PlayMetaFileRecord	Yes	Yes	With restrictions	Yes
SetMetaFileBitsEx	Yes	Yes	No	No
CloseEnhMetaFile	Yes	Yes	No	No
CopyEnhMetaFile	Yes	Yes	No	No
CreateEnhMetaFile	Yes	Yes	No	No
DeleteEnhMetaFile	Yes	Yes	No	No

Table 8.20 Metafile APIs (continued)

GDI APIs	Windows 95	Windows NT	Macintosh	UNIX
EnhMetaFileProc	Yes	Yes	No	Yes
EnumEnhMetaFile	Yes	Yes	No	No
GdiComment	Yes	Yes	No	No
GetEnhMetaFile	Yes	Yes	No	No
GetEnhMetaFileBits	Yes	Yes	No	No
GetEnhMetaFileDescription	Yes	Yes	No	No
GetEnhMetaFileHeader	Yes	Yes	No	No
GetEnhMetaFilePaletteEntries	Yes	Yes	No	No
GetWinMetaFileBits	Yes	Yes	No	No
PlayEnhMetaFile	Yes	Yes	No	No
PlayEnhMetaFileRecord	Yes	Yes	No	No
SetEnhMetaFileBits	Yes	Yes	No	No
SetWinMetaFileBits	Yes	Yes	No	No

Cross-Platform GDI Performance

As we have seen, the Win32 GDI API is very portable between the Win32 hosted platforms. While these cross-platform technologies support a significant amount of Microsoft Windows GDI functionality, the performance of the ported applications can vary significantly. In particular, a ported application should run significantly faster on a high-end RISC workstation than on a typical desktop PC. However, even with the additional CPU power provided by the higher-end systems, bad assumptions in the original Windows application can sometimes limit GDI performance on other platforms.

It is important to note that none of the ideas presented here cause a trade-off of Windows performance for better performance on another platform. In fact, many of these ideas result in a faster Windows application as well, though the speed-up may not be noticeable in most real-world applications. However, the speed-up in other, more complex, graphical environments can be substantial.

Comparing Win32 Platforms Graphics Subsystems

Before we look at specific examples, let's take a quick look at the platforms that support the Win32 API. Table 8.21 classifies the graphics subsystem of each platform as either tightly integrated, micro-kernel based, or distributed.

Table 8.21   Comparison of Graphics Subsystem Architectures of Win32 Platforms

Windows 3.1	Macintosh	Windows NT	UNIX/X
Tightly integrated	Tightly integrated	Micro-kernel–based	Distributed

Tightly Integrated Graphics Subsystems: Windows and Macintosh

Windows and the Macintosh have tightly integrated graphics subsystems. *Tightly integrated* refers to the amount of operating system overhead required for an application to draw something on the screen. For example, in Windows, when an application makes a GDI call, execution proceeds directly from the application, into **GDI.EXE**, and on to the display driver. No context switches are required. The Macintosh also has a relatively short execution path and minimal context switches in its graphics subsystems.

So what *is* the effect of a tightly integrated graphics subsystem on your application? Since the execution path for most graphics calls is very short in these environments, many redundancies and unoptimized logic in your graphics code may not have a large enough performance degradation for your end-users even to notice. For instance, the time that it takes to select a Pen or Brush object into a device context is very small. Even more important, information queries for font metrics, display resolution, color capabilities, and so on, are fast since they are simple function calls from one component of the system to another.

Micro-Kernel Graphics Subsystem: Windows NT

Windows NT has a more complex architecture that adds additional overhead to graphics operations. Because of Windows NT's micro-kernel design, some context switching is required as the execution thread progresses from the Win32 client application, to the Win32 Subsystem, and finally to the NT Executive and device drivers. This execution path is significantly longer than in the tightly integrated graphics subsystems.

Like the simpler architectures, however, the Windows NT graphics subsystem is generally synchronous. That is, when an API completes and returns to the caller, the work to be done by the API is also complete. The Windows NT graphics subsystem does not often queue operations for processing sometime in the future.

Distributed Graphics Subsystem: The X Window System

When people think about graphics on UNIX, they usually are thinking about the X Window System. Though also supported on other platforms, X has become the de facto standard graphics subsystem for most UNIX variants. The X Window System is a distributed graphics system. It allows graphical applications to execute on a UNIX (or other operating system) computer and display their output on any X-compatible graphics display on an attached network.

In the X environment, graphics operations come in two forms: asynchronous and synchronous. An example of an asynchronous operation is the Win32 API LineTo(). Implemented in X, LineTo() translates to a DrawLines protocol request to the X Window Server. Once this request is handed off to the Network Protocol Layer, the application is free to continue executing normally, including submitting additional graphics requests. The application does not block in LineTo() waiting for the X Window Server to respond. It just chugs on its merry way, knowing that the DrawLines protocol request will be processed by the X Window Server sometime in the future (in a few milliseconds or less).

The other form of X graphics operation is a synchronous request. In processing these types of requests, the client application blocks waiting on a response from the X Window Server (in X-speak, this is called a round-trip protocol request). The response includes information that was requested by the application. An example of a synchronous request is GetTextMetrics(). Since all font data is stored at the X Window Server, getting font metrics requires a protocol request to the server; then the application must wait for a response that contains the requested information. Such operations are extremely expensive in the X environment because the application halts processing while waiting for a response.

Because of its distributed nature and reliance on network throughput, the X Window System is the most complex of the Win32 supported platforms, and therefore, is the most performance-sensitive to graphics optimizations. In fact, the number-one performance rule that you should remember when porting applications from Windows to X is: *If it's fast on X, it will be fast everywhere.* Many small optimizations that you might dismiss as insignificant in Windows can result in an order-of-magnitude improvement in performance in X.

Rules for Writing Fast Win32 Cross-Platform Code

Now that we have established some architectural understanding of the different platforms that support the Win32 GDI, let's take a look at specific application examples that are affected by these differences.

We have identified a few rules for writing fast Win32 cross-platform code that are indicative of what we have found to be the most costly or frequently encountered performance problems when attempting to port Windows applications to other platforms. If you follow these rules when you design and code your application, you can expect it to run at native speed on all Win32 supported platforms.

The Sample Application

The CADLIKE sample application demonstrates and quantifies the performance gains of the ideas presented here. This sample application simulates a simple CAD application.

The complete source for CADLIKE is on the disk that accompanies this book. The application was generated with Visual C++ 2.0, so most of the application framework will be familiar to all VISUAL C ++ users.

As you can see CADLIKE is a simple application that demonstrates five rules for writing fast portable Win32 applications. The first three rules deal with high performance graphics rendering, and the fourth and fifth rules demonstrate methods for increasing user interface performance. Let us examine rules 1 through 3, at startup, CADLIKE creates a random series of graphics objects in `CCadlikeDoc::OnNewDocument()`. For simplicity's sake, the list of objects is limited to one of eight colors and consists of lines, rectangles, and circles of varying sizes. When the user selects rule 1, 2, or 3 from the menu bar, the application renders the list of objects into the main application window using, first, an unoptimized algorithm and then the optimized method that demonstrates the rule. The application reports the execution time of each method for comparison in a simple message box.

Rule 1: Make Liberal Use of Device Contexts to Minimize Graphics State Changes

For many applications, when redrawing a window, the possible combinations of GDI attributes are defined and relatively small. For example, in the CADLIKE application, each object type that is rendered has two GDI attributes associated with it: the foreground color (from a set of eight possibilities), and the object type, either a line, a rectangle, or a circle.

Unlike the Windows 3.1 API (commonly known as Win16), Win32 does not have a strict limit on the number of device contexts (DCs) that can be currently allocated with GetDC(). Rather than creating a single DC and repeatedly reconfiguring GDI attributes each time you draw a different object, try to find a way to use multiple preconfigured DCs instead. By allocating a few DCs at the beginning of the rendering logic, you will use up a little more memory, but you eliminate many calls to SelectObject(), SetTextColor(), etc.

As we will see later, eliminating excessive attribute changes in the DC can give exponential performance gains in the X Windows environments where these small requests in the protocol stream can adversely affect the queuing heuristics built into the X Window System protocol.

To demonstrate Rule #1, consider the function CCadlikeViewer:: OnDemonstrationRule1(), listed in Figure 8.9. The function draws the list of objects twice, once using a single DC and again using multiple DCs. Upon completion, OnDemonstrateRule1() reports the times for each method.

```
//
// Demonstrate Rule #1 - Drawing with Multiple DC's
//
void CCadlikeView::OnDemonstrationRule1()
{
    int i;
    CCadlikeDoc *pDoc = (CCadlikeDoc *)m_pDocument;
    CPen Pens[8];
```

```
Clear();

    // create pens for each color
    for (i=0;i<8;i++)
            Pens[i].CreatePen(PS_SOLID,1,pDoc-
            >m_plotterPenRGB[i]);

    WORD SlowTime = LOWORD(GetTickCount());

    // create and initialize the CDC
    CClientDC *pDC = new CClientDC(this);
    CBrush *pBrush = new CBrush();
    pBrush->CreateStockObject(NULL_BRUSH);
    pBrush = pDC->SelectObject(pBrush);

    CPen *pOldPen;

    // Draw using a single DC with state attribute changes on each
       object
    for (i=0;i<NUMELEMENTS;i++) {

            Object_t *pObjects = (Object_t *)LocalLock(pDoc-
            >m_hObjects[i]);
            pOldPen = pDC->SelectObject(&Pens[pObjects-
            >plotterPen]);

            switch (pObjects->objectType) {
            case cadLINE:
                    pDC->MoveTo(pObjects->x1,pObjects->y1);
                    pDC->LineTo(pObjects->x2,pObjects->y2);
                    break;

            ...

            }
```

```
        pDC->SelectObject(pOldPen);
        LocalUnlock(pDoc->m_hObjects[i]);
}


pBrush = pDC->SelectObject(pBrush);


delete pDC;


SlowTime = LOWORD(GetTickCount()) - SlowTime;


Clear();



// Next, draw using multiple DC's to minimize attribute
   changes
WORD FastTime = LOWORD(GetTickCount());


CClientDC *pDCs[8];
CPen *pOldPens[8];


// Create a DC for each of the eight possible colors
for (i=0;i<8;i++) {
        pDCs[i] = new CClientDC(this);
        pOldPens[i] = pDCs[i]->SelectObject(&Pens[i]);
        pDCs[i]->SelectObject(pBrush); // select the null
        brush
}


// Draw each item with the pre-configured CDC, rather than
// change the attributs on a single CDC.
for (i=0;i<NUMELEMENTS;i++) {
```

```
Object_t *pObjects = (Object_t *)LocalLock(pDoc-
>m_hObjects[i]);

switch (pObjects->objectType) {
case cadLINE:
        pDCs[pObjects->plotterPen]->MoveTo(pObjects-
        >x1,pObjects->y1);
        pDCs[pObjects->plotterPen]->LineTo(pObjects-
        >x2,pObjects->y2);
        break;

    ...

    }

    LocalUnlock(pDoc->m_hObjects[i]);
  }

  ...

  FastTime = LOWORD(GetTickCount()) - FastTime;

  ...

}
```

Rule 1: Results

Because of the large number of DC attribute changes that are avoided by creating multiple DCs, Rule 1 resulted in a 11 percent performance improvement on Windows NT 3.5 and Windows 95 (Chicago). In the X Window System, however, the speedup was 87 percent! This much larger increase is a direct result of the network overhead associated with sending the extra attribute change requests to the X Window server.

Rule 2: The Logical Order of Objects from a User's Perspective is not Necessarily the Best Order to Render

Most Windows applications maintain the list of rendered objects in the order that makes the most sense to the user. In the case of a word processor, for example, the list of objects would start with the first word on the first page, and end with the last word on the last page. When it comes time to redraw the list, most applications conveniently draw the objects in the logical order that is maintained for presentation to the user. Often, however, the optimal order for rendering can be different than this logical ordering. Again, in the case of the word processor, the performance of rendering the list of objects (in this case mostly words) in the logical order might mean a font change after every few words. This can be extremely slow.

Consider, instead, the performance speedup of maintaining a second list ordering that is the optimal rendering order. This list would start with an object of a particular attribute combination, and continue through all objects with the same attributes. It would then follow with the next set of attributes and so on. This technique yields the least number of attribute changes necessary to redraw the entire list. It also allows you to use only one DC, which is especially advantageous when you do not have a fixed set of attribute combinations to render.

`CCadlikeDoc::OnNewDocument()` builds the optimal rendering lists in the following lines:

```
// install the optimal rendering order for Rule #2
pObject->hRenderNext = m_hRenderObjects[pObject-
>objectType][pObject->plotterPen];

m_hRenderObjects[pObject->objectType][pObject->plotterPen] =
m_hObjects[i];

m_nRenderObjectsCount[pObject->objectType][pObject-
>plotterPen]++;
```

By linking all of the objects with similar attributes together, an optimized rendering is then straight-forward, as is demonstrated by `OnDemonstrationRule2()` in the following code:

```
//
// Demonstrate Rule #2 - Drawing with optimized rendering order
```

```
//
void CCadlikeView::OnDemonstrationRule2()
{
    int i;
    CCadlikeDoc *pDoc = (CCadlikeDoc *)m_pDocument;
    CPen Pens[8];

 Clear();

    for (i=0;i<8;i++)
            Pens[i].CreatePen(PS_SOLID,1,pDoc-
>m_plotterPenRGB[i]);

... (Same as Rule #1)

    Clear();


    // Next, draw using the optimized rendering order
    WORD FastTime = LOWORD(GetTickCount());
    int objectType;
    int pen;

    for (objectType=0;objectType<3;objectType++) {

            for (pen=0;pen<8;pen++) {

                    HLOCAL hObject = pDoc-
                    >m_hRenderObjects[objectType][pen];
                    pOldPen = pDC->SelectObject(&Pens[pen]);

                    while (hObject) {
                            Object_t *pObject = (Object_t
                            *)LocalLock(hObject);
                            HLOCAL hNextObject = pObject-
                            >hRenderNext;
```

```
            switch (objectType) {

            case cadLINE:
                    pDC->MoveTo(pObject->x1,pObject-
                    >y1);
                    pDC->LineTo(pObject->x2,pObject-
                    >y2);
                    break;


            case cadRECTANGLE:
                    pDC->Rectangle(pObject->x1,

                    pObject->y1,

                    pObject->x2,

                    pObject->y2);
                    break;

            case cadCIRCLE:
                    pDC->Arc(pObject->x1, pObject-
                    >y1, pObject->x2, pObject->y2,
                    0, 0, 0, 0);
                    break;
            }

            LocalUnlock(hObject);
            hObject = hNextObject;


        }
        pDC->SelectObject(pOldPen);
    }
 }

 ...

 }
```

Rule 3: Results

Under Windows NT 3.5 and Windows 95, the results from Rule 2 are very similar to Rule 1 with both showing about an 11 percent speedup. Under the X Window System, however, the speed-up is 279%! The reason for the exponential speed-up under X is due to protocol buffering inside the Xlib software layer. Rather than sending the server lots of protocol requests to draw individual objects with a different graphics context (graphics context in X == device context in Windows), the application can send a single request to draw *hundreds* of objects with a common graphics context. The ability to send batch requests of drawing primitives allows the X protocol to achieve very good performance even on heavily loaded networks.

Rule 4: Eliminate Redundant API Calls

One of the most frequent performance problems that I have found in Windows applications is many redundant API calls for system information. Luckily, this is also one of easiest problems to fix.

When writing Win32 code, be particularly careful about redundantly querying for system information such as font metrics, display resolution, printer capabilities, and display capabilities. Too often applications query this type of information over and over rather than asking the system for it once and storing the result in application memory for repeated use.

`OnDemonstrationRule3()`, shown in Figure 8.11, is a simple example of repeatedly querying information from the system. In particular, the API `GetTextExtent()` is severely abused in the first rendering logic, and is corrected in the faster version that follows.

```
//
// Demonstrate Rule #3 - Show the impact of redundant API calls
//

void CCadlikeView::OnDemonstrationRule3()
{
    CCadlikeDoc *pDoc = (CCadlikeDoc *)m_pDocument;
    CClientDC *pDC = new CClientDC(this);
    int i,j;
    char szString[] = "This is a very long string of words.";
```

```
char *pString = szString;

Clear();

WORD SlowTime = LOWORD(GetTickCount());

for (j=0;j<100;j++) // get enough iterations to make the
timings meaningful
        for (i=0;i<40;i++) {
                CSize StringSize = pDC-
                >GetTextExtent(pString,strlen(pString));
                pDC->TextOut(10,i*20,pString,strlen(pString));
                pDC->MoveTo(10+StringSize.cx,i*20-10); //
                locate at the end of the string
                pDC->LineTo(10+StringSize.cx,i*20-20); // make
                a mark at the end of the sentence
        }
SlowTime = LOWORD(GetTickCount()) - SlowTime;

Clear();
pString = szString; // reinitialize


// Now, don't calculate the string length and size on each
  iteration
WORD FastTime = LOWORD(GetTickCount());

CSize StringSize = pDC-
>GetTextExtent(pString,strlen(pString));
    int len = strlen(pString);

    for (j=0;j<100;j++) // get enough iterations to make the
                        timings meaningful
        for (i=0;i<40;i++) {

                pDC->TextOut(10,i*20,pString,len);
```

```
                    pDC->MoveTo(10+StringSize.cx,i*20-10); //
                    locate at the end of the string
                    pDC->LineTo(10+StringSize.cx,i*20-20); // make
                    a mark at the end of the sentence
          }

     FastTime = LOWORD(GetTickCount()) - FastTime;


     delete pDC;


     char sResults[100];
     sprintf(sResults,"Redraw using:\nUncached: %hu ms\nCached: %hu
     ms",SlowTime,FastTime);
     MessageBox(sResults,"Rule #3 Results", MB_OK);
}
```

Rule 3 Results

The results of Rule 3 vary greatly by platform. On Windows NT 3.5, the speed up was a minimal 6.8 percent, while on Windows 95, the speedup was 32.5 percent. This difference can be largely explained by the 32-bit to 16-bit thunk that is required in the Windows 95 16-bit GDI implementation. The thunking layer makes redundant API calls even more expensive by adding on parameter translations when calling from 32-bit to 16-bit code.

Rule 3 achieves a 35 percent improvement in the X Window System. Luckily for the X developer, the Xlib software layer contains many optimizations and caching techniques that significantly reduce the penalty for redundant API calls.

Summary

In this chapter, we have surveyed the Windows and Windows NT GDI capabilities to determine which capabilities are portable to UNIX and Macintosh platforms. We have also seen that a few simple modifications to native Win32 applications can make them execute much faster in other Win32 hosted environments. Following these five rules will result in dramatic performance increases on some platforms, and will even make your applications somewhat faster on Windows and Windows NT platforms. Best of all, these concepts are completely portable across platforms, are localized to specific pieces of code, and do not trade off Windows performance for better performance on other platforms.

## CHAPTER 9

User APIs

In Windows, the User library provides window management, including the overall Windows graphical environment as well as an application's windows.

This chapter describes cross-platform issues related to the following :

- The API support on each platform for various User library capabilities
- Macintosh window handling differences
- Macintosh extension functions
- UNIX extension functions

Platform-Specific User Capabilities

The User capabilities for Windows 3.1 with Win32s, Windows95, and Windows NT are roughly the same, but there are a few major exceptions. The UNIX and Macintosh User implementations, however, are implemented on top of the native toolkits on each platform. Therefore, there are some limitations on these platforms that are not present on the Windows variants. On the other hand, the UNIX and Macintosh native libraries also provide some additional capabilities that are also not present in the various Windows implementations. This section describes the support status of the User APIs on all of these target platforms.

Caret Handling Functions

All Caret APIs are supported on all platforms, so there will be no differences in the way all versions of your application handle carets.

Table 9.1 Caret Handling APIs

Function	Windows 95	Windows NT	Macintosh	UNIX
CreateCaret	Yes	Yes	Yes	Yes
DestroyCaret	Yes	Yes	Yes	Yes
GetCaretBlinkTime	Yes	Yes	Yes	Yes
GetCaretPos	Yes	Yes	Yes	Yes
HideCaret	Yes	Yes	Yes	Yes
SetCaretBlinkTime	Yes	Yes	Yes	Yes
SetCaretPos	Yes	Yes	Yes	Yes
ShowCaret	Yes	Yes	Yes	Yes

Cursor and Icon Management Functions

Neither the Windows Portability Library nor Wind/U support color cursors on the Macintosh or UNIX platforms. When reading a cursor from a resource file, both toolkits give first preference to 16 x 16 monochrome cursors, followed by 32 x 32 monochrome cursors, which are then scaled down to 16 x 16. You may want to design a custom 16 x 16 monochrome cursor for use in the cross-platform versions of your application.

On the Macintosh, the IDC_ICON and IDC_UPARROW system cursors are not supported.

X Windows supports only the AND mask plane for cursors. Therefore, Wind/U combines the XOR and AND masks into a single AND mask that best approximates the intended view of the cursor.

Table 9.2   Cursor Management APIs

Function	Windows 95	Windows NT	Macintosh	UNIX
ClipCursor	Yes	Yes	No	Yes
CopyCursor	Yes	Yes	Yes	Yes
CopyIcon	Yes	Yes	No	Yes
CreateCursor	Yes	Yes	Yes	Partial
CreateIcon	Yes	Yes	Yes	No
CreateIconFromResource	Yes	Yes	No	No
CreateIconIndirect	Yes	Yes	No	No
DestroyCursor	Yes	Yes	Yes	Yes
DestroyIcon	Yes	Yes	Yes	Yes
GetClipCursor	Yes	Yes	No	Yes
GetCursor	Yes	Yes	Yes	Yes
GetCursorPos	Yes	Yes	Yes	Yes
GetIconInfo	Yes	Yes	No	No
LookupIconIDFromDirectory	Yes	Yes	No	No
LookupIconIdFromDirectoryEx	Yes	No	No	No
SetCursor	Yes	Yes	Yes	Yes
SetCursorPos	Yes	Yes	No	Yes
SetSystemCursor	No	Yes	No	No
ShowCursor	Yes	Yes	Yes	Yes

Dialog Functions

While both toolkits support virtually all dialog box APIs, there are nuances on each platform that you should be aware of when porting code between various platforms. See Chapter 6 for a complete discussion of these differences.

Table 9.3 Dialog Creation and Management APIs

Function	Windows 95	Windows NT	Macintosh	UNIX
CheckDlgButton	Yes	Yes	Yes	Yes
CheckRadioButton	Yes	Yes	Yes	Yes
CreateDialogIndirectParam	Yes	Yes	Yes	Yes
CreateDialogParam	Yes	Yes	Yes	Yes
DefDlgProc	Yes	Yes	Yes	Yes
DialogIndirectParam	Yes	Yes	Yes	Yes
DialogParam	Yes	Yes	Yes	Yes
DlgDirList	Yes	Yes	No	Partial
DlgDirListComboBox	Yes	Yes	No	Partial
DlgDirSelectComboBoxEx	Yes	Yes	No	Yes
DlgDirSelectEx	Yes	Yes	No	Yes
EndDialog	Yes	Yes	Yes	Yes
GetDialogBaseUnits	Yes	Yes	Yes	Yes
GetDlgCtrlID	Yes	Yes	Yes	Yes
GetDlgItem	Yes	Yes	Yes	Yes
GetDlgItemInt	Yes	Yes	Yes	Yes
GetNextDlgGroupItem	Yes	Yes	Yes	Yes
GetNextDlgTabItem	Yes	Yes	Partial	Yes
IsDialogMessage	Yes	Yes	Yes	Yes
IsDlgButtonChecked	Yes	Yes	Yes	Partial
MapDialogRect	Yes	Yes	Yes	Yes
SendDlgItemMessage	Yes	Yes	Yes	Yes
SetDlgItemInt	Yes	Yes	Yes	Yes
SetDlgItemText	Yes	Yes	Yes	Yes

Thread Functions

The Win32 Thread APIs are not supported by the Visual C++ for Macintosh Windows Portability Library. Wind/U, however, does support most of the Windows NT Threads APIs.

Table 9.4 Thread APIs

Function	Windows 95	Windows NT	Macintosh	UNIX
AttachThreadInput	Yes	Yes	No	No
ClientThreadConnect	No	Yes	No	No
CreateThread	Yes	Yes	No	Yes
DeleteCriticalSection	Yes	Yes	No	Yes
EnterCriticalSection	Yes	Yes	No	Yes
EnumThreadWindows	Yes	Yes	No	No
GetThreadDesktop	Yes	Yes	No	No
GetWindowThreadProcessId	Yes	Yes	No	Yes
InitializeCriticalSection	Yes	Yes	No	Yes
LeaveCriticalSection	Yes	Yes	No	Yes
SetThreadDesktop	Yes	Yes	No	No
Sleep	Yes	Yes	No	Yes
SleepEx	Yes	Yes	No	Yes
TlsAlloc	Yes	Yes	No	Yes
TlsFree	Yes	Yes	No	Yes
TlsGetValue	Yes	Yes	No	Yes
TlsSetValue	Yes	Yes	No	Yes

Clipboard Functions

Wind/U defines custom Motif clipboard formats for all Windows clipboard formats except CF_TEXT, which is mapped to the standard Motif format for text. Wind/U does not support the clipboard viewer APIs.

The Macintosh has a much smaller set of standard clipboard formats than does Windows. The CF_TEXT format is mapped to the Macintosh's TEXT format, and CF_METAFILEPICT is mapped to PICT. Note that there is no unique format for the CF_BITMAP, CF_DIB, and CF_PALETTE formats. The Windows Portability Library maps these formats into the PICT format. If your application supports CF_METAFILEPICT, you should disable code in your application that renders or accepts CF_BITMAP, CF_DIB and CF_PALETTE formats.

Table 9.5 Clipboard APIs

Function	Windows 95	Windows NT	Macintosh	UNIX
ChangeClipboardChain	Yes	Yes	Yes	No
CloseClipboard	Yes	Yes	Yes	Yes
CountClipboardFormats	Yes	Yes	Yes	Yes
EmptyClipboard	Yes	Yes	Yes	Yes
EnumClipboardFormats	Yes	Yes	Yes	Yes
GetClipboardData	Yes	Yes	Yes	Yes
GetClipboardFormatName	Yes	Yes	Partial	Yes
GetClipboardOwner	Yes	Yes	Yes	No
GetClipboardViewer	Yes	Yes	Yes	No
GetOpenClipboardWindow	Yes	Yes	Yes	No
GetPriorityClipboardFormat	Yes	Yes	Yes	Yes
OpenClipboard	Yes	Yes	Yes	Yes
RegisterClipboardFormat	Yes	Yes	Partial	Yes
SetClipboardData	Yes	Yes	Yes	Partial
SetClipboardViewer	Yes	Yes	Yes	No

Error Handling Functions

Most Error Handling APIs are supported on all platforms. The MessageBox API does not support the MB_TASKMODAL style.

Table 9.6 Error Handling APIs

Function	Windows 95	Windows NT	Macintosh	UNIX
Beep	Yes	Yes	Yes	Yes
FlashWindow	Yes	Yes	Yes	No
GetLastError	Yes	Yes	Partial	Yes
MessageBeep	Yes	Yes	Yes	Partial
MessageBox	Yes	Yes	Yes	Partial
MessageBoxEx	Yes	Yes	Yes	Yes
SetDebugErrorLevel	Yes	Yes	No	No
SetLastErrorEx	Yes	Yes	Yes	Yes

Hook Functions

Neither the Windows Portability Library nor Wind/U support the journalling, CBT, sysmsgfilter, hardware, and shell hooks. Also, the Windows Portability Library does not support installing system-wide hooks; the thread ID passed to SetWindowsHookEx must be non-NULL (and should be the return value from GetCurrentThreadId). Wind/U currently only supports the hkprc value WH_CALWHNDPROC for the UnhookWindowsHook and UnhookWindows HookEx APIs.

Table 9.7 Hook APIs

Function	Windows 95	Windows NT	Macintosh	UNIX
CallMsgFilter	Yes	Yes	Yes	Yes
CallNextHookEx	Yes	Yes	Yes	Yes
CBTProc	Yes	Yes	No	No
DefHookProc	Yes	Yes	No	Yes
JournalPlaybackProc	Yes	Yes	No	No
JournalRecordProc	Yes	Yes	No	No

Table 9.7 Hook APIs (continued)

Function	Windows 95	Windows NT	Macintosh	UNIX
KeyboardProc	Yes	Yes	No	No
MessageProc	Yes	Yes	Yes	No
MouseProc	Yes	Yes	Yes	No
SetWindowsHook	Yes	Yes	No	Yes
SetWindowsHookEx	Yes	Yes	Yes	Yes
ShellProc	Yes	Yes	No	No
SysMsgProc	Yes	Yes	No	No
UnhookWindowsHook	Yes	Yes	No	Partial
UnhookWindowsHookEx	Yes	Yes	Yes	Partial

System Information Functions

On both the Macintosh and UNIX, FindWindow only searches windows created by the current application, because it does not have access to the windows of other applications.

GetSysColor and GetSystemMetrics are only partially implemented on the Macintosh and UNIX. Not all of the selectors return useful information. Consult toolkit documentation for complete support status of each selector. SetSysColors is not supported in either Visual C++ for Macintosh or Wind/U.

Table 9.8 Window Information APIs

Function	Windows 95	Windows NT	Macintosh	UNIX
AnyPopup	Yes	Yes	Yes	Partial
EnumChildWindows	Yes	Yes	Yes	Yes
EnumTaskWindows	Yes	Yes	No	Yes
EnumThreadWindows	Yes	Yes	No	No
EnumWindows	Yes	Yes	Yes	Yes
FindWindow	Yes	Yes	Yes	Yes

Table 9.8 Window Information APIs (continued)

Function	Windows 95	Windows NT	Macintosh	UNIX
FindWindowEx	Yes	No	No	No
GetNextWindow	Yes	Yes	Yes	Yes
GetParent	Yes	Yes	Yes	Yes
GetSysColor	Yes	Yes	Partial	Yes
GetSystemMetrics	Yes	Yes	Partial	Partial
GetTopWindow	Yes	Yes	Yes	Yes
GetWindow	Yes	Yes	Yes	Yes
GetWindowTask	Yes	Yes	Yes	Yes
IsChild	Yes	Yes	Yes	Yes
IsWindow	Yes	Yes	Yes	Yes
SetParent	Yes	Yes	Yes	Yes
SetSysColors	Yes	Yes	No	No

Input Functions

Both Wind/U and Visual C++ for Macintosh support all of the important keyboard input APIs. Of those that are not supported, most are tied closely to PC hardware and/or Windows keyboard drivers and, therefore, are inherently unportable.

Table 9.9 Input APIs

Function	Windows 95	Windows NT	Macintosh	UNIX
ActivateKeyboardLayout	Yes	Yes	No	No
EnableWindow	Yes	Yes	Yes	Partial
GetActiveWindow	Yes	Yes	Yes	Yes
GetAsyncKeyState	Yes	Yes	Yes	Yes
GetCapture	Yes	Yes	Yes	Yes

Table 9.9 Input APIs (continued)

Function	Windows 95	Windows NT	Macintosh	UNIX
GetDoubleClickTime	Yes	Yes	Yes	Yes
GetFocus	Yes	Yes	Yes	Yes
GetForegroundWindow	Yes	Yes	No	No
GetKeyboardState	Yes	Yes	Partial	Partial
GetKeyboardLayoutName	Yes	Yes	No	No
GetKeyboardType	Yes	Yes	No	No
GetSysModalWindow	Yes	Yes	No	No
IsWindowEnabled	Yes	Yes	Yes	Yes
LoadKeyboardLayout	Yes	Yes	No	No
MapVirtualKey	Yes	Yes	Yes	Yes
RegisterHotKey	Yes	Yes	No	No
ReleaseCapture	Yes	Yes	Yes	Yes
SetActiveWindow	Yes	Yes	Yes	Yes
SetCapture	Yes	Yes	Yes	Yes
SetDoubleClickTime	Yes	Yes	No	Yes
SetFocus	Yes	Yes	Yes	Yes
SetForegroundWindow	Yes	Yes	No	No
SetSysModalWindow	Yes	Yes	No	Partial
SwapMouseButton	Yes	Yes	No	No
UnloadKeyboardLayout	Yes	Yes	No	No
VkKeyScan	Yes	Yes	Yes	Yes
WaitForInputIdle	Yes	Yes	No	No

Menu Management Functions

Almost all menu APIs are supported by all toolkits. The most notable exception is GetSystemMenu, which has significant limitations on both the Macintosh and UNIX.

On the Macintosh, GetSystemMenu returns the Apple menu. This menu is significantly different than the standard Windows system menu, so code that modifies the Windows system menu will likely need to be rewritten for the Macintosh. On UNIX, GetSystemMenu is only supported for child windows, not top-level or popup windows. It returns NULL if the window style is WS_OVERLAPPED or WS_POPUP.

Also, TrackPopupMenu on the Macintosh does not allow your application to position the menu in a window.

Table 9.10 Menu Management APIs

Function	Windows 95	Windows NT	Macintosh	UNIX
AppendMenu	Yes	Yes	Yes	Yes
ChangeMenu	Yes	Yes	Yes	Yes
CheckMenuItem	Yes	Yes	Yes	Yes
CheckMenuRadioItem	Yes	No	No	No
CreateMenu	Yes	Yes	Yes	Yes
CreatePopupMenu	Yes	Yes	Yes	Yes
DeleteMenu	Yes	Yes	Yes	Yes
EnableMenuItem	Yes	Yes	Yes	Yes
FindMenuDefaultID	Yes	No	No	No
GetMenu	Yes	Yes	Yes	Yes
GetMenuCheckmarkDimensions	Yes	Yes	Yes	Yes
GetMenuDefaultItem	Yes	No	No	No
GetMenuItemCount	Yes	Yes	Yes	Yes
GetMenuItemID	Yes	Yes	Yes	Yes
GetMenuItemRect	Yes	No	No	No
GetMenuState	Yes	Yes	Yes	Yes
GetMenuString	Yes	Yes	Yes	Yes
GetSubMenu	Yes	Yes	Yes	Yes
GetSystemMenu	Yes	Yes	Partial	Partial
HiliteMenuItem	Yes	Yes	Partial	No

Table 9.11 Menu Management APIs (continued)

Function	Windows 95	Windows NT	Macintosh	UNIX
InsertMenu	Yes	Yes	Yes	Yes
MenuItemFromPoint	Yes	No	No	No
ModifyMenu	Yes	Yes	Yes	Yes
RemoveMenu	Yes	Yes	Yes	Yes
SetMenu	Yes	Yes	Yes	Yes
SetMenuDefaultItem	Yes	No	No	No
SetMenuItemBitmaps	Yes	Yes	Yes	Yes
SetMenuItemInfo	Yes	No	No	No
TrackPopupMenu	Yes	Yes	Partial	Partial
TrackPopupMenuEx	Yes	No	No	No

Message Functions

Most of the Windows Message APIs are supported in all Win32 environments. The most significant limitation is that both Visual C++ for Macintosh and Wind/U do not allow applications to send messages between processes. Therefore, related APIs like InSendMessage and ReplayMessage are not supported or are stubbed.

Table 9.11 Message APIs

Function	Windows 95	Windows NT	Macintosh	UNIX
CallWindowProc	Yes	Yes	Yes	Yes
DispatchMessage	Yes	Yes	Yes	Yes
FormatMessage	Yes	Yes	No	No
GetCurrentTask	Yes	Yes	No	Partial
GetMessage	Yes	Yes	Yes	Yes
GetMessageExtraInfo	Yes	Yes	No	Partial
GetMessagePos	Yes	Yes	Yes	Yes

Table 9.11 Message APIs (continued)

Function	Windows 95	Windows NT	Macintosh	UNIX
GetMessageTime	Yes	Yes	Yes	Partial
GetQueueStatus	Yes	Yes	No	Partial
InSendMessage	Yes	Yes	Partial	No
PeekMessage	Yes	Yes	Yes	Yes
PostAppMessage	Yes	Yes	Yes	Partial
PostMessage	Yes	Yes	Yes	Partial
PostQuitMessage	Yes	Yes	Yes	Yes
PostThreadMessage	Yes	Yes	No	Yes
RegisterWindowMessage	Yes	Yes	Yes	Yes
ReplyMessage	Yes	Yes	Partial	No
SendAsyncProc	Yes	Yes	No	No
SendMessage	Yes	Yes	Yes	Partial
SendMessageCallback	Yes	Yes	No	No
SendMessageTimeout	Yes	Yes	No	No
SendNotifyMessage	Yes	Yes	No	No
SetMessageQueue	Yes	Yes	Partial	Yes
TranslateAccelerator	Yes	Yes	Yes	Partial
TranslateMDISysAccel	Yes	Yes	Yes	Yes
TranslateMessage	Yes	Yes	Yes	Partial
WaitMessage	Yes	Yes	Yes	Yes

Display and Movement Functions

In the Macintosh environment, the SetWindowPos API has an extra flag named SWP_NOVALIDATEZORDER This flag causes SetWindowPos to bypass the z-order check. Ordinarily if you request SetWindowPos to change the z-order of a window, it examines the window's current z-order and does not change the window if it is already in the correct position. The SWP_NOVALIDATEZORDER flag can be passed to SetWindowPos or DeferWindowPos in the uFlags parameter.

Use SWP_NOVALIDATEZORDER to change the position of an HWND in the Macintosh z-order when the Windows z-order is correct. You can also use SWP_NOVALIDATEZORDER to move a window to the front of the Macintosh z-order when it is already frontmost in the Windows z-order.

The Windows Portability Library for the Macintosh also does not support iconic windows; therefore, CloseWindow and related APIs are not supported.

On the Macintosh, GetWindowPlacement supports two additional flags: WPF_USEDEVICERECT and WPF_CHECKCHILDBOUNDS. WPF_USE DEVICERECT is always set on exit from GetWindowPlacement.

The Windows Portability Library for the Macintosh also supports two additional flags for the SetWindowPlacement API: WPF_USEDEVICERECT and WPF_CHECKCHILDBOUNDS. If the WPF_USEDEVICERECT flag is set, SetWindowPlacement uses the WINDOWPLACEMENT rcDevice field to indicate which monitor the window was originally positioned on, and places the window on a similarly sized and positioned monitor if possible. When WPF_USEDEVICERECT is not set, the rcDevice field is ignored and the window is positioned on the main monitor.

If the WPF_CHECKCHILDBOUNDS flag is set, SetWindowPlacement always places a child window so that it is visible on a monitor. Use this flag with top-level child windows, such as multiple document interface (MDI) windows, that a user might move to a position that is not visible on any monitor.

Table 9.12 Display and Movement APIs

Function	Windows 95	Windows NT	Macintosh	UNIX
ArrangeIconicWindows	Yes	Yes	No	Yes
BeginDeferWindowPos	Yes	Yes	Yes	Yes
BringWindowToTop	Yes	Yes	Yes	Yes
CascadeChildWindows	Yes	No	No	No
CascadeWindows	Yes	No	No	No
ClientToScreen	Yes	Yes	Yes	Yes
CloseWindow	Yes	Yes	No	Yes
DeferWindowPos	Yes	Yes	Yes	Yes
EndDeferWindowPos	Yes	Yes	Yes	Yes

Table 9.12 Display and Movement APIs (continued)

Function	Windows 95	Windows NT	Macintosh	UNIX
EnumChildWindows	Yes	Yes	Yes	Yes
EnumWindows	Yes	Yes	No	Yes
ExitWindowsEx	Yes	Yes	No	No
FindWindow	Yes	Yes	Yes	Yes
FindWindowEx	Yes	No	No	No
FlashWindow	Yes	Yes	Yes	No
GetClientRect	Yes	Yes	Yes	Yes
GetDesktopWindow	Yes	Yes	Yes	Yes
GetShellWindow	Yes	No	No	No
GetWindowPlacement	Yes	Yes	Partial	Yes
GetWindowRect	Yes	Yes	Yes	Partial
GetWindowText	Yes	Yes	Yes	Yes
GetWindowTextLength	Yes	Yes	Yes	Yes
IsChild	Yes	Yes	Yes	Yes
IsIconic	Yes	Yes	Partial	Partial
IsWindowVisible	Yes	Yes	Yes	Yes
IsZoomed	Yes	Yes	Yes	Partial
MoveWindow	Yes	Yes	Yes	Yes
OpenIcon	Yes	Yes	No	Yes
RemovePopup	Yes	Yes	No	Yes
ScreenToClient	Yes	Yes	Yes	Yes
SetWindowPlacement	Yes	Yes	Partial	Yes
SetWindowPos	Yes	Yes	Yes	Partial
SetWindowText	Yes	Yes	Yes	Yes
ShowOwnedPopups	Yes	Yes	Yes	Yes
ShowWindow	Yes	Yes	Yes	Partial
TileChildWindows	Yes	No	No	No
TileWindows	Yes	No	No	No

Property Functions

Only a subset of the property APIs are supported on the Macintosh and UNIX. Avoid unsupported functions in your application whenever possible.

Table 9.13 Property APIs

Function	Windows 95	Windows NT	Macintosh	UNIX
EnumProps	Yes	Yes	Yes	Yes
EnumPropsEx	Yes	Yes	No	Yes
GetProp	Yes	Yes	Yes	Yes
PropEnumProc	Yes	Yes	No	Yes
PropEnumProcEx	Yes	Yes	No	Yes
RemoveProp	Yes	Yes	Yes	Yes
SetProp	Yes	Yes	Yes	Yes

Scroll Bar Functions

Most of the Scroll Bar APIs are supported on all platforms. On the Macintosh, EnableScrollBar supports the ESB_ENABLEBOTH and ESB_DISABLEBOTH constants, but it does not support enabling or disabling only a single scroll bar arrow.

In the UNIX environment, the EnableScrollBar paramenter fuArrowFlags is ignored; the scrollbar is either fully enabled or disabled at all times. Also, the SetScrollRange parameter fRepaint is ignored in the UNIX environment.

Table 9.14 Scrolling APIs

Function	Windows 95	Windows NT	Macintosh	UNIX
EnableScrollBar	Yes	Yes	Partial	Partial
GetScrollInfo	Yes	No	No	No
GetScrollPos	Yes	Yes	Yes	Yes
GetScrollRange	Yes	Yes	Yes	Yes
ScrollWindow	Yes	Yes	Yes	Yes

Table 9.14 Scrolling APIs (comtinued)

Function	Windows 95	Windows NT	Macintosh	UNIX
ScrollWindowEx	Yes	Yes	Yes	Yes
SetScrollInfo	Yes	No	No	No
SetScrollPos	Yes	Yes	Yes	Yes
SetScrollRange	Yes	Yes	Yes	Partial
ShowScrollBar	Yes	Yes	Yes	Yes

Help Functions

On the Macintosh, the WinHelp API starts Microsoft Help, a Macintosh version of the Windows Help engine. This engine supports a significant part of Windows help functionality on the Macintosh using Windows help files. For more information about building help files for the Macintosh, see Chapter 10.

On UNIX, the WinHelp API starts the HyperHelp viewer, a Windows Help engine for Motif. HyperHelp help files are created with the HyperHelp compiler, which reads the same text (.RTF) and project (.HPJ) files as the Windows help compiler. See chapter 10 for more information about creating help files for Motif applications.

Table 9.15 Help APIs

Function	Windows 95	Windows NT	Macintosh	UNIX
GetMenuContextHelpID	Yes	No	No	No
GetWindowContextHelpID	Yes	No	No	No
SetMenuContextHelpID	Yes	No	No	No
SetWindowContextHelpID	Yes	No	No	No
WinHelp	Yes	Yes	Yes	Yes

Timer Functions

All timer functions are fully supported on all platforrms.

Table 9.16 Timer APIs

Function	Windows 95	Windows NT	Macintosh	UNIX
KillTimer	Yes	Yes	Yes	Yes
SetTimer	Yes	Yes	Yes	Yes

Translation Functions

In the Macintosh environment, title bars, size borders, shadows, and other elements of top-level windows are different from their Windows counterparts. Since Macintosh windows do not contain menu bars, the fMenu parameter of AdjustWindowRect is ignored.

For each top-level window, the Windows Portability Library creates an invisible Macintosh window whose portRect field is equal to the top-level window's client rectangle. The top-level window's bounding rectangle is calculated from the dimensions of the Macintosh window. To calculate the size of the bounding rectangle of a window that uses a custom Macintosh window definition identifier (WDEF), you must supply a WHM_PROCID hook during the call to AdjustWindowRectEx to determine what WDEF is passed to the WHM_NEWWINDOW hook.

In the UNIX environment, the window manager controls metrics, such as the width of the window border and the width and height of the window caption, for popup and overlapped windows. Default values for these metrics vary between different window managers, and even between the same window manager on different UNIX platforms. And individual users can configure these metrics with X resources. In addition, an application may call AdjustWindowRect befroe any window (therefore, any widget) is created, thus eliminating the possibility of querying the WMShell for the values of these metrics.

Wind/U determines the values of these metrics as accurately as possible. Given the variable nature of these metrics, however, the values may be off by a few pixels, causing the window appearance to be slightly off.

Table 9.17 Translate APIs

Function	Windows 95	Windows NT	Macintosh	UNIX
AdjustWindowRect	Yes	Yes	Yes	Yes
AdjustWindowRectEx	Yes	Yes	Yes	Yes
ChildWindowFromPoint	Yes	Yes	Yes	Yes
ChildWindowFromPointEx	Yes	No	No	No
WindowFromPoint	Yes	Yes	Yes	Yes

Window Painting Functions

All toolkits support virtually all of the window painting APIs. In the UNIX environment, Wind/U does not support an hwnd value of NULL for the desktop fuRedraw flags RDW_FRAME and RDW_ALLCHILDREN for the RedrawWindow API.

Table 9.18 Window Painting APIs

Function	Windows 95	Windows NT	Macintosh	UNIX
ExcludeUpdateRgn	Yes	Yes	Yes	No
GetUpdateRect	Yes	Yes	Yes	Yes
GetUpdateRgn	Yes	Yes	Yes	Yes
InvalidateRect	Yes	Yes	Yes	Yes
InvalidateRgn	Yes	Yes	Yes	Yes
LockWindowUpdate	Yes	Yes	No	No
RedrawWindow	Yes	Yes	Yes	Partial
UpdateWindow	Yes	Yes	Yes	Yes
ValidateRect	Yes	Yes	Yes	Yes
ValidateRgn	Yes	Yes	Yes	Yes

Window Class Functions

All toolkits provide virtually complete support for all Window Class APIs. In the UNIX environment, Wind/U does not currently support the offset GCW_HMODULE for the GetClassWord function.

Table 9.19 Window Class APIs

Function	Windows 95	Windows NT	Macintosh	UNIX
GetClassInfo	Yes	Yes	Yes	Yes
GetClassLong	Yes	Yes	Yes	Yes
GetClassName	Yes	Yes	Yes	Yes
GetClassWord	Yes	Yes	Yes	Partial
RegisterClass	Yes	Yes	Yes	Yes
SetClassLong	Yes	Yes	Yes	Yes
SetClassWord	Yes	Yes	Yes	Yes
UnregisterClass	Yes	Yes	Yes	Yes

Window Creation and Access

Most window creation and access APIs are supported by all toolkits. There are some limitations in the window styles supported, but both Macintosh and Wind/U toolkits provide support for most APIs.

In the UNIX environment, Motif does not support a border child window style. However, Wind/U provides this functionality through the Wind/U border widget, which provides resize, caption, minimize and maximize buttons, and system menu support to child windows. The internal implementation of the border widget is transparent to Wind/U ported applications. You should be aware, however, that the border widget mimics the look and feel of the Motif Window Manager. Also, the border widget queries X database resources for colors, resize border widths, etc. When running under window managers other than the Motif Window Manager, the border widget resorts to default values.

Table 9.20 Window Creation and Access APIs

Function	Windows95	Windows NT	Macintosh	UNIX
CreateMDIWindow	Yes	Yes	Yes	No
CreateWindow	Yes	Yes	Yes	Partial
CreateWindowEx	Yes	Yes	Yes	Partial
DefFrameProc	Yes	Yes	Yes	Yes
DefMDIChildProc	Yes	Yes	Yes	Yes
DefWindowProc	Yes	Yes	Yes	Yes
DestroyWindow	Yes	Yes	Yes	Yes
GetDesktopWindow	Yes	Yes	Yes	Yes
GetLastActivePopup	Yes	Yes	Yes	No
GetWindowLong	Yes	Yes	Yes	Yes
GetWindowWord	Yes	Yes	Yes	Yes
SetShellWindow	Yes	No	No	No
SetWindowLong	Yes	Yes	Yes	Yes
SetWindowWord	Yes	Yes	Yes	Yes

Windows Messages

Differences between interprocess communiction on the different platforms limits the support for some Windows messages.

In the UNIX environment, for example, there is no concept of idle time because the operating system is preemptive. Therefore, Wind/U only sends WM_ENTERIDLE messages for menus and only when the menu is popped down and as the user traverses the menu. Wind/U never sends WM_ENTERIDLE for dialog boxes.

Wind/U creates controls or child widows in the handling of WM_NCCREATE in DefWindowProc(). If your application handlles WM_NCCREATE, however, Wind/U does nothing. If your application does not get WM_NCCREATE to DefWindowProc(), the hWnd for the child window doesn't exist (except in the handle table) and the child window never gets painted. Therefore, if your applciation handles WM_NNCCREATE, it must send WM_NCCREATE to DefWindowProc().

Table 9.21 Windows Messages

Interface	Windows 95	Windows NT	Macintosh	UNIX
WM_ACTIVATE	Yes	Yes	Yes	Yes
WM_ACTIVATEAPP	Yes	Yes	Yes	No
WM_APP	Yes	No	No	No
WM_ASKCBFORMATNAME	Yes	Yes	No	No
WM_CANCELJOURNAL	Yes	Yes	No	No
WM_CANCELMODE	Yes	Yes	Yes	Yes
WM_CAPTURECHANGED	Yes	No	No	No
WM_CHANGECBCHAIN	Yes	Yes	No	No
WM_CHAR	Yes	Yes	Yes	Yes
WM_CHARTOITEM	Yes	Yes	Yes	Yes
WM_CHILDACTIVATE	Yes	Yes	Yes	Yes
WM_CLEAR	Yes	Yes	Yes	Yes
WM_CLOSE	Yes	Yes	Yes	Yes
WM_COALESCE_FIRST	Yes	Yes	No	No
WM_COALESCE_LAST	Yes	Yes	No	No
WM_COMMAND	Yes	Yes	Yes	Yes
WM_COMMNOTIFY	Yes	Yes	No	No
WM_COMPACTING	Yes	Yes	No	No
WM_COMPAREITEM	Yes	Yes	Yes	Yes
WM_CONTEXTMENU	Yes	No	No	No
WM_COPY	Yes	Yes	Yes	Yes
WM_COPYDATA	Yes	Yes	No	No
WM_CREATE	Yes	Yes	Yes	Yes
WM_CTLCOLOR	Yes	Yes	No	Yes
WM_CTLCOLORBTN	Yes	Yes	Yes	Yes
WM_CTLCOLORDLG	Yes	Yes	Yes	Yes
WM_CTLCOLOREDIT	Yes	Yes	Yes	Yes
WM_CTLCOLORLISTBOX	Yes	Yes	Yes	Yes

Table 9.21 Windows Messages (continued)

Interface	Windows 95	Windows NT	Macintosh	UNIX
WM_CTLCOLORMSGBOX	Yes	Yes	Yes	Yes
WM_CTLCOLORSCROLLBAR	Yes	Yes	No	Yes
WM_CTLCOLORSTATIC	Yes	Yes	Yes	Yes
WM_CUT	Yes	Yes	Yes	Yes
WM_DDE_ACK	Yes	Yes	No	No
WM_DDE_ADVISE	Yes	Yes	No	No
WM_DDE_DATA	Yes	Yes	No	No
WM_DDE_EXECUTE	Yes	Yes	No	No
WM_DDE_FIRST	Yes	Yes	No	No
WM_DDE_INIT	No	No	No	No
WM_DDE_INITIATE	Yes	Yes	No	No
WM_DDE_LAST	Yes	Yes	No	No
WM_DDE_POKE	Yes	Yes	No	No
WM_DDE_REQUEST	Yes	Yes	No	No
WM_DDE_TERMINATE	Yes	Yes	No	No
WM_DDE_UNADVISE	Yes	Yes	No	No
WM_DEADCHAR	Yes	Yes	No	No
WM_DELETEITEM	Yes	Yes	Yes	Yes
WM_DESTROY	Yes	Yes	Yes	Yes
WM_DESTROYCLIPBOARD	Yes	Yes	Yes	No
WM_DEVICEBROADCAST	Yes	No	No	No
WM_DEVMODECHANGE	Yes	Yes	No	No
WM_DISPLAYCHANGE	Yes	No	No	No
WM_DRAWCLIPBOARD	Yes	Yes	Yes	No
WM_DRAWITEM	Yes	Yes	Yes	Yes
WM_DROPFILES	Yes	Yes	Partial	No
WM_ENABLE	Yes	Yes	Yes	Yes
WM_ENDSESSION	Yes	Yes	No	No

Table 9.22 Windows Messages (continued)

Interface	Windows 95	Windows NT	Macintosh	UNIX
WM_ENTERIDEL	Yes	Yes	Yes	Partial
WM_ERASEBKGND	Yes	Yes	Yes	Yes
WM_FONTCHANGE	Yes	Yes	No	No
WM_GETDLGCODE	Yes	Yes	Yes	Yes
WM_GETFONT	Yes	Yes	Yes	Partial
WM_GETHOTKEY	Yes	Yes	No	No
WM_GETICON	Yes	No	No	No
WM_GETMINMAXINFO	Yes	Yes	Yes	Yes
WM_GETTEXT	Yes	Yes	Yes	Yes
WM_GETTEXTLENGTH	Yes	Yes	Yes	Yes
WM_HELP	Yes	No	No	No
WM_HOTKEY	Yes	Yes	No	No
WM_HSCROLL	Yes	Yes	Yes	Yes
WM_HSCROLLCLIPBOARD	Yes	Yes	No	No
WM_ICONERASEBKGND	Yes	Yes	No	Yes
WM_INITDIALOG	Yes	Yes	Yes	Yes
WM_INITMENU	Yes	Yes	Yes	Yes
WM_INITMENUPOPUP	Yes	Yes	Yes	Yes
WM_KEYDOWN	Yes	Yes	Yes	Yes
WM_KEYFIRST	Yes	Yes	Yes	Yes
WM_KEYLAST	Yes	Yes	Yes	Yes
WM_KEYUP	Yes	Yes	Yes	Yes
WM_KILLFOCUS	Yes	Yes	Yes	Yes
WM_LBUTTONDBLCLK	Yes	Yes	Yes	Yes
WM_LBUTTONDOWN	Yes	Yes	Yes	Yes
WM_LBUTTONUP	Yes	Yes	Yes	Yes
WM_MBUTTONDBLCLK	Yes	Yes	No	Yes
WM_MBUTTONDOWN	Yes	Yes	No	Yes

Table 9.21 Windows Messages (continued)

Interface	Windows 95	Windows NT	Macintosh	UNIX
WM_MBUTTONUP	Yes	Yes	No	Yes
WM_MDIACTIVATE	Yes	Yes	Yes	Yes
WM_MDICASCADE	Yes	Yes	Yes	Yes
WM_MDICREATE	Yes	Yes	Yes	Yes
WM_MDIDESTROY	Yes	Yes	Yes	Yes
WM_MDIGETACTIVE	Yes	Yes	Yes	Yes
WM_MDIICONARRANGE	Yes	Yes	No	Yes
WM_MDIMAXIMIZE	Yes	Yes	Yes	Yes
WM_MDINEXT	Yes	Yes	Yes	Yes
WM_MDIREFRESHMENU	Yes	Yes	Yes	No
WM_MDIRESTORE	Yes	Yes	Yes	Yes
WM_MDISETMENU	Yes	Yes	Yes	Yes
WM_MDITITLE	Yes	Yes	Yes	Yes
WM_MEASUREITEM	Yes	Yes	Yes	Yes
WM_MEDIASTATUSCHANGE	Yes	No	No	No
WM_MENUCHAR	Yes	Yes	Yes	No
WM_MENUSELECT	Yes	Yes	Yes	Yes
WM_MOUSEACTIVATE	Yes	Yes	Yes	Partial
WM_MOUSEENTER	Yes	Yes	No	No
WM_MOUSEFIRST	Yes	Yes	Yes	Partial
WM_MOUSELAST	Yes	Yes	Yes	Partial
WM_MOUSELEAVE	Yes	Yes	No	No
WM_MOUSEMOVE	Yes	Yes	Yes	Yes
WM_MOVE	Yes	Yes	Yes	Yes
WM_MOVING	Yes	No	No	No
WM_NCACTIVATE	Yes	Yes	Yes	Yes
WM_NCCALCRGN	No	Yes	No	No
WM_NCCALCSIZE	Yes	Yes	Partial	Yes

Table 9.21 Windows Messages (continued)

Interface	Windows 95	Windows NT	Macintosh	UNIX
WM_NCCREATE	Yes	Yes	Yes	Yes
WM_NCDESTROY	Yes	Yes	Yes	Yes
WM_NCHITTEST	Yes	Yes	Yes	Yes
WM_NCLBUTTONDBLCLK	Yes	Yes	Yes	Yes
WM_NCLBUTTONDOWN	Yes	Yes	Yes	Yes
WM_NCLBUTTONUP	Yes	Yes	Yes	Yes
WM_NCMBUTTONCBLCLK	Yes	Yes	No	Yes
WM_NCMBUTTONDOWN	Yes	Yes	No	Yes
WM_NCMBUTTONUP	Yes	Yes	No	Yes
WM_NCMMOUSEMOVE	Yes	Yes	Yes	Yes
WM_NCPAINT	Yes	Yes	Partial	Yes
WM_NCRBUTTONDBLCLK	Yes	Yes	No	Yes
WM_NCRBUTTONDOWN	Yes	Yes	No	Yes
WM_NCRBUTTONUP	Yes	Yes	No	Yes
WM_NEXTDLGCTL	Yes	Yes	Yes	Yes
WM_NULL	Yes	Yes	Yes	Partial
WM_PAINT	Yes	Yes	Yes	Yes
WM_PAINTCLIPBOARD	Yes	Yes	No	No
WM_PAINTICON	Yes	Yes	No	No
WM_PALETTECHANGED	Yes	Yes	Yes	Yes
WM_PALETTEISCHANGING	Yes	Yes	Yes	Yes
WM_PARENTNOTIFY	Yes	Yes	Yes	Yes
WM_PASTE	Yes	Yes	Yes	Yes
WM_PENWINFIRST	Yes	Yes	No	No
WM_PENWINLAST	Yes	Yes	No	No
WM_POWER	Yes	Yes	No	No
WM_POWERBROADCAST	Yes	No	No	No
WM_PRINT	Yes	No	No	No

Table 9.21 Windows Messages (continued)

Interface	Windows 95	Windows NT	Macintosh	UNIX
WM_PRINTCLIENT	Yes	No	No	No
WM_QUERYDRAGICON	Yes	Yes	No	Yes
WM_QUERYENDSESSION	Yes	Yes	No	Yes
WM_QUERYNEWPALETTE	Yes	Yes	Yes	Yes
WM_QUERYOPEN	Yes	Yes	No	Yes
WM_QUEUESYNC	Yes	Yes	No	No
WM_QUIT	Yes	Yes	Yes	Yes
WM_RBUTTONCBLCLK	Yes	Yes	No	Yes
WM_RBUTTONDOWN	Yes	Yes	No	Yes
WM_RBUTTONUP	Yes	Yes	No	Yes
WM_RENDERALLFORMATS	Yes	Yes	Yes	No
WM_RENDERFORMAT	Yes	Yes	Yes	Yes
WM_SETCURSOR	Yes	Yes	Yes	Yes
WM_SETFOCUS	Yes	Yes	Yes	Yes
WM_SETFONT	Yes	Yes	Yes	Yes
WM_SETHOTKEY	Yes	Yes	No	No
WM_SETICON	Yes	No	No	No
WM_SETREDRAW	Yes	Yes	Yes	Yes
WM_SETTEXT	Yes	Yes	Yes	Yes
WM_SHOWWINDOW	Yes	Yes	Yes	Yes
WM_SIZE	Yes	Yes	Yes	Yes
WM_SIZECLIPBOARD	Yes	Yes	No	No
WM_SIZING	Yes	No	No	No
WM_SPOOLERSTATUS	Yes	Yes	No	No
WM_STYLECHANGED	Yes	No	No	No
WM_STYLECHANGING	Yes	No	No	No
WM_SYSCHAR	Yes	Yes	Yes	Yes
WM_SYSCOLORCHANGE	Yes	Yes	Yes	Yes

Table 9.21 Windows Messages (continued)

Interface	Windows 95	Windows NT	Macintosh	UNIX
WM_SYSCOMMAND	Yes	Yes	Yes	Partial
WM_SYSDEADCHAR	Yes	Yes	No	No
WM_SYSKEYDOWN	Yes	Yes	Yes	Yes
WM_SYSKEYUP	Yes	Yes	Yes	Yes
WM_TIMECHANGE	Yes	Yes	No	No
WM_TIMER	Yes	Yes	Yes	Yes
WM_UNDO	Yes	Yes	Yes	Partial
WM_USER	Yes	Yes	Yes	No
WM_VKEYTOITEM	Yes	Yes	Yes	Yes
WM_VSCROLL	Yes	Yes	Yes	Yes
WM_VSCROLLCLIPBOARD	Yes	Yes	No	No
WM_WINDOWPOSCHANGED	Yes	Yes	Yes	No
WM_WINDOWPOSCHANGING	Yes	Yes	Yes	No
WM_WININICHANGE	Yes	Yes	No	No

Miscellaneous Functions

Some of the newer Win32s APIs are not supported on Macintosh and UNIX. Look for these in future releases.

Table 9.22 Misc User APIs

Function	Windows 95	Windows NT	Macintosh	UNIX
CloseDesktop	No	Yes	No	No
CopyImage	Yes	No	No	No
GetProcessWindowStation	No	Yes	No	No
GetUserObjectSecurity	No	Yes	No	No
MapWindowPoints	Yes	Yes	Yes	Yes

Table 9.22 Misc User APIs (continued)

Function	Windows 95	Windows NT	Macintosh	UNIX
MsgWaitForMultipleObjects	Yes	Yes	No	No
PaintDesktop	Yes	No	No	No
RegisterHotKey	Yes	Yes	No	No
ResetDisplay	Yes	No	No	No
SetUserObjectSecurity	No	Yes	No	No
UnregisterHotKey	Yes	Yes	No	No
wsprintf	Yes	Yes	Yes	Yes
wvsprintf	Yes	Yes	Yes	Yes

Window Management on the Macintosh

In the Macintosh environment, the Windows Portability Library handles windows very similar to the way Windows handles them, with a few differences. Window differences occur mainly in the following areas:

- Resizable Top-Level Windows
- Top-Level Child Windows
- Minimized Windows
- Window Style Restrictions
- Multiple Document Interface (MDI)

Resizable Top-Level Windows

In some cases, the behavior of top-level window under the Windows Portability Library is different than under Windows. This difference is due to interactions with the Macintosh window manager. For example, you cannot change the state (size, position, or z-order) of a top-level window without redrawing the window. Therefore, if you use the SWP_NOREDRAW flag when calling SetWindowPos on a top-level window, the flag is ignored.

The Macintosh uses a size box in the bottom right corner of a window instead of a thick frame to indicate the window is resizable. This difference causes many problems with applications that place user interface elements in this corner of their windows. By default, the Windows Portability Library only draws a size box in a top-level window if the window is resizable (that is, has the WS_THICKFRAME style bit set), and the top-level window or one of its children has at least one frame scroll bar turned on (that is, has the WS_HSCROLL or WS_VSCROLL style bit set), and that scrollbar is aligned to the bottom or right side of the top-level window. These restrictions ensure that the Windows Portability Library only draws a size box if it is guaranteed not to be drawing the size box over a portion of the top-level window that could be drawn on by the application.

Even if the size box is not drawn, however, the bottom right corner of a resizable window still hit-tests as a resizing area. This means that even if your application places a user interface element such as a control in this area, when the user clicks there, the Windows Portability Library will enter a resizing mode for the top-level window instead of passing the click on to your application. For this reason, it is best to redesign your user interface if your existing application uses this corner of a resizable top-level window.

If the Windows Portability Library does not automatically draw a size box for you, you may wish to create a scroll bar control with the SBS_SIZEBOX style bit and place it in this area. A scroll bar created with this style bit draws itself as a size box instead of a scroll bar, and gives the user a visible indication that the window is resizable. Or you can use the WS_EX_FORCESIZEBOX extended window style with CreateWindowEx. This window style forces the Windows Portability Library to draw a Macintosh grow icon in the bottom right corner of the window. You should only use this window style on top-level windows.

Top-Level Child Windows

A child window created with a caption (using the WS_CAPTION style) is not drawn inside its parent window. Instead, it is represented as a separate Macintosh window. The user may freely move the child window about, even moving it outside the bounds of its parent window. When the parent window moves or scrolls, the child window does not move. When the user clicks on the client area of the top-level child window, its z-order does not change; you must call SetWindowPos (possibly by way of BringToFront) to change the child's z-order, just as in Windows. If your ported application creates top-level child windows that you want to be contained by their parent windows, you must create the child windows without a caption and provide your own non-client-area painting to make the child look like a moveable window with a caption.

Some Windows-based applications override the WM_NCCALCSIZE, WM_NCPAINT, WM_NCACTIVATE and other WM_NC... messages to create their own non-client area (frame) styles. For example, your application may implement a window with a small titlebar for its tool palette. Under the Windows Portability Library, if your application changes the frame of a top-level window, the window must be created with an initial style specifying only WS_BORDER. This prevents the Macintosh from drawing a window frame, and allows your application complete control over non-client painting.

Minimized Windows

Neither the Macintosh nor the Windows Portability Library support minimized windows. Passing one of the SW_SHOWMIN... commands to ShowWindow causes the appropriate display and activation of the window, but the window remains in its current size and position and does not minimize.

Window Style Restrictions

Because of differences between Windows and Macintosh windows, not all combinations of window styles are supported when creating a window. Some usages of SetWindowLong to change the style or extended style of a window are not supported, because they would require changing the Macintosh implementation of the window. For example, the Windows Portability Library does not allow adding the WS_CAPTION style to a child window that does not have a caption or system menu, because this would change the child from being drawn inside its parent window to having its own Macintosh window. If you attempt such a change, the Windows Portability Library warns you that changing the host implementation is not allowed, and refuses to make the change. Similarly, you cannot use SetParent on the Macintosh to make the desktop the parent of a child window.

Multiple Document Interface (MDI) Windows

Multiple Document Interface (MDI) is an area where the Windows Portability Library makes many assumptions about your application in order to achieve reasonable Macintosh behavior. As a result, you may encounter compatibility problems where these assumptions are not correct for your application.

The Windows Portability Library requires that an MDI frame window always be maximized, in order to achieve good results when maximizing child windows and positioning child windows of the frame window, such as toolbars and status bars. To enforce this requirement, the Windows Portability Library always maximizes the frame window whenever ShowWindow is called with a show command not equal to SW_HIDE. Also, the DefFrameProc API overrides the WM_WINDOWPOSCHANGING message and changes the window location and size to match the maximized position.

When DefFrameProc receives a WM_ACTIVATEAPP message indicating that the application is being deactivated, it hides all children of the MDI frame window other than the MDICLIENT control. This is done in accordance with the Macintosh user interface convention that windows such as toolbars, status bars, and floating palettes be hidden while the application is in the background. When DefFrameProc receives an activating WM_ACTIVATEAPP message, windows that were hidden by DefFrameProc are shown. If you have a child window of the frame window that you do not want to be hidden, add the WS_EX_NOAUTOHIDE style bit to the child's extended style flags when you call CreateWindowEx.

To work properly, DefFrameProc requires that your application pass the following messages through to it:

- WM_GETMINMAXINFO
- WM_WINDOWPOSCHANGING
- WM_WINDOWPOSCHANGED
- WM_ACTIVATEAPP

The MDI standard for Windows requires that only one child window can be maximized at any time. The Windows MDI APIs enforce this standard by restoring the unmaximized state of the current maximized child whenever a different child is activated, and by maximizing the newly active child.

The Windows Portability Library does not support this standard. On the Macintosh, MDI APIs only change the maximized state of MDI children in response to the WM_MDIMAXIMIZE and WM_MDIRESTORE messages. The WM_MDIMAXIMIZE message handler does not restore any previously maximized child.

The Macintosh window corresponding to an MDI frame window is never made visible, even if the frame window is visible. This means that the MDICLIENT control is not visible either. If your application depends on having a "desktop" area on which to draw, design an alternate user interface, or preferably create a child window on which to draw.

Visual C++ For Macintosh User Extensions

The Visual C++ for Macintosh Windows Portability Library provides a number of user extensions that you can use in the Macintosh version of your application. These extensions allow you take advantage of native Macintosh features that are not available in Windows.

WM_MACINTOSH

The Windows Portability Library uses a new message, the WM_MACINTOSH message. The low word of the wParam of the message is a selector that indicates the particular kind of message. The high word of the wParam and the lParam vary, depending on the value of the selector. Usually, these messages are sent and used internally by the Windows Portability Library, and are handled by DefWindowProc.

```
nCmd = LOWORD(wParam);     // WLM_* constant for the submessage
nCmd1 = HIWORD(wParam);    // Varies according to nCmd
nCmd2 = lParam;            // Varies according to nCmd
```

You can use this Macintosh-specific message to provide a variety of different notifications, depending on the contents of LOWORD(wParam). The following manifest constants represent the valid values that LOWORD(wParam) can take:

WLM_BALLOONHELP

This value is sent to an application when the application is expected to perform a Balloon-Help™ action. It is only sent if Balloon Help is turned on (usually by way of the help menu), and only if no balloon is currently displayed on the screen.

The WLM_BALLOONHELP notification uses the following format:

Location	Contents
HIWORD (wParam)	0
IParam	Pointer to a BALLOONHELPSTRUCT structure.

The members of the BALLOONHELPSTRUCT structure pointed to by IParam are used as follows:

```
struct BALLOONHELPSTRUCT
{
    UINT    BalloonType;        // Set to BHT_MENU, indicating Menu
                                     type.
    UINT    itemID;             // Set to the command for the menu
                                //     item, or zero for pop-up items.
    UINT    itemPos;            // Offset of the menu item within the
                                     menu.
    HWND    hwndItem;           // The HMENU the item is in.
    UINT    itemFlags;          // The menu flags for the given item.
    struct HMMessageRecord* lpMessageRecord;   // Set to NULL.
    struct                      // The rcItem structure, which has
                                     the same
    {                           //     form as a Macintosh rect, is
                                     set up

        short top;              //     to contain the bounding box of
                                     the
        short left;             //     item, in global coordinates.
        short bottom;
        short right;
    } rcItem;
    struct                      // The ptTip structure, which has the
                                     same
    {                           //     form as a Macintosh Point, is
                                     set up
        short v;                //     to contain the suggested tip
```

```
        short h;              //    location, in global
                                    coordinates.

    } ptTip;
} ;
```

Currently, only the BHT_MENU value is supported for BalloonType; Balloon-Help notification for other types of screen objects, such as dialog boxes or windows, may be supported in the future.

The WLM_BALLOONHELP notification is sent when the user's mouse is tracking within a menu or over a menu title in the menu bar, just before an idle state is reached. A menu enters an idle state when it finishes processing a message, and there are no more messages waiting in its queue.

The application is responsible for removing a balloon after it is no longer needed, usually by passing the rcItem rectangle to HMShowBalloon as its alternateRect parameter.

DefWindowProc handles the WLM_BALLOONHELP notification by checking the lpMessageRecord field of the BALLOONHELPSTRUCT. If this field is not NULL, DefWindowProc calls HMShowBalloon with the HMMessageRecord pointed to by lpMessageRecord, using the ptTip and rcItem fields to position the balloons. The following code shows how the call to HMShowBalloon is made:

```
case WLM_BALLOONHELP:
{
    BALLOONHELPSTRUCT* pbh = ((BALLOONHELPSTRUCT*)lParam);
    if (pbh->lpMessageRecord != NULL)
        HMShowBalloon(pbh->lpMessageRecord,
                *(Point*)&pbh->ptTip, (Rect*)&pbh->rcItem,
                NULL, 0, 0,
                pbh->BalloonType == BHT_MENU ? kHMSaveBitsNoWindow :
                    kHMRegularWindow);
}
```

Use khMSaveBitsNoWindow balloons for menu balloons, but be careful not to draw on top of your own balloons. When Balloon Help is enabled, use care in handling WM_PAINT messages and in drawing the menu status bar.

WLM_DEVICECHANGED

This notification is sent to every window that has a corresponding Macintosh window on a Macintosh GDevice that changed. The lparam argument of this notification contains a pointer to a GDEVICEINFO structure that identifies the change.

WLM_CHILDOFFSET

This notification is sent to all the child windows of a window that is being moved. The Windows Portability Library uses this notification internally to update the position of Macintosh controls when their containing parent window moves. The notification uses the following format:

Location	Contents
HIWORD(wParam)	0
LOWORD(lParam)	Change in x position of the parent window
HIWORD(lParam)	Change in y position of the parent window

WLM_HASCCP

This notification is sent to inquire whether the Cut, Copy, and Paste menu items in the window's standard Edit menu should be enabled. The WLM_HASCCP notification is routed to the active window first. DefWindowProc propagates the message to all child windows. By default, the window procedures (WndProc) of edit controls and combo box controls that have editable text fields return TRUE after processing this message.

If a dialog box contains controls whose WndProc returns TRUE for the WLM_HASCCP query in the WM_MACINTOSH message, the Cut, Copy, and Paste menu items in the Edit menu will remain enabled as long as the dialog box is active.

The WLM_HASCCP notification uses the following format:

Location	Contents
HIWORD(wParam)	0
lParam	0

WndProc returns the value TRUE if recipient has Cut, Copy, and Paste, or FALSE if not.

WLM_MACEVENT

This notification is returned to the application when a Macintosh event that has no corresponding Windows message is removed from the event queue. The lParam parameter contains the Macintosh event code contained in the Macintosh EventRecord.what field.

There are several Macintosh event types (such as update, disk, activate, suspend/resume, and high-level) for which there is no corresponding Windows message. In the case of these events, PeekMessage(..., PM_NOREMOVE) returns a WM_MACINTOSH (WLM_MACEVENT) message so that your application can stop passing PM_NOREMOVE to PeekMessage and can instead call GetMessage or PeekMessage(..., PM_REMOVE). PeekMessage also returns the WM_MACINTOSH (WLM_MACEVENT) message if an event is converted into a corresponding Windows message that does not match the HWND or message filters passed to PeekMessage. Again, your application can use the message as a cue to break out of a PeekMessage(..., PM_NOREMOVE) loop, and otherwise ignore its contents. It is unlikely that your application would need to provide any other handling for this message.

The following example shows how you may need to rewrite Windows message latching code to accomodate the WLM_MACEVENT notification. The first code fragment is designed to wait for any message to come in and then retrieve that message from the queue:

```
while (!PeekMessage(&msg, NULL, 0, 0, PM_NOREMOVE))
    NULL;
PeekMessage( &msg, NULL, msg.message, msg.message,
    PM_REMOVE);
// do something with message
```

Under the Windows Portability Library, it is possible that the call to PeekMessage(PM_REMOVE) in the code above will not find the message returned by PeekMessage(..., PM_NOREMOVE). Any message that PeekMessage returns will match the message filter, but if the event located by the call to PeekMessage(..., PM_NOREMOVE) is processed by a WHM_EVENT hook, PeekMessage(..., PM_REMOVE) is not able to convert it into a message and return it. As a result, instead of using the code sequence above, make the following change:

```
while (!PeekMessage(&msg, NULL, 0, 0, PM_NOREMOVE))
    NULL;
if (PeekMessage(&msg, NULL, msg.message, msg.message,
        PM_REMOVE))
{
    // do something with message
}
```

Another example illustrates a similar change to message-filtering code. Message range arguments passed to PeekMessage allow the caller to specify that only a particular subset of messages be returned:

```
while (!PeekMessage(&msg, NULL, WM_KEYFIRST,
        WM_KEYLAST, PM_NOREMOVE))
    NULL;
PeekMessage(&msg, NULL, msg.message, msg.message,
        PM_REMOVE);
// handle the message
```

However, if PM_NOREMOVE is passed to PeekMessage with a given message range, PeekMessage can return a message outside the specified range, namely WM_MACINTOSH (WLM_MACEVENT). To handle this case, alter your code as follows:

```
for (;;)
{
    while (!PeekMessage(&msg, NULL, WM_KEYFIRST,
            WM_KEYLAST, PM_NOREMOVE))
        NULL;
    if (PeekMessage(&msg, NULL, msg.message,
            msg.message, PM_REMOVE))
        break;
```

```
      }
      // handle the message
```

WLM_MENUSTATE

This notification is sent before drawing the menu bar. The value returned by the window procedure (WndProc) that processes the notification determines how the menu bar is enabled:

WndProc Return	Menu enabling
MD_ENABLE	Menu is enabled normally.
MD_DISABLE	Menu is disabled (beeps when you click on it).
MD_GRAY	Menu is grayed.

MD_GRAYCCP Menu is grayed, except for Edit/Cut/Copy/Paste commands; Menu commands are mapped to WM_CUT, WM_COPY, and WM_PASTE and are then routed to the active window.

DefWindowProc returns MD_ENABLE unless the menu owner is disabled. If the window is disabled, DefWindowProc returns MD_GRAY if the active window responded FALSE to the WLM_HASCCP notification, and MD_GRAYCCP if the active window responded TRUE to the WLM_HASCCP notification.

WLM_PARENTACTIVATE

This notification is sent when the highlighted state of the window frame changes in a top-level window or top-level child window. The Windows Portability Library uses this notification internally to show or hide frame scroll bars as appropriate, and to redraw the size box of a window. The WLM_PARENTACTIVATE notification uses the following format:

Location	Contents
HIWORD(wParam)	Boolean: is parent activating/deactivating the window?
lParam	Macintosh WindowPtr pointing to parent window.

WLM_PARENTCHANGED

This notification is sent to a window and all its child windows when the parent of the window is changed using a call to the SetParent function. The Windows

Portability Library uses WLM_PARENTCHANGED internally to destroy and re-create the Macintosh control corresponding to a Windows control class when the containing Macintosh window graphics port (GrafPort) of the control is changed as a result of a call to SetParent. Applications with windows that have native Macintosh implementations can use it for the same purpose. The WLM_PARENTCHANGED notification uses the following format:

Location	Contents
HIWORD (wParam)	0
IParam	0

WLM_SETMENUBAR

This notificatiaon is sent to allow changes to the contents of the Macintosh menu bar. DefWindowProc responds by calling the SetMacMenuBar function to install the menus of the receiving window into the menu bar.

To prevent the menu bar from changing, do not pass the message and notification through to DefWindowProc. To install a different set of menus in the menu bar, call SetMacMenuBar and pass it a different window handle (HWND).The WLM_SETMENUBAR notification uses the following format:

Location	Contents
HIWORD (wParam)	0
IParam	0

Macintosh Hook Functions

The Windows Portability Library supports several hook callback functions not included in Win32. These functions use standard Win32 hook syntax.

A hook is a point in the Microsoft Window message-handling mechanism where an application can install a subroutine to monitor the message traffic in the system and process certain types of messages before they reach the target window procedure.

To take advantage of a particular hook, you must provide a hook procedure and use SetWindowsHookEx to install it into the chain associated with the hook. All hook procedures use the same syntax.

HookProc is a placeholder for an application-defined name. Since Windows must call the hook procedure, the actual name must be exported by listing it and, optionally, its ordinal value, in the EXPORTS statement of the application's module-definition file.

The nCode parameter is a hook code that the hook procedure uses to determine the action to perform. The value of the hook code depends on the type of the hook; each type has its own characteristic set of hook codes. The values of the wParam and lParam parameters depend on the hook code, but they typically contain information about a message that was sent or posted.

SetWindowsHookEx always installs a hook procedure at the beginning of a hook chain. When an event occurs that is monitored by a particular type of hook, Windows calls the procedure at the beginning of the hook chain associated with the hook. Each hook procedure in the chain determines whether to pass the event to the next procedure. A hook procedure passes an event to the next procedure by calling CallNextHookEx. Hook procedures for some types of hooks can only monitor messages. Windows passes messages to each hook procedure, regardless of whether a particular procedure calls CallNextHookEx.

The Windows Portability Library hook extensions are listed under the names of the manifest constants passed to SetWindowsHookEx when registering them.

WHM_ACTIVATE

This value is passed to SetWindowsHookEx as the nHookType parameter to register a hook callback function provided by the application. The Windows Portability Library calls this hook function when it receives an activate or deactivate event relating to a Macintosh window not under its control. There is no default behavior for the function. This callback function must use standard Win32 hook callback syntax:

```
LRESULT CALLBACK ActivationHookProc( int nCode, WPARAM wParam,
LPARAM lParam )
```

ActivationHookProc is a placeholder for the actual name defined by your application. The wParam argument is not used, and the lParam argument points to an Apple EventRecord containing an activate or deactivate event. The return value is ignored.

WHM_ALLOCWINDOWRECORD

This value is passed to SetWindowsHookEx as the nHookType parameter to register a hook callback function provided by the application. The Windows Portability Library calls this hook function to allocate memory for a Macintosh WindowRecord. If no hook is installed, NewPtr is used to allocate the memory. The callback function must use standard Win32 hook callback syntax:

```
LRESULT CALLBACK AllocWindowRecordHookProc( int nCode, WPARAM
wParam, LPARAM lParam )
```

AllocWindowRecordHookProc is a placeholder for the actual name defined by your application. The wParam argument contains the window handle of the window being created, and the lParam argument contains the number of bytes to allocate. The callback function must return a pointer to the block of memory allocated.

WHM_CLOSEWINDOW

This value is passed to SetWindowsHookEx as the nHookType parameter to register a hook callback function provided by the application. The Windows Portability Library calls this hook function when a native Macintosh window needs to be closed. If no hook is installed, the CloseWindow routine is used to close the window. The callback function must use standard Win32 hook callback syntax:

```
LRESULT CALLBACK CloseWindowHookProc( int nCode, WPARAM wParam,
LPARAM lParam )
```

CloseWindowHookProc is a placeholder for the actual name defined by your application. The wParam argument is unused, and the lParam argument contains the Macintosh WindowPtr of the native window to be closed. The return value is ignored.

The hook function should use either the CloseWindow or DisposeWindow traps to close the window, depending on how the storage for the window was allocated. Typically this hook will be used in conjunction with custom WHM_ALLOCWINDOWRECORD and WHM_FREEWINDOWRECORD callback functions.

WHM_CTLUNDERLINE

This value is passed to SetWindowsHookEx as the nHookType parameter to register a hook callback function provided by the application. The Windows Portability Library calls this hook function when a control window is being drawn, to determine whether the accelerator character in the title of the control window should be underlined. If no hook is installed, the accelerator is not underlined.

The callback function must use standard Win32 hook callback syntax:

LRESULT CALLBACK CtlUnderlineHookProc(int nCode, WPARAM wParam, LPARAM lParam)

CtlUnderlineHookProc is a placeholder for the actual name defined by your application. The wParam argument is unused, and the lParam argument contains the handle (HWND) of the window being drawn. The callback function must return TRUE if the accelerator in the window title should be underlined, or FALSE if not.

WHM_CUSTOMMENUSETUP

This value is passed to SetWindowsHookEx as the nHookType parameter to register a hook callback function provided by the application. The Windows Portability Library calls this hook function before drawing a menu to determine whether a WHM_MENUSETUP hook callback function needs to be called to modify any items on the menu. There is no default behavior. The callback function must use standard Win32 hook callback syntax:

```
LRESULT CALLBACK CustomMenuSetupHookProc( int nCode, WPARAM
wParam, LPARAM lParam )
```

CustomMenuSetupHookProc is a placeholder for the actual name defined by your application. The wParam argument contains the handle (HWND) of the window that owns the menu to be drawn, and the lParam argument contains the handle (HMENU) of the menu itself. The callback function must return TRUE if the menu requires a WHM_MENUSETUP callback, or FALSE if not.

WHM_DIALOGHOOK

This value is passed to SetWindowsHookEx as the nHookType parameter to register a hook callback function provided by the application. The Windows

Portability Library calls this hook function when the Macintosh Dialog Manager calls the common dialog callback function. The callback function must use standard Win32 hook callback syntax:

```
LRESULT CALLBACK DialogHookProc( int nCode, WPARAM wParam, LPARAM
    lParam )
```

DialogHookProc is a placeholder for the actual name defined by your application. The wParam argument is unused, and the lParam argument contains a pointer to a DIALOGHOOKINFO structure. The callback function must return the index for the item that should be considered as having been hit. Your hook can cause a different item to be hit than the one indicated in the DIALOGHOOKINFO structure.

There is no default behavior. This hook is never called for hits in the subsidiary Macintosh standard file dialog boxes (Replace/Cancel, New Folder, and so forth).

An application can provide its own Macintosh DLOG and DITL resources for file common dialog boxes. Your hook function can then use the information passed to it in order to control specific items that you have added to a common dialog box. To use custom DLOG and DITL resources that have different resource identifiers than the default common dialogbox resources, set the OFN_ENABLEMACTEMPLATE flag in the flags field of the OPENFILENAME structure and place either the resource identifier or the resource name into the lpTemplateName member of the OPENFILENAME structure.

WHM_DRAGBOUNDS

This value is passed to SetWindowsHookEx as the nHookType parameter to register a hook callback function provided by the application. The Windows Portability Library calls this hook function when a Macintosh window is being dragged by the user. A hook function may modify the drag boundary rectangle (that is, adjust the bounds rect passed to _DragGrayRgn) when a window is dragged, to prevent the window from being dragged into certain areas of the screen. There is no default behavior.

The area in which a top-level window or top-level child window can be dragged is the area of the entire desktop.

The callback function must use standard Win32 hook callback syntax:

```
LRESULT CALLBACK DragBoundsHookProc( int nCode, WPARAM wParam,
LPARAM lParam )
```

DragBoundsHookProc is a placeholder for the actual name defined by your application. The wParam argument contains the handle (HWND) of the window being dragged, and the lParam argument contains a pointer to a QuickDraw rectangle bounding the region in which the window may be dragged. The return value is ignored.

This hook is called in response to a user dragging a window by clicking the title bar. The dragging occurs in DefWindowProc while the SC_MOVE WM_SYSCOMMAND is being handled.

WHM_EVENT

This value is passed to SetWindowsHookEx as the nHookType parameter to register a hook callback function provided by the application. The Windows Portability Library calls this hook function when an EventRecord is received from the Macintosh Toolbox. The default hook passes the event to the TSMEvent routine of the Macintosh Text Services Manager. The callback function must use standard Win32 hook callback syntax:

```
LRESULT CALLBACK EventHookProc( int nCode, WPARAM wParam, LPARAM
lParam )
```

EventHookProc is a placeholder for the actual name defined by your application. The wParam argument contains one of the following event codes, indicating the circumstances under which the event was retrieved from the Macintosh event queue:

Code	How the event was retrieved
HEVT_GETMSG	Retrieved by GetMessage.
HEVT_PEEKREMOVE	Retrieved by PeekMessage(PM_REMOVE).
HEVT_PEEKNOREMOVE	Retrieved by PeekMessage(PM_NOREMOVE).
HEVT_SWP	Retrieved by SetWindowPos; definitely an update event.
HEVT_DLGFILTER	Passed to the Windows Portability Library's modal-dialog event filter.
HEVT_AEIDLE	Passed to Windows Portability Library's AppleEvent idle event filter.

The lParam argument contains a pointer to the Macintosh EventRecord. The callback function must return TRUE if the hook handled the event, or FALSE if not.

WHM_FREEWINDOWRECORD

This value is passed to SetWindowsHookEx as the nHookType parameter to register a hook callback function provided by the application. The Windows Portability Library calls this hook function to free memory that is being used to hold a Macintosh WindowRecord. If no hook is installed, DisposePtr is used to free the memory. The callback function must use standard Win32 hook callback syntax:

```
LRESULT CALLBACK FreeWindowRecordHookProc( int nCode, WPARAM
wParam, LPARAM lParam )
```

FreeWindowRecordHookProc is a placeholder for the actual name defined by your application. The wParam argument contains the handle (HWND) of the window being destroyed, and the lParam argument contains a pointer to the memory to be freed. The return value is ignored.

WHM_GROWWINDOW

This value is passed to SetWindowsHookEx as the nHookType parameter to register a hook callback function provided by the application. The Windows Portability Library calls this hook function when a user interface is needed for resizing a Macintosh window. The default hook function invokes the Macintosh Window Manager user interface by calling _GrowWindow. An application can provide its own hook function to provide a different user interface. This callback function must use standard Win32 hook callback syntax:

```
LRESULT CALLBACK GrowWindowHookProc( int nCode, WPARAM wParam,
LPARAM lParam )
```

GrowWindowHookProc is a placeholder for the actual name defined by your application. The wParam argument points to a GROWWINDOWINFO structure that describes the sizing parameters. The lParam argument contains the WindowPtr of the window to be sized. The callback should return the same information as _GrowWindow would: zero if the window's size did not change, or the window's new height in the high word and the new width in the low word.

A GROWWINDOWINFO structure is defined as follows:

```
typedef struct tagGROWWINDOWINFO
{
    Point ptStart;        // Mouse global coordinates when button
                          // was pressed.
    Rect* prctLimits;     // Limits on minimum and maximum sizes of
                          // the window.
} GROWWINDOWINFO;
```

WHM_MENUSELECT

This value is passed to SetWindowsHookEx as the nHookType parameter to register a hook callback function provided by the application. The Windows Portability Library calls this hook function after the MenuSelect routine returns. The default hook passes the return value from MenuSelect to the TSMMenuSelect routine of the Macintosh Text Services Manager. The callback function must use standard Win32 hook callback syntax:

```
LRESULT CALLBACK MenuSelectHookProc( int nCode, WPARAM wParam,
LPARAM lParam )
```

MenuSelectHookProc is a placeholder for the actual name defined by your application. The wParam argument is unused, and the lParam argument contains the return value from MenuSelect. The callback function must return TRUE if the hook handled the menu selection, or FALSE if not.

WHM_MENUSETUP

This value is passed to SetWindowsHookEx as the nHookType parameter to register a hook callback function provided by the application. The Windows Portability Library calls this hook function for each item in a menu if a WHM_CUSTOMMENUSETUP hook returned TRUE for that menu. The hook function should modify the state of the current GrafPort data structure as necessary for the menu item passed to it and then return. There is no default behavior.

This hook could be used, for example, to allow Japanese font names in a font menu to appear in Osaka (the Japanese system font) instead of in Chicago (the Roman system font). When the application draws the names of the fonts, the hook function could set the font of each menu item to be the system font for the script owning each menu item's font. The callback function must use standard Win32 hook callback syntax:

```
LRESULT CALLBACK MenuSetupHookProc( int nCode, WPARAM wParam,
LPARAM lParam )
```

MenuSetupHookProc is a placeholder for the actual name defined by your application. The wParam argument is unused, and the lParam argument contains a pointer to a MENUSETUPINFO structure. The return value is ignored.

A MENUSETUPINFO structure has the following members:

```
struct MENUSETUPINFO {
    HWND  hwnd;     // The window that owns the menu being drawn.
    HMENU hmenu;    // The popup menu being drawn.
    DWORD iitem;    // 0-based index of the hmenu item being
                    // drawn.
} ;
```

WHM_MOVEWINDOW

This value is passed to SetWindowsHookEx as the nHookType parameter to register a hook callback function provided by the application. The Windows Portability Library calls this hook function when a Macintosh window needs to be moved. The default hook function calls _MoveWindow. An application's hook function may provide its own implementation for moving a window. This callback function must use standard Win32 hook callback syntax:

```
LRESULT CALLBACK MoveWindowHookProc( int nCode, WPARAM wParam,
LPARAM lParam )
```

MoveWindowHookProc is a placeholder for the actual name defined by your application. The wParam argument points to a POSWINDOWINFO structure that describes the new location to which the window should be moved. The lParam argument contains the WindowPtr of the window to be moved. The return value is ignored.

A POSWINDOWINFO structure is defined as follows:

```
typedef struct tagPOSWINDOWINFO
{
    short h;                    // The window's new horizontal
                               // position.
    short v;                    // The window's new vertical position.
    BOOL fActivateOrUpdate;    // True if the window should be
                               // activated,
} POSWINDOWINFO;               //    or false if not.
```

WHM_NEWWINDOW

This value is passed to SetWindowsHookEx as the nHookType parameter to register a hook callback function provided by the application. The Windows Portability Library calls this hook function when a new Macintosh window needs to be initialized.

The default hook function calls either NewWindow or NewCWindow to initialize the window, depending on whether its wParam argument indicates that the Macintosh supports color. For example, you could use a WHM_NEWWINDOW hook to create black and white windows only, even on a color Macintosh, or to modify parameters passed to NewWindow or NewCWindow.

The callback function must use standard Win32 hook callback syntax:

```
LRESULT CALLBACK NewWindowHookProc( int nCode, WPARAM wParam,
LPARAM lParam )
```

NewWindowHookProc is a placeholder for the actual name defined by your application. The wParam argument returns TRUE if a color window should be created, or FALSE if a black-and-white window should be created.

The lParam argument contains a pointer to a NWINFO structure. The members of a NWINFO structure correspond to the parameters of NewWindow and NewCWindow that have the same names:

```
struct NWINFO {
    void*              wStorage;
    Rect               boundsRect;
    Str255             title;
    Boolean            visible;
    short              theProc;
    struct GrafPort*   behind;
    Boolean            goAwayFlag;
    long               refCon;
} ;
```

The hook function can either call NewWindow or NewCWindow directly, or modify the NWINFO members as necessary and then use CallNextHookEx to call the default hook. The hook function must return a Macintosh WindowPtr pointing to the new window.

WHM_PROCID

This value is passed to SetWindowsHookEx as the nHookType parameter to register a hook callback function provided by the application. The Windows Portability Library calls this hook function to determine what Macintosh window definition (WDEF) identifier to use when creating a new Macintosh window. The default hook returns the identifier of the WDEF that most closely matches the window styles given in the PROCIDINFO, as follows:

dwStyle	dwExStyle	procID
0	WS_EX_DLGMODALFRAME	dBoxProc
WS_CAPTION	0	noGrowDocProc
WS_CAPTION | WS_MAXIMIZEBOX	0	zoomNoGrow
WS_CAPTION | WS_THICKFRAME	0	documentProc
WS_CAPTION | WS_MAXIMIZEBOX | WS_THICKFRAME	0	zoomDocProc
WS_CAPTION	WS_EX_DLGMODALFRAME	movableDBoxProc
WS_DLGFRAME	[ignored]	dBoxProc
WS_BORDER	[ignored]	plainDBox

The callback function must use standard Win32 hook callback syntax:

```
LRESULT CALLBACK ProcIDHookProc( int nCode, WPARAM wParam, LPARAM
lParam )
```

ProcIDHookProc is a placeholder for the actual name defined by your application. The wParam argument is unused, and the lParam argument contains a pointer to a PROCIDINFO structure:

```
struct PROCIDINFO {
    HWND    hwndParent;   // The parent of the window to be created.
    DWORD   dwStyle;      // Window style of the new window.
    DWORD   dwExStyle;    // Extended window style of the new window.
    BOOL    fCloseBox;    // Should there be a close box? (Set on
                          // exit).
} ;
```

The callback function must return the Macintosh WDEF identifier to be used in creating the window.

WHM_SETCURSOR

This value is passed to SetWindowsHookEx as the nHookType parameter to register a hook callback function provided by the application. The Windows Portability Library calls this hook function before sending a WM_SETCURSOR message. The default hook passes the mouse position to the SetTSMCursor routine of the Macintosh Text Services Manager.

The callback function must use standard Win32 hook callback syntax:

```
LRESULT CALLBACK SetCursorHookProc( int nCode, WPARAM wParam,
LPARAM lParam )
```

SetCursorHookProc is a placeholder for the actual name defined by your application. The wParam argument is unused, and the lParam argument contains the position of the mouse, expressed as a QuickDraw point using global coordinates. The callback function must return TRUE if the hook function changed the cursor, or FALSE if not.

WHM_SHUFFLERECT

This value is passed to SetWindowsHookEx as the nHookType parameter to register a hook callback function provided by the application. The Windows Portability Library calls this hook function when multiple document interface (MDI) child windows are being shuffled (tiled or cascaded). The hook function can adjust the rectangle inside which the windows will be positioned. The hook function will be called once for each monitor connected to the Macintosh that has an MDI child window positioned on it. There is no default behavior.

Use this hook to prevent MDI child windows from being placed over certain screen areas, such as toolbars or status bars, by adjusting the input rectangle accordingly.

The callback function must use standard Win32 hook callback syntax:

```
LRESULT CALLBACK ShuffleRectHookProc( int nCode, WPARAM wParam,
LPARAM lParam )
```

ShuffleRectHookProc is a placeholder for the actual name defined by your application. The wParam argument contains a GDHandle for the device on which the windows are being arranged, and the lParam argument contains a pointer to a QuickDraw rectangle, expressed in global coordinates, bounding the region in which to place windows. The return value is ignored.

WHM_SIZEWINDOW

This value is passed to SetWindowsHookEx as the nHookType parameter to register a hook callback function provided by the application. The Windows Portability Library calls this hook function when a Macintosh window needs to be resized. The default hook function calls _SizeWindow. An application's hook function may provide its own implementation for sizing a window.

This callback function must use standard Win32 hook callback syntax:

```
LRESULT CALLBACK SizeWindowHookProc( int nCode, WPARAM wParam,
LPARAM lParam )
```

SizeWindowHookProc is a placeholder for the actual name defined by your application. The wParam argument points to a POSWINDOWINFO structure that describes the new size of the window. The lParam argument contains the WindowPtr of the window to be sized. The return value is ignored.

A POSWINDOWINFO structure is defined as follows:

```
typedef struct tagPOSWINDOWINFO
{
    short h;                    // The window's new width.
    short v;                    // The window's new height.
    BOOL fActivateOrUpdate;     // TRUE if the window should be
                                // activated,
} POSWINDOWINFO;                //    or FALSE if not.
```

WHM_SLEEPTIME

This value is passed to SetWindowsHookEx as the nHookType parameter to register a hook callback function provided by the application. The Windows Portability Library calls this hook function to determine value of the sleepTime parameter to pass to WaitNextEvent. If no hook is installed, the default time is LONG_MAX.

The callback function must use standard Win32 hook callback syntax:

```
LRESULT CALLBACK SleepTimeHookProc( int nCode, WPARAM wParam,
LPARAM lParam )
```

SleepTimeHookProc is a placeholder for the actual name defined by your application. Neither the wParam argument nor the lParam argument is used. The callback function must return the maximum sleep time (in ticks) that should be passed to WaitNextEvent.

WHM_UPDATE

This value is passed to SetWindowsHookEx as the nHookType parameter to register a hook callback function provided by the application. The Windows Portability Library calls this hook function when an update event is received for a window not under Windows Portability Library control. The default hook calls BeginUpdate and EndUpdate for the window.

The callback function must use standard Win32 hook callback syntax:

```
LRESULT CALLBACK UpdateHookProc( int nCode, WPARAM wParam, LPARAM
lParam )
```

UpdateHookProc is a placeholder for the actual name defined by your application. The wParam argument is unused, and the lParam argument contains a pointer to an EventRecord containing an update event. The return value is ignored.

WHM_ZOOMWINDOW

This value is passed to SetWindowsHookEx as the nHookType parameter in order to register a hook callback function provided by the application. The Windows Portability Library calls this hook function when a Macintosh window needs to be moved and sized simultaneously. The default hook function calls _ZoomWindow. An application's hook function may provide its own implementation for zooming a window.

This callback function must use standard Win32 hook callback syntax:

```
LRESULT CALLBACK ZoomWindowHookProc( int nCode, WPARAM wParam,
LPARAM lParam )
```

ZoomWindowHookProc is a placeholder for the actual name defined by your application. The low word of the wParam argument contains the window part code, which must be either inZoomIn or inZoomOut. The high word of the wParam argument is TRUE if the window should be activated, or FALSE if not. The lParam argument contains the WindowPtr of the window to be zoomed. The return value is ignored.

Macintosh API Extensions

In addition to these messages, the Windows Portability Library provides a number of Macintosh-specific APIs. These functions allow the Macintosh verison of your application to access native Macintosh system objects.

Ports

The following APIs facilitate the direct use of Macintosh GrafPorts:

- WrapPort creates a device context handle (HDC) from a GrafPort.
- UnwrapPort destroys a wrapped HDC.
- CheckoutPort and CheckinPort access the GrafPort underlying any HDC.

- ResetMacDC, SetMacPort, and InitDC all affect a wrapped port.

Printing

The Windows Portability Library provides direct access to Macintosh print records. The WrapPint, UnwrapPrint, CheckoutPrint, and CheckinPrint APIs provide translation between printer HDCs and Print records.

Pictures

The WrapPict, UnwrapPict, CheckoutPict, and CheckinPict APIs provide direct access to Macintosh Pictures and translation between bitmaps and PICT files.

Menus

The WrapMenuCommand, CheckoutMenu, and CheckinMenu APIs provide direct access to Macintosh menus and translation between Windows Portability Library menus and Macintosh menus.

Windows

The Windows Portability Library provides several Macintosh extension APIs for wrapping and unwrapping Macintosh windows.

WrapWindow

```
BOOL WrapWindow( WindowPtr wp, HWND* phwnd, DWORD dwExStyle,
LPCSTR szClassName, DWORD dwStyle, HWND hwndParent, HMENU hmenu,
HINSTANCE hinstance, void* lpParam )
```

This function creates a Windows-style window handle from an existing Macintosh window. On entry, wp points to the existing Macintosh window and phwnd points to a location where the new window handle (HWND) should be placed. The remaining arguments have the same meaning and syntax as those passed to CreateWindowEx, which WrapWindow calls. This function returns TRUE if successful, or FALSE if not.

To prevent conflicts regarding the activation state of a Macintosh window, make the window invisible before wrapping it. Also, register the window class to be used for the new HWND, and pass the class name to WrapWindow as the szClassName parameter. The resulting HWND has a Windows z-order corresponding to the Macintosh window's z-order in the Macintosh window list.

Do not use Macintosh Window Manager calls to access a Macintosh window after it has been wrapped. WrapWindow changes the windowKind, wRefCon, and windowDefProc fields of the Macintosh window to values used internally by the Windows Portability Library, and UnwrapWindow does not necessarily restore these fields to their original values.

Do not pass the WS_CHILD style flag to WrapWindow. WrapWindow cannot create child windows.The WS_BORDER, WS_CAPTION, WS_DLGFRAME, WS_MAXIMIZEBOX, WS_SYSMENU, WS_THICKFRAME, WS_VISIBLE, and WS_EX_DLGMODALFRAME style flags are ignored when passed as part of the dwStyle or dwExStyle parameters. These flags are set dynamically by WrapWindow by examining the Macintosh window.Internally, WrapWindow calls CreateWindowEx. Therefore your WndProc procedure for the wrapped window will receive WM_MINMAXINFO, WM_NCCREATE, and WM_CREATE messages, as if the HWND had just been created.

GetWindowWrapper

```
HWND WINAPI GetWindowWrapper( WindowPtr wp )
```

This API returns the Windows Portability Library handle corresponding to a Macintosh window, or NULL if there is no corresponding handle. On entry, wp points to the Macintosh window.

GetwrapperContainerWindow

```
WindowPtr WINAPI GetWrapperContainerWindow( HWND hWnd )
```

This API returns the Macintosh window that contains hWnd, or NULL if hWnd is not contained by a Macintosh window (for example, if it identifies the desktop window). A Macintosh window is said to contain hWnd if the window identified by hWnd is drawn within the Macintosh window's graphics port (GrafPort).

UnwrapWindow

```
BOOL UnwrapWindow( HWND hwnd, WindowPtr* pwp )
```

This API destroys a Windows Portability Library handle without affecting the underlying Macintosh window. Places the Macintosh window pointer in *pwp. Returns TRUE if successful, or FALSE if not. UnwrapWindow can be used on any window handle for which GetWrapperWindow returns a non-NULL value. The window handle need not have been created using WrapWindow. UnwrapWindow cannot be used on window handles that do not have a directly corresponding Macintosh window.

Internally, UnwrapWindow calls DestroyWindow; therefore the window handle's WndProc procedure will receive WM_DESTROY and WM_NCDESTROY messages, just as if the window handle had been destroyed normally.

Wind/U User Extensions

Some applications may need to access the underlying X Window System/Motif components of Wind/U. Wind/U extension functions give developers fast and easy access to Motif widgets and X Window System displays, screens, etc.

The Wind/U extension functions allow you to mix X/Motif with your Microsoft Windows code. These functions return Motif widgets, from which you can then get windows, displays, etc. This chapter describes the Wind/U extension functions. To access these functions, include wuExten.h in your source files.

wuBitmapReadCoreHeaderFromFile

```
extern int wuBitmapReadCoreHeaderFromFile(HFILE hFile,
BITMAPCOREHEADER *lpBmc)
```

This API reads a DIB core header from a binary file and performs the necessary byte swapping. The hFile parameter is the handle of the binary file to read; lpBmc is the pointer to the DIB core header.

wuBitmapSwapCoreHeader

```
extern int wuBitmapSwapCoreHeader(char *original, BITMAPCOREHEADER
*lpBmc)
```

This API converts a DIB core header read from a binary file and performs the necessary byte swapping. The original parameter is a pointer to the memory block to convert. The lpBmc parameter is a pinter to the DIB core header.

wuBitmapWriteCoreHeaderToFile

```
extern int wuBitmapWriteCoreHeaderToFile(HFILE hFile,
BITMAPCOREHEADER *lpBmc)
```

This API writes a DIB core header to a binary file and performs the necessary byte swapping. The hFile parameter is the handle of the binary file to write. The lpBmc parameter is the pointer to the DIB core header.

wuDCToGC

```
GC wuDCToGC(HDC hDC)
```

This function takes a Windows HDC and returns the associated X GC. The hDC parameter is the handle of the Windows device context.

wuEnableMotifTabbing

```
void wuEnableMotifTabbing()
```

Enables Motif-style tabbing in your application instead of the default Windows-style tabbing. Call this function in your def.c or def.C file before wu_main().

wuEnablePalettes

```
void wuEnablePalettes()
```

Enables color palette support in your application. Call this function in your def.c or def.C file before wu_main().

wuFontName

```
char *wuFontName(LOGFONT *lf)
```

Returns a comma-separated list of one or more XLFD font names that satisfy the font set requirements for the current locale. The last font is a wild-card so that at least one font will always be returned.

wuGetAppContext

```
XtAppContext wuGetAppContext(void);
```

Returns the AppContext of the Wind/U-ported application.

wuGetAppShellWidget

```
Widget wuGetAppShellWidget(void)
```

Returns the application shell widget for the application.

wuGetBkColor

```
COLORREF wuGetBkColor(HWND, HDC);
```

Returns the window background color of a control. This function is equivalent to the Windows GetBkColor() function. The HWND parameter is the handle of the window to return the background color for. The HDC parameter is the device context associated with the window handle specified by HWND.

wuGetEnumFontsTextMetrics

```
BOOL wuGetEnumFontsTextMetrics(void)
```

Specifies whether or not to include text metrics information. To improve X server performance, you can specify not to pass text metrics information to the EnumFonts callback function.

wuGetVersion

```
wuVersion_t *wuGetVersion(void)
```

Returns the following structure:

```
typedef struct {
    char *version_release;
    int version_api;
    char *version_os;
    char *version_compile_date;
    char **version_user;
    char **version_gdi;
    char **version_kernel;
} wuVersion_t;
```

You can also get the same information by invoking any Wind/U ported application with the -version flag. The application displays the Wind/U version information and exits, as in the following example:

```
$ appname -version
Wind/U Version 2.0.B2
Copyright (c) 1991-1994 Bristol Technology Inc.
Windows API: Win16
Operating System: HPUX Release 9.0
Bottled On: May 13 1994
USER: May 13 1994
GDI: May 13 1994
KERNEL: May 13 1994
```

The Bottled On field is the date that Wind/U was compiled. Each DLL also contains its own date stamp, in case it is updated in a patch release after the rest of Wind/U.

wuGetXFontSetName

```
char *wuGetXFontSetName(hDC hDC, HFONT hFont);
```

This function returns the actual X font set name mapped by the Wind/U font mapping algorithm for the given font handle. The hDC parameter is the device context to be considered. If this value is NULL, Wind/U uses the screen DC==GetDC(0). The hFont parameter is the font handle used to query the XFontSetName from.

wuhWndToCanvasWidget

```
Widget wuhWndToCanvasWidget (HWND hWnd)
```

Returns a canvas widget given a window handle. For main windows, the canvas widget is an application shell. For dialogs, the canvas widget is a dialog shell. For controls, the canvas widget is a form widget.

wuhWndToControlWidget

```
Widget wuhWndToControlWidget (HWND hWnd)
```

Returns a control widget given a window handle. For main windows, the control widget is a Motif Main window. For dialogs, the control widget is a bulletin board. For controls, the control widget corresponds to the control (for example, for a scrollbar control, it is a Motif scrollbar widget).

wuhWndToDrawingWidget

```
Widget wuhWndToDrawingWidget (HWND hWnd)
```

Returns a drawing widget given a window handle. For main windows and dialogs, the drawing widget is a Motif bulletin board. For controls, the drawing widget is the same as the control widget.

wuODComboboxGetShadowOffset

```
BOOL wuODComboboxGetShadowOffset(HWND hWnd)
```

In Motif, the three-dimensional shadow around the combobox is considered to be part of the widget. Therefore, when Wind/U sends out a WM_DRAWITEM message for an ownerdrawn widget, the rectangle for the item is generally shrinked to take this border into account. In general, the left edge is greater than zero.

Some Windows applications, however use the assumption that the ownerdrawn left edge is at zero, and use this as a criteria to determine whether the given window is a combobox control. Therefore, Wind/U allows you to switch between the two modes. This function returns the mode for the specified window. A return value of 0 means the left edge is always at position zero. A return value of 1 means the shadow is considered when the rectangle coordinate is computed.

wuODComboboxSetShadowOffset

```
BOOL wuODComboboxSetShadowOffset(HWND hWnd, BOOL nMode)
```

In Motif, the three-dimensional shadow around the combobox is considered to be part of the widget. Therefore, when Wind/U sends out a WM_DRAWITEM message for an ownerdrawn widget, the rectangle for the item is generally shrinked to take this border into account. In general, the left edge is greater than zero.

Some Windows applications, however use the assumption that the ownerdrawn left edge is at zero, and use this as a criteria to determine whether the given window is a combobox control. Therefore, Wind/U allows you to switch between the two modes with this function.

An nMode value of 0 means the left edge is always at position zero. An nMode value of 1 means the shadow is considered when the rectangle coordinate is computed.

wuODListboxGetShadowOffset

```
BOOL wuODListboxGetShadowOffset(HWND hWnd)
```

In Motif, the three-dimensional shadow around the listbox is considered to be part of the widget. Therefore, when Wind/U sends out a WM_DRAWITEM message for an ownerdrawn list, the rectangle for the item is generally shrinked to take this border into account. In general, the left edge is greater than zero.

Some Windows applications, however use the assumption that the ownerdrawn left edge is at zero, and use this as a criteria to determine whether the given window is a combobox control. Therefore, Wind/U allows you to switch between the two modes. This function returns the mode for the specified window.

A return value of 0 means the left edge is always at position zero. A return value of 1 means the shadow is considered when the rectangle coordinate is computed.

wuODListboxSetShadowOffset

```
BOOL wuODListboxSetShadowOffset(HWND hWnd, BOOL nMode)
```

In Motif, the three-dimensional shadow around the listbox is considered to be part of the widget. Therefore, when Wind/U sends out a WM_DRAWITEM message for an ownerdrawn list, the rectangle for the item is generally shrinked to take this border into account. In general, the left edge is greater than zero.

Some Windows applications, however use the assumption that the ownerdrawn left edge is at zero, and use this as a criteria to determine whether the given window is a combobox control. Therefore, Wind/U allows you to switch between the two modes with this function.

An nMode value of 0 means the left edge is always at position zero. An nMode value of 1 means the shadow is considered when the rectangle coordinate is computed.

wuReadBitmapFileHeaderFromFile

```
extern int wuReadBitmapFileHeaderFromFile(HFILE hFile,
BITMAPFILEHEADER *lpBfh)
```

Reads a DIB file header from a binary file and performs the necessary byte swapping. The hFile parameter is the handle of the binary file to read. The lpBfh parameter is a pointer to the DIB file header.

wuReadBitmapInfoHeaderFromFile

```
extern int wuReadBitmapInfoHeaderFromFile(HFILE hFile,
BITMAPINFOHEADER *lpBmi)
```

Reads a DIB info header from a binary file and performs the necessary byte swapping. The hFile parameter is the handle of the binary file to read. The lpBmi parameter is a pointer to the DIB info header.

wuSetEnumFontsTextMetrics

```
BOOL wuSetEnumFontsTextMetrics(BOOL include)
```

Specifies whether or not to include text metrics information. If include==true, text metrics information is included. To improve X server performance, you can specify not to pass text metrics information to the EnumFonts callback function. The wuSetEnumFontsTextMetrics function allows the application to control this setting at runtime.

wuSetEventHook

```
typedef Boolean (*wuXtEventProc)(XEvent *);
wuXtEventProc wuSetEventHook(wuXtEventProc);
```

This function registers a function to be called immediately after Wind/U calls XtAppNextEvent(). This function gives the application access to the Xt event queue which may be necessary to integrate other X/Xt/Motif packages with Wind/U. If a function was previously registered by another call to wuSetEventHook(), the pointer to that function is returned; otherwise it returns NULL.

The registered function should return True if it has processed the XEvent. Returning False causes normal Wind/U event processing to take place.

Since this function returns the previously registered function, your application can chain subsequent calls, if necessary.

wuSetFallbackResources

```
void wuSetFallbackResources(char **)
```

This function lets you specify default X resource values in your application. You do not need to specify a default value in your app-defaults file; however, users can override the fallback value by specifying a different value for the resource in the app-defaults file.

The following example, in def.c before wu_main is called, sets the background resource to blue and the shadowThickness resource to 2:

```
main(int argc, char **argv)
{
    char *afbr[] = {
        "*background:blue",
```

```
            "*XmText*shadowThickness:2",
            NULL
            };

    void wuSetFallbackResources(afbr);

    return wm_main(argc,argv);
}
```

wuSetWindowBackground

```
    int wuSetWindowBackground(HDC,HBRUSH)
```

Use this function to draw your own window background rather than having Windows draw it for you. Most applications specify a brush handle or system color value for the class background brush when registering the window class; Windows uses the brush or color to draw the background. However, Windows sends a WM_ERASEBKGND message to your window procedure whenever the window background must be drawn, letting you draw a custom background. In Wind/U, the class background brush is used to notify the Motif library of the window background color. The reason you would want to use this API is that without it, applications that handle WM_ERASEBKGND will sometimes flicker between the default Motif background color and the brush color used by your application to erase the background.

In the following example, the window procedure draws a large checkerboard pattern that fits neatly in the window. The procedure fills the client area with a white brush and then draws thirteen 20-by-20 rectangles using a gray brush. The display DC to use when drawing the background is specified inthe wParam parameter for the message. The #ifdef WU_APP areas define the changes necessary for Wind/U.

```
    HBRUSH hbrWhite, hbrGray;
    #ifdef WU_APP
    BOOL XbackgroundNeedsSet;
    #endif
    .
    .
    .case WM_CREATE:
        hbrWhite= GetStockObject(WHITE_BRUSH);
```

```
        hbrGray = GetStockObject(GRAY_BRUSH);
#ifdef WU_APP
        XbackgroundNeedsSet=TRUE;
#endif
        return 0L;



    case WM_ERASEBKGRND:
        hdc=(HDC)wParam;
#ifdef WU_APP
        /* since the class background brush was not defined, inform
         WU what it should be the first time */
        if(XbackgroundNeedsSet) {
                XbackgroundNeedsSet=FALSE;
                wuSetWindowBackground(hdc,hbrWhite);
        }
#endif
        GetClientRect(hwnd,&rc);
        SetMapMode(hdc,MM_ANISOTROPIC);
        SetWindowExtEx(hdc,,100,100,NULL);
        FillRect(hdc,&rc,hbrWhite);


        for(i-0;i<13;i++) {
                x=(i*40)%100;
                y=((i*40)/100)*20;
                SetRect(&rc,x,y,x+20,y+20);

                FillRect(hdc,&rc,hbrGray);
        }
    return 1L;
```

wuSWAP16

```
    unsigned int wuSWAP16()
```

Swaps bytes of a signed or unsigned 16-bit integer value.

wuSWAP32

```
    unsigned int wuSWAP32()
```

Swaps bytes of a signed or unsigned 32-bit integer value.

wuSwapBitmapFileHeader

```
extern int wuSwapBitmapFileHeader(char *original, BITMAPFILEHEADER
*lpBfh)
```

Converts a DIB file header read from a binary file and performs the necessary byte swapping. The original parameter is a pointer to the memory block to convert. The lpBfh parameter is a pointer to the DIB file header.

wuSwapBitmapInfoHeader

```
extern int wuSwapBitmapInfoHeader(char *original, BITMAPINFOHEADER
*lpBmi)
```

Converts a DIB info header read from a binary file and performs the necessary byte swapping. The original parameter is a pointer to the DIB core header.

wuWriteBitmapFileHeaderToFile

```
extern int wuWriteBitmapFileHeaderToFile(HFILE hFile,
BITMAPFILEHEADER *lpBfh)
```

Writes a DIB file header to a binary file and performs the necessary byte swapping. The hFile parameter is the handle of the binary file to write. The lpBfh parameter is a ponter to the DIB file header.

wuWriteBitmapInfoHeaderToFile

```
extern int wuWriteBitmapInfoHeaderToFile(HFILE hFile,
BITMAPINFOHEADER *lpBmi)
```

Writes a DIB info header to a binary file and performs the necessary byte swapping. The hFile parameter is the handle of the binary file to write. The lpBmc parameter is a pointer to the DIB info header.

Summary

Most User Library APIs are supported across both the Macintosh and UNIX platform, with the main exception being hardware-related APIs. However, window manager differences between Windows, the Macintosh, and UNIX platforms require you to use care when creating and accessing windows in your application. In addition, both the Visual C++ for the Macintosh Windows Portability Library and Wind/U provide extension functions that you can use in your application to take advantage of native features on each platform.

## CHAPTER 10

Cross-Platform
On-Line Help

One aspect of cross-platform development that affects more than just the development team is on-line help. It is very important that you be able to maintain a single set of help source files for all target platforms. This chapter discusses the following issues related to on-line help for cross-platform applications:

- Requirements for cross-platform on-line help tools
- Available cross-platform on-line help tools for UNIX and Macintosh
- Cross-platform issues you should be aware of
- Alternative help development strategies
- Visual C++ support for creating on-line help

On-Line Help Requirements

In the Windows and Windows NT environments, any number of tools are available for creating on-line help source files in Rich Text Format (RTF).You can use almost any Windows-based word processor to create RTF files, inserting the necessary hypertext codes yourself, or you can use any number of tools to help automate the coding process. Examples of these tools include ForeHelp, RoboHelp, and Doc-to-Help.

The Windows help compilers **HC31.EXE, HC35.EXE**, or **HCP.EXE** compile the RTF files and a help project (**.HPJ**) file to create a binary help (**.HLP**) file. Applications use the **WinHelp**() function call to display on-line help via the WinHelp viewer application. **WinHelp**() parameters allow you to display context-sensitive on-line help; that is, help text that applies to the specific part of your application that the user wants to know about. Figure 10.1 shows a typical Windows help screen.

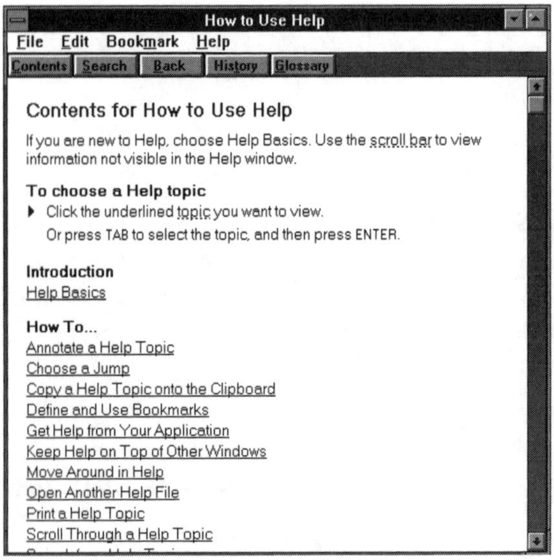

Figure 10.1 Sample Windows help display.

The requirements for cross-platform on-line help tools are as follows:

- They support the use of a single source file base.
- They are accessed by the **WinHelp**() API.
- They provide context-sensitive capabilities.

Single Source File Base

The most important requirement for cross-platform help tools is the capability to use a single set of help source files for all target platforms. Because you are likely to be porting an existing Windows application, this means the help tool on other platforms must read either RTF or compiled Windows help files.

The reasons for requiring a single source file base for your help system are the same reasons you want to maintain a single source file base for the rest of your application. Maintaining a single set of files reduces the initial development effort, because you need to create the files only once, and you do not need to be concerned about the cost, time, or risk of errors associated with translation from one format to another. Having a single set of help source files for all platforms ensures that the information is consistent throughout all versions of your application. You need not worry about making a correction in one version's help system and forgetting to make it in another. Therefore, a single source file base is much easier to maintain than a different source base for each target platform.

The WinHelp() API

If you are porting an existing Windows application, it accesses on-line help with the **WinHelp**() function. Any on-line help tools you use on other platforms must also use the **WinHelp**() function call so that you won't have to change your code. Even if you are developing your application for all platforms in parallel, the **WinHelp**() function is still the most common way to access on-line help from an application, so you will want to use it.

In addition to being the most common on-line help interface, **WinHelp**() has other advantages. For example, if you use **WinHelp**(), it is the only API you need to access help. Some help viewers have different APIs to access different parts of your help file, such as the contents. **WinHelp**(), however, enables you to access any point in your help file with a single API. Another advantage of **WinHelp**() is the easy way it enables you to add context-sensitive help to your application.

Context-Sensitive Help

Context-sensitive help is on-line help that provides information about a specific topic when the user wants it. For example, if a user is working in a specific dialog and accesses help, the help information displayed will be about that particular dialog. Windows help uses a context mapping to associate help topics to **WinHelp**() calls in the code that accesses them. When you port your application and on-line help to a different platform, you want to make sure that the same mappings can be used for all platforms.

Context-sensitive help is a particularly important requirement if you are using MFC for your application development. MFC automatically provides context-sensitive help in most dialogs. Because it is so easy to add context-sensitive help to your applications with MFC, you want to be sure that you provide context-sensitive help on your target platforms as well. The details of how to leverage this MFC support for on-line help across platforms is discussed.

Available Cross-Platform Help Tools

On the Macintosh, the Visual C++ for Macintosh toolkit provides MacHelp, which is a Macintosh version of the WinHelp viewer. MacHelp supports a significant subset of Windows help functionality. MacHelp even reads help files compiled with the Windows help compiler. So, except for the differences noted in the "MacHelp Cross-Platform Issues" section of this chapter, your compiled Windows help files will look exactly the same on the Macintosh as in Windows or Windows NT. Figure 10.2 shows a Windows help file displayed by the MacHelp viewer on a Macintosh.

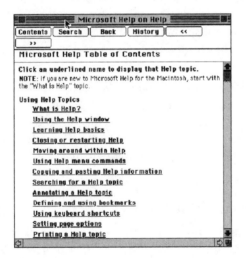

Figure 10.2 Sample MacHelp viewer display.

In the UNIX environment, however, Microsoft does not provide a WinHelp-compatible help viewer. Because the Windows help file format is proprietary, you must recompile your RTF and help project file on the target UNIX platforms. The most robust tool for compiling and viewing on-line help in UNIX is HyperHelp. HyperHelp supports all Windows help hypertext features and virtually all Windows help macros and compile options. In addition, HyperHelp is very closely integrated with the Wind/U cross-platform development toolkit. If you are using Wind/U to run your application on UNIX platforms, it is very easy to distribute the HyperHelp viewer with the UNIX version of your application. Except for the differences noted in the "HyperHelp Cross-Platform Issues" section of this chapter, your compiled HyperHelp files will look exactly the same on UNIX platforms as in Windows or Windows NT.

HyperHelp is the best tool available for cross-platform help in UNIX for a number of reasons. First of all, it reads the same RTF, bitmap, and segmented bitmap files used to compile the Windows help file. There is no need to change your help source files or convert them to a different format. HyperHelp is also completely compatible with the **WinHelp**() API. It uses the same context map for context-sensitive help as Windows help. Figure 10.3 shows a Windows help topic displayed by the HyperHelp viewer in Motif.

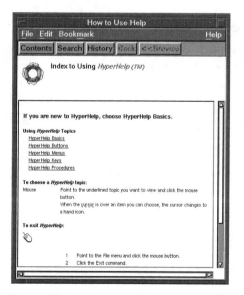

Figure 10.3 Sample HyperHelp viewer display.

MacHelp Cross-Platform Issues

The Microsoft Visual C++ for Macintosh toolkit includes the **HC35.EXE** help compiler and the MacHelp viewer. Although the MacHelp viewer reads help files compiled in the Windows environment, there are some issues you should be aware of.

First, you must use the **HC35.EXE** help compiler to compile your help files in Windows or Windows NT. This compiler features support for the Macintosh platform, including better bitmap scaling and PICT graphics. Note, however, that this compiler does not support RTF files created with Word for Windows release 6.*x*; if you use Word for Windows to create your RTF files, you must use release 2.*x*.

To use MacHelp, you must have a Motorola 680*x*0 (or higher) CPU and at least 4 MB of RAM (8 MB is recommended). However, MacHelp will run under Macintosh System 6.0.7 or later. You can install your help file in any folder on the Macintosh. However, the MacHelp file must be installed in the System Folder Extensions under Microsoft:Help.

Creating a Help File for MacHelp

The process for creating a help file for Macintosh is the same as for creating a help file for Windows or Windows NT. You plan the organization of your help system, write your help topic files with a word processor that creates RTF output, create a help project file, and compile these files to produce a binary help file. When you create your help project file for MacHelp, however, you must do the following:

- Make sure that the [OPTIONS] section is the first section in the help project file.
- If your help file includes graphics, add **PLATFORM = MAC** as the first line in the [OPTIONS] section.

Note that if you are transporting an existing Windows help file to the Macintosh, and if your help file contains graphics, you must add **PLATFORM = MAC** to the [OPTIONS] section of the help project file, and then recompile with Help Compiler version 3.5.

After you have compiled your help file for MacHelp, you must transfer it to the Macintosh. The Visual C++ for Macintosh toolkit provides the MFILE utility to transfer a help file from a PC, which has Visual C++ for Macintosh installed, to a remote Macintosh.

After you transfer your help file to the Macintosh, you can view it in any of the following ways:

- Clicking a help file icon in a Macintosh folder. This launches the Microsoft help engine and opens the help file.
- Choosing the Help menu, or other options, in an application that provides help support. This method requires using the Windows Portability Library **WinHelp**() function within the application code.

You can also preview your Macintosh help file with the Windows help engine, even if you have included the **PLATFORM = MAC** option in the help project file. Instead of transferring your file to the Macintosh and finding errors, you can save time by testing and fixing your help file under Windows or Windows NT on your PC.

Help for the Macintosh does not support all the features the Help Compiler allows. In addition, graphics are treated differently on the Macintosh than in Windows. If you want to include features in your Windows help file that are not supported in your Macintosh help file, you need to change the help project file or the topic files.

Features supported by Windows help but not by help for the Macintosh include the following:

- Secondary windows
- Customizable menus
- DLLs
- Some Windows help macro commands

Displaying Graphics on the Macintosh

If you are developing a cross-platform application, you have two options for creating help files that include graphics:

- If the help file does not include detailed graphics, you can decrease maintenance by building the help file from a single help project (.HPJ) file. Your help file will be fully supported by Windows help, but any graphics you use will be scaled differently on the Macintosh.

- If the help file includes detailed graphics, you can build two different help files from the same source files. To do this, create one .HPJ file for Windows and one .HPJ file for the Macintosh. The two .HPJ files can then control how graphics are displayed on each platform.

MacHelp can display **PICT** files, bitmaps (.BMP files), and device-independent bitmaps (.DIB files), but not Windows metafiles (.WMF files). Likewise, **PICT** files cannot be displayed in Windows. Instead, the message **Cannot display picture** is displayed. For cross-platform help files, then, restrict your graphics to simple .BMP files and .DIB files that display well on both platforms. If you want to take advantage of .WMF files or **PICT** files, use a separate help project file for each platform.

Using Segmented Hypergraphics

MacHelp supports segmented hypergraphics (.SHG files) that are saved with the Hotspot Editor version 3.5 (**SHED.EXE**). However, it does not support hypergraphics that contain Windows metafiles or unsupported help macros. Hypergraphics have the same scaling problems as bitmaps. To ensure that hypergraphics appear correctly on the Macintosh, fulfill these requirements when working with the Hotspot Editor:

- Include the following line in the **SHED.INI** file:
  ```
  ResBasedOnExt = 1
  ```
- Save hypergraphics with a .MAC filename extension. This instructs the Hotspot Editor to save special scaling information for the Macintosh in the hypergraphic. After the hypergraphic has been saved with the .MAC extension, you can rename it.

Help Macro Commands Supported on the Macintosh

When you view a help file in MacHelp, only the Help macros in the following list are supported. If your help file contains any other macros, they are silently ignored. Details specific to the Macintosh, if any, are listed with each macro.

- About()

- Back()

- BrowseButtons()

- CopyDialog()

- CreateButton() or CB(). The "&" character, used in Windows to signify a keystroke accelerator, is stripped from button labels in Help for the Macintosh because keystroke accelerators are not supported. The button name **btn_browse** is reserved and cannot be used for authored buttons (see **DestroyButton**).

- DestroyButton(). MacHelp automatically creates browse buttons when a help file is opened. To remove the browse buttons, use **DestroyButton("btn_browse")**. Windows Help displays browse buttons only if you create them with the **CreateButton()** macro.

- Exit()

- History()

- JumpId() or JI(). When interfile jumps are used on the Macintosh, the target help file must be installed in the same folder as the source help file; otherwise, the jumps do not work.

- PopupId() or PI(). When interfile pop-ups are used on the Macintosh, the target help file must be installed in the same folder as the source help file; otherwise, the pop-ups do not work.

- PositionWindow() or PW(). In Help for the Macintosh, the window position does not correspond to the full size of the monitor, but rather to the position the window would assume if the user were to click the window's zoom box.

- Print()

- Search()

HyperHelp Cross-Platform Help Issues

Just as MacHelp requires you to recompile to take advantage of native graphics formats, HyperHelp also requires you to recompile RTF files to get optimal functionality and performance under UNIX. If your application supports more than one UNIX variant (for example, HP-UX and Solaris), you can compile your help files on either platform, but you must distribute the HP-UX version of the

HyperHelp viewer to your HP customers and the Solaris version of the viewer to your Sun customers. All viewers, however, can display help file created by any version of the HyperHelp compiler.

Creating a Help File for HyperHelp

In order to use HyperHelp to create the UNIX version of your application's help system, simply transfer your RTF files, graphic files, and help project file to the UNIX platform where you have installed the HyperHelp compiler. You can then compile these files with the HyperHelp compiler to produce a binary help file.

After you have compiled your help file for HyperHelp, you can view it in any of the following ways:

- Using the **hyperhelp** command. This command starts the HyperHelp viewer and opens the help file.
- Choosing the Help menu, or other options, in an application that provides help support. This method requires you to use the **WinHelp()** function in the application code.

Other than a few macros, HyperHelp supports all the features of Windows help, including secondary windows and customizable menus. However, HyperHelp does not support all the graphics formats supported by Windows help, and there are portability issues with DLLs that you must be aware of.

Displaying Graphics in HyperHelp

With Windows Help, you can use several different graphics formats: bitmaps (**.BMP**), device-independent bitmaps (**.DIB**), segmented bitmaps (**.SHG**), Windows metafiles (**.WMF**), and multiple resolution bitmaps (**.MRB**). All of these file formats, however, are not portable to UNIX platforms.

On UNIX platforms, HyperHelp supports .BMP, .SHG, .WMF, and .XPM formats; it does not support .MRB. If you want to include .MRB files in the Windows version of your help file, you must either replace them with supported file types or remove them from the UNIX version of your RTF file. However, since neither HyperHelp or MacHelp support them, it is best to avoid them altogether.

Also, all graphics must be included in your RTF files by reference; that is, with **bmc**, **bml**, or **bmr** commands. They cannot be included in your RTF file directly.

Including graphics by reference is sound development practice anyway, because it reduces the size of your RTF files and ensures consistency should you make changes to a drawing that is used more than once in your help file.

Using Macro Commands

Although HyperHelp supports most Windows help macros and compiler options, there are some that it does not support. If you use these macros or options in the Windows version of your on-line help, HyperHelp ignores them:

- AddAccelerator()
- RemoveAccelerator()
- HelpOnTop()

Using DLLs

Like Windows help, HyperHelp supports the use of DLLs to extend the functionality of the viewer. You can either register your DLLs as macro commands with the **RegisterRoutine**() macro, or you can use them with embedded windows and external data sources. When you use DLLs, however, keep in mind that you cannot simply copy your Windows DLLs to a UNIX platform and use them. They are executable files and, as such, must be recompiled under UNIX. Before you can use your Windows DLLs with the UNIX version of your help system, you must port them to UNIX, just as you are porting your application.

Using X Resources

Just like Windows applications use .INI files to control the appearance and behavior of the application, UNIX applications rely on X resources. The HyperHelp viewer depends on a number of X resources for controlling its appearance. Help users can use the default X resources without change, or they can change them to customize the appearance of the viewer on their system. Examples of viewer aspects that can be changed with X include the hypertext link colors, menu fonts, and viewer background and foreground colors. When you distribute your application and its help system to your customers, you should also distribute an app-defaults file that specifies default X resource values for the HyperHelp viewer. HyperHelp provides an app-defaults file that you can distribute as-is or customize for your help system.

Using WinHelp()

Although the HyperHelp viewer supports most of the **WinHelp**() command options supported by the Windows help viewer, there are a few that it does not support. If the following unsupported commands are included in your WinHelp calls, HyperHelp ignores them:

- HELP_MULTIKEY
- HELP_SETCONTENTS
- HELP_CONTEXTPOPUP
- HELP_SETWINPOS
- HELP_FORCEFILE

MFC Support for On-Line Help

The MFC application framework was designed to make it easy to support world-class on-line help in your applications. When using MFC, the framework is responsible for communicating with the appropriate help viewer: WinHelp on Windows, MacHelp on the Mac, and HyperHelp on UNIX. The application programmer does not need to know the name of the on-line help viewer. In the following sections, WinHelp refers to the generic on-line help viewer application. The MFC framework supports the following aspects of on-line help:

- F1 Help involves launching WinHelp with the appropriate context based on the currently active object.
- Shift+F1 Help invokes a special help mode in which the cursor changes to a Help cursor.
- Help Index launches WinHelp to show the help index for the application.
- Using Help launches WinHelp to show help on using the on-line help tool.
- Quitting Help notifies WinHelp that the application is shutting down.

WinHelp API

Like all Windows application, on-line help in MFC is built around the WinHelp API. The WinHelp function starts Windows help (**WINHELP.EXE**, MacHelp, or

HyperHelp) and passes additional data indicating the nature of the help requested by the application. The application specifies the name and, if required, the directory path of the help file to display.

```
BOOL WinHelp(
    HWND    hwnd,      // handle of window requesting Help
    LPCTSTR lpszHelp, // help filename string
    UINT    uCommand, // type of Help
    DWORD   dwData     // additional data
    );
```

In most applications the first two parameters, the application window handle and the help filename, are the same for all WinHelp API calls. The power of this API is in the third parameter, the help command. The following table lists the help commands, the actions they perform, the data associated with the command, and the MacHelp and HyperHelp support level.

Table 10.1 Cross-Platform Support For WinHelp Commands

Command	Action	dwData	Supported on Mac	Supported on UNIX
HELP_COMMAND	Executes a Help macro or macro string.	Address of a string that specifies the name of the Help macro(s) to execute. If the string specifies multiple macros names, the names must be separated by semicolons. You must use the short form of the macro name for some macros because Help does not support the long name.	Yes	Yes
HELP_CONTENTS	Displays the topic specified by the Contents option in the [OPTIONS]	Ignored, set to 0.	Yes	Yes

Table 10.1 Cross-Platform Support For WinHelp Commands(continued)

Command	Action	dwData	Supported on Mac	Supported on UNIX
	section of the .HPJ file. This is for backward compatibility. New applications should provide a .CNT file and use the HELP_ FINDER command.			
HELP_CONTEXT	Displays the topic identified by the specified context identifier defined in the [MAP] section of the .HPJ file.	Unsigned long integer containing the context identifier for the topic.	Yes	Yes
HELP_CONTEXT-POPUP	Displays, in a pop-up window, the topic identified by the specified context identifier defined in the [MAP] section of the .HPJ file.	Unsigned long integer containing the context identifier for a topic.	No	No
HELP_FORCEFILE	Ensures that WinHelp is displaying the correct help file. If the incorrect help file is being	Ignored, set to 0.	Yes	No

Table 10.1 Cross-Platform Support For WinHelp Commands(continued)

Command	Action	dwData	Supported on Mac	Supported on UNIX
	displayed, WinHelp opens the correct one; otherwise, there is no action.			
HELP_HELPON-HELP	Displays help on how to use Windows Help, if the **WINHELP.HLP** file is available.	Ignored, set to 0.	Yes	Yes
HELP_INDEX **HELP_CONTENTS**	Displays the Index in the Help Topics dialog box. This command is for backward compatibility. New applications should use the **HELP_FINDER** command.	Ignored, set to 0.	Yes	Partial, maps to
HELP_KEY	Displays the topic in the keyword table that matches the specified keyword, if there is an exact match. If there is more than one match, displays the	Address of a keyword string.	Yes	Yes

Table 10.1 Cross-Platform Support For WinHelp Commands(continued)

Command	Action	dwData	Supported on Mac	Supported on UNIX
	Index with the topics listed in the Topics Found list box.			
HELP_MULTIKEY	Displays the topic specified by a keyword in an alternative keyword table.	Address of a MULTIKEYHELP structure that specifies a table footnote character and a keyword.	No	No
HELP_PARTIAL-KEY	Displays the topic in the keyword table that matches the specified keyword, if there is an exact match. If there is more than one match, displays the Index tab. To display the Index without passing a keyword (the third result), you should use a pointer to an empty string.	Address of a keyword string.	Yes	Yes
HELP_QUIT	Informs the Help application that it is no longer needed.	Ignored, set to 0.	Yes	Yes

Table 10.1 Cross-Platform Support For WinHelp Commands(continued)

Command	Action	dwData	Supported on Mac	Supported on UNIX
	If no other applications have asked for help, Windows closes the Help application.			
HELP_SET-CONTENTS	Specifies the Contents topic. The Help application displays this topic when the user clicks the **Contents** button.	Unsigned long integer containing the context identifier for the Contents topic.	Yes	No
HELP_SETINDEX	Specifies a keyword table to be displayed in the Index of the Help Topics dialog box.	Unsigned long integer containing the context identifier for the I ndex topic.	Yes	No
HELP_SETWINPOS	Displays the Help window, if it is mini mized or in memory, and sets its size a nd position as specified.	Address of a HELPWININFO structure that specifies the size and position of either a primary or secondary help window.	Yes	No

The five types of on-line help in the MFC framework build on the following commands:

- F1 Help implemented using the **HELP_CONTEXT** command

- Shift+F1 Help implemented using the **HELP_CONTEXT** command
- Help Index implemented using the **HELP_INDEX** command
- Using Help implemented using the **HELP_HELPONHELP** command
- Quitting Help implemented using the **HELP_QUIT** command

Starting at the Top with AppWizard

When you use the AppWizard to create an MFC application you can create all of the base functionality for the five types of MFC help. Use the following steps to create an on-line help enabled application:

1. From the File menu, select **New**, select **Project**, and then select **OK**.
2. In the **Project Type:** field of the New Project dialog, select **MFC AppWizard (exe)** or **MFC AppWizard (dll)**. Complete the other fields and select **OK**.
3. MFC AppWizard, Step 1, Step 2, Step 3. Choose the appropriate settings for your application.
4. MFC AppWizard, Step 4. Select **Context Sensitive Help** (see Figure 10.5)
5. MFC AppWizard, Step 5, Step 6. Select the appropriate settings for your application.

AppWizard creates the application template supporting the five types of MFC help and generates initial RTF files to get you started.

These simple steps generate a complete context-sensitive application. Figure 10.4 illustrates the major features visible to the user.

When AppWizard created this application, it created the following items for on-line help:

- Message-map entries in your derived frame window class (CMainFrame) for handler functions to handle Help menu items and F1 and Shift+F1 help. These handlers are predefined by the framework:

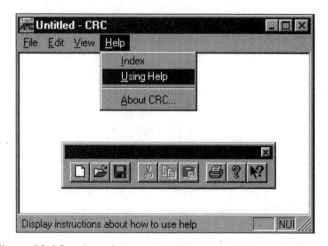

Figure 10.4 Sample appliction with help menu and help toolbar button.

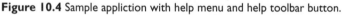

```
BEGIN_MESSAGE_MAP(CMainFrame, CMDIFrameWnd)
...
    // Global help commands
    ON_COMMAND(ID_HELP_INDEX, CMDIFrameWnd::OnHelpIndex)
    ON_COMMAND(ID_HELP_USING, CMDIFrameWnd::OnHelpUsing)
    ON_COMMAND(ID_HELP, CMDIFrameWnd::OnHelp)
    ON_COMMAND(ID_CONTEXT_HELP, CMDIFrameWnd::OnContextHelp)
    ON_COMMAND(ID_DEFAULT_HELP, CMDIFrameWnd::OnHelpIndex)
END_MESSAGE_MAP()
```

• Index and Using Help items in the menu definitions:

```
POPUP "&Help"

BEGIN
    MENUITEM "&Index",                    ID_HELP_INDEX
    MENUITEM "&Using Help",               ID_HELP_USING
```

```
        MENUITEM SEPARATOR
        MENUITEM "&About Testing...",              ID_APP_ABOUT
    END
```

- Status-bar command prompts and toolbar hints for the help items. These appear when the user clicks the mouse on one of the menu commands or pauses over a toolbar button:

```
    ID_CONTEXT_HELP          "Display help for clicked on buttons,
menus and windows\nHelp"
    ID_HELP_INDEX            "List Help topics\nHelp Index"
    ID_HELP_USING           "Display instructions about how to use
help\nHelp"
    ID_HELP                 "Display help for current task or
command\nHelp".
```

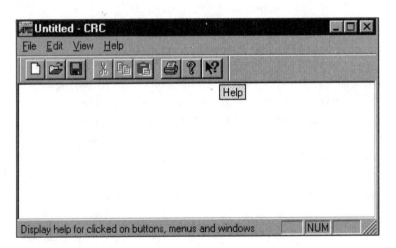

Figure 10.5 Sample appliction with one line help and toolbar hint.

- Accelerator items for the frame window class to map F1 and SHIFT+F1 to commands:

```
IDR_MAINFRAME ACCELERATORS PRELOAD MOVEABLE
BEGIN
...
```

```
    VK_F1,          ID_CONTEXT_HELP,        VIRTKEY,SHIFT
    VK_F1,          ID_HELP,                VIRTKEY
END
```

- A batch file called **MAKEHELP.BAT** that you can use to compile the help.
- A Windows help project file with an **.HPJ** extension.
- Two or more RTF files containing standard help contexts.
- Several bitmap files used in the help files.

Supporting F1 Help

The MFC framework supports F1 Help for windows, dialog boxes, message boxes, menus, and toolbar buttons. If the cursor is over a window, dialog box, or message box when the user presses the **F1** key, the framework opens Windows help for that window. If a menu item is highlighted, the framework opens Windows help for that menu item. And if a toolbar button has been pressed (but the mouse not released yet), the framework opens Windows help for that toolbar button. This processing is extensible, and additional hot spots in the application windows can be identified. Also, no special help mode is involved.

The F1 key is usually translated to an ID of **ID_HELP** by an accelerator placed in the main window's accelerator table. But, when a menu or model dialog box is active and the user presses **F1**, the keystroke is detected by a message filter that has hook all messages. This avoids added extract code to every dialog to detect that **F1** has been pressed. Like other areas, the message filter generates an **ID_HELP** command. The following code segment contains most of the MFC message filter logic looking for **F1** key:

```
From .../MFC/SRC/THRDCORE.CPP
BOOL CWinThread::ProcessMessageFilter(in code, LPMSG lpMsg)
{
...
    switch (code)
    {
...
    case MSGF_MENU:
...
```

```
                if (pMainWnd != NULL && pFrameWnd->IsTracking() &&
                    pFrameWnd->GetTopLevelFrame()->m_bHelpMode &&
                    (IsEnterKey(lpMsg) || IsButtonUp(lpMsg)))
                {
                    pMainWnd->SendMessage(WM_COMMAND, ID_HELP);
                    return TRUE;
                }
            }
            // fall through...

        case MSGF_DIALOGBOX:    // handles message boxes as well.
            pMainWnd = AfxGetMainWnd();
            if (pMainWnd != NULL && IsHelpKey(lpMsg))
            {
                pMainWnd->SendMessage(WM_COMMAND, ID_HELP);
                return TRUE;
            }
...
            }
            break;
    }

    return FALSE;    // default to not handled
}
```

After the **ID_HELP** message is generated, it is routed as a normal command until it reaches the command handler of the window, normally CWinApp::OnHelp. After the help context is resolved, CWinApp::OnHelp attempts to launch WinHelp in the following order:

1. It checks for an active AfxMessageBox call with a Help ID. If a message box is currently active, WinHelp is launched with the context appropriate to that message box.

2. If no message box is active, CWinApp::OnHelp sends a **WM_COMMANDHELP** (a message private to the Microsoft Foundation

classes) to the active window. If that window does not respond by launching WinHelp, the same message is then sent to the parent of that window until the message is processed or the current window is a top-level window (and therefore does not have a parent window).

3. If the message remains unprocessed, then the default Help is invoked. This is done by sending a **ID_DEFAULT_HELP** command to the main window. This command is generally mapped to CWinApp::OnHelpIndex.

To override this standard functionality and the way that a Help context is determined, an application should handle the **WM_COMMANDHELP** message. You may want to provide more specific help routing than the framework provides; it only goes as deep as the current MDI child window. Or you may want to provide more specific help for a particular window or dialog—perhaps based on the current internal state of that object or the active control within the dialog.

```
LPARAM WM_COMMANDHELP
    afx_msg LRESULT CWnd::OnCommandHelp(WPARAM, lParam)
```

WM_COMMANDHELP is an MFC private Windows message that is received by the active window when help is requested. When the window receives this message, it may call CWinApp::WinHelp with context that matches the window's internal state. **LParam** should be set to a nonzero number when the help context has been determined. **WParame** is not used and should be zero.

   If the OnCommandHelp handler calls CWinApp::WinHelp, it should return TRUE. Returning TRUE acknowledges that the help context search is over and the routing of this command to other classes (base classes) and to other windows should be stopped.

Supporting SHIFT+F1 Help

If the user presses **Shift+F1** at any time when the application is active (or uses an equivalent toolbar or menu operation), the framework puts the application into Help mode and changes the cursor to a Help cursor (see Figure 10.6).

Figure 10.6 MFC help cursor and Shift+F1 toolbar button.

This mode is not available when a modal dialog box or menu is active. The next object the user clicks determines what Help context the framework opens in Windows Help. When the user presses **Shift+F1**, the framework routes the command **ID_CONTEXT_HELP** through the normal command routing. The command is mapped to the CWinApp member function OnContextHelp, which captures the mouse, changes the cursor to a Help cursor, and puts the application into Help mode. The Help cursor is maintained as long as the application is in Help mode but reverts to a normal arrow cursor if it is not over the application that is in Help mode. Activating a different application cancels Help mode in the original application. While in Help mode, the application determines what object the user clicks and calls the CWinApp member function WinHelp with the appropriate context, determined from the object clicked on. After an object has been selected, Help mode ends and the cursor is restored to the normal arrow.

If the user chooses a command from the menu, it is handled as help on that command (through **WM_COMMANDHELP**). If the user clicks a visible area of the applications window, a determination is made as to whether it is a non-client click or a client click. OnContextHelp handles mapping of non-client clicks to client clicks automatically. If it is a client click, it sends a **WM_HELPHITTEST** to the window that was clicked. Thus, to create a window-specific help context, add **WM_HELPHITTEST** to your message map and process the resulting OnHelpHitTest commands. If your window returns a nonzero value, the value is used as the context for help. If the window returns zero, OnContextHelp tries the parent window (and failing that, its parent, and so on). If a Help context cannot be determined, the default is to send an **ID_DEFAULT_HELP** command to the main window, which is then mapped to CWinApp::OnHelpIndex.

```
WM_HELPHITTEST
afx_msg LRESULT CWnd::OnHelpHitTest(WPARAM, LPARAM lParam)
```

WM_HELPHITTEST is an MFC private windows message that is received by the active window clicked during the Shift+F1 Help mode. When the window receives this message, it returns a DWORD Help ID for use by WinHelp. **LParam** contains the X and Y coordinates of where the mouse was clicked. The coordinates are relative to the client area of the window. If your application already performs hit testing, you should be able to leverage this to provide help for each object as well.

MFC provides hit testing for:

- control bars, CControlBar—hit testing identifies any button
- dialogs, CDialog—anywhere in the dialog is a hit
- windows, CFrameWindow—anywhere in the window is a hit

The following code segment shows how CControlBar hit testing leverages its prebuilt command hit testing to provide context-sensitive help for every part of the CControlBar:

```
File: .../MFC/SRC/BARCORE.CPP
LRESULT CControlBar::OnHelpHitTest(WPARAM, LPARAM lParam)
{
    ASSERT_VALID(this);

    UINT nID = OnCmdHitTest((DWORD)lParam, NULL);
    if (nID != -1)
        return HID_BASE_COMMAND+nID;

    nID = _AfxGetDlgCtrlID(m_hWnd);
    return nID != 0 ? HID_BASE_CONTROL+nID : 0;
}
```

Supporting Help Index

Unlike supporting **F1** and **Shift+F1** help, there is little magic required in the MFC framework to support **HELP_INDEX**. Selecting the **Help Index** menu item simply issues an **ID_HELP_INDEX** command. The default CWin::OnHelpIndex function calls the MFC WinHelp function, which in turn calls the WinHelp API sending the **HELP_INDEX** command. The MFC WinHelp function deals with determining the application help file pathname and handling error codes from the WinHelp API. The following code segment is the generic OnHelpIndex member function:

```
File: .../MFC/SRC/APPHELPX.CPP
void CWnd::OnHelpIndex()
{
    AfxGetApp()->WinHelp(0L, HELP_INDEX);
```

```
}
```

Supporting Using Help

Like supporting Help Index, supporting help on how to use help is simply a matter of the Using Help menu item issuing an **ID_HELP_USING** command. This command is mapped to OnUsingHelp, which calls the MFC WinHelp function, which in turn calls the WinHelp API. The following code segment is the generic OnHelpUsing member function:

```
File: .../MFC/SRC/APPHELPX.CPP
void CWinApp::OnHelpUsing()
{
    WinHelp(OL, HELP_HELPONHELP);
}
```

Supporting Quitting Help

When an application terminates, it should send a message to WinHelp indicating that help is no longer needed. This little busy work is missing from many commercial applications. Now, with MFC 3, all applications will do this because it is buried in the MFC framework and requires no programmer changes—or even knowledge. The following code segment illustrates the framework doing the right thing by sending the **HELP_QUIT** message when it is shut down:

```
File: .../MFC/SRC/WINFRM.CPP
void CFrameWnd::OnDestroy()
{
    DestroyDockBars();

    // reset menu to default before final shutdown
    if (m_hMenuDefault != NULL && ::GetMenu(m_hWnd) !=
m_hMenuDefault)
    {
        ::SetMenu(m_hWnd, m_hMenuDefault);
        ASSERT(::GetMenu(m_hWnd) == m_hMenuDefault);
```

```
    }

    // Automatically quit when the main window is destroyed.
    if (AfxGetApp()->m_pMainWnd == this)
    {
        // closing the main application window
        ::WinHelp(m_hWnd, NULL, HELP_QUIT, OL);

        // will call PostQuitMessage in CWnd::OnNcDestroy
    }
    CWnd::OnDestroy();
}
```

Help Context Ids

With the MFC framework, the help context is based on the ID of the active program element. Although the framework knows the type of the program element—Commands (ID_* and IDM_*), Prompts (error messages) (IDP_*), Resources (IDR_*), Dialogs (IDD_*), special purpose (non-client hit testing), or Frame Controls (IDW_*)—the framework cannot ensure that the IDs are unique. The framework solves this overlap problem by adding an element type in the ID before calling WinHelp, creating help context ranges. The help context ranges hard-coded into MFC 3 are listed in Table 10.2.

Table 10.2 Help Context Ranges

Program Element	ID Prefix	Help Context ID Prefix	Range
User defined	any	H...	0x00000000 - 0x0000FFFF
Commands	ID_	HID_	0x00010000 + ID_
Windows and Dialogs	IDR_, IDD_	HIRD_, HIDD_	0x0002000 + ID[RD]_
Prompts	IDP_	HIDP_	0x00030000 + IDP_
Special purpose	any	H...	0x00040000 + H...
Controls	IDW	HIDW_	0x00050000 + IDW

For example, the dialog IDD_ABOUTBOX (0x0064) will be identified in the on-line help systems as HIDD_ABOUTBOX (0x20064).

Help Mapping File

To automate the mapping of normal application IDs to help Ids, Visual C++ supplies the **makehm.exe** program and generates the **makehelp.bat** batch file to run **makehm.exe**. The **makehm.exe** program parses files looking for IDs and creates a help mapping file with the new help ID names and values. Following is the **makehelp.bat** file generated by App Wizard:

```
@echo off
REM -- First make map file from Microsoft Visual C++ generated
resource.h
echo // MAKEHELP.BAT generated Help Map file.  Used by CRC.HPJ.
>hlp\CRC.hm
echo. >>hlp\CRC.hm
echo // Commands (ID_* and IDM_*) >>hlp\CRC.hm
makehm ID_,HID_,0x10000 IDM_,HIDM_,0x10000 resource.h >>hlp\CRC.hm
echo. >>hlp\CRC.hm
echo // Prompts (IDP_*) >>hlp\CRC.hm
makehm IDP_,HIDP_,0x30000 resource.h >>hlp\CRC.hm
echo. >>hlp\CRC.hm
echo // Resources (IDR_*) >>hlp\CRC.hm
makehm IDR_,HIDR_,0x20000 resource.h >>hlp\CRC.hm
echo. >>hlp\CRC.hm
echo // Dialogs (IDD_*) >>hlp\CRC.hm
makehm IDD_,HIDD_,0x20000 resource.h >>hlp\CRC.hm
echo. >>hlp\CRC.hm
echo // Frame Controls (IDW_*) >>hlp\CRC.hm
makehm IDW_,HIDW_,0x50000 resource.h >>hlp\CRC.hm
REM -- Make help for Project CRC

echo Building Win32 Help files
call hc31 CRC.hpj
if exist windebug copy CRC.hlp windebug
if exist winrel copy CRC.hlp winrel
```

```
EndLocal
```

Running makehelp.bat creates the following **HM** (help mapping) file:

```
// MAKEHELP.BAT generated Help Map file.  Used by CRC.HPJ.

// Commands (ID_* and IDM_*)
// Prompts (IDP_*)

// Resources (IDR_*)
HIDR_MAINFRAME                          0x20080

// Dialogs (IDD_*)
HIDD_ABOUTBOX                           0x20064

// Frame Controls (IDW_*)
```

This help mapping information is integrated into the help project file with the standard MFC framework help information. The AppWizard-created help project file:

```
[OPTIONS]
CONTENTS=main_index
TITLE=CRC Application Help
COMPRESS=true
WARNING=2

[FILES]
hlp\afxcore.rtf
hlp\afxprint.rtf

[BITMAPS]
; toolbar buttons for File commands
hlp\filenew.bmp
hlp\fileopen.bmp
hlp\fileprnt.bmp
```

```
hlp\filesave.bmp

; toolbar buttons for Edit commands
hlp\editcopy.bmp
hlp\editcut.bmp
hlp\editpast.bmp
hlp\editundo.bmp

; toolbar buttons for Record commands
hlp\recfirst.bmp
hlp\recprev.bmp
hlp\recnext.bmp
hlp\reclast.bmp

; cursors
hlp\curarw4.bmp
hlp\curarw2.bmp
hlp\curhelp.bmp

; system command icons
hlp\scmenu.bmp
hlp\scmax.bmp
hlp\scmin.bmp

; miscellaneous
hlp\bullet.bmp
hlp\appexit.bmp
hlp\hlpsbar.bmp
hlp\hlptbar.bmp

[ALIAS]
HIDR_MAINFRAME = main_index
HIDD_ABOUTBOX = HID_APP_ABOUT

HID_HT_SIZE = HID_SC_SIZE
```

```
HID_HT_HSCROLL = scrollbars
HID_HT_VSCROLL = scrollbars
HID_HT_MINBUTTON = HID_SC_MINIMIZE
HID_HT_MAXBUTTON = HID_SC_MAXIMIZE
AFX_HIDP_INVALID_FILENAME        = AFX_HIDP_default
AFX_HIDP_FAILED_TO_OPEN_DOC      = AFX_HIDP_default
AFX_HIDP_FAILED_TO_SAVE_DOC      = AFX_HIDP_default
AFX_HIDP_ASK_TO_SAVE             = AFX_HIDP_default
AFX_HIDP_FAILED_TO_CREATE_DOC    = AFX_HIDP_default
AFX_HIDP_FILE_TOO_LARGE          = AFX_HIDP_default
AFX_HIDP_FAILED_TO_START_PRINT   = AFX_HIDP_default
AFX_HIDP_FAILED_TO_LAUNCH_HELP   = AFX_HIDP_default
AFX_HIDP_INTERNAL_FAILURE        = AFX_HIDP_default
AFX_HIDP_COMMAND_FAILURE         = AFX_HIDP_default
AFX_HIDP_PARSE_INT               = AFX_HIDP_default
AFX_HIDP_PARSE_REAL              = AFX_HIDP_default
AFX_HIDP_PARSE_INT_RANGE         = AFX_HIDP_default
AFX_HIDP_PARSE_REAL_RANGE        = AFX_HIDP_default
AFX_HIDP_PARSE_STRING_SIZE       = AFX_HIDP_default
AFX_HIDP_FAILED_INVALID_FORMAT   = AFX_HIDP_default
AFX_HIDP_FAILED_INVALID_PATH     = AFX_HIDP_default
AFX_HIDP_FAILED_DISK_FULL        = AFX_HIDP_default
AFX_HIDP_FAILED_ACCESS_READ      = AFX_HIDP_default
AFX_HIDP_FAILED_ACCESS_WRITE     = AFX_HIDP_default
AFX_HIDP_FAILED_IO_ERROR_READ    = AFX_HIDP_default
AFX_HIDP_FAILED_IO_ERROR_WRITE   = AFX_HIDP_default
AFX_HIDP_STATIC_OBJECT           = AFX_HIDP_default
AFX_HIDP_FAILED_TO_CONNECT       = AFX_HIDP_default
AFX_HIDP_SERVER_BUSY             = AFX_HIDP_default
AFX_HIDP_BAD_VERB                = AFX_HIDP_default
AFX_HIDP_FAILED_MEMORY_ALLOC     = AFX_HIDP_default
AFX_HIDP_FAILED_TO_NOTIFY        = AFX_HIDP_default
AFX_HIDP_FAILED_TO_LAUNCH        = AFX_HIDP_default
AFX_HIDP_ASK_TO_UPDATE           = AFX_HIDP_default
AFX_HIDP_FAILED_TO_UPDATE        = AFX_HIDP_default
```

```
AFX_HIDP_FAILED_TO_REGISTER         = AFX_HIDP_default
AFX_HIDP_FAILED_TO_AUTO_REGISTER    = AFX_HIDP_default

[MAP]
#include <D:\MSVC20\MFC\include\afxhelp.hm>
#include <hlp\CRC.hm>
```

Although this is complex, the process of building your application's help file is as simple as running the single **makehelp.bat** file. There are three major parts to creating an application with world-class on-line help:

1. Creating context-sensitive application (support F1 and Shift+F1 help).
2. Writing a help file with quality information on all contexts.
3. Building the help file with automatic integration of these two qualities.

Visual C++ with the MFC application framework offers a nearly turnkey solution to part 1, making the application context-sensitive. If you follow framework ID naming conventions, part 3 is automated. This leaves part 2, writing the help file, as the part you need to add to ship a great cross-platform on-line help solution.

Alternative Help Development Tools

The most common cross-platform development strategy is to port an existing Windows application to Windows NT, UNIX, and the Macintosh. In this case, you would have an existing help file that you must also port to these new target platforms. All the information in this chapter so far has dealt with using existing RTF help topic files to create help for UNIX and the Macintosh. However, if you are developing a new application and you are performing your cross-platform development in parallel, there may be other alternatives for on-line that you want to explore.

If you are doing parallel cross-platform development—and therefore creating an on-line help system—the first step is to choose your help writing tool. Due to resource limitations, most companies want to be able to leverage their existing documentation to create on-line help.

If your existing documentation was created with word processing software that can generate RTF files, then you would use the same process already discussed for porting existing help files. That is, you would insert the hypertext codes into your word processor files, either by hand or using one of the many tools available to help you. Next, you would save the file in RTF format, create a help project file, and compile your on-line help for all target platforms.

Although software documentation is often written with tools that provide RTF conversion, this is not always the case. For example, many companies use an SGML editor to create documentation in SGML format. Other companies often use sophisticated electronic publishing software, such as Interleaf or FrameMaker, to create documentation. If your existing documentation is in one of these formats, the process for creating on-line help from existing documentation is not so simple.

One solution is to convert your existing documentation to a word processor format, such as Word for Windows. This solution can be very expensive in terms of software you must purchase, including the word processing software you are converting to and some type of conversion software to actually perform the conversion. It can also be very time-consuming, since conversion tools generally require some type of reformatting once they are converted.

You can also develop your on-line help information from scratch. Although this solution may be ideal in that you can create information specifically designed for on-line display, it doesn't allow you to take advantage of any of the existing documentation you have already invested significant resources to produce. Your on-line help developers may spend quite a bit of time re-creating information that has already been developed and tested.

HyperHelp provides a different solution that allows you to leverage from existing documentation in SGML, FrameMaker, or Interleaf format to create on-line help for UNIX, Windows, Windows NT, and Macintosh platforms. In addition to the RTF compiler (which can compile help files created with Interleaf), HyperHelp also provides an SGML compiler and an MIF compiler (which compiles help files created with FrameMaker). You can use these compilers to create a binary on-line help file for the UNIX version of your application.

What about the Windows and Macintosh versions of your application? HyperHelp provides an optional utility called HyperHelp Bridge. After you have used the HyperHelp compiler to create a UNIX version of your binary help file, you can use HyperHelp Bridge to convert the compiled help file to RTF files, which you can then compile with the Windows help compiler. As already discussed, you can view these files with the WinHelp viewer on Windows and Windows NT platforms, or with MacHelp on the Macintosh. The only limitation with this solution, however, involves graphics. The HyperHelp Bridge converts all graphics in the UNIX binary help file into Windows metafiles (**.WMF**), which are not supported on the Macintosh. However, you can copy the original bitmap files that you used to create the compiled HyperHelp file to the Windows or Windows NT platform and use those files when you compile the Macintosh version of your help file.

Summary

Although the Windows help format is essentially a proprietary format, tools are available that let you port existing Windows help source files to UNIX and the Macintosh. Just as you want to do with your application source code, you can maintain a single set of help source files for all versions of your application. If you do not have existing help files that you are porting to target platforms, tools are available that allow you to leverage existing documentation in most common documentation formats.

Both MacHelp and HyperHelp work seamlessly with Visual C++ and MFC applications. All Win32 platforms support the **WinHelp()** API, so you need not make any changes to your application to provide on-line help across platforms. In fact, MFC provides methods for on-line help in all classes where it is pertinent.

## CHAPTER 11

Win32 Communications

This chapter describes how to use the Win32 Communications APIs for cross-platform development of Visual C++ applications. In particular, it addresses the following topics:

- Inter-application communications through the Dynamic Data Exchange Management Library (DDEML)
- Using the Winsock APIs in cross-platform applications
- Cross-platform Open Database Connectivity (ODBC)
- Implications of using OLE 2 in portable applications
- Using Remote Procedure Calls in cross-platform applications

The Dynamic Data Exchange Management Library (DDEML)

Dynamic data exchange (DDE) is a form of interprocess communication that uses shared memory to exchange data between applications. Applications can use DDE for one-time data transfers and for ongoing exchanges in which the applications send updates to one another as new data becomes available.

DDE differs from the traditional clipboard data-transfer mechanism in that DDE transactions typically continue without the user's further involvement, whereas clipboard transactions are usually initiated each time by the user.

DDE was first introduced in Windows 3.0, but at that time an application had to implement DDE by posting low-level windows and performing its own memory management. Due to the complexity of implementing DDE, most application programmers found it difficult to create compliant and robust DDE applications.

In an effort to simplify the task of coding DDE applications, Microsoft Windows 3.1 introduced the Dynamic Data Exchange Management Library (DDEML). The DDEML provides an application programming interface (API) that simplifies the task of adding DDE capability to a Windows application. Instead of sending, posting, and processing DDE messages directly, an application uses the functions provided by the DDEML to manage DDE conversations.

The DDEML also provides a facility for managing the strings and data that are shared among DDE applications. Instead of using atoms and pointers to shared memory objects, DDE applications create and exchange string handles, which identify strings, and data handles, which identify global memory objects. DDEML provides a service that makes it possible for a server application to register the service names that it supports. The names are broadcast to other applications in the system, which can then use the names to connect to the server.

The biggest advantage of the DDEML is that it ensures compatibility among DDE applications by forcing them to implement the DDE protocol in a consistent manner.

Another significant (and possibly unanticipated) advantage of the DDEML is that it abstracts the details of the DDE implementation from the developer by wrapping it in a well-defined API. This approach allows the underlying implementation of DDE to be tailored for optimal performance and functionality on all Win32 hosted platforms. For instance, in the Wind/U implementation of DDEML, all DDEML APIs are mapped to native X protocol messages rather than to higher-level Windows messages. This implementation has the following advantages in the X Window System environment:

- By implementing DDEML directly is the X protocol, optimal performance in achieved and interoperability between different architectures is guaranteed.
- Since the X Window System is distributed, applications running on different hosts can communicate with each other via the X Server.

- Through the Wind/U Native DDEML Extension, applications written to native UNIX and X Window System APIs can communicate with Wind/U ported Win32 applications.

The Wind/U Native DDEML Extension is a separate library that can be linked to native UNIX applications to allow them to communicate with Wind/U ported applications via the DDE protocol. This extension is important for developers who are porting newer Win32 applications to the X Window System, but who must also maintain and interact with legacy applications written to native UNIX APIs. The Native DDEML Extension exports the DDEML APIs, as well as a few extensions that are needed to initialize the library in the native environment.

The Windows dynamic data exchange management library (DDEML) is not supported on the Macintosh.

N O T E

In Windows for Workgroups 3.11, Microsoft introduced Network DDE, which allows applications running on different systems to communicate via the DDE protocol over a local area network. Neither the Macintosh nor UNIX Win32 toolkits support the Network DDE APIs. Consider using the Winsock APIs (described later in this chapter) for a more portable and standards-based solution.

Table 11.1 DDE APIs

API	Windows NT	Windows 95	Macintosh	UNIX
DdeAbandonTransaction	Yes	Yes	No	Yes
DdeAccessData	Yes	Yes	No	Yes
DdeAddData	Yes	Yes	No	Yes
DdeCallback	Yes	Yes	No	Yes
DdeClientTransaction	Yes	Yes	No	Yes
DdeCmpStringHandles	Yes	Yes	No	Yes
DdeConnect	Yes	Yes	No	Yes
DdeConnectList	Yes	Yes	No	Yes
DdeCreateDataHandle	Yes	Yes	No	Yes

Table 11.1 DDE APIs (continued)

API	Windows NT	Windows 95	Macintosh	UNIX
DdeCreateStringHandle	Yes	Yes	No	Yes
DdeDisconnect	Yes	Yes	No	Yes
DdeDisconnectList	Yes	Yes	No	Yes
DdeEnableCallback	Yes	Yes	No	Yes
DdeFreeDataHandle	Yes	Yes	No	Yes
DdeFreeStringHandle	Yes	Yes	No	Yes
DdeGetData	Yes	Yes	No	Yes
DdeGetLastError	Yes	Yes	No	Yes
DdeInitialize	Yes	Yes	No	Yes
DdeKeepStringHandle	Yes	Yes	No	Yes
DdeNameService	Yes	Yes	No	Yes
DdePostAdvise	Yes	Yes	No	Yes
DdeQueryConvInfo	Yes	Yes	No	Yes
DdeQueryNextServer	Yes	Yes	No	Yes
DdeQueryString	Yes	Yes	No	Yes
DdeReconnect	Yes	Yes	No	Yes
DdeSetUserHandle	Yes	Yes	No	Yes
DdeUnaccessData	Yes	Yes	No	Yes
DdeUninitialize	Yes	Yes	No	Yes

WinSock in Cross-Platform Applications

The Windows Sockets (WinSock) specification defines a network programming interface for Microsoft Windows which is based on the "socket" paradigm popularized in the Berkeley Software Distribution (BSD) from the University of California at Berkeley. It encompasses both familiar Berkeley socket style routines and a set of Windows-specific extensions designed to allow you to take advantage of the message-driven nature of Windows.

The Windows Sockets Specification provides a single API to which application developers can program and multiple network software vendors can conform. Furthermore, in the context of a particular version of Windows, it defines a binary interface (ABI) such that an application written to the Windows Sockets API can work with a conformant protocol implementation from any network software vendor. This specification thus defines the library calls and associated semantics to which an application developer can program and which a network software vendor can implement.

The WinSock Library is quickly becoming the API of choice for network-based applications. WinSock and TCP/IP provide the greatest interoperability among different systems and also allow applications to interoperate seamlessly over the Internet. For complete network interoperability within a Win32 framework, no toolkit would be complete without support for Winsock.

The Windows Portability Library does not directly support the WinSock APIs on the Macintosh. However, native Macintosh support is available for these APIs through add-on network software.

Table 11.2 WinSock APIs

API	Windows 95	Windows NT 3.5	Macintosh	UNIX
accept	Yes	Yes	Yes	Yes
bind	Yes	Yes	Yes	Yes
closesocket	Yes	Yes	Yes	Yes
connect	Yes	Yes	Yes	Yes
gethostbyaddr	Yes	Yes	Yes	Yes
gethostbyname	Yes	Yes	Yes	Yes
gethostname	Yes	Yes	Yes	Yes
getpeername	Yes	Yes	Yes	Yes
getprotobyname	Yes	Yes	Yes	Yes
getprotobynumber	Yes	Yes	Yes	Yes
getservbyname	Yes	Yes	Yes	Yes
getservbyport	Yes	Yes	Yes	Yes

Table 11.2 WinSock APIs (continued)

API	Windows 95	Windows NT 3.5	Macintosh	UNIX
getsockname	Yes	Yes	Yes	Yes
getsockopt	Yes	Yes	Yes	Yes
htonl	Yes	Yes	Yes	Yes
htons	Yes	Yes	Yes	Yes
inet_addr	Yes	Yes	Yes	Yes
inet_ntoa	Yes	Yes	Yes	Yes
ioctlsocket	Yes	Yes	Yes	Yes
listen	Yes	Yes	Yes	Yes
ntohl	Yes	Yes	Yes	Yes
ntohs	Yes	Yes	Yes	Yes
recv	Yes	Yes	Yes	Yes
recvfrom	Yes	Yes	Yes	Yes
select	Yes	Yes	Yes	Yes
send	Yes	Yes	Yes	Yes
sendto	Yes	Yes	Yes	Yes
setsockopt	Yes	Yes	Yes	Yes
shutdown	Yes	Yes	Yes	Yes
socket	Yes	Yes	Yes	Yes
WSAAsyncGetHostByAddr	Yes	Yes		Yes
WSAAsyncGetHostByName	Yes	Yes		Yes
WSAAsyncGetProtoByName	Yes	Yes		Yes
WSAAsyncGetProtoByNumber	Yes	Yes		Yes
WSAAsyncGetServByName	Yes	Yes		Yes
WSAAsyncGetServByPort	Yes	Yes		Yes
WSAAsyncSelect	Yes	Yes		Yes
WSACancelAsyncRequest	Yes	Yes		Yes
WSACancelBlockingCall	Yes	Yes		Yes

Table 11.2 WinSock APIs (continued)

API	Windows 95	Windows NT 3.5	Macintosh	UNIX
WSACleanup	Yes	Yes		Yes
WSAGetLastError	Yes	Yes		Yes
WSAIsBlocking	Yes	Yes		Yes
WSASetBlockingHook	Yes	Yes		Yes
WSASetLastError	Yes	Yes		Yes
WSAStartup	Yes	Yes		Yes
WSAUnhookBlockingHook	Yes	Yes		Yes

Open Database Connectivity (ODBC)

The Open Database Connectivity (ODBC) interface allows applications to access data in database management systems (DBMS) using Structured Query Language (SQL) as a standard for accessing data. The interface permits maximum interoperability—that is, a single application can access different database management systems. Therefore, an application developer can develop, compile, and ship an application without targeting a specific DBMS. Users can then add modules called *database drivers* that link the application to their choice of database management systems.

The ODBC interface defines the following:

- A library of ODBC function calls that allow an application to connect to a DBMS, execute SQL statements, and retrieve results.
- SQL syntax based on the X/Open and SQL Access Group (SAG) SQL CAE specification (1992).
- A standard set of error codes.
- A standard way to connect and log on to a DBMS.
- A standard representation for data types.

The ODBC interface is flexible in that:

- Strings containing SQL statements can be explicitly included in source code or constructed on the fly at run time.

- The same object code can be used to access different DBMS products.

- An application can ignore underlying data communications protocols between it and a DBMS product.

- Data values can be sent and retrieved in a format convenient to the application.

The ODBC interface provides two types of function calls:

- *Core functions* are based on the X/Open and SQL Access Group Call Level Interface specification.

- *Extended functions* support additional functionality, including scrollable cursors and asynchronous processing.

The Windows Portability Library does not provide wrapper functions for Apple's implementation of ODBC, level 1 on the Macintosh, although Macintosh-specific calls to these functions can be included in an application. The header files and documentation needed for creating ODBC applications are included. Support in Macintosh MFC will be in the next release of the product. For information about Apple ODBC support, see Apple's documentation.

On UNIX, Wind/U provides stub functions for all of the ODBC level 2 APIs. The APIs are stubbed to return error codes that inform the calling application that the called API did not execute properly. For applications that require ODBC support, Wind/U provides a mechanism for replacing the default stubs with an ODBC library from one of a few vendors that provide ODBC on UNIX. The two most notable vendors of ODBC on UNIX are:

INTERSOLV	Visigenics, Inc.
5540 CenterView Drive	951 Mariner's Island Boulevard, Suite 460
Raleigh, NC 27606	San Mateo, CA 94404

Wind/U MFC includes the ODBC classes, and when combined with the ODBC libraries from one of the above vendors, provides support for ODBC in MFC applications.

Table 11.3 ODBC APIs

API	Windows 95	Windows NT 3.5	Macintosh	UNIX
SQLAllocConnect	Yes	Yes	Yes	Yes
SQLCancel	Yes	Yes	Yes	Yes
SQLAllocEnv	Yes	Yes	Yes	Yes
SQLColAttributes	Yes	Yes	Yes	Yes
SQLAllocStmt	Yes	Yes	Yes	Yes
SQLColumnPrivileges	Yes	Yes	Yes	Yes
SQLBindCol	Yes	Yes	Yes	Yes
SQLColumns	Yes	Yes	Yes	Yes
SQLBrowseConnect	Yes	Yes	Yes	Yes
SQLConnect	Yes	Yes	Yes	Yes
SQLDataSources	Yes	Yes	Yes	Yes
SQLError	Yes	Yes	Yes	Yes
SQLDescribeCol	Yes	Yes	Yes	Yes
SQLExecDirect	Yes	Yes	Yes	Yes
SQLDescribeParam	Yes	Yes	Yes	Yes
SQLExecute	Yes	Yes	Yes	Yes
SQLDisconnect	Yes	Yes	Yes	Yes
SQLExtendedFetch	Yes	Yes	Yes	Yes
SQLDriverConnect	Yes	Yes	Yes	Yes
SQLFetch	Yes	Yes	Yes	Yes
SQLGetCursorName	Yes	Yes	Yes	Yes
SQLForeignKeys	Yes	Yes	Yes	Yes
SQLGetData	Yes	Yes	Yes	Yes
SQLFreeConnect	Yes	Yes	Yes	Yes
SQLGetFunctions	Yes	Yes	Yes	Yes
SQLFreeEnv	Yes	Yes	Yes	Yes
SQLGetInfo	Yes	Yes	Yes	Yes
SQLFreeStmt	Yes	Yes	Yes	Yes

Table 11.3 ODBC APIs (continued)

API	Windows 95	Windows NT 3.5	Macintosh	UNIX
SQLGetStmtOption	Yes	Yes	Yes	Yes
SQLGetConnectOption	Yes	Yes	Yes	Yes
SQLGetTypeInfo	Yes	Yes	Yes	Yes
SQLMoreResults	Yes	Yes	Yes	Yes
SQLPrepare	Yes	Yes	Yes	Yes
SQLNativeSql	Yes	Yes	Yes	Yes
SQLPrimaryKeys	Yes	Yes	Yes	Yes
SQLNumParams	Yes	Yes	Yes	Yes
SQLProcedureColumns	Yes	Yes	Yes	Yes
SQLNumResultCols	Yes	Yes	Yes	Yes
SQLProcedures	Yes	Yes	Yes	Yes
SQLParamData	Yes	Yes	Yes	Yes
SQLPutData	Yes	Yes	Yes	Yes
SQLParamOptions	Yes	Yes	Yes	Yes
SQLRowCount	Yes	Yes	Yes	Yes
SQLSetStmtOption	Yes	Yes	Yes	Yes
SQLSetConnectOption	Yes	Yes	Yes	Yes
SQLSpecialColumns	Yes	Yes	Yes	Yes
SQLSetCursorName	Yes	Yes	Yes	Yes
SQLStatistics	Yes	Yes	Yes	Yes
SQLSetParam	Yes	Yes	Yes	Yes
SQLTablePrivileges	Yes	Yes	Yes	Yes
SQLSetPos	Yes	Yes	Yes	Yes
SQLTables	Yes	Yes	Yes	Yes
SQLSetScrollOptions	Yes	Yes	Yes	Yes
SQLTransact	Yes	Yes	Yes	Yes

What about OLE 2?

The Visual C++ Cross Development Edition for Macintosh includes the necessary documentation and header files for creating OLE 2 applications using the native OLE 2 SDK for the Macintosh. However, support for OLE 2 in AppWizard and support for OLE 2 classes in MFC are not currently supported. The next release of Visual C++ for Macintosh will include support for the Windows OLE 2 interfaces and MFC classes, as well as AppWizard tools for creating OLE 2 applications.

The current release of Wind/U provides stubs for the OLE 2 APIs so that applications that use the OLE 2 APIs directly or link to the OLE 2 classes in MFC will execute properly, with the exception that OLE 2 features will be inoperative.

In the near future, Wind/U will provide native support for OLE 2 applications. The Wind/U implementation of OLE 2 is based on the source code for OLE 2 in Windows NT 3.51, and will include features of OLE 2 such as in-place activation, automation, drag-and-drop, and OLE compound documents.

The Windows95, Windows NT, UNIX, and Macintosh implementations of OLE 2 are all derived from a single source base, which provides for maximum portability and interoperability of the three platforms.

Remote Procedure Calls (RPC)

The Win32 API provides remote procedure calls (RPC) to enable applications to call functions remotely. With RPC, communication with other processes becomes as easy as calling a function. RPC operates between processes on a single computer or on different computers on a network. One way to think of RPC is as a DLL that works on a network.

The RPC provided by the Win32 API is compliant with the Open Software Foundation (OSF) Distributed Computing Environment (DCE). This means that RPC applications written using the Win32 API are able to communicate with other RPC applications running with other operating systems that support DCE. RPC automatically supports data conversion to account for different hardware architectures and for byte-ordering between dissimilar environments.

The RPC APIs are only available on Windows95, Windows NT, and UNIX; they should not be used in applications that need to support the Macintosh. Table 11-4 shows the support status of all RPC APIs in Windows 95, Windows NT, the Windows Portability Library for the Macintosh, and Wind/U for UNIX.

Table 11.4 Remote Procedure Calls (RPC) APIs

Function	Windows 95	Windows NT	Macintosh	UNIX
DceErrorInqText	Yes	Yes	No	Yes
RpcAbnormalTermination	Yes	Yes	No	Yes
RpcBindingCopy	Yes	Yes	No	Yes
RpcBindingFree	Yes	Yes	No	Yes
RpcBindingFromStringBinding	Yes	Yes	No	Yes
RpcBindingInqAuthClient	Yes	Yes	No	Yes
RpcBindingInqAuthInfo	Yes	Yes	No	Yes
RpcBindingInqObject	Yes	Yes	No	Yes
RpcBindingReset	Yes	Yes	No	Yes
RpcBindingServerFromClient	Yes	Yes	No	Yes
RpcBindingSetAuthInfo	Yes	Yes	No	Yes
RpcBindingSetObject	Yes	Yes	No	Yes
RpcBindingToStringBinding	Yes	Yes	No	Yes
RpcBindingVectorFree	Yes	Yes	No	Yes
RpcEndExcept	Yes	Yes	No	Yes
RpcEndFinally	Yes	Yes	No	Yes
RpcEpRegister	Yes	Yes	No	Yes
RpcEpRegisterNoReplace	Yes	Yes	No	Yes
RpcEpResolveBinding	Yes	Yes	No	Yes
RpcEpUnregister	Yes	Yes	No	Yes
RpcExcept	Yes	Yes	No	Yes
RpcExceptionCode	Yes	Yes	No	Yes
RpcFinally	Yes	Yes	No	Yes
RpcIfIdVectorFree	Yes	Yes	No	Yes

Table 11.4 Remote Procedure Calls (RPC) APIs (continued)

Function	Windows 95	Windows NT	Macintosh	UNIX
RpcIfInqId	Yes	Yes	No	Yes
RpcIfRegisterAuthInfo	Yes	Yes	No	Yes
RpcImpersonateClient	Yes	Yes	No	Yes
RpcMgmtEnableIdleCleanup	Yes	Yes	No	Yes
RpcMgmtEpEltInqBegin	Yes	Yes	No	Yes
RpcMgmtEpEltInqDone	Yes	Yes	No	Yes
RpcMgmtEpEltInqNext	Yes	Yes	No	Yes
RpcMgmtEpUnregister	Yes	Yes	No	Yes
RpcMgmtInqComTimeout	Yes	Yes	No	Yes
RpcMgmtInqDfltAuthnLevel	Yes	Yes	No	Yes
RpcMgmtInqIfIds	Yes	Yes	No	Yes
RpcMgmtInqServerPrincName	Yes	Yes	No	Yes
RpcMgmtInqStats	Yes	Yes	No	Yes
RpcMgmtIsServerListening	Yes	Yes	No	Yes
RpcMgmtSetAuthorizationFn	Yes	Yes	No	Yes
RpcMgmtSetCancelTimeout	Yes	Yes	No	Yes
RpcMgmtSetComTimeout	Yes	Yes	No	Yes
RpcMgmtSetServerStackSize	Yes	Yes	No	Yes
RpcMgmtStatsVectorFree	Yes	Yes	No	Yes
RpcMgmtStopServerListening	Yes	Yes	No	Yes
RpcMgmtWaitServerListen	Yes	Yes	No	Yes
RpcNetworkInqProtSeqs	Yes	Yes	No	Yes
RpcNetworkIsProtSeqValid	Yes	Yes	No	Yes
RpcNsBindingExport	Yes	Yes	No	Yes
RpcNsBindingImportBegin	Yes	Yes	No	Yes
RpcNsBindingImportDone	Yes	Yes	No	Yes
RpcNsBindingImportNext	Yes	Yes	No	Yes
RpcNsBindingInqEntryName	Yes	Yes	No	Yes

Table 11.4 Remote Procedure Calls (RPC) APIs Continued)

Function	Windows 95	Windows NT	Macintosh	UNIX
RpcNsBindingLookupBegin	Yes	Yes	No	Yes
RpcNsBindingLookupDone	Yes	Yes	No	Yes
RpcNsBindingLookupNext	Yes	Yes	No	Yes
RpcNsBindingSelect	Yes	Yes	No	Yes
RpcNsBindingUnexport	Yes	Yes	No	Yes
RpcNsEntryExpandName	Yes	Yes	No	Yes
RpcNsEntryObjectInqBegin	Yes	Yes	No	Yes
RpcNsEntryObjectInqDone	Yes	Yes	No	Yes
RpcNsEntryObjectInqNext	Yes	Yes	No	Yes
RpcNsGroupDelete	Yes	Yes	No	Yes
RpcNsGroupMbrAdd	Yes	Yes	No	Yes
RpcNsGroupMbrInqBegin	Yes	Yes	No	Yes
RpcNsGroupMbrInqDone	Yes	Yes	No	Yes
RpcNsGroupMbrInqNext	Yes	Yes	No	Yes
RpcNsGroupMbrRemove	Yes	Yes	No	Yes
RpcNsMgmtBindingUnexport	Yes	Yes	No	Yes
RpcNsMgmtEntryCreate	Yes	Yes	No	Yes
RpcNsMgmtEntryDelete	Yes	Yes	No	Yes
RpcNsMgmtEntryInqIfIds	Yes	Yes	No	Yes
RpcNsMgmtHandleSetExpAge	Yes	Yes	No	Yes
RpcNsMgmtInqExpAge	Yes	Yes	No	Yes
RpcNsMgmtSetExpAge	Yes	Yes	No	Yes
RpcNsProfileDelete	Yes	Yes	No	Yes
RpcNsProfileEltAdd	Yes	Yes	No	Yes
RpcNsProfileEltInqBegin	Yes	Yes	No	Yes
RpcNsProfileEltInqDone	Yes	Yes	No	Yes
RpcNsProfileEltInqNext	Yes	Yes	No	Yes

Table 11.4 Remote Procedure Calls (RPC) APIs (continued)

Function	Windows 95	Windows NT	Macintosh	UNIX
RpcNsProfileEltRemove	Yes	Yes	No	Yes
RpcObjectInqType	Yes	Yes	No	Yes
RpcObjectSetInqFn	Yes	Yes	No	Yes
RpcObjectSetType	Yes	Yes	No	Yes
RpcProtseqVectorFree	Yes	Yes	No	Yes
RpcRaiseException	Yes	Yes	No	Yes
RpcRevertToSelf	Yes	Yes	No	Yes
RpcServerInqBindings	Yes	Yes	No	Yes
RpcServerInqIf	Yes	Yes	No	Yes
RpcServerListen	Yes	Yes	No	Yes
RpcServerRegisterAuthInfo	Yes	Yes	No	Yes
RpcServerRegisterIf	Yes	Yes	No	Yes
RpcServerUnregisterIf	Yes	Yes	No	Yes
RpcServerUseAllProtseqs	Yes	Yes	No	Yes
RpcServerUseAllProtseqsIf	Yes	Yes	No	Yes
RpcServerUseProtseq	Yes	Yes	No	Yes
RpcServerUseProtseqEp	Yes	Yes	No	Yes
RpcServerUseProtseqIf	Yes	Yes	No	Yes
RpcSsDestroyClientContext	Yes	Yes	No	Yes
RpcStringBindingCompose	Yes	Yes	No	Yes
RpcStringBindingParse	Yes	Yes	No	Yes
RpcStringFree	Yes	Yes	No	Yes
RpcTryExcept	Yes	Yes	No	Yes
RpcTryFinally	Yes	Yes	No	Yes
RpcWinSetYieldInfo	Yes	Yes	No	Yes
UuidCompare	Yes	Yes	No	Yes
UuidCreate	Yes	Yes	No	Yes
UuidCreateNil	Yes	Yes	No	Yes

Table 11.4 Remote Procedure Calls (RPC) APIs (continued)

Function	Windows 95	Windows NT	Macintosh	UNIX
UuidEqual	Yes	Yes	No	Yes
UuidFromString	Yes	Yes	No	Yes
UuidHash	Yes	Yes	No	Yes
UuidIsNil	Yes	Yes	No	Yes
UuidToString	Yes	Yes	No	Yes
YieldFunctionName	Yes	Yes	No	Yes

Summary

Win32 provides several sets of APIs that can be used to implement interprocess and network communications. While cross-development with these APIs are still relatively new, there are already solutions available or under development for Winsock, ODBC, DDEML, OLE 2, and RPC.

CHAPTER 12

Cross-Platform Testing Strategies

Introduction

Software quality is a competive advantage. In the 1970s quality transformed the automobile industry; in the 1980s quality transformed the semiconductor industry. Now, in the 1990s, quality is transforming the software industry. With the highly competive software market, delivering a high quality product is more important that ever. Using a good testing methodolgy and appropriate cross-platform testing tools is the most effective way to deliver a high quality product.

Delivering a low quality software product is costly in time and resources. Adding quality after development creates the following problems:

- Your engineers are required to work on patchs, not developing the next release or a new product.

- Your support team is buried in a flood of user problems

- Your sales and marketing teams are spending their time fighting overheated customers and not finding new customers.

Insuring quality as part of the development process helps in the following ways:

- It makes product delivery dates more predicatble.

- It makes engineering more effective, spending less time on patches and support issues

- It improves the image of your company

To help deliver a quality product, serveral automated tools are available, from tools to test GUI interaction, to runtime error checking, to performance analysis. While these tools help you deliver a quality product, they are not magic elixirs. They help, but commitment by everyone involved to deliver a high quality product is the key ingrediant.

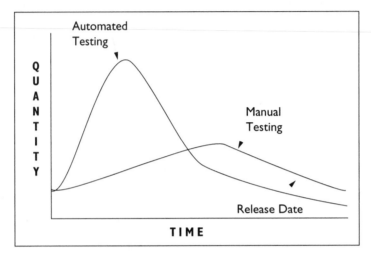

Figure 12.1 Catching defects earlier

This chapter is divided into four related aspects of cross-platform testing strategies:

- Client application testing,
- Multi-user testing,
- System testing, and
- Quality process management

Client Application Testing

The software created with Visual C++ and MFC tends to be feature-rich, sophisticated, graphical user-interface–based applications. While these GUI applications are targeted to enhance the user's productity, they make testing an arduous and time-consuming task.

Automated testing tools

Several tools are available for automated testing of GUI applications. A few of these tools are available for cross-platform testing. Mercury Interactive's WinRunner and XRunner tools, along with Segue Software's QA Partner are the cross-platform market leaders. These tools let you test GUI applcations faster, more accurately, and more thoroughly than ever before. After the suite of regression tests has been created, these tools can run an automated nightly test suite that would have required weeks of manual testing. With automated testing tools, tests you create:

- Are independent of the absolute or relative position of GUI objects on the screen.
- Are independent of the speed of the application and the timing of events.
- Can be used over and over, on several platforms
- Can be designed to be robust and failure-resistant

The following is a high-level view of the automated testing process.

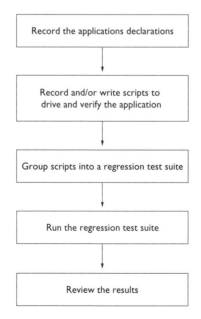

Figure 12.2 Automated Testing Process

As shown in Figure 12.2, you start by recording declarations for the GUI objects in your application. These declarations provide the names that you use in tests to access the object. Normally, the testing tool can automaticly extract these declarations for you. Next, you record, and optionally create, a series of testcases, a script, to test the application. These scripts drive the application and observe and verify its output—Just as a human would, picking menu items, clicking on buttons, reading text on the screen, and entering text into fields. Then you group the scripts into an ordered suite. Now, you can consistently execute the regression test suite and review the results looking for inconsistencies.

Creating Regression Tests

A thorough automated regression test can be quite large. Like any large project, it is important that the regression test be created using a structured, modular approach. Depending on the complexity of your WinAPI/MFC application, there may be hundreds of components in the full regression test suite. The regression test will contain declarations, test cases, and various tools and utilities needed to ensure that the regression test is robust. A good modular approach is to use a three-tiered structure, composed of:

1. test cases—a test for a single application feature
2. scripts—a collection of one or more testcases for releated features
3. test suites—a collection of scripts required to completly test an application

If your application has several distinct components, DLLs, or executables, you should create test suites for each component.

When creating a test case, use the following design principles:

- The test case should have a single principle
- The test case should start at a known base state
- The test case should return the application to the known base state
- The test case should be independent of any other testcase

A test case should have only one of two possible outcomes: pass or fail. Thus, it should only address one test requirement, since only one single output is possible. For example, a test case may be designed to verify that a menu item is enabled if an object is on the clipboard. Another test case would be created to verify that the menu item is disabled if no objects were on the clipboard. This single principle/pass-or-fail test case design makes it easy to determine specifically what aspects of the target application are either working or not working. In order for a test case to be able to consistently drive an application to a state to be tested, the application must be in a known state when the test case begins to execute. Therefore, it is important that the testcase return the application to a known state after testing the application. Lastly, the test case should be independent of all other testcases. It should not rely on the successful, or unsuccessful, completion of another test case, or on the side effect of another test case. For example, the *delete* test case should not assume that the *insert* testcase successfully inserted an object and left it lying around. Having dependencies on other test cases will result in a lot of test case failures. For example, if the *delete* testcase relied on the *insert* testc ase, if the insert testcase failed, the *delete* testcase would fail, but there might not be any problems with the applications' delete logic.

While these design principles are sound, they can lead to an explosion for test cases. While all of these test cases are needed, what is not needed is duplication of the logic to set up the test case and restore the application to a known state. The automated testing tools minimize this duplication by allowing you to generalize and parameterize the testcase. This allows you to reuse the testcase with different parameter values to test different aspects of the application.

Testing Application Features

By using an automated testing tool it is possible to exercise an application regorously, testing each feature with many possible combinations of actions and data. The goal of this level of testing is to determine if the application works the way the designers intended, and to be able to repeat this testing in a quick and efficient manner. When determining your test requirements, the goal is to rigorosuly test each application feature. To rigorously test a feature, you need to determine all the possible combinations of data an user can input. These test requirements should include both positive and negative testcases—(that is, a test with valid data, the function passes; and a test that with invalid data, the function fails.)

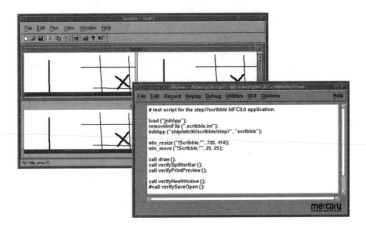

Figure 12.3 Automated Testing Tool

Testing the Applications GUI

After testing your application's features, you need to test if the GUI objects are behaving as defined for your application. Items to test include:

- Do the expected GUI objects exist?
- Is the default enabled/disabled state correct?
- Is the default value or selection correct?

To demonstate the variety of tests involved, here are some of the GUI test requirements for the *Pen Widths* dialog in the MFC Scribble sample application:

- Verify that the Pen Widths dialog appears when menu Pen -> Pen Widths is selected.
- Verify the contents of the dialog
  - a static text string for *Thin Pen Width:*
  - a text input field for the thin pen width, with the default number 2 in it
  - a static text string for *Thick Pen Width:*
  - a text input field for the thick pen width, with the default number 5 in it
  - a pushbutton for *OK*
  - a pushbutton for *Cancel*

- a pushbutton for *Default*

- Verify that the three pushbuttons are enabled, as well as that the two edit fields are enabled

- Verify that the *OK* pushbutton is the default pushbutton

- Verify that each object receives the focus in the correct tab order

- Verify that error checking is working for the text input fields

  - That non-integer values display an error dialog when OK pressed

  - That integer values must be in the range of 1 to 20

- Verify that, if the pen width values are changed, that re-invoking the dialog displays the current widths, not the default widths.

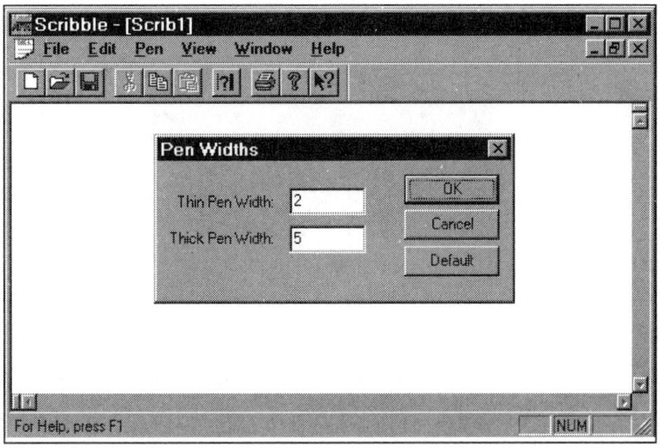

Figure 12.4 Scribble Pen Widths Dialog

Testing across GUIs

When using automated testing tools across Windows NT, Macintosh, and UNIX, the amount of changes in the testing scripts is roughly equivalent to the number of changes you have in your application. Testing application features will have very few differences across platforms. But testing the applications GUI may require some changes in the test cases. For example, if your Macintosh version replaces the File -> Exit menu item, with the File -> Quit menu item, any test cases that verify that the Exit menu item exists, will need to check that the Quit menu item exists when running on the Macintosh. Use the following guidelines as you design your regression test suite:

- The command to start the application is different, for example. `c:\msvc\samples\mfc\scribble\step7\windebug\scribble.exe` or `$WUHOME\samples\mfc\scribble\step7\$ARCH\scribble`
- Captions and labels may be different
- The menu hierarchy may be different, for example. File -> Exit vs File -> Close.
- Dialogs may contain extra controls, for example. the File Open common dialog does not have a drive letters section on UNIX.

Using automated testing tools in a cross-platform environment allows you to leverage the majority of your QA effort directly to the other platforms.

Run-time testing tools

Using run-time testing tools futher increases your product's quality. Oftentimes, problems such as run-time errors and memory leaks are not spotted by automated testing tools. For example, the automated testing tool can verify that the dialog pops up and is fully functional, but it cannot spot memory leaks in the dialog logic. By using tools such as Pure Software's Purify on UNIX and Nu-Mega Technologies' Bounds-Checker you can find additional quality problems.

These tools monitor your application as it runs and report memory-access errors and memory leaks—memory that has been allocated but can no longer be accessed because there are no pointers to it. Purify intercepts each memory access and inserts instructions into your executable before every load and store instruction. These insertions enable Purify to detect memory corruption just before it happens. This allows Purify to precisely identify the orgin of the problem, including the line number in the source code where the error occurred. Purify detects the following types of run-time errors:

- Reading or writing beyond the bounds of an array
- Reading or writing freed memory
- Freeing memory multiple times
- Reading and using uninitialized memory
- Reading and writing through null pointers

- Reading and writing beyond the end of the stack
- Overflowing the stack by deeply recursive function calls

Bounds-Checker, like Purify, runs under-the-hood, looking for problems that automated testing tools can overlook. Bounds-Checker detects the following types of run-time errors:

- Calling Windows APIs with invalid parameters
- Having memory leaks
- Having resource leaks
- Reading and writing freed memory
- Reading and writing through null or invalid pointers
- Processor faults
- Ignoring bad Windows API return values

How Run-Tme Tools Detect Memory Access Errors

Purify monitors your program, making sure that each memory access performed is legal. Every read, write, allocation and free of memory is checked to make sure that the operations are legal. A table is maintained to track the state of each byte of memory used by the program. The table has two bits of information on every byte, allowing for four distinct states per byte, increasing run-time memory usage by about 25 percent. One bit is used to represent whether the corresponding byte may be accessed. It can be accessed if it has been allocated as part of a malloc or new operation. The other bit is used to record whether the memory has been initialized. The four states can be conveniently described as colors of memory:

- *Red*. The heap memory is initially read. Red means that the memory is unallocated and uninitialized. It has either never been allocated or it has been allocated and subsequently freed. It is illegal to read, write or free red memory becuase it is not owned by the application.
- *Yellow*. Memory returned by malloc is yellow. Yellow means that the memory has been allocated, but is unititialized. The program now owns this memory. It is legal to write yellow memory, or free it if allocated by malloc/new, but it is illegal to read it because it is uninitialized. Stack frames are also set to yellow when a function is entered.

- *Green.* Once yellow memory has been written, it becomes green. Green means that the memory is allocated and initialized. It is legal to read or write green memory, or free it if it was allocated with malloc/new. The data and bss sections of memory, which represent initialized or zeroed global memory and static data) are automatically initialized to the green state.

- *Blue.* Memory which has been freed after it was initialized and used is blue. Blue means that the memory has been initialized, but is no longer valid for access. It is illegal to read, write, or free blue memory.

Using this per-byte memory status information, Purify can report a variety of messages with differing severity levels. There are four levels of messages:

- *Fatal,* indicating imminent abnormal program termination

- *Corrupting,* indicating a major program malfunction

- *Warning,* indicate anomalous program behavior. Programs with Warning level errors tend to fail sporadically and ofter mysteriously.

- *Informational,* provide additional debugging data

Table 12.1 indicates the major messages displayed by Purify:

Table 12.1 Message Overview

Message	Description	Severity
ABR	Array Bounds Read	Warning
ABW	Array Bounds Write	Corrupting
BRK	Misuse of Brk or Sbrk	Corrupting
BSR	Beyond Stack Read	Warning
BSW	Beyond Stack Write	Warning
COR	Core Dump Imminent	Fatal
FIU	File Descriptors In Use	Informational
FMR	Free Memory Read	Warning
FMW	Free Memory Write	Corrupting
FNH	Freeing Non-Heap Memory	Corrupting

Table 12.1 Message Overview (continued)

Message	Description	Severity
FUM	Freeing Unallocated Memory	Corrupting
MAF	Malloc Failure	Informational
MIU	Memory In-Use	Informational
MLK	Memory Leak	Warning
MRE	Malloc Reentrancy Error	Corrupting
MSE	Memory Segment Error	Warning
NPR	Null Pointer Read	Fatal
NPW	Null Pointer Write	Fatal
PAR	Bad Parameter	Warning
PLK	Potential Leak	Warning
SBR	Stack Array Bounds Read	Warning
SBW	Stack Array Bounds Write	Corrupting
SIG	Signal	Informational
SOF	Stack Overflow	Warning
UMC	Uninitialized Memory Copy	Warning
UMR	Uninitialized Memory Read	Warning
WPF	Watchpoint Free	Informational
WPM	Watchpoint Malloc	Informational
WPN	Watchpoint Entry	Informational
WPR	Watchpoint Read	Informational
WPW	Watchpoint Write	Informational
WPX	Watchpoint Exit	Informational
ZPR	Zero Page Read	Fatal
ZPW	Zero Page Write	Fatal

The run-time testing tools can be used in combination with the automated testing tools to increase the quality of your application. Since the automated regression suite is designed to test the complete application functionality and GUI, executing this regression suite on an executable instrumented with run-time checking is a major step in producing a high-quality application.

Figure 12.5 Runtime Testing Tool

Code coverage tools

The ideal regression suite executes all of your applications code, but how can you be sure? With code coverage tools you get a quantitative measurement of the amount of your application code that is executed by a regression suite. Currently, there are no cross-platform code coverage tools, but there are good tools on every platform. The Pure Software's PureCoverage tool on UNIX is a easy to use and highly productive code coverage tool. There is also an simple integrated code coverage tool in Visual C++.

PureCoverage lets you:

- Identify areas of code that were not exercised by your regression suite.
- Accumulate coverage data from several sessions of your application, since the regression suite may start and stop your application several times.
- Merge data from different applications that share common code, since your application may be composed of several separate components.

PureCoverage works by inserting usage-tracking instructions into the object code of your application. If your application has been compiled without source line number information, PureCoverage can provide information on all of the functions in your application. With debugging source line number information, PureCoverage can provide information on all basic blocks of code. A basic block of code is an indivisible sequence of instructions always executed together in succession.

Using automated testing tools and having a regression suite is a great start. Using code coverage tools to identify areas that need additonal test cases improves the quality of your application.

```
                                    PureCoverage
 File   View   Actions                                              Help

 Sorting order:                        _____FUNCTIONS_____  _____LINES____
 Unused lines             Runs Calls  unused   used used%   unused  used u

 ▼ Total Coverage                       2353     749   24%    22521   8004
   ▶ .../amal/windu/gdi/                  331      90   21%     7306   1775
   ▶ .../amal/windu/wmi/                  218     191   46%     5804   3300
   ▶ .../amal/windu/ssi/                  335      58   14%     3735    766
   ▶ .../amal/windu/controls/             73      60   45%     3587   1424
   ▶ .../amal/windu/c7lib/                156       8    4%      777     88
   ▼ .../samples/multipad/                 23      17   42%      526    249
     ▶ multipad.c            2     4       8   66%      142    134
     ▶ mpfile.c              2     4       4   50%      117     39
     ▶ mpprint.c            2     4       1   20%      116     20
     ▶ mpopen.c             2     5       1   16%       72     22
     ▶ mpfind.c             2     6       0    0%       69      0
     ▶ mpinit.c             2     0       2  100%       10     32
     ▶ def.c                2     0       1  100%        0      2
   ▶ .../amal/windu/help/                  6       0    0%      230      0
   ▶ .../amal/windu/ssi/                  13       3   18%      212     33
   ▶ .../amal/windu/wmi/                  28       9   24%      199    208
   ▶ .../amal/windu/gdi/                   4       7   63%      105    150
   ▶ .../amal/windu/msgs/                  9       3   25%       40     11
   ▶ .../SC3.0.1/lib/                    157      10    5%        0      0
   ▶ .../SC3.0.1/lib/cg89/                 0       1  100%        0      0
   ▶ .../multipad/sun4-g/                  0       0   --         0      0
   ▶ .../media32/lib.sun4/               982     287   22%        0      0
   ▶ .../windu2/lib.sun4/                  5       5   50%        0      0
```

Figure 12.6 Code Coverage Tools

Visual C++ contains utilities for function and line code coverage analysis. The code coverage is part of the profiling package built into Visual C++. The Tools->Profile dialog is used to select function coverage or line number coverage.

The output from the profiling tools is stored in the Profile tab at the bottom of the Visual C++ integrated development environment.

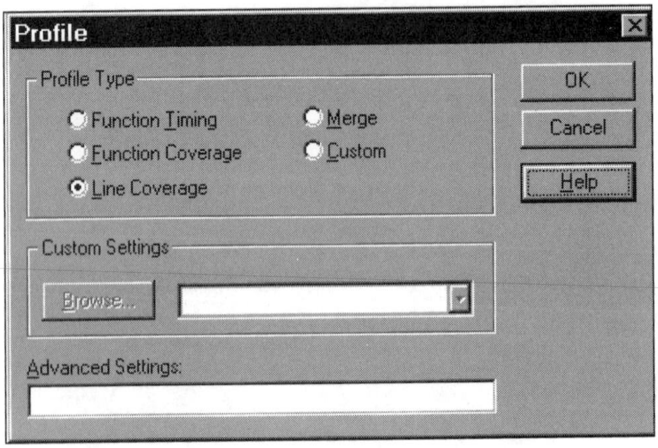

Figure 12.7 VC++ Tools -> Profile Dialog Box

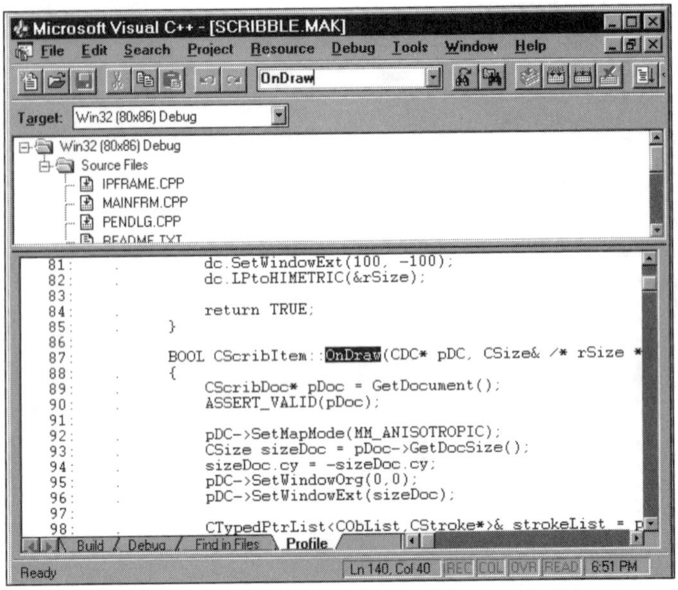

Figure 12.8 VC++ Profile Output Window

Using the Scribble sample application shows the following coverage results when exercising the following features:

- Start Scribble
- Miximize MDI window
- Draw a complex scribble
- Save the scribble
- Exit

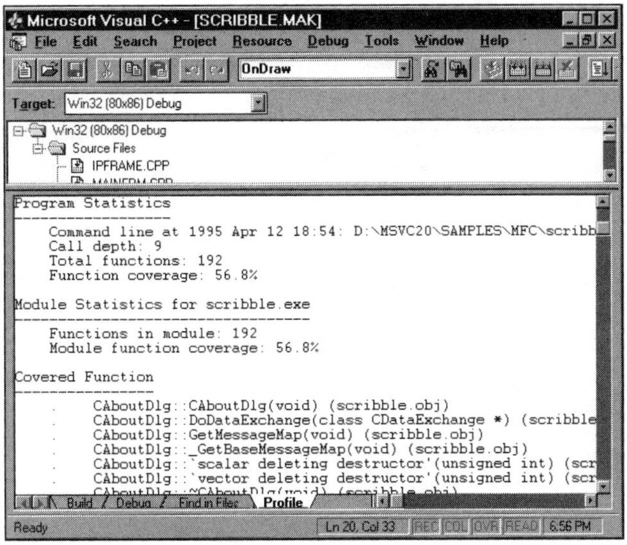

Figure 12.9 Scribble Function Profile Results

Since on 58 percent of the functions we executed, lets use a more complex test, consisting of:

- Start Scribble
- Load a scribble file
- Tile two MDI windows
- Draw a complex scribble in the new window
- Use the Pen Widths... dialog
- Split the new window
- Save the new scribble
- Exit

Figure 12.10 Expanded Scribble Function Profile Results

By exercising more features the code coverage now reports 82 percent. But this is only function-level code checking. Now, switching to line coverage profiling with this same expanded functionality produces the results shown in Figure 12.11.

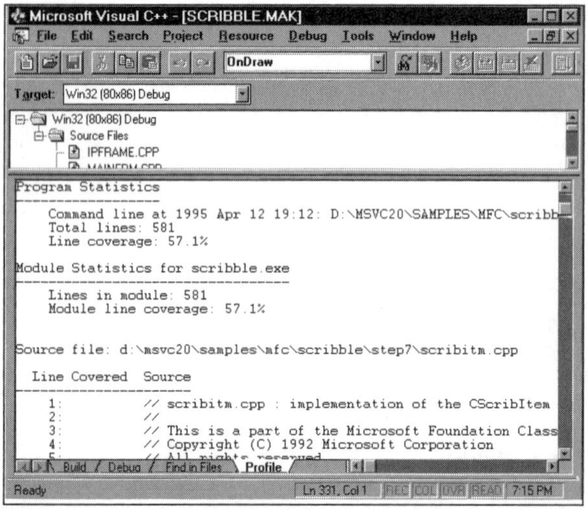

Figure 12.11 Expanded Scribble Line Profile Results

On a line-by-line code coverage bases, this expanded scribble test utilized on 75 percent of the source lines. This number is significantly lower than function profiling since only part of most functions were exercised. For example, the

Performance Analysis Tools

There are a lot of aspects of quality—automated testing tools, run-time testing tools, and code coverage tools all help improve the quality of the application. But not of these tools address the issue of application performance and whereby performance bottlenecks are. Not only do customers want feature-rich applications that don't have bugs, but they also want the fastest possible software. They want the application to work instanteneously and make the most of their computing resources. Inferior performance degrades their satisfaction with the features you worked so hard to include. Before jumping into performance analysis tools, you need to understand what causes slow software.

What Causes Performance Bottlenecks

There are at least four major causes of performance bottlenecks:

- Useless computation,
- Needless recomputation,
- Excessive requests for services, and
- Waiting for service requests to complete.

As programs evolve and algorithms are refined, some code that was needed in earlier versions may not be removed. For example, a function may have required its data to be sorted, but a new implemenation allows data in any order. Most likely, there are still areas in your application that are doing useless computation to sort the data before calling the new function. The end result is that many large programs might be performing computations whose results are never used. Performance bottlenecks are caused by time wasted on this dead code. Another common source of useless computations are those made automatically or by default, even when not required—For example, applications that needlessly free data structures during the shutdown of a program, or allocate resources that are never used.

Programs sometimes recompute values rather than storing (caching) them for later use. Here, performance bottlenecks are caused by spending time recomputing values that should have been cached. The classic example is a loop over each character in a string, that recomputes the string length each time through the loop:

```
// Performance bottleneck city
for ( int i = 0; i < strlen(my_string); i++) {
    // do something
}

for ( char *p = my_string; *p; p++ ) {
    // do something
}
```

There are times, of course, when you must continually re-compute values because the cost (in terms of memory)of caching a value exceeds the cost of re-computation.

Applications can make unnecessary requests for services, slowing down execution time and leading to bottlenecks. Excessive requests for operating system services are especially costly because, in addition to the time required to perform the service, the operating system must context-switch to make the request and return the result. This context-switch is a lot slower than a normal function call.

When applications request services, they typically block, waiting for the system to return. Waiting for the operating system service request to complete is a common performance bottleneck. Performance bottlenecks occur whenever a computation or request is performed needlessly or inefficiently.

Reducing and Eliminating Perforamance Bottlenecks

When you identify a performance bottleneck, in most cases you can elimate, or reduce it, using one of the following approaches:

- To avoid useless or unnecessary computation, stop doing it. Most unnecessary computation can be avoided by simply restructuring the application. If it isn't necesary—for example, freeing data structures during the shutdown of an applicaton—stop doing it.

- Make fewer calls for operating system services. By making fewer calls you reduce the number of context switches that can dramatically slow down your application. For example, instead of using the default buffered file input/output of 512 bytes, switch to a size that is better for your application by using setvbuf(). If you switch to an 8192 byte buffer, you can cut context-switches by 16-fold on most systems.

- By delaying computations or requests until they are needed or solicited, you can do them later. If your program can wait and make the calls for service during what would otherwise be use idle time, then the performance penality of the context-switch and service delay can be effectively hidden from the user. For example, when the user is moving the mouse over menu items, MFC does not update the status bar until the user is idle for a fraction of a second.

- You can also solve performance bottlenecks caused by needlessly recomputing a value over and over. For example, computing a string's length value once outside of a loop, storing it as a variable, then using the stored length when needed will dramatically improve performance for the loop.

- Finally, "do it, but in a more efficient way" has the potential for the most improvement. That is, by making small changes, such as caching results and making few operating system service requests may double the performance of a given algorithm. Switching to a better algorithm might make areas ten times faster. For example, switching from searching for items in a large linked list, to searching for items in a balanced binary tree could make the search ten times faster.

Finding Performance Bottlenecks

The first step to fixing a performance bottleneck is to find the code that is creating the bottleneck. Never assume you know where the slow code is—always instrument and profile your application first. Not only are most guesses wrong, but you need a baseline to compare your results to. Visual C++ includes a profiling tool to identify performance bottlenecks. Pure Software's Quantify tool for UNIX can also be used to identify performance bottlenecks.

Figure 12.12 A & B Performance Analysis Tools

After you have identified and fixed a performance bottleneck, you need to verify the improvement over several test cases and across all platforms.

INDEX

About the Diskette

The diskette that accompanies this book contains the source code for the examples that are presented in the book. The following projects are inluded on the diskette:

> chap3/scribble - sample demonstrates Wind/U porting utilities and build process
>
> chap4/mfcpower - sample application showing MFC features
>
> chap5/scribble - sample used to demonstrate cross-platform object persistence
>
> chap6/slider - demonstrates using Motif widgets inside a Wind/U ported application
>
> chap8/cadlike - CDI performance demonstration

Several of theses directories also include screen shots of the application in TIFF format.

On-Line Information

In addition to the source code samples on the accompanying disk, we also maintain an area on our WWW site that will contain the following additional information:

- An up-to-date errata with any correction once the book is in production,
- Complied examples for Windowa, Macintosh, and Unix platforms,
- Third-party and unsupported utilities for porting Win32 code.
- Other relevant information to porting Win32 application to other platforms.

To access the WWW server, open the following URL:

> http://www.bristol.com./CrossPlatformVCPP.html